ON BECOMING HUMAN

A model of the transition from ape to human
& the reconstruction of early human social life

On Becoming Human

Nancy Makepeace Tanner

CAMBRIDGE UNIVERSITY PRESS
Cambridge
London   New York   New Rochelle
Melbourne   Sydney

Published by the Press Syndicate of the University of Cambridge
The Pitt Building, Trumpington Street, Cambridge CB2 1RP
32 East 57th Street, New York, NY 10022, USA
10 Stamford Road, Oakleigh, Melbourne 3166, Australia

First published 1981
Reprinted 1981, 1983, 1986

Printed in the United States of America

Library of Congress Cataloging in Publication Data
Tanner, Nancy Makepeace.
On becoming human.
Bibliography: p.
Includes index.
1. Human evolution.   2. Social evolution.
I. Title.
GN281.4.T36   573.2   80-21526
ISBN 0 521 23554 5 hard covers
ISBN 0 521 28028 1 paperback

The cover photograph is of Lake Naivasha in Kenya, eastern Africa. It is reproduced here with the kind permission of Diane Gifford.

Contents

Illustrations

x   *Illustrations*

Preface

On Becoming Human presents a new theory on the transition from an ape-like primate ancestor to the early hominids. The book develops a model for the reconstruction of the lifeways of the ancestral ape population, the transitional population, and the early hominids. It suggests that plant gathering with tools by females for obtaining sufficient food to share with their offspring was a very early innovation, and one that played a critical role in the transition from ape to human.

Four things stand out about this model of human origins. First, it examines the roles of women and children, as well as of men, during human evolution. In exploring the roles of members of my own sex along with the roles of males in early human social life, this model seeks to correct what has been both a ludicrous and a tragic omission in evolutionary reconstructions. Second, this model stresses the sequential development of important economic innovations — initially, the invention of food gathering, followed much later by hunting. The inventions of gathering and of hunting occurred at different times, and this had important evolutionary implications. Third, the model presents a method for reconstruction of social behavior (which, of course, does not fossilize), as suggested not only by the fossils themselves but also by the study of present-day gatherer-hunters and the investigation of social behavior among our ape cousins, especially of the very closely related chimpanzees. The importance of developing a biocultural anthropology — that is, of integrating data and concepts from fossil studies with those from primate behavior research and the perspectives and understandings of cultural and social anthropology — is emphasized. Fourth, the model delineates the interaction of gathering, food sharing with offspring, and natural and sexual selection in a new environment in order to suggest the actual dynamics of becoming human.

Nancy Makepeace Tanner

Acknowledgments

Of the many friends and scholars whose ideas have influenced me and whose encouragement has sustained me, I wish to make special mention of those who, each in his or her own way, had a particularly important impact on the development of this model.

Clifford Geertz was my first anthropology teacher. The four years I spent doing ethnographic work among the matrilineal Islamic Minangkabau of the highlands of western Sumatra during the mid-1960s and early 1970s were, in large measure, due to his inspiration. Even more important to me, however, was the range of his scholarship, as exemplified in the essays now collected in *The Interpretation of Cultures* (1973). His work strengthened my conviction that it is still humanly possible to be an anthropologist in the full sense of the word: that it is still feasible to integrate concepts and data from social, cultural, and physical anthropology and archeology in a meaningful way. Of his writings, my favorite essays have always been "The Growth of Culture and Evolution of Mind" and "The Impact of the Concept of Culture on the Concept of Man," first published in 1962 and 1966, respectively. The impact of these essays on my own thinking is evident throughout this book.

Before he died, Lloyd (Tom) Fallers used part of an early unpublished essay on the transition from ancestral ape to early hominid written by Adrienne Zihlman and myself (see also Tanner and Zihlman, 1976a), which first put forward some of the basic ideas I have built upon in Chapter 7, for a graduate course at the University of Chicago. I doubt there was anything else that this wise man whom I so deeply respected could have done that would have been more meaningful to me at that point in the early development of this new model.

Sherwood Washburn, in his lectures at the University of Chicago in the early 1950s when I was still very young (and a premed student) and, later, when I was a graduate student in anthropology at the University of California, Berkeley, in the early 1960s, gave me an evolutionary perspective and introduced me to the range of data useful for reconstructing the social life of our hominid ancestors. I could never really forget the excitement over evolutionary puzzles that he engendered. Our approaches are quite different, but he showed me what tools I needed to acquire.

In the early and mid-1970s Adrienne Zihlman, a physical anthropology colleague at the University of California, Santa Cruz, rekindled my old interest in human evolution. She reintroduced me to the literature and with a sure hand guided my initial explorations in the burgeoning scholarship of today. She is a careful and exacting researcher, and her high standards of documentation on our joint work (Tanner and Zihlman, 1976a, b; Zihlman and Tanner, 1979) proved to be an inspiration and a challenge in my combing of the literature for this book. Many of the ideas in the present book were first developed in conversations with her and were set forth in preliminary form in an unpublished and unfinished manuscript we worked on from 1973 through the summer of 1975. Jointly and singly we published on a number of topics growing out of that thought, discussion, and writing (Zihlman, 1974; Tanner and Zihlman, 1976a, b; Zihlman, 1978a, b; Zihlman and Tanner, 1979). In early 1976 I determined to give first priority to working through the model in complete, fully developed form. The present book is the result of that effort. I must of course take full responsibility for the formulation as it is presented here, for interpretations of data, and for any inaccuracies that might exist; however, my intellectual debt to Adrienne Zihlman is great. During the period in which we worked jointly, her enthusiasm, her effort, her carefulness were unfailing. Above all, I have rarely enjoyed intellectual discourse with anyone else so fully.

A different type of influence came from Hildred Geertz. In the early 1970s, in the course of two field trips back to the Minangkabau of Indonesia (the people I had lived with and studied from 1963 to 1966), I became interested in looking at the roles of women cross-culturally in several societies (Tanner, 1974), largely inspired by the example of Hildred Geertz's research on the Javanese family (1961). I valued her encouragement of my work, "Minangkabau Women in Historical Perspective" (a project funded by the Ford Foundation, 1973–1974), and of further cross-cultural comparisons. A cross-cultural perspective on the roles of women formed the immediate context from which I began to explore the roles of women in human evolution.

Special thanks are due Mary Hilger and Tina de Benedictis for their expert, long-term research assistance over a considerable period of time. Tina de Benedictis, a primatologist who was completing her Ph.D. in anthropology at the University of California, Berkeley, performed extremely thorough library searches on a vast array of topics. She assisted with both the initial research and the subsequent verification and checking of data for the charts, diagrams, and illustrations in a highly professional, competent, and careful manner and made many pertinent suggestions regarding their format and content. In addition to the work that could be done in Berkeley, she also gallantly commuted to Santa Cruz twice monthly for nearly two academic years; and her responsible, consistent, scholarly assistance on many aspects of the project was deeply appreciated. Mary Hilger, a professional librarian, assisted me with all phases of the work. Her daily troubleshooting on a wide variety of topics and tasks, good sense, library expertise, and organizing ability contributed more than I know how to express. Her skill and resourcefulness as a professional librarian were invaluable in reference searches and the compilation of the extensive bibliography. Both Tina de Benedictis and Mary Hilger were involved with almost every aspect of the research at one point or another; they read and reread the manuscript, along with many references, and made numerous useful suggestions as to both content and presentation. I also want to acknowledge the research assistance of Sjamsir Sjarif, Elna Brunckhorst, Michael Brezel, Rick Topkins, Jane Huskins, Gary Glasser, Laurie Stuart, Ruth Arnold, and Laura Martinez, who worked in early phases of the project, and of Marilyn Hing, Margot Gerber, John Olmsted, Barbara Sironen, Joan McAdams, Dave Merkel, and especially at the very end, Patricia Ballard for assistance in later stages.

The illustrations and figures are the work of the artist Dee Anne Hooker. She translated the concepts and data into visual form — a difficult task that took many long hours, inspiration, and humor, as well as a great deal of thought and talent. Her ingeniousness and many ideas were a constant source of inspiration and delight. Suzanne Copeland also assisted with the illustrations.

I especially appreciated the suggestions made by friends and colleagues who read all or part of the manuscript at various stages — Clifford Geertz, Hildred Geertz, Tom Fallers, Diane K. Lewis, A. Kay Behrensmeyer, Diane Gifford, Jack Cronin, F. Clark Howell, John Pfeiffer, George Stocking, Marta J. Devins, Theresa Harned, Ernest Callenbach, and Jim Moore. I thank F. Clark Howell for loaning out many pertinent articles and manuscripts and Alice Davis for consultation; and thanks also to colleagues consulted on specific points, including F. Clark Howell, Jack Cronin, Claudia Carr, Leo Laporte, Eli Silver, Don Johanson, A. Kay Behrensmeyer, Garnes Curtis, and Dan Livingston.

The staffs of many libraries, at both UCSC and UCB, were consistently helpful. I am grateful to the Merrill and College Eight Steno Pools, UCSC, and to Bobbi Pearson and Elaine Morgan for typing early drafts, and especially to Lynn Galiste for prompt, effective typing of the final draft. Copy Machine Xeroxing in Santa Cruz was very accommodating, and Prism Publishing took real care in the preparation of stats for the illustrations. I thank the Research Committee of the University of California at Santa Cruz for several research grants that helped fund the research without which this book could not have been written, and the Regents of the University of California for sabbatical leave during spring 1976 and fall 1978, which contributed precious time to the project. I also appreciate the time for thinking at the beginning of my interest in this topic that was provided by a research grant from the Ford Foundation (for research on "Minangkabau

Women in Historical Perspective") during 1973–1974. I especially thank Marta J. Devins, Diane K. Lewis, Peggy Theobald, and Jim Moore for their encouragement, advice, empathy, and friendship through the hard times as well as the good. Most of all I thank my daughters, Elna and Elizabeth, for their acceptance and understanding of the energy, attention, and love I have put into this effort.

Nancy Makepeace Tanner

ONE

Darwin and the descent of "man"

A MAJOR gap exists in most reconstructions of the social life of our pongid and early hominid ancestors. Females and young are omitted. Or a more subtle fallacy is incorporated: Traditional Western beliefs are read back into the past. Like Social Darwinism in the late nineteenth and early twentieth centuries, naive imagery springing from unexamined evolutionary assumptions about early social behavior can, even today, act as an origin myth.

Evolution as an origin myth

MORE than a century ago Darwin intimated human origins were with simpler and "lower" forms. Darwin suggested a mechanism – natural selection – to explain evolutionary change. This concept was developed and elaborated in *The Origin of Species by Means of Natural Selection* (1859); many species of plants and animals – living as well as fossil – were used to illustrate how this mechanism operated. Although Darwin's only comment on the human species was in his closing chapter where he stated, "Much light shall be thrown on the origin of man and his history," the implication was understood (Darwin, 1859, as reprinted 1936:373). In *The Descent of Man and Selection in Relation to Sex* (1871), published 12 years later, Darwin not only made explicit that humans descended from animals but also pointed out that, in addition to natural selection, sexual selection was an important aspect of the evolutionary process.

Since the publication of *The Origin of Species* (1859) and *The Descent of Man* (1871), the idea of human evolution has consistently generated interest, excitement, and controversy. The topic carries an aura that goes far beyond simple scientific curiosity. The subject fascinates people, yet often elicits strong negative response: Recall the furor surrounding Darwin's work. The quick reception by many contrasts vividly with the extremely long time it has taken for Darwin's ideas to be generally accepted by others. Even today, despite a well-established and rapidly increasing hominid fossil record, there are religious sects for which the concept of biological evolution is still anathema.

The extraordinary interest in Darwin's theories of biological evolution through natural and sexual selection of continuous intraspecies variability cannot be understood as merely deriving from the ingenuity of his argument from phylogeny at a time when an early human fossil record scarcely existed. True, his theory was so persuasive and well argued that it provided an effective paradigm for the interpretation of subsequent hominid fossil finds. Its intellectual acuity hardly explains the popular response, however. The theory was readily, rapidly, and widely embraced but also encountered strong and persisting resistance. Darwinian evolutionary theory has had social implications from the very beginning.

The social and intellectual context of the times provides an understanding of the enthusiastic acceptance of evolutionary theory, whereas religious beliefs in special creation buttressed its rejection in other camps. Evolutionary approaches to a variety of phenomena were part of the mid-nineteenth century intellectual climate (Bock, 1955). Almost simultaneously with Darwin, Wallace presented essentially the same thesis regarding biological evolution (Wallace, 1855, 1858). Ideas of economic, political, and cultural "progress" and "development" (often joined with biological racism), in which the white men of western Europe imagined themselves at the apex of "progressive social evolution," arose after the West's "discovery" of the rest of the world and were still current in Darwin's era (Bock, 1955; Stocking, 1968); and Spencer, in three of his early writings (1852a, 1857), had already incorporated an idea of biological evolution (albeit by Lamarckian processes) along with the idea of social and cultural evolution into a grand schema that offered a direct alternative to the prevailing but already faltering religious view. Among those who accepted Darwin's ideas were, therefore, many who, like Spencer, saw biological evolution as but part of a perspective that was largely social and political.

The opposition was largely grounded in adherence to religious beliefs on human origins. Darwin's theorizing had led him not only to trespass but to stake out claim on sacred ground. His theory offered an explanation of human origins. In so doing, Darwin's theory came into direct competition with his culture's religious origin myth. And eventually the theory of evolution was to contribute to the creation of contemporary myths that, surprising as it might seem, bear certain similarities to the religious origin story that preceded it.

Just as Eve was formed from Adam's rib, once "scientific" speculation began on human origins, the Western preoccupation with "man" – rather than with humans of both sexes – became evident. The English language, in which *man* can refer to humans in general as well as be used in its more restricted sense to refer to the male gender per se, reflects and reinforces the Western cultural tendency to focus on males. There has, in fact, been very little direct exploration or reconstruction of women's activities during the course of human evolution. Although this is understandable in view of the cultural background of many Western scholars, it is poor science. There is a great deal of data that cannot be adequately analyzed if scientists fail to examine the activities of one half of the human species (see Figure 1:1).

Reconstruction of early human social activities – with the identification of "man" or "man the hunter" as the prime actor – can, like the primacy of Adam, serve to mythically legitimize traditional Western cultural patterns of sexual stratification. Similarly, what was once called the problem of the origin of evil in theology has come to be accounted for through evolutionary reconstruction (Montagu, 1976). Attempts have been made to comprehend the reasons for Western sexual inequality, social hierarchies, competition, conflict, and even warfare between industrial nation-states by reference to the supposed qualities of our animal ancestors (Lorenz, 1966; Morris, 1967; Tiger, 1969; Tiger and Fox, 1971).

That scientific theories on human evolution (and particularly their popularized rephrasings) should, in this instance, come to fulfill some of the same functions as the religious origin myths they have largely replaced is not really surprising. Every human society endeavors to understand its own existence and way of life. Origin myths are an integral part of most such attempts. They relate to a people's understanding of the meaning of their lives and provide guidelines for social behavior. With the partial demise of earlier origin myths, Western peoples formed a new evolutionary myth that could both satisfy their curiosity as to human origins and provide an image of how humans "should" behave – or, more accurately for the new myths, how they "inevitably" do behave.

Darwin perhaps sensed that he was proposing a theory that would ultimately revolutionize humanity's image of itself. If so, one can better understand the attention he gives to the question of the development of the "moral faculties" during "primeval times" in *The Descent of Man* (1871). As with the physical aspects of evolution, so with the social aspects: Darwin was particularly interested in origins. Although he saw some forms of interpersonal behavior as more adaptive than others, his framework for the understanding of ethics was developmental and probabilistic rather than prescriptive. Nonetheless, like Western explorers and colonists before him and especially like the philosopher Herbert Spencer (1864), Darwin sug-

FIGURE 1:1. Cross-cultural views of women. There is a great deal of data that cannot be adequately analyzed if scientists fail to examine the economic and other activities of one half of the human species.

gested that in the course of time some societies came to have an advantage over others, only to be superseded later by other, even more "successful" and more "moral" societies (1871). This mild Darwinian speculation was to be a precursor of Social Darwinism—a set of beliefs that in actuality owed at least as much to Spencer as to Darwin. Social Darwinism, the new Western "origin myth," in turn, made it possible for the peoples of the expanding West to consider themselves the chosen people of social evolution.

Despite vast changes in biological evolutionary thought since Darwin, he still stands as a giant figure in intellectual history. His monumental work on speciation was exemplary in terms of scientific investigation, and his proposal of change through natural and sexual selection formed the basis for *the* new paradigm within which the biological sciences have operated for the past century. But, in Darwin's day, at least equally important was the immense influence of social evolutionary theory on Western folk beliefs. In hindsight, we now realize that Social Darwinism has no connection with the process of biological evolution. This insight is largely the product of several generations of research in genetics and anthropology. Biological racism and ethnocentrism are no longer scientifically respectable.

Darwin was, of course, to some extent a product of his culture and his time. It is not difficult to find racist or sexist assumptions in his writings or to see a reflection of the competitive Victorian social milieu in his concept of natural selection (Sahlins, 1977). Ironically it was this cultural baggage, which he carried with him (but did not focus on) in his biological work, that proved to be so attractive to Western society. Biological Darwinism was interpreted, extended, and its thrust changed subtly but surely in ways that made Darwin's ideas particularly attractive to the rising bourgeoisie and compatible with the ideas of competition, free enterprise and capitalism at home, and with colonialism abroad (Hofstadter, 1959).

With Herbert Spencer's equation of "Progress" and "Evolution" (1857), E. B. Tylor's (1871) and Lewis Henry Morgan's (1877) ranking of the societies of the world into an ascending series from "savagery" through "barbarism" to "civilization," and the then current anthropological assumptions of a sort of hierarchy of human races (Stocking, 1968), the major elements of a new origin myth were complete. Social Darwinism extended Huxley's portrayal of warfare in nature (Huxley, 1888) to warfare in the marketplace; this gave the burgeoning industrial world of the time a "scientific" sanction for free, unregulated, and often quite ruthless competition. This was the era of industrialization in the West and of colonial exploitation in the rest of the world.

"The survival of the fittest" was coined by Spencer (1866), subsequently picked up by Darwin in later editions of *The Origin of Species* (1869), and also used by Huxley (1894). The phrase caught the popular imagination of the time and even today still evokes a powerful response. Darwin (1869) adopted it as a metaphor for natural selection. For him it referred to the individual organism's life-maintaining activities – among which were cooperation and interdependence – and to its success in bearing, nurturing, and leaving healthy progeny. Huxley (1894), however, echoed his times when he presented as synonyms "the survival of the fittest," "the struggle for existence," and "the competition of each with all." For the Social Darwinists and their audience, the term came to encapsulate a new ideology:

"The survival of the fittest" was for the industrial barons at once the inspiration and the justification of their policies and their actions: on the one hand, explosive growth in the industrialization of society, which was naturally seen by the beneficiaries as "progress"; on the other hand, social approval of the personal qualities that made this possible – personal ambition, greed, self-aggrandizement, competitiveness, exploitation of others and indifference to their plights.   [Montagu, 1976:46]

In the popular mind of the day, Darwinism per se (i.e., the theory of biological evolution through natural and sexual selection) joined with Social Darwinism: A new origin myth, along with a set of guidelines for human behavior, had arisen.

This new origin myth – the sociocultural as well as the biological "survival of the fittest" – integrated two potentially discordant features: (1) It was universalistic in the sense that all contemporary peoples came to be seen as members of one species, *Homo sapiens sapiens,* and (2) it simultaneously provided a justification for Western imperialism, for colonial and neocolonial expansion, and for exploitation of both material and human "resources." Biological universalism combined with the legitimization of increasing social differentiation along class, ethnic, and national lines was characteristic of a historical period that saw intensified economic and political interdependency of the peoples of the world on increasingly unequal terms. As Western societies became more technologically sophisticated, capitalistic, urban, class structured, ethnically diverse, and secular, the theory of human evolution combined with Social Darwinism came to be a peculiarly apt origin myth. Its rapid and wide acceptance in the West, like the initial (and in some camps persisting) opposition, must be understood in the context of broad cultural and social trends.

Today, Social Darwinism is largely a doctrine of the past. Indeed, many scholars would look back upon its florescence as an unscientific aberration

(Alland, 1974; Freeman, 1974; Gould, 1974). Yet the fact that a doctrine so deeply related to Western history and society could be at least partly inspired by and, as it were, adhere to the scientific theory of biological evolution should prove instructive with regard to the potential for building ideology at the expense of science when scholars deal with matters so culturally loaded as human origins.

Scientists, no less than others, are cultural beings. Many "evolutionary" reconstructions dealing with early human social interaction have, therefore, come out of Western values and Western perspectives about human nature and not only reflect but reinforce common social patterns. Reconstructions of past social behavior—in the absence of both substantial evidence and a culturally relativistic perspective—tend to simulate a modified and simplified version of the culture and society of the reconstructor.

Reopening the question: "human nature" from an evolutionary perspective

The influence of the sexual attitudes of the Victorian era is evident in a curious reversal in one part of Darwin's argument. When describing the process of sexual selection (1871) among all animals save the human species, he not only discusses competition among males for females but also stresses the importance of female choice. The secondary sexual characteristics of the males, such as bright coloration, fine plumage, special vocal qualities, and so forth, are seen as being important to the extent that they are attractive to the females: "The females are most excited by, or prefer pairing with, the most ornamented males, or those which are the best songsters, or play the best antics . . . Thus the more vigorous females, which are the first to breed, will have the choice of many males" (1871, as reprinted 1936:573). However, when Darwin approaches the discussion of sexual selection among humans, male choice is now assumed, and it is female beauty that is seen as attracting the male. In accounting for this apparent shift, he writes: "Man is more powerful in body and mind than woman, and in the savage state he keeps her in a far more abject state of bondage than does the male of any other animal; therefore, it is not surprising that he should have gained the power of selection" (1871, as reprinted 1936:901).

In a centennial volume edited by Campbell (1972a) commemorating Darwin's *The Descent of Man and Selection in Relation to Sex* (1871), the framework Darwin set forth is still utilized and his approach to female choice is very much in evidence (Zihlman, 1974). The articles in the Campbell volume range in their interpretations from those by Trivers and

FIGURE 1:2. Victorian women: no female choice?

Selander, which discuss the role of female choice, to those of Fox and Crook, which neglect it. Birds and insects are the primary subject matter of Trivers's and Selander's articles; Crook and Fox deal with primates and humans—as if the closer the human condition is approached, the less female choice is confronted and dealt with directly. Fox combines his views with those of Levi-Strauss (1949) on the "exchange of women" in marital "alliance systems" and does not consider active female roles in society during evolution. His approach is similar to that part of Darwin's argument that stressed female beauty so that she would be selected by males. When the attributes of females are seen in this light, as existing for male choice, it also appears "logical" to view females as passive and, by extension, to assume women had an insignificant part in the formation and development of human society during our several-million-year evolutionary history.

The assumption of an uninitiating role for females was intimated by Darwin who was doubtless influenced by the social milieu of Victorian England where women were treated and characterized as passive. Even today this view permeates much of what has been written concerning early human social behavior. This illustrates how ideas that were formulated in a particular cultural period can persist even though the context has changed. Ideas do eventually catch up with social reality, and it is now time for us to begin to explore the role of women, along with the role of men, in evolution.

Human evolution includes men, women, and children

All aspects of evolution have their fascination, but it is our social life that marks us off as human. We have enormous potential for learning any one of myriad specific cultural patterns for social interaction and ecological adaptation. As a species our communities are incredibly variable – ranging from tiny gathering–hunting camps to massive industrialized nation–states. Humans rely on learning, on culture, to know how to perform even the very basics of survival – how to give birth, feed the young, obtain food, attract a sexual partner. Learned patterns and skills guide the construction of shelters and of social meeting places for conversation, trade, ritual, or politics (see Figure 1:3). Culture informs the arrangement of physical structures and social roles into the differing configurations appropriate to a tiny hamlet of shifting cultivators, a substantial village of wet rice farmers, a provincial town that is a seat of trade and local government, or a large urban industrial center. In some societies women have more than one husband simultaneously; in others men have more than one wife. In our society's past, permanent monogamy ("till death do us part") was customary; today, serial monogamy has become quite common. The essential question in human evolution is: How did this enormous plasticity develop? How did the great capacity for human learning and communication come to be?

Social action is not preserved in the fossil record: Language, mother love, environmental lore, kinship systems, faith, and children's games do not fossilize. In trying to understand the social life of early hominids – those "pre-people" so long ago and far away – there is a tendency to see them as modified, simplified, or idealized versions of ourselves. Sadly, what this has meant in practice, until very recently indeed, has been an almost

FIGURE 1:3. A !Kung San woman, 8 months pregnant, of the Dobe area, southern Africa, with her husband, her small daughter, and a visiting uncle (*on left*).

exclusive emphasis on adult male behavior. This book develops a model of
early human social life that takes into account both sexes and the young as
well as adults.

The present social and scientific context is one that permits, even en-
courages, asking new questions. From a theoretical standpoint this proves
to be enormously exciting: By asking these new questions – questions
about the specific roles of each sex and how they interacted during the
course of human evolution – data that once seemed anomalous can now
be fitted into the evolutionary picture. Further, by examining the activities
of both sexes it becomes possible to construct a sequential model of human evolution – in other words, to hypothesize how behavior changed
through time. When both sexes are included, the lifeways of the transitional population that was diverging from ape ancestors and of the early
hominids can be reconstructed in a manner consistent with the fossil and
archeological evidence. It is, in short, now feasible to reassess the process
of human evolution in a more considered manner.

What this book is all about

The necessity, excitement, and utility of model building are presented in
Chapter 2.

Chapter 3 reviews molecular and fossil evidence to establish a phylogeny relevant to ape and human evolution. This chapter is, necessarily, rather technical, and some readers may prefer to skim or skip parts of it on their first time through the book. The data and their evaluation are, however, important in determining what the ancestral population was like. The question of whether there are living primates that can serve as effective models of the population from which the human line diverged is explored.

It is probable that the chimpanzee, one of the African apes, provides the most useful primate model of the population ancestral to the human line. Chapters 4, 5, and 6 describe chimpanzee locomotion, tool use, and diet; patterns of chimpanzee social interaction and organization and variation relating to ecological and situational factors; and the relationship of chimpanzee communication, social organization, and the ecological adaptivity observed in the wild to the extraordinary mental and "linguistic" capacities demonstrated in laboratory studies. Chimpanzees use tools far more than previously assumed, have flexible social organization, and exhibit impressive cognitive and communicatory capacities. These features, along with many others, prove helpful in building a model of the ancestral population.

Going on from this base, Chapter 7 presents a model of the social life of the transitional hominids that were probably moving from the tropical forests onto the eastern African savanna and adapting to this new environment some time between 8 million and 3.5 million years ago. Chapter 7 therefore forms the core of the book. It suggests how natural and sexual selection could work together for a rapid transition from ancestral apes to the earliest hominid genus, *Australopithecus,* which lived in the new ecological niche. A long-range gathering and foraging strategy in which adults consistently carried babies, tools, and food over a wide range, thus necessarily coming to walk upright, was basic to the new adaptation. The hypothesis, in brief, is that transitional hominid mothers were beginning to gather and share plants with offspring and that this female tool use, gathering, carrying, and mother–child food sharing became essential for the transitional population's adaptation to the new environment.

Chapter 8 delves into the difficult question of whether there are transitional fossils: Possible candidates dating from before 4 million years ago are identified. And the earliest known hominids, from Laetoli and Afar in eastern Africa, are examined to ascertain what they can reveal about the ancestral population and the nature of the transition.

In Chapter 9, a model for the generic adaptation of *Australopithecus* is presented. This genus inhabited the mosaic savanna environment in eastern and southern Africa from at least 3.5 million to less than 1.5 million years ago, was bipedal with a small brain, had a dentition characterized by small canines but with large molars and premolars, and used and ulti-

FIGURE 1:4. Three generations of Dobe area !Kung San. The adults are preparing plant food gathered in the Kalahari Desert of southern Africa. Information on living peoples who gather and hunt their food can be useful in evolutionary reconstruction.

mately made stone tools. At this stage, it is highly likely that gathering of plant food combined with some insect collecting and predation on small animals, rather than hunting large animals with tools, was basic to their adaptation (see Figure 1:4).

Chapter 10 reviews the fossil evidence on *Australopithecus,* with particular attention to the variation among the australopithecines and to the sequence of change. This chapter attempts to show how the rather confusing array of evidence on early hominid variability can be made intelligible in the context of the gathering hypothesis.

In Chapter 11, the final chapter, the gathering hypothesis is reviewed and the overall argument summarized. In conclusion, the implication of this model of human origins (as worked out in the specific models of the ancestral, transitional, and early hominid populations) for the understanding of the nature of the human adaptation is explored, and the integral role of the development of the capacity for culture is highlighted.

This book, then, offers a sequential model of human origins and presents an interpretation of the nature of the human adaptation. It integrates information from a variety of fields—cultural and social anthropology, primate behavior, physical anthropology and paleontology, archeology, molecular biology, geology, and the study of paleoenvironments—to facilitate the reconstruction of behaviors critical to the transition from pongid to hominid. In particular, the roles of females and of children, as well as of males, are explored in order to explicate the dynamics of the ape–human divergence.

TWO

Models in evolution

WHAT is needed, at this point, is a comprehensive model of early human evolution—a model that takes both sexes seriously, a model that incorporates and integrates the critical but highly specialized information relevant to human evolution appearing in many disciplines and, in particular, a model which can explain the transition from ape to human.

The data: the necessity of an interdisciplinary approach

THIS book, as a whole, can be considered an exercise in biocultural anthropology, one in which both biology and culture are taken very seriously. It is an effort to bridge some of the chasms resulting from disciplinary overspecialization to produce a more effective model of early human evolution. Because of a rapidly multiplying body of information on fossil hominids, it is possible to trace human origins back several million years. A fossil sequence has been established. Many detailed studies have been made on the behavior of nonhuman primates as well as on the social and economic life of contemporary humans whose subsistence still depends upon gathering plants and hunting. Excellent data therefore exist about our closest primate relatives and on humans who still utilize their environment in ways much more like that of our early human ancestors than we do. This information provides a substantial base for interpretation of the way of life of the early hominids. Fossil evidence on the Miocene apes and its analysis assist with an understanding of primate evolution. Genetics and molecular biology shed light on the speciation process and on the times of divergence of the human line from ape ancestors. Information on paleoenvironments provides clues to the types of environments in which primate ancestors and early hominids may have lived. Comparative geological, faunal, and paleomagnetic data assist in establishing relative dates, and other dating techniques can establish absolute dates for some of the sites. Archeological associations give indirect information on early human activi-

15

ties. Finally, the fossils themselves reveal a great deal about hominid anatomy, which in turn can provide important clues to the behavior of the early hominids themselves. The question is how to reason about this wealth of data in the reconstruction of early hominid anatomy and behavior. Interpreting the relevance of this proliferating evidence is a particularly acute problem in the reconstruction of patterns of social interaction.

Attempts at integration of diverse fields and subdisciplines are fraught with dangers. Much of what passes for "sociobiology," for example, is neither good sociology nor good biology, let alone a synthesis of the two. Rather, powerful metaphor – such as "the selfish gene" – often replaces powerful analysis, and there is frequent recourse to reductionist formulations. Reductionist thinking – that is, the belief that cultural arrangements are due to our biology – is most often encountered when scientific work is popularized and overgeneralized. Similar problems also can arise when specialists on the behavior of animals that are phylogenetically distant from humans, such as birds or insects, for instance, begin to write about evolutionary aspects of human behavior without first familiarizing themselves adequately either with the plentiful data on our close primate relatives or with the extensive cross-cultural research on human behavior itself.

Vast leaps up the evolutionary ladder not only distort one's understanding of the nature of the human adaptation but also make it impossible to trace in detail how humans could have evolved from ape ancestors. Primate behavior studies can assist in filling this gap. And social and cultural anthropology examine the differences and similarities in human action and systems of meaning that are found from society to society.[1] Cross-cultural research can therefore be an invaluable aid, although hardly an infallible one, in avoiding Eurocentrism in evolutionary reconstructions. Cross-cultural research on human societies and on primate behavior studies must, together, form the context for any attempt to scientifically reconstruct the social life of early humans.

When existing information on the apes and on the many different lifeways found throughout the world among members of the human species is ignored, "evolutionary" reconstructions are especially prone to transfer Western values and patterns of social interaction back in time. Failure to incorporate an understanding of human social and cultural variability

---

[1] In my own case, I spent four years (three research trips) during the 1960s and early 1970s in the highlands of West Sumatra, Indonesia, doing research among the matrilineal, Islamic Minangkabau on conflict and dispute settlement patterns, sociolinguistics, and women's roles (in the context of their economic and kinship systems) prior to beginning work about 1973 on (1) cross-cultural comparisons of women's roles and (2) evolutionary and primate behavior topics.

gained from cross-cultural research and to effectively utilize evidence on the social behavior and ecological adaptation of primates living in undisturbed natural settings can lead to an impoverished and Westernized picture of early human social life.

I endeavor here, not without trepidation, to avoid these pitfalls and to build a model that is process oriented, considers the behavior of females as well as males, and integrates the plentiful information relevant to human evolution now available in a number of disciplines and subdisciplines. This book therefore presents, step-by-step, the evidence and reasoning fundamental to the development of a framework for the reconstruction of the social and economic life of the ancestral pongids, the transitional population, and the early hominids.

The importance of an explicit, process-oriented model

Vastly increased information now exists concerning the fossil record, about animal behavior and in particular the social behavior of the great apes, and concerning contemporary humans who live in small groups and gather and hunt in a manner perhaps still reminiscent of earlier *Homo sapiens* populations. These extensive bodies of information pose a challenge. What sort of model of early human social life can appropriately build on the data already in hand and generate important questions for further inquiry? To narrow the possibilities requires that the model of origins and of each stage of human evolution be specific. Such a model is, of course, more controversial because assumptions are distinctly noted and clear-cut interpretations are made. This means that the model can be evaluated, argued about, examined for logical coherence, and inspected for fit with data. Consistency and interconnectedness between the components provide a way to test its overall logic. When a model is explicit, its usefulness in interpreting and assessing the significance of new data is enhanced. Similarly, the formulation of further elaborations or modifications of the model in the light of subsequent evidence is facilitated.

Illuminating insights do not simply emerge from "facts"; rather, facts are intelligible only when they are viewed in a theoretical framework. Facts are like pieces of a puzzle. In a sense, a model is analogous to the completed picture. The key is to visualize what the finished puzzle might look like in order to figure out how to put the pieces together. Rather than occurring separately, data collection and interpretation interact. An effective model ties the data together and makes sense out of them, generates novel questions and new paths of research, and provides a framework in which hypotheses may be checked against existing data and new information as it appears.

The central analytic task in developing a model of early human evolution is to build a process orientation into the model itself. Questions of how and in what sequence behaviors arose and were transmitted are integral to the logic of the model presented in this book. Early theorists postulated several stages in the development of human society, but these did not go back far in time and were necessarily highly speculative because little evidence for reconstruction was available (Morgan, 1877; Engels, 1891, 1895–1896). A common difficulty of many of the reconstructions put forward in this century has been their essentially static quality. Little attempt has been made to differentiate earlier from later behavior or to ascertain how the latter might develop from the former. In order to build an effective model of human evolution, it is necessary to have a specific starting point – in this case the ancestral ape population. One must then go on to hypothesize how the changes developed that led to the transition from apes to early human. In other words, dealing with behavioral sequences is essential. Such a process-oriented model can be built only if the whole population is considered. Both sexes and all ages were part of the evolving population. A viable model cannot be constructed if, as has so often been the case, the subsistence and social activities of women – half the species – are ignored (Figure 2:1).

The requirements for construction of a useful and effective evolutionary model are of several kinds: It must be process oriented, deal with the adaptation of the total species, and consider interrelationships of environment, biology, social organization, and both the material and the nonmaterial aspects of culture. This book as a whole is an exercise in working with this sort of model for understanding the processes involved in becoming human (Geertz, 1973). It focuses on the transition from an ape ancestor to the early hominid, *Australopithecus*.

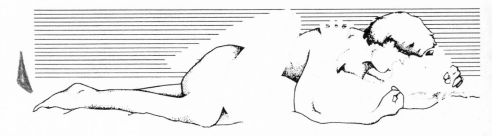

FIGURE 2:1. A viable model cannot be constructed if half the species remains invisible, with its sexual, economic, protective, and other activities unexamined.

More specifically, I present a model of the social life of three critical stages: the primate population directly ancestral to the hominid line; the transitional population; and that of the earliest hominid genus, *Australopithecus*. These specific explorations follow directly from the broader framework; they are the detailed, sequential working out of this model for the reconstruction of early hominid social life.

Primate models in human evolution: problems with the baboon model

Various primate species have been used as models. Until Jane Goodall and her associates effectively presented an African ape, the chimpanzee, as a model for the ancestral ape population, both scholarly and popular attention was largely concentrated on African monkeys — initially the common or savanna baboon (Goodall and Hamburg, 1975). One reason for the frequent reliance on savanna and, later, hamadryas baboons in reconstruction was that they are easily visible on the open African grasslands and therefore have been studied by many researchers. Also, early zoo studies had seemed to indicate that baboons fit Western notions of how societies — particularly those giving rise to humans — should be organized (Zuckerman, 1932; Haraway, 1978).

Another reason for use of data on baboons in the reconstruction of early hominid social life deserves more serious consideration. The argument was framed: Transitional hominids, in moving out of a heavily forested environment, had to deal with problems similar to those of other ground-dwelling primates in the savanna today (Washburn and DeVore, 1961a; DeVore and Washburn, 1963). These problems included predator pressure from lions, leopards, cheetahs, hyenas, jackals, and wild dogs, as well as much more scattered resources than in the tropical forest. The implication, therefore, was that early hominid social life resembled baboon social life in the wild as described by the earlier field researchers.

There are several fallacies to this argument. First, the transitional hominids of both sexes could doubtless throw branches and leaves at potential predators at least as effectively as chimpanzees today (see Chapters 4 and 7). Second, as John Pfeiffer has suggested, the new upright posture and gait of the transitional hominids confronted predators with a strange thing: An upright animal may have discouraged predation on the principle that strangeness works versus ingrained predation patterns (pers. com.). Third, with regard to baboons themselves, their extreme sexual dimorphism is very different from the minimal sexual dimorphism in humans. Fourth, the earlier picture of savanna baboon social life was so incomplete as to be misleading.[2] Fifth, the complexity and variety of various savanna-living species' anatomical, social, and ecological adaptations were not explored, resulting in an oversimplified comparison. There are actually a variety of ways that monkeys deal with the savanna environment, and early hominids might be expected to develop further strategies. Sixth, baboons are phylogenetically quite removed from the hominid line, and a great deal is now known about the social behavior and ecological ranges of the African apes, which are much more closely related to the hominid line than are monkeys.

Among savanna baboons, which inhabit the open grasslands of sub-Saharan Africa from eastern to southern Africa, great sexual dimorphism is evident. Males are twice the body size of females and have very large canine teeth, much larger than those of females (which, compared to those of hominids, are also very large). This high degree of physical sexual dimorphism is correlated with contrasts in male and female baboon behavior. Savanna baboons live in multimale, multifemale groups. The baboon troop, averaging 40 to 80 members in some areas, moves as a unit for long distances on the ground throughout the day and sleeps together in trees at night. Both of these features enhance the species' ability to deal with predators. Further, some of the adult males form a group that functions for the protection of the whole troop. These males were seen as the focus of attention and social interaction (Hall and DeVore, 1965), and this was picked up on in the popularization of the baboon model (Tiger, 1969).

Multimale, multifemale savanna baboon troops with a male protective unit exist in an environment that can support relatively large groups traveling together but that has heavy predator pressures. To generalize from this example to hominids is misleading, however. Postulation of too tight or too rigid a correlation of ecology and social structure is erroneous. Environmental factors can be dealt with in a variety of ways. Patas monkeys — which, like savanna baboons, inhabit relatively open country — have adapted to predator pressure through concealment and silence, occasionally combined with the use of the adult male as a decoy, and anatomical specializations for speed (Hall, 1965a; Struhsaker and Gartlan, 1970).

[2] Interestingly, the more recent researchers — who have moved on from initial studies that tended to be primarily concerned with the large males — have found that, even among baboons, female behavior is more significant to group life than previously realized (Rowell, 1969, 1972). In addition, Rowell has demonstrated that the concept of social dominance is not particularly useful for studies of primate behavior in the wild (Rowell, 1974; Haraway, 1978). Rather, extremely submissive and aggressive behavior is more applicable to the abnormal conditions found in zoo situations. "Thus a rigid hierarchy may with some justification be regarded as a pathological condition . . . brought about by too high stress levels" (Rowell, 1974:151).

They deal with predators by hiding, subterfuge, and running rather than by aggression.[3] Patas monkeys and savanna baboons have similar environments and are exposed to similar predator pressure but have developed quite different anatomical and social modes of responding. Conversely, the same general social organizational types can be found in different settings. For instance, social structures similar to that of hamadryas baboons, namely, one-male, multifemale groups, occur among several monkey species in African forest habitats where the problems of resources and predators are very different from those on the savanna (Struhsaker, 1969; Aldrich-Blake, 1970).

There certainly is no reason to suppose that early human society was structured in the same way as that of savanna baboons. With regard to some of the popularized uses that have been made of his own work on baboons, Sherwood Washburn has stated:

Because of my early research on the social organization of baboons, my work is often cited to support theories about the animal origins of human behavior. Obviously, we studied animal behavior to find both possible similarities and possible differences. As time has passed it is the differences that seem more important, especially when considering social behavior. [1978:70]

There are many different life patterns among mammalian savanna dwellers. The ungulates, carnivores, and primates that live today in the African savannas exhibit a variety of modes for dealing with their common environment. And the late middle and late Miocene "ape," *Ramapithecus* — thought by some to have lived in open country and to have been a hominid ancestor — exhibits neither large canine teeth with major sexual dimorphism nor any evidence of tool use for protection (Pilbeam, Meyer, et al., 1977; Pilbeam, 1978a).

A species's ecological adaptation and social organization are related not only to features of the environment — such as food availability and location or predator pressure — but also to the evolutionary history and potentialities of the species itself. Even though a species may inhabit a range of environments, species-typical social characteristics are recognizable. African baboons in the forest and in the savanna or Indian langur monkeys on the plains or mountain slopes have distinctive, though variable, social patterns compared to other monkey species (DeVore and Hall, 1965; Hall and DeVore, 1965; Rowell, 1966; Yoshiba, 1968; Dolhinow, 1972; Curtin

---

[3] Considerable sexual dimorphism is evident, comparable to that in savanna baboons, but this appears to function to keep other male patas monkeys out of the group rather than for predator protection as in savanna baboons (Gartlan, 1975).

and Dolhinow, 1978). The interaction between phylogeny and environment must be examined for each population (Gartlan, 1973). The African apes are the primates most intimately related to us phylogenetically – far more so than any of the Old or New World monkeys. African apes are also more closely related to the human line than are Asian apes.

The most distinctive feature of the human adaptation is the ability to deal with what for other species would be a variety of ecological niches and, indeed, the ability to create our own environments. We do this through learned behavior. Humans are culture-bearing and culture-dependent animals not only in myth, ritual, and art forms but also in social structure, technology, and use of the environment. The symbol-creating and symbol-structuring potential of the human brain and the physiological and social extension of infancy in which learning is mediated by intense affective ties and long-term interaction with the mother (and, gradually, other members of the immediate social group) provide humans with unique learning capacities and opportunities. It is possible for each human child to master the language, attain the technical skills, map out the environment and ways to deal with it, and learn the specific patterns of social action and values characteristic of his or her culture. Recent experiments comparing two species of New World monkeys, *Saimiri sciureus* and *Saguinus nigricollis,* one Old World monkey species, *Macaca mulatta,* and one African ape species, *Pan troglodytes* (the common chimpanzee) demonstrate that "the closer taxonomically a species is to man the greater the deceleration of growth during the first postnatal year" (McKim and Hutchinson, 1975:495). In other words, for the species observed, the closer a primate is to humans, the slower the infants grow during the first year after birth. Therefore, for the special extended mother–child interresponsiveness so important to human learning, apes are much better models than are monkeys.

In selecting a primate species as a model for the population ancestral to the hominid line, the species's anatomical and behavioral potential must be the starting point. Evolutionary history needs to be taken into account. African apes are phylogenetically much closer to humans than are baboons. Even in terms of decelerated early growth, so critical to a species for which learning is essential to the adaptation, it is chimpanzees, as opposed to baboons, that are most likely to be similar to the ancestral population. This, then, is the foundation on which we must build.

Why a new model is needed: early human social life – science and myth

After Darwin, the search for origins shifted from priests and philosophers to geologists and biologists, whose solutions were often no less naive

than those of their predecessors. First, Social Darwinism and, more recently, a spate of pseudobiological tracts have become the functional
equivalents of origin myths for Western man. From the time of Spencer
and Darwin to the present, the evolutionary writings that have captured
the popular imagination – regardless of whether they were serious scholarly works or popularized formulations – have utilized metaphors that
keyed into cultural themes of long standing (Hyman, 1962). Sometimes
these metaphors have rested on powerful poetic imagery; sometimes they
have been merely catchy and essentially trite. What they have in common is that, given our culture, they have been quite effective. Recall, for
example, evolutionary slogans such as "survival of the fittest" (Spencer,
1866; Darwin, 1869); "nature red in tooth and claw" put forward in a
poem by Tennyson (1850) and still extant over a century later (de Beer,
1958); popular titles from the 1960s and 1970s such as "the imperial
animal" (Tiger and Fox, 1971), "the naked ape" (Morris, 1967), "men in
groups" (Tiger, 1969), or a sociobiological metaphor, "the selfish gene"
(Dawkins, 1976). Thematically, many such metaphors bear a striking resemblance to images promulgated by the entertainment industry – also a
product of Western culture (see Figure 2:2). Twentieth century evolutionary myths, like Social Darwinism in the nineteenth century, are often no
more than backward projections of features of our own culture. They thus
serve to interpret and justify aspects of the Western economic system and
some of Western society's particularly chauvinistic, hierarchical, and war-
like characteristics.

Any discipline is profoundly affected by the culture in which it arises.
Until recently, most anthropologists and students of animal behavior were
Western and, with a few notable exceptions, male. Because observers
naturally look at things from their own perspectives, there has been a
pronounced tendency to approach social behavior with the implicit question: How did Western adult male behavior evolve? Even in animal behavior studies, sex stereotyping has been prevalent: the male as hunter,
provider, protector; the female as nest builder and devoted mother. But
recent observations have revealed the fallaciousness of such uncritical assumptions. A beaver colony, for instance, is organized around the adult
female, who most often repairs the dam, maintains the lodge, builds food
caches, and gives warning signals, whereas male activity primarily consists
of checking the dam for leaks (Hodgson and Larson, 1973). Similarly,
Schaller's four-year study of lions in the African Serengeti revealed that the
females are the most active predators and share the meat with the males
and young. The males kill only for themselves (Schaller, 1972).

So too with human evolution; the concept "man the hunter" pervades

FIGURE 2:2. King Kong: a cultural metaphor from the movies of the 1930s.

most of the earlier reconstructions of the lifeways of the first hominids (Read, 1920; Zuckerman, 1933; Dart, 1949; Bartholomew and Birdsell, 1953; Etkin, 1954; Washburn and Lancaster, 1968; Lee and DeVore, 1968). Assumptions regarding early hominid hunting and the emphasis placed on it in the anthropological literature of one to several decades ago are now undergoing reevaluation among scholars. Many scholars already realize how unlikely full-scale hunting would have been among the early hominids and recognize that gathering played a critical role. Popularists

FIGURE 2:3. Images of australopithecine "hunting." The original appeared as the lead illustration for an article entitled "A Definition of Man" (Oakley, 1962).

have, however, picked up the hunting idea; and they have exaggerated it far beyond what had been assumed by an earlier generation of anthropologists, before sufficient data for examining the idea were available. Robert Ardrey, for example, goes so far as to claim: "While we are members of the intelligent primate family, we are uniquely human even in the noblest sense, because for untold millions of years we alone killed for a living" (Ardrey, 1976: Preface). John Napier, in reviewing Ardrey's book, effectively expresses just how unlikely such a claim is.

There is no doubt that to have been a hunter in open country was an unlikely career for a basal hominid unless he were already endowed with three major advantages – bidepalism, tool and weapon use, and an organisational brain sufficiently evolved to be able to substitute skill for speed and strength. Anything less than the full expression of these characters would have left the basal hominid in the awkward position of being incompletely adapted for a hunting life. A more vulnerable state for a hominid, fresh from the boon-docks, in competition with the full paid-up carnivores of the grasslands, is hard to imagine. Yet this is the situation that Ardrey is asking us to accept.　　　　　　　　　[Napier, 1976:242]

Unfortunately, Ardrey's prose is an illustration of the sort of press that can result as a popular by-product when scholars employ unexamined assumptions, based largely on their cultural background rather than on the evidence.

Huxley, in his essay "Evolution and Ethics" (1893) and his subsequent introduction (1894) to the republished essay, was to disavow the extremes of Social Darwinism by the end of the nineteenth century. Though never dreaming that the course of evolution in the animal world might be anything but vicious, he became horrified at the thought that what he imagined as the brutality of the biological selective process should govern human social life. Apparently rather vainly, he therefore attempted to put forward a concept of human ethics that stood in opposition to what he conceived as the laws of nature:

The practice of that which is ethically best . . . involves . . . conduct which . . . is opposed to that which leads to success in the cosmic struggle for existence . . .

Its influence is directed, not so much to the survival of the fittest, as to the fitting of as many as possible to survive. It repudiates the gladiatorial theory of existence . . .

It is from neglect of these plain considerations that the fanatical individualism of our time attempts to apply the analogy of cosmic nature to society . . .

The intelligence which has converted the brother of the wolf into the faithful guardian of the flock ought to be able to do something towards curbing the instincts of savagery in civilized men.
　　　　　　　　　[Huxley, 1893, as reprinted 1896:81, 82, 85]

Huxley, toward the end of his life, thus came to regret the excesses of Social Darwinism that unfortunately followed from some of his assumptions. What he did not understand is that it is ineffective to disavow the social side

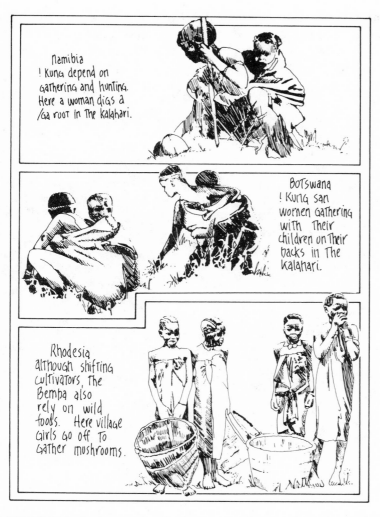

Namibia
!Kung depend on gathering and hunting. Here a woman digs a /Ga root in the Kalahari.

Botswana !Kung san women gathering with their children on their backs in the Kalahari.

Rhodesia although shifting cultivators, the Bemba also rely on wild foods. Here village girls go off to gather mushrooms.

FIGURE 2:4. Among most gathering and hunting peoples today, gathering efforts provide roughly 70 percent of the food. Women are extremely actively engaged in gathering wild foods. Were women's economic activities any less important among the early hominids?

effects of one's assumptions while still maintaining the same basic ideas. Today scholars are also beginning to feel some sense of responsibility for aspects of popular doctrines that earlier evolutionary assumptions may have inadvertently spawned. Efforts are underway to counteract some of the current extremes. But the more basic task, I believe, is the reexamination of elemental assumptions and the building of a new model.

Female behavior and the behavior of the young — in whom, for example, the early development of intelligence and the evolution of crying, smiling, and gurgling may well have been important bases for survival — were, until this last quarter of the twentieth century, largely neglected. Women's reproductive role, of course, had been acknowledged, but their part in subsistence, protection, play, communication, and tool making had been almost ignored. Gathering plants for subsistence, an activity far more certain of result than predation on or hunting of animals, is of such basic importance in the food quest that it is simply amazing that there has been so little inquiry into its invention, development, and effects for the evolving hominids (Figure 2:4). One thing seems clear: Plant gathering was and is an arena in which females exercised their ingenuity and expended their energy.

This book attempts to present a well-documented reconstruction of our human past that incorporates both sexes and the young as well as adults in a context determined by the ascertainable conditions of their own existence rather than as a flashback of ours. An evolutionary sequence is proposed: It differentiates early from later behavior; integrates economic, technological, organizational, communicatory, and affective aspects with the anatomical and physiological capacities of the organism; and relates these features to the ecological context in which early populations were evolving.

THREE
African apes and human evolution

BUT it is not I who seek to base man's dignity on his great toe.

Thomas H. Huxley, 1863

FROM what sort of pongid ancestor did the earliest hominids diverge? How long ago did this occur? These have been hotly debated issues, with experts in molecular evolution often having reached different conclusions from primate fossil specialists. This chapter deals with these issues and attempts to weigh the evidence and assess to what extent it may be possible to reconcile the two bodies of evidence. I then return to the question, posed in Chapter 2, of whether there is a living primate – and, if so, which one – that can serve as an effective model of the ancestral ape population from which the hominid line diverged.

Apes and humans: an anatomical and behavioral perspective

Shortly after Darwin's proposal of evolutionary mechanisms in 1859, Thomas Henry Huxley speculated explicitly on the course of human evolution in *Evidence as to Man's Place in Nature* (1863, as reprinted 1959). Huxley demonstrated anatomical similarities between apes and humans and argued for evolutionary continuity; Darwin postulated the selective factors that could make such continuity possible. Huxley, a comparative anatomist, juxtaposed humans and the great apes. He recognized the extent of our similarities with African apes and concluded that humans evolved from an ape-like ancestor. Comparative anatomy was a primary method in evolutionary reconstruction because, during the last half of the nineteenth century when Huxley and Darwin were writing, little fossil evidence was available.

In comparing apes and humans, Huxley identified three sets of structures as crucial in the hominid evolutionary process: (1) the pelvis and lower limbs – these changed during the development of upright posture, with the pelvis becoming shorter and broader, the legs longer, and the feet less flexible; (2) the canine teeth and associated muscles—human canines are small and almost identical in size for both sexes, as contrasted to the large ones of common chimpanzees and gorillas, with males' canines larger than females'; and (3) the brain, which increased in volume to become two to three times the size of the African ape brain. The evolutionary importance of the three anatomical systems identified by Huxley has been confirmed from the fossil record (see Figure 3:1), and it is now apparent that these systems evolved at different times and rates (Washburn, 1950; McHenry, 1975). The dentition and locomotor structures were the first to change as they are directly related to the feeding adaptation. Brain size increased subsequent to the establishment of the hominid line.

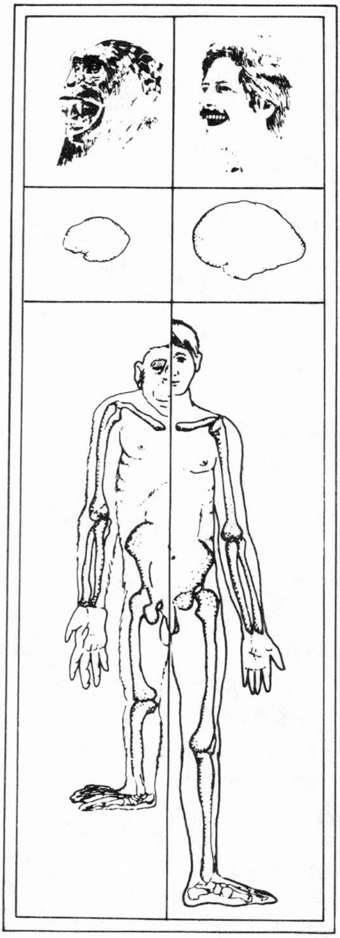

In *The Descent of Man and Selection in Relation to Sex* (1871), Darwin built upon Huxley's slender outline to expand his own earlier suggestion (1859) that the human species was a product of evolution. Some scientists stressed human distinctiveness from apes in features such as the large human brain, small canine teeth, well-developed thumbs, unique pelvis, and two feet adapted to walking upright. What Darwin argued was that selective processes had transformed these structures from those of an ape ancestor to those that exist today.

FIGURE 3:1. Three important anatomical systems differ between chimpanzee and human: dentition; brain; and locomotor structures, especially pelvis, legs and feet. Hands also differ (although arms and shoulders are very similar).

The relationship of the lower limb complex to bipedal locomotion, initially pointed out by Huxley, was elaborated by Darwin. He maintained that as our ancestors began to walk upright and hands and arms came to enhance survival through tool use, the individuals most effective at bipedalism survived in greater numbers. Darwin thought that free use of hands was partly the cause and partly the result of erect posture, which indirectly led to the modification of the anatomy of the pelvis, lower limb, and foot. He further suggested that early humans acquired the habit of utilizing clubs and weapons with their freed hands and arms, thus using jaws and teeth less for fighting. He proposed that this could account for the reduced size of canine teeth, jaws, and associated muscles, and the more gracile skull in humans. This rationale for the gracile human skull and reduced canine tooth and jaw size, as compared with apes, has been widely accepted – as might be expected given the emphasis on weaponry in Western society. For reasons to be presented later I favor an explanation that, although including some role for protective activities, emphasizes functions of the teeth related to food processing and communication.

Darwin also emphasized the close relationship between brain size and development of intellectual faculties. Like Huxley, he believed there was no fundamental difference in the structure of human and ape brains and thought the critical factor was simply an expansion in size. As Darwin (1871) saw it, the ape brain was capable of memory, emotion, and imagination but not language, which is of paramount significance in humans. He realized that the elaboration of the brain as a basis for language was the single most outstanding human characteristic. Thus Darwin viewed human origins in terms of modification of behaviors and their correlated structures through time. He showed that evolution could be understood as the contributions of successful behaviors – through selection of biological bases – to the formation of new species and new ways of life. In spite of oversimplifications and misunderstandings (particularly, his Lamarckian interpretations), Darwin's perspective was essentially sound. Today, additional lines of evidence support Darwin's and Huxley's proposal that humans evolved from an ape-like predecessor.

Ape social behavior and intelligence

Today, studies of apes in the wild and in laboratory situations have begun to demonstrate remarkable similarities between humans and apes – even in the realm of intelligence, tool use, and communication. Early studies of captive chimpanzees on Tenerife, Canary Islands, in about 1915 by the German scientist Köhler (1927, translated), showed that chimpanzees can make and use tools. About this time the American psychologists Yerkes and Yerkes (1929) were also exploring chimpanzee mental abilities; and

FIGURE 3:2. Learning through play: Here, a young chimpanzee plays with its mother's stem tool.

in Russia, Kohts was studying chimpanzee communication, particularly facial expressions, and comparing ape and human infants (1935). These initial laboratory studies focused on mental capacities, especially tool use and communication, and highlighted the intelligence of apes. The first field studies on African apes in natural settings were encouraged by the Yerkeses and carried out by Nissen (1931) on chimpanzees and by Bingham (1932) on gorillas. These investigations, though brief, called attention to the importance of studying animals in the wild where the full range of individual and group behavior could be observed.

Some 30 years later, during the 1960s, a number of more extensive field studies on chimpanzees and gorillas were finally undertaken in a variety of African habitats, and they illustrate the diversity, variability, and complexity of behavior present in wild populations. Jane Goodall began her famous long-term study of Gombe Stream chimpanzees in Tanzania in 1960. Soon after, the Kyoto University African Primatological Expedition began work in Tanzania, followed by Adriaan Kortlandt in central and western Africa and

FIGURE 3:3. There are many similarities in chimpanzee and human nonverbal communication. Here, chimpanzees touch palms, engage in a mouth-to-mouth greeting, and embrace.

Frances Reynolds in Uganda. During the 1970s, many other researchers have continued the African field research begun in the previous decade and have made extremely valuable further contributions on diet, tools, and social behavior. (See Figure 3:12 for information on these recent studies.)

That chimpanzees were clever and capable of using objects as tools in a variety of ways had been documented in Köhler's early work. Recent field observations further show that chimpanzees select raw materials, fashion them into tools, and use them in a variety of circumstances and that there also are indications that patterns of tool use may show regional variation. In group composition, mother–offspring interaction, communication, conflict, sexual behavior, and play, chimpanzees are variable, flexible, and "human-like." For example, the number and form of greeting patterns and reassurance gestures—such as "kissing," palm touching, shoulder patting, and embracing—strike human observers (Goodall, 1976). This is not a matter of simple anthropomorphism: Chimpanzee gestures remind us of ourselves because they are used in similar interactional contexts and, at least in that sense, have "meanings" similar to those in our communication (Goodall, 1968b).

African apes and human evolution: the story molecules tell about genetic affinity

The close relationship between *Homo sapiens* and the African apes, originally deduced by Huxley and Darwin from anatomical comparisons, has been further confirmed by comparing molecules between the species to obtain a quantitative measure of relative genetic distance. This "distance" has been measured in a variety of plants and animals for many of the common proteins that make up organisms, as well as for nucleic acids (Goodman and Lasker, 1975).[1] At this molecular level of comparison a relatively fine-grained assessment of degrees of evolutionary closeness can be made.

In different species, what appear to be functionally and structurally very similar (i.e., homologous) proteins nonetheless differ somewhat in their precise sequence of constituent amino acids. The more distant the evolutionary relationship between two organisms, the more differences there will be in the amino acid sequences of these proteins. The rate of evolutionary change for any one type of protein molecule is thought to be relatively constant over time (Wilson et al., 1977). From one type of molecule to another, however, rates differ greatly. Therefore, degrees of similarity and difference can be measured between distantly related organisms, such as plants and animals, by comparing slowly changing molecules like cytochrome C; and the extent of similarity between closely related forms can be determined from faster-changing molecules, such as fibrinopeptides or transferrins.

Numerous comparisons of homologous proteins, and of nucleic acids, have demonstrated the extremely close genetic relationship among humans, chimpanzees, and gorillas. Further, human and African ape chromosomes have similar shapes (Klinger et al., 1963; Bender and Chu, 1963) and nearly identical banding patterns (Miller, 1977). African apes and humans share susceptibility to many of the same diseases and parasites (Hsiung et al., 1964; McClure and Guilloud, 1971). They have such similar immunological responses and reactions to medication that one African ape, the chimpanzee, is the preferred testing subject for some drug firms — an eventuality that may prove disastrous to the chimpanzee. Chimpanzees are so much in demand in the United States for testing of medication for human use that they are currently being captured (to capture a baby, the mother is shot because she protects her infant and will not willingly allow its capture), smuggled across national borders, and sold to drug firms. As

[1] Nucleic acids are essentially the basic genetic material and are of two major types, DNA or deoxyribonucleic acids and RNA or ribonucleic acids (Barry and Barry, 1973).

Jane Goodall and Geza Teleki have pointed out, chimpanzees are being exported at such a rate that some populations are in danger of severe reduction in size or even extinction (Wade, 1978).

Similarities between humans and African apes at the molecular level, in chromosome shape and banding,[2] in susceptibility to parasites, and in response to diseases and medications, coupled with similarities in anatomy, learning patterns, and modes of nonverbal communication, make the African apes (and especially the chimpanzee, for reasons to be explained later) particularly interesting. In the new field of molecular evolution, it is now possible to trace the extent of genetic affinity between humans and apes in considerable detail. Comparisons of protein molecules (such as hemoglobin and myoglobin, albumin, transferrin, fibrinopeptides), as well as of nucleic acids, show about the same amount of accumulated change in the three lines leading to (1) the common and pygmy chimpanzees, (2) the gorilla, and (3) humans (Sarich and Wilson, 1967; Wilson and Sarich, 1969; Cronin, 1975, 1977a; Sarich and Cronin, 1976). It is evident from findings such as these that the relationship between humans and African apes is evolutionarily very close. The molecular evidence strongly supports a divergence of humans and African apes from a common ancestor not very many millions of years ago.

Genes, appearance, and behavior

People tend to judge closeness or distance of relationship among animals by their external appearance and behavior. Indeed, the basis for the Linnaean system of classification is appearance. But molecular studies amply illustrate that actual genetic relationship and, therefore, evolutionary histories cannot be determined from appearance alone. There are, for example, two kinds of frogs (*Rana* and *Hyla*) where the species within each genus look almost identical, but their albumins differ by 20 to 30 times as much as between chimpanzee and human (King and Wilson, 1975).

Humans and apes (particularly the great apes) are genetically about as different from each other as closely-related species . . . in other groups of organisms . . . [For example], we have obtained estimates of genetic differentiation between humans and the great apes no greater than, say, those observed between morphologically indistinguishable (sibling) species of *Drosophila* flies.   [Bruce and Ayala, 1978:265]

---

[2] There is a "striking resemblance of the subbanding pattern of most chromosomes" (Yunis, Sawyer, and Dunham, 1980:1146). In fact, these researchers find "the fine structure and genetic organization of the chromosomes of man and chimpanzees . . . so similar that it is difficult to account for their phenotypic differences" (1980:1145).

The paradox of the human—chimpanzee relationship is how they can be so close genetically yet appear quite different in external morphology and behavior. Although numerous anatomical similarities were noted a century or more ago by Huxley and Darwin, many have thought evolutionary separation to be quite long. To some extent, of course, this may have been influenced by an understandable tendency to want to see our own species widely separated from the animal world. Huxley sensed this when he wrote:

On all sides I shall hear the cry—"We are men and women, not a mere better sort of apes, a little longer of leg, more compact in the foot, and bigger in brain than your brutal Chimpanzees and Gorillas . . . "

But, it is not I who seek to base man's dignity on his great toe, or insinuate that we are lost if an Ape has a hippocampus minor. On the contrary, I have done my best to sweep away this vanity.

[1863, as reprinted 1959:129]

However, in addition to some degree of ascientific wistfulness that may occasionally encourage an exaggeration of human—ape differences, there is also the real matter of fairly large phenotypic distinctions between the African apes and ourselves, whereas genetic differences appear to be quite minor. In other words, humans do not look or act as much like apes as might be expected, given the molecular similarities. How is it possible for ape and human phenotypes, as reflected in anatomy and behavior, to appear quite distinctive, despite the molecular evidence for a close genetic relationship? King and Wilson (1975) suggest that changes in relatively few regulatory genes plus shifts in gene arrangement could account for this phenomenon. Much of the human genetic code could thereby remain similar to that of apes, but with a few significant changes accounting for anatomical differences or making feasible the major behavioral differences (largely related to the human capacity for language and culture) that do exist between humans and apes.

Methods

How can the degree of genetic affinity, as distinct from phenotypic similarities and differences, be measured? A variety of macromolecules—proteins and nucleic acids—have been compared, and research on an array of species has been carried out (Ayala, 1976; Goodman et al., 1976). This account will concentrate on studies comparing chimpanzee and human macromolecules.

Four methods are available for comparing macromolecules (Cronin, 1975; Nei, 1975; Sarich and Cronin, 1976; Almquist and Cronin, 1977;

Wilson et al., 1977): (1) Direct amino acid sequencing of proteins, or of the nucleotide sequences of DNA, is possible. Indirect means of examining amino acid sequences in proteins to determine the degree of molecular similarity also exist and include (2) immunological techniques and (3) electrophoresis. In addition, (4) DNA, which carries the genetic code, can be studied through DNA hybridization.

Amino acid sequencing determines the actual arrangement of amino acids in a particular protein. In sequencing, the linear chains of amino acids that comprise homologous proteins in different species can be directly compared and the changes counted. Similarly, the sequence of the four nucleotides that make up the genetic code in DNA can be examined (Nei, 1975). Direct sequencing is of limited applicability because the costs are high and both amino acid and nucleotide sequencing are very time consuming.

Immunology is simpler and nearly as informative. Indirect measures of amino acid differences between homologous proteins from two species can be obtained relatively easily. The protein molecule to be compared is used as an antigen. Antibodies are produced in a host, and then homologous protein molecules from another species are reacted with these antibodies. The amount of reaction reflects the degree of "recognition" by the antibody. For the hominids, the phylogenetic group that includes humans and apes, immunological results for many protein molecules have proved extremely consistent. The greatest amount of reaction is, as would be expected, between human antigens and human antibodies. Next in degree of reaction are African apes–humans (i.e., chimpanzee–human and/or gorilla–human). Last are Asian apes–humans (i.e., gibbon–human or orangutan–human). Despite some variation in the intensity of reactions for the different molecules tested, the overall branching order remains constant–with humans and African apes more closely related than humans and Asian apes– no matter which molecules are compared (Cronin, 1977a).

Electrophoresis is a technique that can be used in comparing closely related organisms. Proteins are placed in an electric field and are discriminated by the degree of differential migration in the medium. (Only part of the amino acids in a protein are charged, so a correlation factor must be calculated for the remaining amino acids.) Charge changes occur in only about one fourth of mutations, and the net charge can remain constant while the primary sequence varies. In electrophoresis, then, one can note only a proportion of the actual changes that have occurred during the evolution of homologous proteins in different lines.

DNA strands (which carry the genetic code) can be compared by *DNA hybridization* (Kohne, 1970; Kohne et al., 1972). The first step is to break the links between the double strands by heating the DNA. As the DNA cools, the strands realign and pair again. The extent of relatedness of DNA strands is evident in the degree to which strands reassociate. Single DNA strands from different species, such as humans and chimpanzees, can be placed together to see whether they will link up again. For humans and chimpanzees, the single strands do bond again; this is called DNA hybridization. The next step is to compare human double-strand DNA (that has bonded again) to this hybridized chimpanzee–human double-strand DNA. Similarities and differences are measured in terms of relative thermal stability, that is, in terms of the difference between the dissociation temperature of hybridized chimpanzee–human DNA and the dissociation temperature of reannealed human DNA. By comparing the temperatures at which human DNA and hybridized chimpanzee–human DNA chains dissociate, the percentage of identity (in the nucleotide base pair sequences that form DNA) can be determined. This method is useful for organisms not too distantly related, for example, those in the same mammalian order. If the organisms are too distant the single strands of DNA will not hybridize.

Findings

For humans and chimpanzees, identity in amino acid sequences has been demonstrated for several proteins: cytochrome C, fibrinopeptide A and B, and the alpha, beta, and gamma chains of hemoglobin. Some difference is noted for albumins, myoglobin, and transferrin (also proteins), for the enzyme carbonic anhydrase I, and for DNA (DeJong, 1971; Goodman and Lasker, 1975; Sarich and Cronin, 1976).

Cytochrome C is necessary for oxidation in cells and is part of the common heritage of all organisms with nucleated cells, both plants and animals. It has been studied in some 50 species from humans to fruit flies to bread mold (Goodman, 1976; Moore et al., 1976; Fitch, 1977). Cytochrome C changes extremely slowly, and identity in humans and chimpanzees would be expected. Its extremely conservative nature means that it is not particularly useful for comparing closely related organisms.

In contrast, fibrinopeptides, which function to keep the blood-clotting protein in a nonaggregating molecule until it is needed, change very rapidly.[3] All are identical in humans and chimpanzees (Doolittle and Mross, 1970). By way of comparison, fibrinopeptides in four species of Old World monkeys differ from humans in 5 to 8 of the 30 amino acid

---

[3] The unit evolutionary period (UEP) of fibrinopeptide A is 1.7 million and of fibrinopeptide B only 1.1 million (Wilson et al., 1977). The UEP is a standard measure whereby molecules of different size can be compared. The UEP of a protein molecule is the average time it takes for a 1 percent change to accumulate in an amino acid sequence.

positions. The identity of chimpanzee and human fibrinopeptides is of note, as these are among the fastest-changing molecules known. Other mammalian pairs with identical fibrinopeptides are sheep and goats, and llamas and vicunas. Humans and chimpanzees are closer in fibrinopeptides than horse–donkey, water buffalo–Cape buffalo, cat–lion, or dog–fox pairs (Doolittle and Mross, 1970; Doolittle et al., 1971).

There are only a few differences between chimpanzees and humans in the globins, which change fairly rapidly (although more slowly than fibrinopeptides, transferrins, or albumins). Hemoglobin molecules carry oxygen in the red blood cells and are longer than fibrinopeptides but smaller than transferrins or albumins. There is one amino acid difference between chimpanzees and humans in the delta chain of hemoglobin and in myoglobin, a muscle protein (King and Wilson, 1975). The amino acid composition of the alpha, beta, and gamma hemoglobin chains in chimpanzees and humans is indistinguishable (DeJong, 1971; Goodman and Lasker, 1975).[4]

Transferrin is a large blood plasma protein that transports iron to the sites of synthesis. Next to fibrinopeptides, transferrin is one of the faster-changing molecules.[5] On the average, human and chimpanzee transferrins differ by only about 9 "transferrin units" (a type of immunological unit) compared to 49 between apes and Old World monkeys (Sarich and Cronin, 1976). Albumin, also a blood plasma protein, changes more slowly than transferrin.[6] Humans and chimpanzees differ in just 7 "albumin units," (also immunological units) as compared to 34 to 36 units between apes and Old World monkeys (Sarich and Cronin, 1976). These molecules are a sample of the many that have been studied. Others include haptoglobin, lysozyme, and lactate dehydrogenase (see King and Wilson, 1975, for review). For all, the close relationship between chimpanzee and human is evident.

Molecular "clocks"

Chimpanzees and humans obviously shared a common ancestor. Zuckerkandl and Pauling (1962) suggested that molecular comparisons might serve as an evolutionary clock; and this is an idea that has generated considerable discussion and experimentation since then. How might such study of macromolecules indicate when two groups separated? In the construction of an evolutionary picture, three components are present: (1)

---

[4] The UEPs for some of the globins are: myoglobin, 6 million; and alpha and beta hemoglobins, 3.7 million and 3.3 million, respectively (Wilson et al., 1977).
[5] The UEP of transferrin is 2 million (Cronin, 1975).
[6] The albumin UEP is 3 million (Wilson et al., 1977).

cladistics, or the branching order of various groups, (2) patristics, or measurement of change in a specific characteristic of a lineage, and (3) chronistics, dating divergent events (Cronin, 1977a). I am considering cladistics and chronistics here.

From the study of several proteins in a number of species it has become apparent that each type of molecule evolves on the average, over long periods of time, at what has been termed "a statistically constant rate" (Almquist and Cronin, 1977). This statistical regularity through time is an observed and measured phenomenon, not an assumption (Sarich and Wilson, 1967; Sarich, 1973; Sarich and Cronin, 1976; Wilson et al., 1977; Carlson et al., 1978). Thus, molecules of the same type change, on the average, at a fairly regular rate. This averaging out over long periods of time does not negate the likelihood that, in the short run, molecular changes may occur at quite irregular intervals (Lewontin, 1974). In order to most accurately calculate a divergence time for any two lineages, several molecules should be used.

A set of branching relationships (i.e., a cladogram) is constructed from the molecular "ratios of closeness" for living species (Sarich and Cronin, 1976). The next step is to choose a calibration point. Dates from the fossil record for a number of divergences can provide reference points in time. Those used here for calibration are 70 million years ago for the "lower"–"higher" primate (prosimian–anthropoid) divergence and 35 million to 40 million years for the Old World monkeys/apes and the New World monkey divergence (Sarich and Cronin, 1976).[7] With calibration points

[7] Establishing calibration points is the most difficult aspect in the construction of a molecular clock. The divergence dates used here are not yet firmly established (Radinsky, 1978).

For the lower primate–higher primate divergence, dates from about 70 Mya to 45 Mya could fit the fossil records, depending on interpretation. In support of a date at the earlier end, fossil primates were already in existence by about 65 Mya (Hill, 1972), and Butzer (1978) and Simons (1976) think that the primates may have diverged from other placental mammals as early as 80 Mya to 100 Mya. An estimate of 65 Mya to 70 Mya for the divergence of "lower" and "higher" primates (i.e., prosimians and anthropoids) therefore is not unreasonable. Alternatively, the anthropoids may have diverged from the prosimians at a somewhat later period. This interpretation is favored by Romero-Herrera et al. (1973), who think it most likely that the anthropoids arose from one branch of the prosimians – the Tarsiiforms. Tarsiiforms are present in the fossil record in the early Eocene, which probably was some 50 or so millions of years ago (Berggren, 1972). At the most recent end of the scale, the earliest known anthropoid (higher primate) fossils found appear in the late Eocene, early Oligocene, perhaps 40 Mya to 35 Mya (Simons, 1972; Berggren, 1972; Campbell and Bernor, 1976). According to Radinsky, a divergence date more recent than 45 Mya "is highly unlikely, since by those times (or very shortly thereafter), we have undoubted fossils of the relevant groups involved" (1978:1182).

For the divergence of New World monkeys from the ancestors of Old World monkeys and apes, interpretations also differ. New World monkey fossils dating from the early Oligocene have been found in Bolivia (Simons, 1976). The early Oligocene is generally thought

superimposed on the set of branching relationships, molecular changes become "evolutionary clocks" (see Figure 3:4).

Molecular changes, therefore, provide a basis for calculating relationships. When a date from the fossil record is plugged into the set of branching relationships (cladogram) that was constructed according to degrees of molecular similarity, the dates for divergences are thereby determined. Each date for branching is therefore as "valid" as another. Thus, if one estimates the divergence of higher from lower primates at about 70 million years ago and of the New World monkeys from the Old World monkeys and apes at between 35 million and 40 million years ago, it becomes extremely difficult to discard a date of 5 million years ago for the ape–human divergence.

From the eastern African fossil evidence, the dating of the divergence between humans and African apes can be narrowed even further. Fossils that are clearly hominid date from the Hadar Formation, Afar Triangle, Ethiopia, about 3 million to 3.7 million years ago. There is an exceptional lower jaw from the Laetolil formation near Garusi, Tanzania, that has distinctive hominid features but has a canine about the size of that of a female pygmy chimpanzee (see Figure 8:7). It dates from 3.77 to 3.59 million years ago. There are very fragmentary remains of possible early hominid or transitional fossils from over 4 million years ago. But dental remains at Lothagam probably dating from about 5.5 million years ago, which were previously assumed to be hominid, have now been shown to have measurements that fall within the ape range (Eckhardt, 1977). This combined evidence is compatible with the estimate of 5 million to 4 million years for the *Homo–Pan–Gorilla* divergence derived from molecular studies (Sarich, 1973; Sarich and Cronin, 1976, 1977).

to have dated from about 38 Mya to 32 Mya (Berggren, 1972). However, Simons (1976) believes a considerably earlier divergence, about 55 Mya, is likely based on his understanding of continental shifts. Szalay, in contrast, thinks that the ancestor of the Old World monkeys and apes may have diverged from the New World monkeys (who, in his view, could have evolved first) and reached Africa "not much earlier than the latest Eocene" (1975:20). This would be about 43 Mya to 38 Mya or somewhat before but fairly close in time to the discovery of fossils of the ancestors of New World monkeys.

Sarich's and Cronin's (1976) estimate of 70 Mya for the lower–higher primate divergence and of 40 Mya to 35 Mya for the New World monkey–Old World monkey/ape split is based on further calculations from molecular evidence, which were, in turn, calibrated to a marsupial–placental divergence in the early Cretaceous about 135 Mya (Lillegraven, 1974; Cronin, pers. com.). Their estimate is also consistent with a relatively straightforward reading of the currently known fossil record. Primate fossils dating from as long ago as 65 Mya exist, and Sarich and Cronin apparently think that an early divergence of prosimians and anthropoids occurred about that time. And, New World monkey-like fossils dating from 35 Mya to 40 Mya have been found. Therefore, the fossil evidence, if taken at face value, also provides a basis for calibration of the split of New World monkeys from Old World monkeys and apes that is consistent with Sarich's and Cronin's (1976) estimate.

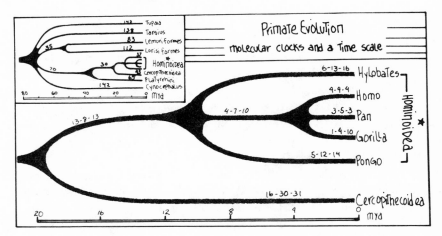

FIGURE 3:4. This molecular "clock" for the primates shows how very closely related humans (*Homo*) are to the African apes – the chimpanzee (*Pan*) and *Gorilla* – as compared with the evolutionary relationships among other apes and monkeys. The numbers on the branches refer to the amount of molecular change for certain common protein molecules in each of the various primate lines. From these data, a set of branching relationships can be constructed to illustrate molecular change over time. The large diagram is a blowup of a section of the smaller diagram (*inset*) and shows the relationship of the primates closest to humans. *Above left,* a phylogeny of the primates utilizes a combination of albumin and transferrin to show relative molecular "distances" for humans and apes (*Hominoidea*), Old World monkeys (*Cercopithecoidea*), New World monkeys (*Platyrrhini*), and the various "lower" primates or prosimians such as *Tupaia, Tarsius,* etc. *Below,* cladistic analysis based on albumin, transferrin, and DNA differences shows the relatively small molecular differentiation between *Homo* and the African apes (*Pan* and *Gorilla*), the greater distance between these three hominoids and the Asian apes (*Hylobates* and *Pongo*), and the large difference between the hominoids as a group and the cercopithecoids (the Old World monkeys).

Summary

Comparative studies of proteins through amino acid sequencing and immunology show that "the average human polypeptide (i.e., protein molecule) is more than 99 percent identical to its chimpanzee counterpart" (King and Wilson, 1975:114, 115). This molecular similarity indicates common ancestry and divergence so recent that relatively few genetic changes (of the sort that code for the amino acid sequence of proteins) have had a chance to occur. The relatedness of chimpanzees and humans and the time of their divergence can therefore be judged in the same context as for other closely related pairs (horse–donkey; water buffalo–cape buffalo; cat–lion, etc.), all of which are thought to have diverged in

Pleistocene or recent times (Doolittle and Mross, 1970) – that is, within the last 2 million years.

The biochemical evidence demonstrates impressive genetic affinities between African apes and humans. These "ratios of closeness," when arranged into a "tree" and calibrated to a divergence of lower and higher primates at 70 million years ago, and of New World monkeys from Old World monkeys and apes at 35 million to 40 million years ago, suggest a time scale within which the radiation of primates and the divergence of the hominid line took place (Figure 3:4). From this molecular evidence the ape–human divergence would appear to be a very recent one, perhaps only 4 million or 5 million years ago. These dates are consistent with the existence of uncontested hominids in eastern Africa by at least 3 million and very probably by 3.77–3.59 million years ago. Molecular evolutionary studies confirm the close relationship of humans and African apes that Darwin and Huxley suggested a century ago, further the understanding of phylogenetic relationships, and provide a basis for calculating the times of divergence of living forms.

Ape evolutionary history

The "higher" primates of today (anthropoids) include monkeys, apes, and humans. They contrast in many ways with the "lower" primates or prosimians – tree shrews, tarsiers, lemurs, lorises, and galagos. Most prosimians have small, procumbent incisors and sharp-cusped molars and premolars, are usually nocturnal, and rely heavily on the sense of smell. All the higher primates have special visual refinements – color vision (more developed in Old World monkeys, apes, and humans than among New World monkeys) and a high degree of stereoscopic vision, both of which promote depth perception. They are almost all day living and, compared to most prosimians, relatively social. In the primate fossil record, the so-called Miocene ape fossils (which date from about 20 million to 9 million years ago) actually may be ancestral to Old World monkeys as well as to apes and to humans.

A time line is essential for the study of fossils relevant to ape and human evolution. Absolute dating of volcanic rocks (in which the proportions of potassium and argon change over time after a volcanic eruption) is now feasible. Geological sequences from different areas can sometimes be matched by examining their patterns of magnetism. (Some periods have normal magnetic polarity, whereas others show reversed polarity.) Further, the contemporaneity of sites in the same general locale can be recognized when they contain similar fossil fauna. Paleomagnetic and faunal sequences therefore provide an important means of cross-checking isolated potassium–argon radiometric dates. Correlational "dates" can be determined for areas without datable volcanic rocks when good paleomagnetic and faunal correlations with areas where volcanic rocks have been dated exist. By the combination of these and other techniques, the establishment of a solid chronological sequence for fossils at most sites can be anticipated in the near future.

Even today, a general outline of the time sequence pertinent to ape and human evolution can be constructed. Epochs that are particularly relevant with regard to ape and human evolution are the *Miocene,* which now extends into more recent times than previously assumed and is dated at 23.5 million to 5 million years ago, with the middle Miocene starting at 16 million years ago and the late Miocene at 12 million to 10.5 million years ago; the *Pliocene,* which is even more recent and now appears to be a much shorter period than had been thought, extending from only 5 million to 1.8 million years ago; and the *Pleistocene,* 1.6 million years ago to the present (J.A.H. and J.A. Van Couvering, 1976; Haq et al., 1977).

Important fossil "ape" remains, initially from Africa and subsequently from southern and eastern Asia and Eurasia, date from the Miocene (see Figure 3:9). These are the so-called dental apes that may have been ancestral to both monkeys and apes. Much later fossil finds in Africa, which show some resemblances to both pongids and hominids, date from the Mio-Pliocene border and the Pliocene. From the Pliocene are also some very early hominid remains. Fossils that are clearly *Australopithecus,* the first hominid genus, appear in eastern Africa in the Pliocene and continue well into the Pleistocene. *Homo erectus* and, of course, eventually *Homo sapiens* appear later in the Pleistocene. Figure 3:5 summarizes this chronological information on Miocene ape to human fossils.

Once hominid-like and hominid fossils began to appear in the African Pliocene, hominid fossils became numerous and widespread surprisingly rapidly. By 3 million years ago hominids were established in Africa, and it is possible to trace their subsequent evolution there in time and space. There is some evidence that hominids had spread to Southeast Asia by the early Pleistocene, moving first eastward through the tropics to Indonesia (Jacob and Curtis, 1971; Jacob, 1972, 1976; Ninkovich and Burckle, 1978), then northward from Southeast Asia to China, and north from Africa to Circum-Mediterranean regions by the Middle Pleistocene.

An early "higher" primate radiation – early to middle Miocene fossils

The line leading to both Old World monkeys and apes was probably part of an early to middle Miocene higher primate radiation that may have started some 20 million years ago. Dental remains are primarily ape-like, with U-shaped or V-shaped dental arcades, somewhat procumbent incisors, fairly large canines, and Y-5 cusp patterns on the molars (Simons and Pilbeam, 1965; Pilbeam, 1969; Bilsborough, 1971; Swindler, 1976, Poirier, 1977; Greenfield, 1978). However, fossils with monkey-like teeth also have been found from the early Miocene in Africa (Delson, 1975a, b). Features of the limbs (and the sacrum of one species) are often quite monkey-like or intermediate between monkeys and apes (Washburn, 1963; Ankel, 1965; Morbeck, 1972, 1975a; Preuschoft, 1973). These anatomical data are consistent with molecular evidence placing the divergence between Old World monkeys and apes in the early Miocene, about 20 million to 22 million years ago (Sarich and Cronin, 1977; Cronin, 1977a).

The limb skeletons of living monkeys and apes are easily distinguished and relate to their differing locomotor adaptations: quadrupedalism on the top of branches for monkeys, sometimes combined with the use of a tail for swinging and balancing; and for apes, brachiation, a below-branch hanging, swinging, and climbing pattern (Figure 3:6).

The locomotion of the early to mid-Miocene primates differed from both modern monkeys and modern apes (see Figure 3:7). The few preserved limb bones and joints of these Miocene "dental apes" were intermediate, possessing some features like monkeys, others like apes. Brachiation is a distinguishing behavior of apes as we know them today: Mobile shoulder and wrist joints make hanging and swinging from branch to branch possible. Humans also have similar types of mobile shoulder and wrist joints. Although wrist joints for some Miocene dental apes indicate a beginning capacity for suspensory locomotion, brachiation was not yet fully developed (Lewis, 1972a). Morbeck has effectively summarized the locomotor patterns of these Miocene "apes":

The Miocene post cranial evidence, in general, indicates quadrupedalism and these animals were certainly capable of a variety of postures and locomotor behavior both in the trees and on the ground. Like modern monkeys where differences are related to frequencies of these actions, they probably could walk, run, gallop, leap, climb, sit, reach, and hang or swing for short periods of time.   [1972:144]

Overall, the postcranial evidence points to an eclectic quadrupedal lifestyle, more like that of monkeys than that of apes, "and few well-defined key features of the ape-like climbing-reaching, as defined with regard to contemporary genera, are present in the known fossil record" (Morbeck, 1972:145).

Epoch		Dates (Mya)	Sites
Pleistocene 1.6 Mya to present		±1.9–0.04	Indonesia and Malaysia
		>2–0.02	Tanzania: Olduvai
Plio-Pleistocene		Probably after 2	S. Africa: Swartkrans
		Somewhat before and after 1.8	Kenya: E. Turkana
		±3–0.9	Ethiopia: Omo
Pliocene 5–1.8 Mya		Estimated 3–2.5 or less	S. Africa: Makapansgat
		About 3.7–3	Ethiopia: Afar/Hadar
		3.77–3.59	Tanzania: Laetoli
		4 (faunal 4.5–4)	Kenya: Kanapoi
		About 5.5	Kenya: Lothagam
Mio-Pliocene		About 6.5	Kenya: Baringo/Lukeino
Miocene 23.5–5 Mya		8 (bounded by 12.5–5): Khaur, Pakistan	Asia: Pakistan, India, Turkey
		14.0–12.5: Ft. Ternan, Africa No other dates	E. Africa: Kenya Europe: Greece, Hungary
		14.0–12.5: Ft. Ternan, Africa 19.6: Koru, Africa 19.8: Songhor, Africa No other dates (est. 23–9)	E. Africa: Kenya, Uganda Asia: Pakistan, India, Turkey, China Europe: France, Germany, Spain, Austria, Greece, Hungary, Czechoslovakia

FIGURE 3.5. Trends in primate and hominid evolution: time sequence for selected fossils and sites from the Miocene to the present. *Figure 3.5 continued on facing page.*

Map	Classification, Comments
	"*Meganthropus*"; *Homo erectus; Homo sapiens*
	A./H. habilis and/or *A. africanus; A. robustus/boisei; Homo erectus; Homo sapiens*
	Australopithecus robustus
	Australopithecus: great variability (gracile, robust, and an early large-brained form); *Homo erectus* appears
	Australopithecus: considerable variability (gracile, robust); *Homo erectus*
	Early gracile hominid: *Australopithecus africanus*
	Basal hominid: *A. afarensis;* bipedal, dentition still some pongid features
	Basal hominid: *A. afarensis;* bipedal, dentition still some pongid features
	Uncertain: could be hominid
	Perhaps transitional
	Probably pongid
	Ramapithecines, gigantopithecines, and sivapithecines: shorter faces than dryopithecines; thick molar enamel; great differential molar wear
	Dryopithecines: Miocene "apes"; dentition similar to living apes'; postcranial skeleton has features of both apes and monkeys

Miocene "ape" sites in Africa and Eurasia and hominid sites in Africa and Southeast Asia are shown. Both the Miocene ape fossils and the hominid fossils appear earlier in Africa than elsewhere. Our genus, *Homo*, does not appear until the Pleistocene.

FIGURE 3:6. Spider monkey, vervet monkey, and young chimpanzee moving in trees. Note four-legged locomotion and use of tail for hanging or balancing for the monkeys and armswinging (brachiation) for the chimpanzee.

The early primates of this period were widespread and successful (Morbeck, 1972; Simons, 1972).[8] They appear first in eastern Africa in the early Miocene and continue there until the beginning of the late Miocene (see Figures 3:5, 3:7, and 3:9). Similar fossil fragments appear in Eurasia about the middle Miocene (Walker, 1976; Andrews et al., 1978). Much of the eastern African environment of the early Miocene was – unlike the bush and grasslands dominating the area today – apparently a continuation of heavily forested lowlands extending eastward from the Congo Basin (Andrews and A. H. Van Couvering, 1975; Van Couvering and Van Couvering, 1976). Only in the middle Miocene, when massive uplifting and rifting occurred, was the eastern African rift system completed. A series of elongated basins with rivers and lakes was created, along which there may have been an interconnected network of gallery forests leading northward. A similar web of rain forests may have rimmed the bordering highlands and volcanos. Van Couvering and Van Couvering suggest that these eastern African forest networks of the middle Miocene may have created a "high road" and a "low road between equatorial Africa and the forested mountains and plains of Asia Minor" (1976:163, 164). As this is about the same time that Miocene ape fossils first appear outside Africa, they think this was the forest bridge that was used in expanding out of Africa.

David Pilbeam (1978a) has suggested that the fossils described above as part of an early Miocene radiation all be considered members of one family, which he would call "dryopithecids." This general category would include forms that have been known as *Dryopithecus* (including *Proconsul* and *Rangwapithecus*) as well as *Pliopithecus* (including *Limnopithecus*) (see note 8 to this chapter). On the basis of his belief that these forms have thin tooth enamel as compared with other fossil "apes" later in the Miocene and to hominids, Pilbeam suggests that these dryopithecids were forest adapted (the type of environment where plentiful succulent plant foods would be readily available). If the climate of the early to middle Miocene was generally warm and moist, as is thought to be the case, it is indeed likely that forests would have been widespread. For eastern Africa, a range of evidence

[8] Most have been classified into three genera: *Dryopithecus*, including *Proconsul* with six to nine species; *Pliopithecus*, including *Limnopithecus* with several species and *Ramapithecus*, including *Kenyapithecus wickeri* (Simons, 1972; Andrews, 1974). *Oreopithecus* and *Gigantopithecus* appear less closely related to the first three. The fossils range in body size and tooth size from the small *Pliopithecus* and *Dryopithecus africanus* to *Dryopithecus major*, perhaps as large as gorillas. Although the forms previously were thought to have given rise to modern gibbons (*Pliopithecus*), chimpanzees (*D. africanus*), gorillas (*D. major*), and hominids (*Ramapithecus*) (Pilbeam, 1966; Uzzell and Pilbeam, 1971; Simons, 1972), this may not be the case as the early conclusions were based on dental similarities only (Corruccini et al., 1976).

FIGURE 3:7. The Miocene "dental apes" had locomotor capacities intermediate between monkeys and apes today.

has been presented that indicates lowland rain forests were dominant there during the early to middle Miocene (J. A. H. Van Couvering, 1975; Andrews and A. H. Van Couvering, 1975). In this type of ecological context, a dentition similar to contemporary apes (whether or not thin tooth enamel was an important feature) could well relate to eating soft forest foods.

A later "higher" primate radiation – late middle and late Miocene fossils

Climatic deterioration began in the late middle Miocene and continued into the late Miocene; drier and somewhat cooler weather gradually re-

placed the earlier lush, moist, warm climate. The forests shrank and grasslands spread. It was during this period that *Hipparion,* the ancestor of the
horse, evolved and spread explosively over much of the globe into the new
grassy environments awaiting it about 11.5 million years ago (Walker,
1976).

In this environmental context a later radiation of Miocene "apes" may
have occurred (Kennedy, 1978). David Pilbeam (1978a) would call all the
ape fossils from this period "ramapithecids." He would divide them into
two groups – those with large, sexually dimorphic canines (the *Sivapitheci-
nae*) and those with less dimorphic canines (the *Ramapithecinae*). In the
latter, in addition to *Ramapithecus,* he includes Gigantopithecus and *Rudapithecus* (Pilbeam, Meyer, et al., 1977). All of these forms, like those
from earlier in the Miocene, are now extinct.

Controversy rages over the *ramapithecids.* Pilbeam claims they have
thicker tooth enamel than the early Miocene apes (Pilbeam, Meyer, et al.,
1977; Pilbeam, 1978a). But Frayer (1976) disputes this assessment, and his
critique of some fossils is quite telling. The issue is an important one
because one of these forms, *Ramapithecus,* has been suggested as a hominid ancestor partly on the basis of its supposed thicker tooth enamel, and
because of probable overall differences in the functioning of its jaws (with
its relatively large molars, heavy mandibles, and small canines) as compared to living apes (Pilbeam, 1969; Andrews, 1971; Uzzell and Pilbeam,
1971; Simons, 1972, 1977). If *Ramapithecus* had thicker tooth enamel
than both the earlier Miocene fossil "apes" and living apes, the argument
is that this could mean it was adapting dentally to a diet based on foods
found in relatively dry woodlands and open grasslands – a situation similar
to that postulated for early hominids.

The evidence on both tooth enamel thickness and the environment is
inconclusive. Extensive recent excavations in Pakistan have unearthed
many new *Ramapithecus* and other primate fossils there (Pilbeam, Meyer,
et al., 1977; Pilbeam, Barry, et al., 1977). Most are from Khaur region
sites dated about 8 million years ago (Tauxe, 1979). The particular combination of fauna found at these sites suggests woodlands and bush, with
patches of grassland.

In the eastern African rift zone, woodlands had probably already
largely replaced the earlier tropical forests (J. A. H. Van Couvering,
1975). But the particular environment of finds there is still unclear. Butzer
states: "The mid- and late Miocene specimens come from contexts that
were partly wooded, and partly open. In each case a mosaic of vegetation must be assumed, and in every case geological processes could
potentially have derived a particular fossil from either a closed or open
habitat" (1978:199). And in at least two areas outside Africa –

Rudabánya, Hungary and Keiyuan, southern China – ramapithecine remains have been "found in lignite deposits indicative of very moist, heavily vegetated conditions" (Kennedy, 1978:12).

The situation with regard to tooth enamel comparisons is even more obscure. Gantt, Pilbeam, and Steward (1977) compared the enamel prism patterns for living apes, the fossil *Ramapithecus,* and *Homo sapiens.* They found a similar keyhole pattern for *Ramapithecus* and *Homo sapiens* and suggested that "differences in prism packing may be correlated with differences in prism thickness" (Gantt et al., 1977:1157). Subsequently, Vrba and Grine (1978) examined the dental enamel prism patterns of several living apes (the chimpanzee, gorilla, and orangutan), an early hominid sample (gracile and robust australopithecines), and *Homo sapiens.* "On all hominid and pongid specimens . . . the keyhole pattern was found to predominate . . . The occurrence by itself of a prismatic keyhole pattern in *Ramapithecus* suggests no closer kinship of that taxon to *H. sapiens* than to the extant apes" (Vrba and Grine, 1978:890, 892).

More important than tooth enamel characteristics, or even the environmental context, is the question of whether the ramapithecids had a type of locomotor skeleton that could have been ancestral to hominids. In other words, we need to know whether the ramapithecids were already brachiators, that is, whether or not they exhibited the features of the arm and shoulder that living humans and apes share. Very little is known about the locomotor adaptation of the various late middle Miocene apes, but some postcranial bones have been discovered recently (Pilbeam, Meyer, et al., 1977). Reconstruction of ramapithecid locomotor behavior is now essential. It will not be possible to understand their relationships either to the earlier Miocene apes – for whom locomotor analyses have already been made – or to living genera without knowing whether ramapithecid locomotion was still intermediate between monkeys and apes or whether apelike brachiation had already developed.

The development of brachiation

At some point, the hominoid survivors developed brachiation, a specialized locomotor feeding system adapted to hanging and swinging in trees to obtain fruit and tender leaves from the ends of branches (Avis, 1962; Washburn, 1963; Napier, 1963; Washburn and Moore, 1974). In this adaptation the arms are considerably longer than the legs; there is no tail, and the fingers are long and curved. Shoulder and wrist bones, and forelimb and shoulder muscles, differ from those of quadrupedal monkeys (Oxnard, 1963). This radiation of brachiators has African descendants (the chimpanzees and gorillas), as well as Asiatic survivors (the gibbons and orangutans). The Asian apes, like the African apes, are brachiators; but the former are more arboreal. The Asian apes' arboreal hanging and feeding system is especially well suited to the tropical rain forests in which they live. Molecular comparisons indicate that the Asian apes diverged from the ancestral line considerably earlier than did the African apes. Similarly, from anatomical evidence, it seems apparent that Asian apes diverged from ancestral apes before the African apes did (Lewis, 1972a, b). The anatomical evidence is, therefore, consistent with molecular data.

The development of this ability to swing through the trees is critical for understanding human evolution. Anatomically, the adaptation is marked by certain features of the shoulder, arm, and wrist that make this movement feasible. Humans share many of these anatomical features with African and Asian apes. This indicates that the divergence of the hominid line occurred *after* the evolution of brachiation (see Figures 3:1 and 3:6).

Dating the development of brachiation is therefore a matter of considerable interest. Exciting fossil evidence has been recovered in Rudabánya, Hungary, by Miklós Kretzoi and his associates and studied and reported on in the United States by M. E. Morbeck (1979). Postcranial material has been found that shows important similarities with living apes in the locomotor capabilities of the arms. These are *Hipparion* (horse ancestor) age fossils and therefore probably date from about 11.5 million years ago. From molecular evidence, the divergence of gibbon and orangutan (the Asian apes) from their common primate ancestor can be estimated at roughly 11 million to 7 million years ago.[9] Based on fossil and molecular data, one reasonable hypothesis, therefore, is that brachiation developed shortly before 11 million years ago. This could have been about the same period as the radiation of the ramapithecids in the late middle and late Miocene. Did they share in the development of brachiation or not?

At Rudabánya there is dental and facial evidence of several forms, *Rudapithecus, Bodvapithecus,* and *Pliopithecus.* Pilbeam, Meyer, and their colleagues (1977) consider *Rudapithecus* to be a ramapithecid. Unfortunately the postcranial material studied by Morbeck (1979) was not associated with the dental and facial material above. Thus the critical question of whether *Ramapithecus* was a brachiator or not cannot yet be answered. If *Ramapithecus* does prove to be a brachiator, dental similarities (Simons, 1978) with hominids will have to be taken seriously. If it was not a brachiator, the presence of *Ramapithecus* on the line leading to humans is unlikely.

[9] This combines an estimate of 11 Mya to 9 Mya for DNA (Sarich and Cronin, 1977) with the estimate of 9.6 Mya to 7.2 Mya for albumin and transferrin (Cronin, 1977a).

Molecular clocks and fossil "apes": is the discrepancy more apparent than real?

Proponents of *Ramapithecus* as a hominid ancestor have suggested a pongid–hominid divergence of some 15 million years ago, whereas the molecular clock best-guess estimate based on comparison of several molecules comes out about 5 million to 4 million years ago, just before the clear appearance of hominid fossils in eastern Africa some 3.77–3.59 million to 3 million years ago. There has, therefore, been a general air of controversy between some paleontologists and some molecular evolutionists (Simons, 1978). This controversy, however, may be cooled somewhat by David Pilbeam's proposal (1978a) that the fossil "ape" picture is far more complex than many paleontologists, himself included, had formerly recognized. He no longer thinks that clear ancestor–descendant lines can be drawn from early Miocene fossil apes to contemporary apes. Frayer (1976) has pointed out that, at least in overall jaw configuration, *Ramapithecus* differs more than had been anticipated from hominids. Pilbeam (1978a) goes on to note that the V-shaped jaw of *Ramapithecus* differs from *both* the U-shaped jaws of today's pongids and from the parabolic shape of contemporary human jaws. However, a comparison of the jaws of *Ramapithecus* and of the very early basal hominid *Australopithecus afarensis* does show an interesting similarity in shape (Figure 3:8).

In any case, the "discrepancy" between the molecular and fossil evidence may well be more apparent than real. Estimates of ape–human divergence times for individual molecules do range from zero to 10 million years ago (Cronin, 1975). And Korey (1979) has shown there is a mathematical tendency for systematic underestimation of divergence times for recent speciation events. Also, if new postcranial evidence from Pakistan should show that *Ramapithecus punjabicus* had an ape-like locomotor system some 8 million years ago, then it was still an ape in the sense I use the term.

If *Ramapithecus punjabicus,* which was living in Pakistan as recently as 8 million years ago (Tauxe, 1979), should prove to be a brachiating ape living away from the tropical forests, it might be an ape that was ancestral to the hominid line. Or it could be an ape adapting to somewhat more open country, which, like the other ramapithecids, left no descendants. Alternatively, if *Ramapithecus* was not a brachiating ape but had eclectic motor capacities similar to the early to middle Miocene dental apes, it probably was a dead end. That is, although it still might prove to be an example of higher primate adaptation to relatively open country, it was

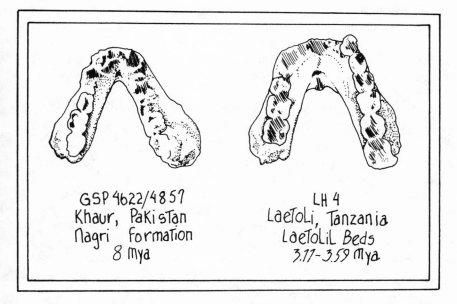

FIGURE 3:8. Comparison of the lower jaw of the late Miocene ape, *Ramapithecus (left)* – sometimes thought to be a hominid ancestor – with that of the basal hominid, *Australopithecus afarensis (right)*.

one that was to be superseded by terrestrial monkeys and, even later, by the hominids themselves (who subsequently evolved from a population of brachiating apes).

The African ape radiation

After brachiation was well established among the forest pongids in Asia and ancestors of the African pongids had developed further refinements (Lewis, 1972a, b), another radiation occurred, perhaps some 8 million to 4 million years ago. The ability to brachiate was retained and continued to be used when feeding in trees. What was new in this radiation was a terrestrial component: The brachiating ancestors of the African apes developed ways to move effectively on the ground. As this parental population radiated, some became knuckle walkers, and some became bipedal. The descendants of the knuckle walkers are chimpanzees and gorillas. The bipeds evolved into *Australopithecus,* the first known hominid. Today, chimpanzees and gorillas are found only in Africa, primarily in the forest belt stretching across the center of that continent (Figure 3:9). All the earliest hominid remains have also been found in Africa, somewhat to the east of the forest belt, in the mosaic savannas. These extensive African savanna grasslands and bush, with some woodlands, may not have been present until the Plio-Pleistocene (J. A. H. Van Couvering, 1975), the period in which the earliest known hominid fossils have been found. The spread of these savannas in eastern Africa may, itself, have been a factor in the hominid divergence.

Possibly, this relatively recent radiation in Africa about 8 million to 4 million years ago began with brachiating apes coming into Africa from Asia as suggested by Sarich and Cronin (1976). To date, there is almost no fossil record in Africa for either Miocene apes or for apes as we know them today from 12 million years ago to the present time. This could be partially explained by extinction of the Miocene apes in Africa after their Eurasian dispersion and by a recent reentry to Africa. Alternatively, if the African Miocene apes are direct ancestors of present-day African apes, they may have followed the rain forests to the west as they receded, which could account for the absence of fossils after 12 million years ago in the excavated areas of eastern Africa (see Figure 3:9). More research is needed.

The radiation of common and pygmy chimps, of gorillas, and of hominids could have occurred in at least two ways. One would be to speciate and radiate rapidly when they came in, as did Darwin's finches in the Galápagos Islands (Lark, 1953). If there was a recent ape entry into Africa from Asia 8 million to 6 million years ago this explanation is plausible. However, if the African Miocene apes were direct ancestors of African apes today or if any reentry into Africa from Asia were earlier, then a forest stem population may have become well established there, followed by a later development of forms (both hominid and pongid) with terrestrial components to their locomotion. The transitional hominids would have evolved among an isolated population at the edges of the range of the ape stem population, as a direct solution to the question of how a brachiating ape can become terrestrial. In the hominid case, it was by becoming bipedal instead of knuckle walking like chimpanzees and gorillas.

One component of the radiation was dietary. The apes that began to concentrate on forest leaves and stems, and that developed physiological and anatomical characteristics suited to this specialized diet, became gorillas. The conservative chimpanzees (common and pygmy) continued an omnivorous capacity, with a concentration on fruits. The hominids also maintained an omnivorous capacity but obtained less succulent and probably harder-to-find plant foods in the new environment – the eastern African savanna. They specialized by becoming more intelligent and bipedal, and by using tools.

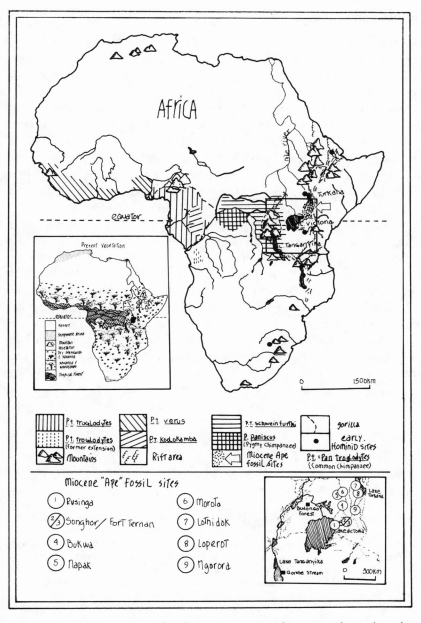

FIGURE 3:9. Miocene "ape" fossil sites in eastern Africa. Note how close these sites are to the ranges of contemporary African apes – the gorillas and chimpanzees. The Miocene sites, although located in what are now relatively dry savannas, are situated in what once were forested areas. Contemporary apes range in tropical forests to savanna forest mosaics.

Summary and conclusions

There was an early "higher" primate radiation where a number of features of the masticatory apparatus, but only some characteristics of the upper limbs, are similar to those of living apes. These so-called Miocene apes or dryopithecids were primarily quadrupedal, like monkeys (Morbeck, 1972; Preuschoft, 1973; McHenry, 1975), but had some ability to suspend themselves from tree branches (Lewis, 1972a, b). Most of these early forms became extinct in the middle Miocene, and probably only a few left descendants. They were followed briefly by later Miocene apes that may have radiated in response to environmental changes. The critical question with regard to these ramapithecids is whether they were already brachiators, and therefore possibly ancestral to hominids, or whether their locomotion was like that of the earlier Miocene apes—in which case they probably were a dead end, with their niche likely filled today by terrestrial monkeys. Brachiation developed among those Miocene apes still living in the forests, and, about 11 million to 7 million years ago in the late Miocene, there was a further radiation of which the Asian apes are living survivors. As part of this radiation of brachiating apes there was an African form (or a form that entered Africa). I think it likely that modern pygmy and common chimpanzees, gorillas, and hominids arose from this parental stem population in a fourth radiation in Africa in the late Miocene or in the early Pliocene, 8 million to about 4 million years ago (Figure 3:10). The form giving rise to the radiation of African apes and early hominids may have resembled a small chimpanzee (Sarich, 1968; Zihlman, 1979).

Which African ape?

At the present time, the best available model for the "prospective adaptations" of the ancestral population from which the hominid line diverged is the common chimpanzee.[10] Many studies of behavior in the wild exist (see

[10] As long ago suggested by Coolidge (1933), it is quite possible that the pygmy chimpanzee, *Pan paniscus*—when more data are available on behavior in the wild—might serve as an even more specific model than the common chimpanzee. Pygmy chimpanzee and hominid anatomy are particularly close in some respects (Zihlman, 1977; Zihlman et al., 1978; Cramer and Zihlman, 1978; Zihlman and Cramer, 1978; Zihlman, 1979). An unexpected diversity of molecular findings (despite overall closeness to *Pan troglodytes*) has even led one researcher to "entertain the intriguing notion that *Pan paniscus* . . . may represent a primitive relic stock from which *Gorilla, Pan troglodytes*, and the hominid line diverged" (Cronin, 1977b).
    It will be most interesting to know more about behavioral aspects. At present research is underway at Yerkes Primate Laboratory, Georgia, on three pygmy chimpanzees on loan from the Zaire government (Savage et al., 1976; Savage and Bakeman, 1978; Savage-Rumbaugh and Wilkerson, 1978; Savage-Rumbaugh et al., 1977). Even more significant, observations of pygmy chimpanzees in their natural habitat have now begun (Nishida, 1972b; MacKinnon, 1976; Badrian and Badrian, 1977; Kano, 1979, 1980).

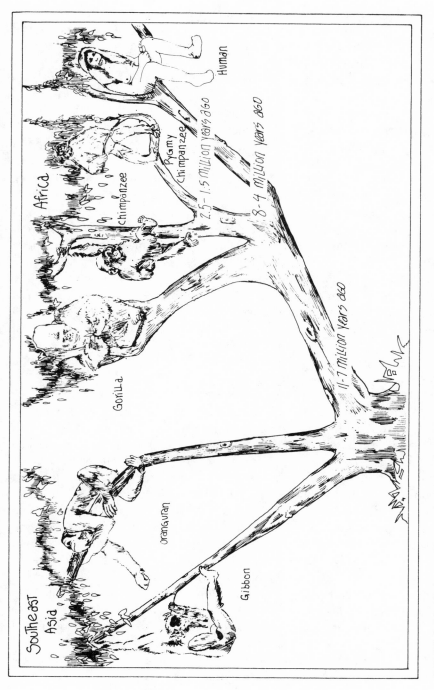

FIGURE 3:10. Phylogenetic tree showing relationships of humans to African and Asian apes.

Figure 3:12). The common chimpanzee inhabits a variety of forest habitats – riverine forests, montane forests, and savanna woodlands – from Guinea in western Africa through central Africa and as far east as Tanzania near Lake Tanganyika (Hill, 1969; Sabater Pí, 1974), and extensive data on the behavior of populations in various habitats have been collected. For the common chimpanzee years and years of field observation by many researchers provide adequate data for model building, particularly regarding the critical realm of social behavior. With a chimpanzee model of the ancestral population, it becomes feasible to specify the probable nature of the behaviors available for selection to operate on during the transition from a fruit-eating, forest-living ancestral form to the transitional one adapting to the mosaic savanna away from the tropical rain forests. Chimpanzees demonstrate a constellation of behaviors that would seem to have been necessarily present in an ape population ancestral to the first hominids. They exhibit a range of critical capacities, including some bipedal behavior and carrying, tool use in the food quest, food sharing, reliance on plant foods plus limited insect collecting and predatory behavior, long-term mother–offspring interaction and the important role of play for learning in the young, effective communication, general intelligence, a flexible social organization, and an ability to utilize a range of habitats (Goodall and Hamburg, 1975; Goodall, 1976; Tanner and Zihlman, 1976a, b; Zihlman and Tanner, 1979). Such capacities are necessary precursors to the evolution of hominid behavior.

In the latter part of the Miocene, a parental stem population probably similar to living chimpanzees was developing. Molecular evidence suggests that this population diverged from the Asian apes about 11 million to 7 million years ago and shared a common history prior to the beginning of the African ape radiation perhaps some 8 million to 4 million years ago. From this stem population, gorillas diverged and changed moderately; the common and pygmy chimpanzees diverged from the stem population but remained morphologically similar to each other and probably to the stem population as well; and the hominid line diverged and changed very rapidly. Further information on molecular comparisons of pygmy and common chimpanzees, lowland and mountain gorillas, and humans can be expected to clarify the question of whether (1) gorillas diverged first, with chimpanzees and hominids together a bit before diverging from each other, or whether (2) gorillas, chimpanzees, and hominids diverged about the same time. In either case, chimpanzees provide the most specific model for the characteristics of the population immediately preceding the early hominids.

Gorillas, although similar to chimpanzees in many respects and also found in Africa, provide a less useful model because they are more specialized behaviorally and anatomically than chimpanzees. Their specialized

SEXUAL DIMORPHISM			
BODY WEIGHT	male	female	female as % of male
gorilla	140 - 180 Kg	75 - 110 Kg	54 - 61 %
chimpanzee	49 Kg	41 Kg	84 %
human	48 - 90 Kg	40 - 77 Kg	83 - 86 %
BODY LENGTH	male	female	female as % of male
gorilla (trunk length)	693 mm	523 mm	75 %
chimpanzee (trunk length)	469 mm	432 mm	92 %
human (total height)	1575 - 1930 mm	1473 - 1829 mm	94 - 95 %

FIGURE 3:11. Humans and chimpanzees show very little sexual dimorphism (with females 83 to 95 percent of male weight and length), whereas gorillas are quite dimorphic by sex (with females 54 to 75 percent of male weight and length).

features include an herbivorous diet, with a digestive system that can regularly process vast quantities of relatively unnutritious food; a comparatively small home range and restricted habitat; large body size; marked sexual dimorphism, with males twice the size of females (Figure 3:11); and small, stable, rigidly structured social groups.

This is not to imply that gorillas are not adaptable and intelligent. In captivity, both African apes show similar high performance on many laboratory tests (Rumbaugh, 1970; Patterson, 1978a, b). The gorilla adaptation is the more limited, however. Chimpanzees, not gorillas, use their abilities in the wild in ways that enable us to conceptualize how the ape population directly ancestral to the hominids may have behaved and to delineate those behaviors upon which natural selection could have worked.

Chimpanzees are more generalized and represent a relatively conservative lineage. The very similar anatomy and adaptation of pygmy and common chimpanzees—despite the fact that they may have separated from each other nearly 3 million years ago—increases the likelihood that each is patterned on the basic ape that was ancestral to both of them and to hominids. The hominids adapted to a distinctive habitat where evolutionary change occurred rapidly, whereas both chimpanzee lines remained forest fruit eaters. Chimpanzees, then, are probably similar to the generalized and highly successful stem population that gave rise to gorillas, both chimpanzee lines, and hominids. They exhibit the sorts of behavioral potentials that probably characterized the population ancestral to hominids.

Site	Habitat	Dates	Species	Provisioning	Habituated to humans	Researchers
UGANDA Kigezi Gorilla Sanctuary: Kisoro	?	1959	?	?	?	N.Bolwig
Budongo Forest	Forest	1960, 1966–70	P.t.	No	Yes	J.Itani, Y.Sugiyama, A.Suzuki, T.Suzuki
Budongo Forest (Busingiro Hill) and Siba Forest	Rain forest with selective logging	1960–62	P.t.s.	No	No	F.Reynolds, V.Reynolds
Kibale Forest	?	1970–78	P.t.	?	?	M.Ghiglieri, L.L.Struhsaker, T.T.Struhsaker
TANZANIA Gombe National Park: Kasakela, Kakombe Valley.	Mosaic grass-land/woodland forest	1960–present	P.t.s.	Periodically since 1962 (daily in 1960s, less in 1970s)	Since 1961	H.Albrecht, D.Anderson, L.Baldwin, R.Barnes, H.Bauer, C.D.Busse, D.Bygott, C.Clark, C.Coleman, R.Davis, E.Drake, J.Goodall (van Lawick-Goodall), M.Hankey, L.Hobbett, E.E.Hunt, Jr., H.C.Kraemer, P.Marler, P.McGinnis W.C.McGrew, K.Morris, C.Packer, J.H.Pfifferling, A.Pusey, G.Rilling, D.Riss, Y.Selemani, S.Sheehan, I.B.Silk, A.Simpson, M.Simpson, A.Simpson-Shouldice, A.Sorem/Ford, D.Starin, G.Teleki, M.Thorndahl, C.E.G.Tutin, R.Wrangham
Kahama Community,	Mosaic grass-land/woodland forest	1974–75	P.t.s.	No	Some animals	A.Pierce
Nyasanga Valley		1969–70	P.t.s.	?	?	L.Baldwin, C.Gale
Kabogo Point: Mukuyu	Forest to woodland	1961–63	P.t.s.	Yes, but no success	Beginning to be	S.Azuma, K.Imanishi, J.Itani, A.Toyoshima
Kasakati Basin: Masito	Mosaic grass-land/woodland	1963–67	P.t.	Yes	Yes	K.Imanishi, J.Itani, K.Izawa, T.Kano, M.Kawabe, T.Nishida, A.Suzuki
Filabanga Basin: Masito Hills, Ishanda, neighboring areas	Woodland, grassland, savanna, riverine forest	1965–66	P.t.s.	No	No	J.Itani, T.Kano, A.Suzuki

	Habitat	Years	Species	Provisioning	Hunted	Researchers
Mahali Mountains: Kasoge	Mosaic grassland/woodland/forest	1965–present	P.t.	Some groups	Yes	J.Hasegawa, J.Itani, M.Kakeya, K.Kawanaka, K.Kitamura, A.Mori, T.Nishida, K.Norikoshi, S.Uehara
Tumbatumba	?	1971	?	?	?	A.Suzuki
ZAIRE/CONGO						
Beni Chimpanzee Reserve, in North Kivu Province, and Parc National Albert	Forest edge/plantation	1960, 1963–64	P.t.	Some for experimentation	No	A.Kortlandt
?	High and low, open and forest	1976–?	P.t.	?	?	T.Kano et al.
GABON						
?	?	Near end of 19th century	?	?	?	R.L.Garner
CAMEROON						
Korup Forest Reserve	Lowland forest	1974–78	P.t.	?	?	M.Demment, J.S.Gartlan, S.Gartlan, F.Namata, Struhsaker, D.W.Thomas, J.Thomas
IVORY COAST						
Tai Forest Reserve	Forest	1970–71	P.t.v.	?	?	P.Hunkeler, U.Rahm, T.T.Struhsaker
GUINEA						
Fouta Djallon Region, Kindia area	Woodland	1930	?	No	No	H.W.Nissen
Fouta Djallon	Savanna to forest	1965–66	P.t.	?	?	D.de Bournonville
Rio Muni: Mt. Alen, Okorobikó Mountains	Lowland evergreen forest	1966–69	P.t.t.	No	No	C.Jones, J.Sabater Pi
Bossou (Sacred Hill) and Kindia area (Kanka Sili)	Forest and savanna	1966–69	P.t.	Yes	Partly	H.Albrecht, S.C.Dunnett, R.Pfeiffers, J.van Orshoven, J. C. J. van Zon
Kanka Donga	Low, open forest	1976–77	P.t.v.	?	?	Y.Sugiyama
SENEGAL						
Mont Assirik, Parc National du Niokolo-Koba	Low, open forest	1973–present	P.t.v.	No	?	P.J.Baldwin, B.Bessanine, R.Bouang, S.Brewer, S.Harrison, W.C.McGrew, J.I.Pollock, R.Savinelli, M.J.Sharman, C.E.G.Tutin et al.

Key to species:

P.t. = *Pan troglodytes*
P.t.t. = *Pan troglodytes troglodytes*
P.t.s. = *Pan troglodytes schweinfurthi*
P.t.v. = *Pan troglodytes verus*

FIGURE 3:12. Field studies of common chimpanzees.

FOUR

Chimpanzees as a model of the ancestral population: locomotion, tools, and diet

A THEORY of human evolution is only as good as its component parts: Each stage of the evolutionary sequence must be explicitly reconstructed. Where we start is critical. Chimpanzees, in genetics, anatomy, behavior, and environment, present a total configuration that provides the best available model for suggesting features of the ancestral ape population.

In their utilization of the environment, they exhibit considerable variability in social and dietary patterns. Thus, although chimpanzees live primarily in the forested areas of western and central Africa, their ranges also extend eastward into savanna woodlands relatively near the savannas where the earliest hominid fossils are found.

Chimpanzees are particularly exciting because their whole behavioral range – from tool using to social interaction – can actually be observed in the wild. The dynamic interrelationships of anatomy, behavior, tools, and environment can be, and have been, investigated. When we turn to hominid fossils, and archeological and other remains that exist from the past, there is no direct information on social behavior and its relation to tool use, communication, or ecology. By using the conservative chimpanzees as a model of the ancestral population, we gain a starting point. It is then feasible to postulate the ways behavior remained unchanged and in what ways it did change for, first, the transitional population and, then, for the sequence of early hominids.

Chimpanzees have been studied by a wide variety of researchers, over many years, in habitats that vary from lowland rain forest to savanna woodlands. Observational conditions have also differed, with some workers provisioning chimpanzees to keep them near the research station and other researchers following regional populations over wide ranges (see

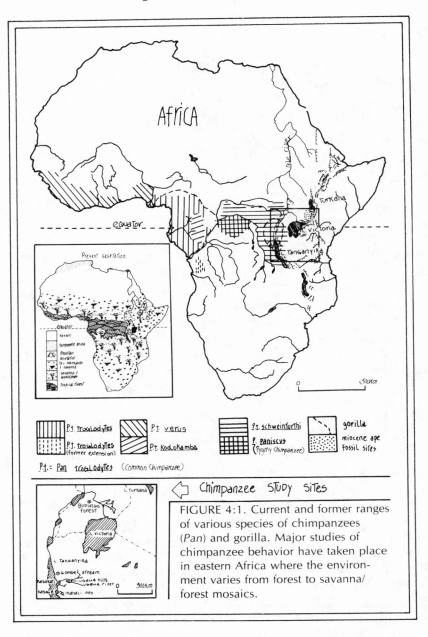

FIGURE 4:1. Current and former ranges of various species of chimpanzees (*Pan*) and gorilla. Major studies of chimpanzee behavior have taken place in eastern Africa where the environment varies from forest to savanna/forest mosaics.

Figure 3:12). The common chimpanzee (*Pan troglodytes*) is, at this time, by far the most thoroughly studied of all apes.

Locomotion: jack-of-all-trades

Chimpanzees have versatile locomotor abilities and in important senses are both terrestrial and arboreal. They spend about 50 percent of their day feeding in trees and sometimes also mate, display, groom, play, and sleep there. Their grasping feet and long, mobile arms, with flexible shoulder and wrist joints, evolved for climbing, hanging, and feeding in trees (Figure 4:2). Chimpanzees also move effectively on the ground; they walk quadrupedally, on their feet and their knuckles, with flexed fingers stabilizing their mobile wrist joints (Figure 4:3). Knuckle walking is a unique method of locomotion with anatomical correlates: in particular, the well-developed ridges of the finger bones to hold the stronger flexor tendons (Tuttle, 1967, 1969).

Of particular interest for human evolution is the fact that chimpanzees also exhibit bipedal behavior as part of their locomotor repertoire in a variety of contexts not observed for other primates. Chimpanzees of all ages and both sexes stand and move bipedally in many situations, especially when arms and hands are occupied with nonlocomotor activities.[1] They may carry food or objects with both hands while walking bipedally (Figure 4:4). Even more frequent is "tripedal" behavior—one-handed knuckle walking, with something in the other hand. Females may walk upright (or tripedally) when supporting their newborn infants. Bipedalism is also used for better visibility when walking short distances through tall grasses, in nest building when reaching for branches, in aggressive displays, for carrying food, or simply for looking around. When chimpanzees stand up, they gain height and have relatively good balance compared to monkeys.

Bipedal behavior occurs, but the chimpanzee does not possess specialized structures for efficient bipedalism: Its foot, with its grasping first toe and mobile ankle joint, is adapted for climbing and not for stability and support; its pelvis is that of a quadrupedal animal, with an ilium that is long and narrow rather than bowl-shaped as in humans (Figure 4:5). Nonetheless, a chimpanzee-like pelvis and foot could have been remodeled to form those of bipedal hominids (Morton, 1935; Gregory, 1949; Washburn, 1968b).

---

[1] A few individuals at Gombe whose upper limbs became paralyzed through disease have been observed walking frequently on two legs (Bauer, 1977).

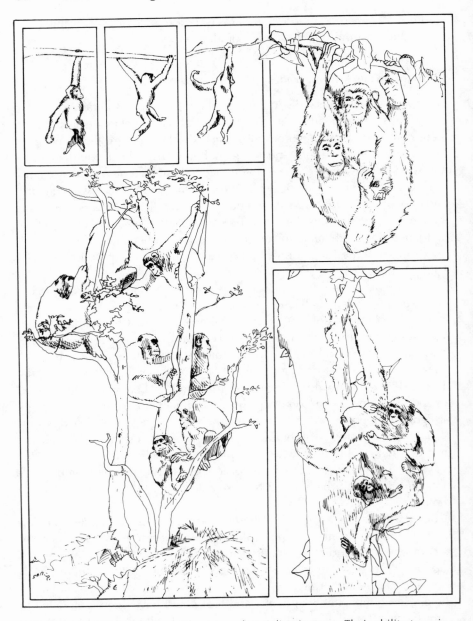

FIGURE 4:2. Chimpanzees feed, rest, and socialize in trees. Their ability to swing through the branches (brachiate) and to hold on with feet as well as hands is important, particularly in the food quest.

FIGURE 4:3. Knuckle walking:
Chimpanzees use their hands when moving on the ground.

Tool use by a small-brained primate

Making and using tools have been described as the fundamental hominid activity (Oakley, 1961). For a time during the 1930s and 1940s, when stone tools were found in deposits as old as those of *Australopithecus* from South Africa, people doubted that the australopithecines made them. Australopithecine brains were not much larger than those of apes, and so initially these early hominids were thought to lack sufficient intelligence to make tools. This position is no longer tenable. Köhler's early work (1927) demonstrated that chimpanzees could use and make tools in a laboratory setting, but before field data were available it was questionable whether tool use was part of their adaptation in the wild. With the growing body of field data on tool use, chimpanzees' generalized ability to modify and utilize objects as tools has become clear (see Figure 4:6). This capacity is not restricted to a particular object or class of objects used for a specific task, as is the case in the use of rocks by sea otters for cracking open shells, or the twig probes used by finches to get grubs (Lancaster, 1968a; Goodall, 1970). The generalized tool using ability of chimpanzees differs from the limited and highly particularistic tool use of other animals. Chimpanzees use tools in multiple contexts – in water and food getting, in displays and defense, and in grooming. Goodall's findings on chimpanzee object modification and tool use in the wild lent credence to the idea that the early hominids (the australopithecines) were at least as intelligent as living apes, and that even with small brains tool making and using were possible. Chimpanzees have the genetic base for generalized object use and modification. This behavioral capacity also appears to be present in gorillas, orangutans, and gibbons and likely was present in the ancestral ape population (Hall, 1963b; Jay, 1968; Goodall, 1970).

FIGURE 4:4. Chimpanzees can walk upright when their hands are occupied.

Much has been written on the hominid hand and its evolution for tool use. However, the anatomy of chimpanzees' hands – specifically their long fingers and short but well-developed thumb – does not preclude or prevent fine manipulation of objects. Chimpanzees' manipulative skills, combined with their conceptual abilities, expand their tool-using and tool-making domain. Remarkably, Viki, the chimpanzee trained by the Hayeses, had the manual dexterity, ability to learn new skills, and requisite concentration to sew, albeit with ribbon and large darning needles on a mesh sack (Hayes, 1951). Hayes also remarks that

On a recent occasion a gentleman stood beside our car, telling me that Viki's short thumb was the whole answer to man's superiority. As he discoursed, Viki turned the ignition off and on, worked the windshield wiper, shifted gears, and rolled down the window, the better to swat the gentleman's little boy.   [Hayes, 1951:233]

Ground living was once thought to be a prerequisite for the development of hominid tool use. Tools are used by chimpanzees in trees as well as on the ground, however; for example, the chimpanzees obtain arboreal ants for food by poking sticks into the ant nests (for this, chimpanzees break off twigs in a manner similar to that employed in their own nest building).

The line between tool using and tool making, once thought so firm, becomes more and more tenuous as data accumulate. Chimpanzees do

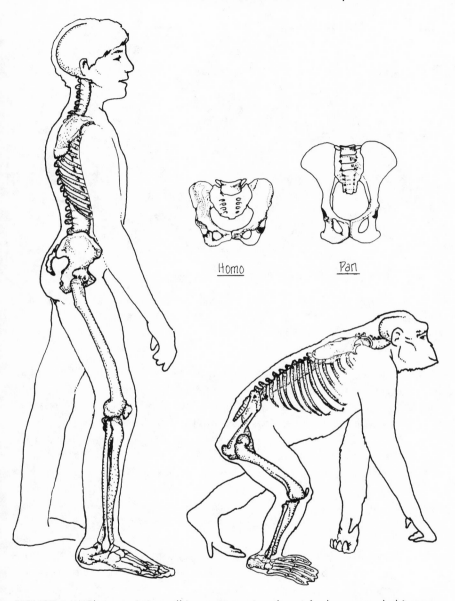

Homo   Pan

FIGURE 4:5. Characteristic walking postures (*as above*) for human and chimpanzee emphasize differences in limb proportions, pelvis, and foot. However, chimpanzees are also capable of assuming bipedal postures (Figure 4:4).

FIGURE 4:6. Chimpanzees modify objects and use tools in their natural habitat. Both of these chimpanzees are using grass stalks to collect termites. *Center,* a light branch is being stripped, also for termiting.

modify objects before using them. Leaves are torn from trees, crumpled, and chewed to form an effective sponge. For termiting or probing tools, leaves and bark are stripped from stems or twigs by hand or with the lips, or a bent end is bitten off to make it straight.

The many ways that chimpanzees use objects in connection with food and water constitute a fascinating array. For example, sticks, twigs, strips of bark, and grasses are used for obtaining termites, several species of ants, and honey (Suzuki, 1966, 1969; Goodall, 1968a; Hladik, 1973; Nishida, 1973). Chimpanzees in the Ivory Coast, western Africa, were noted using rocks as hammers for cracking open fruits and nuts (Struhsaker and Hunkeler, 1971; Rahm, 1971), and Gombe chimpanzees have been seen smashing hard shelled fruits against embedded rocks until the rinds crack open (Goodall, 1973b). Crumpled leaves have served as sponges to collect water from crevices between tree branches. Jane Goodall tried this method and found it to be seven or eight times more effective than licking water from her fingers, the usual way chimpanzees drink. Teleki (1973b) also observed a wad of vegetation being used as a sponge to extricate the brains of a prey animal from its skull. In the food quest, tools are sometimes used to obtain insects, water, honey, and to open fruit and nuts.

"Foresight" is also exhibited in tool use to obtain food, and tools are used regularly in some activities. In insect collecting, chimpanzees actually seek materials for tools and carry them several yards for a specific purpose. Goodall (1970) observed a chimpanzee select several sticks, then carry them to termite hills where they were used in succession. The spares were used after the worn ones were discarded. Chimpanzees even go one step further to prepare a perch for "ant dipping." When no natural elevation such as a fallen log or overhanging branch is conveniently located, a chimpanzee may bend a nearby sapling and sit on it while collecting the ants to avoid being bitten by them. For ant dipping, then, tool use can include both the implement for dipping and the facility from which it is done (McGrew, 1974).

From observing tool remains as well as insect collecting activities, it is known that termite collection with tools takes place in several widespread spots (McGrew et al., 1979). Termites can actually be an important food source. One type of termite, for example, builds very large mounds that can persist some 700 years and contain as many as 2 million individuals totaling about 20 kilograms in weight.

Females frequently prepare tools and facilities for termite "fishing," "dipping" for driver ants, and "fishing" for arboreal ants. Females engage in termiting and ant collecting—finding, modifying, and using tools for these food-getting activities—frequently and for long periods (Nishida, 1973; McGrew, 1977, 1979). They are able to focus their attention long enough to obtain significant quantities. McGrew (1979) reports that a female chimpanzee may obtain as much as 20 grams of ants in a typical session of ant dipping. From preliminary observations, females engage in these insect collecting activities with tools for longer periods and more often than do males (Nishida, 1973; McGrew, 1979).

If the ancestral and transitional populations and the early hominids likewise collected insects with tools, and found them a significant protein source, the "hunting" image might need considerable revision! What if early hunting largely consisted of australopithecine females with tools sitting for long periods collecting insects, rather than of those long-imagined ferocious groups of half-human males racing after big animals?

Chimpanzees also modify and use objects in a number of other ways. For example, they build nests for sleeping. They may use leaves for wiping off feces from the anal region and water and other foreign materials from their hair (Goodall, 1968a), and they sometimes use sticks as toothpicks (McGrew and Tutin, 1973) and leafy twigs to fan away flies from the genital area after copulation (Sugiyama, 1969) and so groom with tools. Twigs and grasses can become "olfactory aids"; they are poked into termite holes and the ends are sniffed (Goodall, 1970). Sticks are also used as

FIGURE 4:7. Bipedal tool use. *Left,* a male chimpanzee brandishes a stick at his reflection in a mirror. *Right,* throwing by a juvenile chimpanzee.

levers. Köhler observed this in the laboratory; and chimpanzees at Gombe use sticks or twigs to pry open the boxes of bananas provided by researchers. Captive chimpanzees in a fenced enclosure used logs for ladders so successfully that they managed to escape (Menzel, 1973b).

Handfuls of vegetation, fronds, stones, branches, or sticks are often used in aggressive displays. These frightening displays may be directed toward other species, such as baboons, bushpigs, or leopards, or at other chimpanzees. Both female and male chimpanzees direct such agonistic behavior toward animals from different species; usually only males engage in displays directed at other chimpanzees. In most displays, materials appear to be thrown at random (Goodall, 1968a), although aimed throwing, particularly when directed at other species, does occur. We know from zoos that with practice chimpanzee aim can be quite accurate, though probably in the wild this skill is not often achieved.

In dramatic experiments in West Africa, upon seeing a stuffed leopard both female and male chimpanzees became excited and threw vegetation and available objects at it; a chimpanzee mother used a long stick to hit the leopard and a shorter one to throw at it (Kortlandt and Kooij, 1963; Kortlandt, 1965, 1967; Reynolds, 1967; Albrecht and Dunnett, 1971). Not only do chimpanzees recognize potential predators but both sexes have an appropriate defensive response. Protection of offspring appears to be an important factor in skill and intensity of defense with tools. Kortlandt (1967:218) reports that "the fierceness of attacks and the performance level of agonistic tool use were definitely higher in the mothers than in the males" (see Figure 7:7).

Hall (1963b) has classified animal object use by function. Preparation of living sites, grooming, and feeding account for 90 percent of all cases; object use in agonistic behavior completes the usual list and is found only in monkeys and apes. Both unaltered materials such as rocks or modified objects (e.g., stripped twigs or leaves) are used by chimpanzees in a variety of contexts and for several purposes. Very few species use tools in more than one of the ways designated by Hall; chimpanzee tool use covers the entire range. In addition, preparation of perches for ant dipping and tool use in investigative behavior, prying, digging, and escaping have all been observed but are not subsumed under any of Hall's categories. Furthermore, the extent and kinds of tool use exhibited by chimpanzees vary geographically. These regional variations in tool use partially accord with environmental exigencies. Partly, however, there are regional stylistic differences (McGrew et al., 1979). It has been suggested that perhaps it is "those traditions which are practiced mainly by migrant females (e.g., probing with tools for termites) that are . . . most likely to disseminate throughout a regional population" (Teleki, in press:186). Environmental variables, social tradition, and social migration may all play a part in determining what insect species are sought with tools, what kinds of objects are used, and in what context. Only humans also use tools in all the ways in which chimpanzees use them.

Chimpanzees: incipient omnivores

Although their food consists mainly of fruit, chimpanzees eat a variety of plant parts, insects, and animals (Reynolds and Reynolds, 1965; Goodall, 1968a; Suzuki, 1969; Jones and Sabater Pí, 1971). At Kasoge in Tanzania, for example, Nishida (1968) noted a collection of 66 different types of plant food from 51 species of plants and trees; at Gombe 77 plant species are eaten consistently (Riss and Busse, 1977). Specifics differ from area to area, but the total inventory is extensive: fruits, leaves, blossoms, seeds, stems, bark, honey, insects, birds, eggs, and mammals. Proportions of feeding time for various types of foods for Figan, an adult male observed at

A crumpled wad of leaves is used to spoon brains from a baboon skull.

Leaves are sometimes used in grooming. This female is wiping blood from her clitoris, which was bitten during a squabble.

Prying with a stick -- trying to get bananas from a concrete box at Gombe National Park.

Dipping for ants with a stick.

FIGURE 4:8. Chimpanzees use objects as tools in a wide variety of contexts.

Gombe for 50 consecutive days, were: fruit, 52 percent; leaves, 27 percent; seeds, 16.4 percent. This is a total of 95.4 percent feeding time for plant food. He also ate soil, insects (mostly ants), five monkeys, one bushbuck, and one guinea fowl (Riss and Busse, 1977).

Six to eight hours a day are spent in feeding; most of the chimpanzees' food grows in trees, and they feed there over half of the daylight hours (Goodall, 1965, 1968a). The proportion of time spent in subsistence activities is greatest for female heads of matrifocal units, that is, females with offspring (69.2 percent), with single females next (60 percent), and males least (53.1 percent) (Teleki, in press). This probably reflects the greater nutritional stress on females, particularly those who are pregnant or lactating. Each chimpanzee normally forages for itself and eats food where it is found. Occasionally fruits and stems are shared (Sugiyama, 1972; Hladik, 1973). Sometimes food – such as blocks of mineral salts, fruit, eggs, sugar cane or meat – is carried away to another place for more leisurely consumption (Goodall, 1965; Albrecht and Dunnett, 1971; Teleki, 1973a) or for "preparation" as in extracting "nut meats" or seeds from fruits (Rahm, 1971).

Chimpanzee populations in different locales vary as to which foods are utilized and with what frequency, a pattern also observed for gorillas (Schaller, 1963) and baboons (DeVore and Hall, 1965). Termites are eaten at least at Gombe and in the Kasakati Basin in eastern Africa, and in western Africa at Mount Assirik, West Cameroon, Dipikar Island, Ayamiken, and Okorobikó (McGrew et al., 1979). In Gabon, western Africa, the main source of animal protein appears to be ants (Hladik, 1973). Local "tradition," individual preference, and availability probably all influence diet.

Range and seasonality of plant food

Fruit, the main food source, is seasonal. Chimpanzees eat mostly mature, well-ripened fruits. Birds, monkeys, and other animals also eat fruit; once a tree ripens, the fruit disappears quickly. So, in order for chimpanzees to use this food source effectively, they must be at a particular tree or area when the fruit is available. Other foods, such as blossoms or tender shoots, are also seasonal. Similarly, termites are most available at Gombe during three weeks in the early part of the rainy season (Goodall, 1963). The seasonality of major foods influences where chimpanzees travel and when.

An adequate, year-round food supply requires detailed knowledge of a large range. Chimpanzee memory for locating food is well developed. More important than memory per se is their ability to "map" an area in their minds. Menzel's experiments (1973c, 1974) show that chimpanzees not only remember where food is hidden in an acre enclosure but also organize this information in such a way that the foods they like best are usually obtained and eaten first. In the wild, chimpanzees also appear to seek out preferred foods; when these foods run out, they turn to other available though less desired sources.

Protein sources

A variety of insects are eaten, and they provide an important protein source. For example, at Kasoge near the Mahali Mountains in Tanzania, Nishida (1973) noted chimpanzees eating eight species of insects—four species of arboreal ants, one species of termite, one species of sand cricket, one species of cicada, and one species of moth—with ants and termites eaten most frequently. Over a 10 year period, chimpanzees at Gombe also were observed killing an average of 9 or 10 mammals per year (Teleki, 1973a). Meat has been estimated to form from 1 percent to 5 percent of the diet at Gombe (Teleki, 1975).

Despite their minimal significance in the overall diet, predation and meat eating are of interest as behavioral potentialities likely present in the ancestral population. For chimpanzees, the potential exists, but the specific prey species and amount of predation vary. Seasonal and environmental factors, in particular those affecting the availability of other protein sources such as insects, may play a role (Teleki, 1973b). In a chimpanzee reserve near Beni in Zaire (then the Congo), Adriaan Kortlandt carried out food experiments with interesting results:

To test the carnivorous tendencies of forest dwelling chimpanzees, such incentives as large live snails, live chameleons, live tortoises, live hen chicks, a dead wild bird, a dead baby antelope . . . goats . . . a live mongoose, and a young monkey . . . were placed along the path. In all trials, none of the chimpanzees showed the slightest indication of any interest in any of these objects as food. On the contrary the live monkey was treated rather as a pet, and attempts were made to release it . . . and take it with them.   [1965:329]

Kortlandt's experiments plus his data on stomach contents of apes shot by museum collectors indicate that, in the rain forest habitat he investigated, chimpanzees subsisted primarily on plants. Similarly, Reynolds and Reynolds (1965), in their study of unprovisioned chimpanzees in the Budongo Forest, found no evidence of predation; nor did Nissen (1931) in his early study of wild, unprovisioned chimpanzees. However, at Gombe National Park, Tanzania, Geza Teleki (1973b) and others have observed fairly regular, if infrequent, predation on small animals.

What characterizes chimpanzee meat eating when it does occur? The prey is always small, less than 9 kilograms and usually less than 5 kilograms. The range of animals consumed is fairly extensive, with other primate species probably the most frequently caught and eaten. At Gombe, where the environment is a savanna woodland mosaic, meat sources include young baboons, red colobus monkeys, blue monkeys, red-tail monkeys, young bushbucks, and young bushpigs (Teleki, 1973b). Red colobus monkeys are the main prey there (Riss and Busse, 1977). The heightened contact and competition with baboons because of provisioning at the Gombe provisioning station may have artificially heightened predation on infant baboons (Teleki, 1973b, in press; Wrangham, 1974). A chimpanzee in another savanna woodlands community from Kasoge near the Mahali Mountains in Tanzania was observed killing a young pygmy antelope but not eating it (Nishida, 1968). Greater galago, vervet monkeys, and a dead red-tail monkey possibly killed by chimpanzees were also found (Nishida, 1972a). In the savanna woodlands of the Kasakati Basin, Tanzania, Kawabe (1966) noted predation on red-tail monkeys, although Suzuki (1966) says meat eating only rarely occurs there.

Patterns of pursuit, capture, and consumption in predatory episodes among Gombe chimpanzees have been described by Teleki (1973b). Pursuit may consist of simple seizure – a sudden lunge and grab, covering only about a meter and taking only seconds. Chases, sometimes involving a dash of 90 meters or more, also occur. From time to time chimpanzees stalk potential prey, a cautious process that can take hours. Most successful predatory episodes involve simple seizure of the prey; only 6 of the 11 observed chases were successful, and all stalking efforts seen to date have failed. Predatory activity can be solitary but often includes several chimpanzees. They do not communicate by vocalizations (Teleki, 1973a) or by any obvious gestures; yet, their movement and positioning appear coordinated. When several individuals are involved, the likelihood of success is increased, as it also is among carnivores: The quarry has less chance to escape (Schaller, 1972; Kruuk, 1972).

Capture – including acquisition, killing, and initial division – usually lasts less than five minutes. In four ways of killing prey described by Teleki, only one involved the teeth; the hands were utilized in the other three. A chimpanzee may wring the prey's neck or grasp it by the legs and strike its head and body against a tree; or two or more chimpanzees may each grasp a limb and literally tear the prey apart, killing and dividing it simultaneously. Tools are not used either to kill or to divide the prey.

Consumption is social and lasts a long time. The kill is widely, though not necessarily equally, shared among group members. Individuals gather around the possessor. They reach out to touch the carcass or the lips or hands of the possessor, or they hold out their hands palms up (Teleki, 1973a, b). The possessor may threaten, turn away, or allow the other animals to feed from the carcass, or occasionally may detach pieces and hold them toward the begging individuals. Small bones are eaten, the larger ones cleaned and sucked; the brains are scooped out with the fingers or with leaf wads and eaten. Meat is consumed slowly, usually with several individuals participating.

Other primates, particularly baboons, also occasionally eat meat (De-Vore and Washburn, 1963; DeVore and Hall, 1965; Rowell, 1966; Alt-mann and Altmann, 1970; Strum, 1975; Harding and Strum, 1976). Although baboons and chimpanzees eat a similar range of prey species, social aspects contrast. Adult baboon males frequently fight among themselves over the spoils. Which baboon eats meat depends largely upon its status, and the dominant males eat most of the meat. Even if a female baboon kills an animal, adult males – particularly the most dominant ones – usually appropriate the prey for themselves. Unlike the situation among chimpanzees, there is little "begging" or sharing among baboons, and the meat is eaten quickly.

Both male and female chimpanzees engage in catching and killing small animals. For example, Kawabe (1966) observed one instance in which the predatory group was composed of an old female, an adult male, an adult female, two young adult females, and one juvenile female. Both sexes and all ages participate in consumption.

Chimpanzees occasionally appropriate baboon kills. In fact, from information available, it appears that an appreciable number of baboon kills are taken over by chimpanzees (Morris and Goodall, 1977). Despite the fact that baboons have been observed intimidating large carnivores and even killing a leopard, they seem to be no match for either female or male chimpanzees. In one instance, two adult female chimpanzees (each carrying an infant ventrally and one also accompanied by a dependent juvenile) grabbed a dead bushbuck fawn from a young male baboon, then succeeded in keeping it despite extended harassment from several male baboons (Morris and Goodall, 1977). During this harassment from the baboon males, the two female chimpanzees effectively defended themselves and their prey bushbuck. They barked at the baboons repeatedly; and one of the females swung the carcass at a male baboon, and also stamped on a branch and raised her arm threateningly.

Chimpanzee killing of small animals for meat has frequently been termed "hunting." Use of this term engenders confusion; for chimpanzees, predatory behavior is the most accurate phrasing. Hunting by humans implies a specialized technology. Chimpanzees never used tools to obtain or kill an animal in any predatory activities observed to date. Once, however, an old chimpanzee at Gombe threw a large rock at some bushpigs, which succeeded in dispersing the adults. The rock hit one of them, and the adult bushpigs fled. The chimpanzees then chased, captured, killed by hand, and ate a defenseless piglet (reported as pers. com. to McGrew, 1979). Chimpanzee predation without tools on small animals, meat eating, and sociable sharing of the spoils suggest that these behaviors were habitual, although not frequent, among the pongid ancestral population prior to the divergence of the hominid line. Killing animals and eating meat were not what was new in the initial divergence (Teleki, 1975; Tanner and Zihlman, 1976a).

FIVE

Chimpanzees as a model of the ancestral population: social organization and interaction

CHIMPANZEES generally associate in open, flexible, loosely structured groups.[1] Individuals do not join into cohesive units that move together all the time; yet their intelligence, rich affective responses to other chimpanzees, and effective nonverbal communication facilitate coordinated and patterned interaction. Two types of chimpanzee groupings exist: (1) temporarily formed small congregations termed "party," "band," or "subgroup"; and (2) larger aggregations of individuals that share a home range and are variously referred to as a "community," "large-sized group," "regional population," "unit group," or "nomadic group" (reviewed in Sugiyama, 1968; Goodall, 1975a; Teleki et al., 1976; Teleki, in press). Composition of the small parties is diverse and variable: They can be made up of adults of both sexes, of females with young, of males, or of mixed ages and sexes. Composition changes continually from hour to hour and day to day. The larger communities of about 15 or 30 to 80 or 85 chimpanzees constitute relatively stable associations over time; these regional populations range over a known area. Within the larger communities are found the continually changing small parties varying from 1 or 2 to 30 individuals.

In one sense, chimpanzees do not have permanent or fixed groups. At another level, in terms of a population relative to a general region, chimpanzee communities are comparatively stable, yet open, and fluctuate with regard to the composition of subgroupings in time and space. Both females and males do occasionally change communities temporarily or

[1] Chimpanzee social organization has been discussed by many researchers, for example: Reynolds and Reynolds, 1965; Goodall, 1965, 1968a, 1973a, b, 1975a, b; Itani and Suzuki, 1967; Nishida, 1968, 1970; Sugiyama, 1968, 1969, 1972, 1973a, b; Suzuki, 1969; Izawa, 1970; Mason, 1970; Jones and Sabater Pí, 1971; Albrecht and Dunnett, 1971; Nishida and Kawanaka, 1972; Kawanaka and Nishida, 1974; McGrew, 1977; Sugiyama and Koman, 1979; Bygott, 1979; Teleki, in press.

permanently (Nishida and Kawanaka, 1972; Goodall, 1973a, 1975a; Kawanaka and Nishida, 1974; Teleki et al., 1976; Pusey, 1979; Nishida, 1979; Sugiyama and Koman, 1979).

Party size, composition, and amount of movement per day vary situationally, particularly with regard to available food in an area.[2] When a fig tree is ripe, many animals gather to eat from it. For more dispersed foods that are not available in large quantities, chimpanzees forage alone, or a few who are friends or genealogically related (in various age and sex combinations) move together over a wide range. Fairly large parties may migrate from one area to another (Reynolds and Reynolds, 1965).

In traveling and feeding, mothers and young ordinarily remain within a smaller range, whereas adults without young may range over a wider area. Reynolds and Reynolds (1965), for example, report parties of mothers and young remaining for long periods within a core area of about 15 square kilometers compared to a range of at least 26 square kilometers for other types of parties.

Females, mothers with infants, or males may move about alone from time to time (Goodall, 1968a). Such occasional isolation is rare for ground-living primate species. The chimpanzee's large body size, substantial canines, and, apparently, the minimal predator pressure may offer a partial explanation. Food, curiosity, sexual interests, and "individuality" may also be factors. Even though chimpanzees are solitary from time to time, it is for brief periods. Overall, they are intensely social and spend most of their time in the company of others. In this they differ from the Asian apes: the almost solitary orangutan and the paired gibbons. Chimpanzees' specific companions do vary, though, in contrast to gorillas or baboons where group composition remains quite stable over time.

Environment and social structural flexibility

Vegetation, amount and distribution of food, and whether chimpanzees are relatively stationary or traveling all influence group patterns. Suzuki (1969) described three modes – "concentration," "linkage," and "dispersal." Concentration of up to 50 chimpanzees occurs in two contrasting contexts: (1) in areas (usually forest) where the food supply is concentrated, or (2) in savanna woodlands, particularly when a group travels over a long distance. In the hilly Kasakati Basin, Tanzania, where woodland or open forests with savanna grasslands and riverine forests characterize the

[2] The Reynoldses (1965) noted several contingencies that brought subgroups together in the Budongo Forest: concentration of food; sexual behavior and grooming; attraction to calls and drumming of neighbors; use of habitual routes and regions of activity; and large scale movements to a new place, usually related to the decrease of food supply in one area.

landscape, Izawa (1970) observed about 30 to 40 individuals of both sexes and all ages moving together often. Their relatively extensive movements and frequent congregation may be related to the multiplicity and irregularity of food "seasons" in this area. Linkage of two or three subgroups, each ranging in size from 6 to 13 individuals, which move 100 to 1,000 meters from each other and continually exchange calls, was observed frequently in riverine forests and on occasion in savanna woodlands. Dispersal of one, two, or three chimpanzees spread out away from other individuals or from other small groups of two or three also occurs; there are almost no vocalizations. Such dispersal was noted when food was dwindling in a riverine forest and when food was abundant and the chimpanzees were staying in the area for a long time. No one mode of social patterning correlates in a rigid way to a particular environmental situation.

Social flexibility, with patterning, enables the species to utilize a range of environments: A community can thereby deal with seasonal and other variations within its habitat. Food supplies change according to season in both forest and savanna woodland habitats (Reynolds and Reynolds, 1965; Suzuki, 1969).

Chimpanzee ranges and their population densities vary considerably, depending on the environment. At one end of the spectrum, in the Budongo *tropical forest* of Uganda, one regional population studied over a number of years includes about 40 to 80 chimpanzees (Reynolds and Reynolds, 1965; Sugiyama, 1968). Small groups of less than 10 often stay within an area of 5 square kilometers or so for several months (Sugiyama, 1973a). They have a small nomadic range of about 7 or 8 to 20 square kilometers (Reynolds and Reynolds, 1965; Sugiyama, 1968, 1973a) and a fairly high population density, estimated to average about 4 to 5 chimpanzees per square kilometer (Sugiyama, 1973a). In contrast, in *savanna woodlands,* ranges are wider and densities lower. A survey of a large savanna woodlands area of about 20,000 square kilometers along the eastern coast of Lake Tanganyika, Tanzania, included well studied areas such as the Kasakati Basin and Gombe National Park (Kano, 1972). On the average, Kano estimates regional populations at about 30 to 50 animals, range size about 190 square kilometers, and mean densities of around 0.2 chimpanzees per square kilometer for this area.[3] In one *unusually arid region* in Ugalla, Tanzania, Itani (1979) estimates the nomadic range of

[3] The number of chimpanzees in a regional population, range size, and population density is difficult to ascertain for savanna woodlands. Regional populations range over a wide area but use some areas more intensely than others, and traveling companions vary from time to time according to individual preference. This means that it is hard to identify a regional community and to be sure how large an area it ranges over. Further, some savanna woodlands areas are utilized more intensely than others. For all these reasons, figures for the "same" savanna woodlands regions tend to differ somewhat from study to study.

a group of 15 to 40 chimpanzees to be as high as 700 to 750 square kilometers. This would make their population density only 0.07 to 0.08 head per square kilometer.

Thus, range size differs greatly with environment – small in the forest, extensive in savanna woodlands, and very high indeed for especially arid regions. Chimpanzees' savanna woodlands ranges are the widest known for any nonhuman primate (Kano, 1972). Within arid regions, however, certain forested areas are most intensively utilized (Suzuki, 1969; Kano, 1972).

Significantly, the total size of any one community or regional population varies within far narrower limits (approximately 15 to 85 for savanna woodlands, and 40 to 80 for tropical forests) than does the range such a community covers (from only about 7 to 8 km^2 to some 750 km^2). From an evolutionary perspective, this is intriguing for three quite different reasons.

First, in savanna woodlands, the range is a great deal larger and the population much less dense than in the forest (Itani and Suzuki, 1967; Sugiyama, 1968; Suzuki, 1969). Such a situation may well have characterized the population transitional between ancestral apes and early hominids as it adapted to a new ecological niche on the savannas of eastern Africa.[4] Second, chimpanzees have some access to savannas but do not utilize them intensively. In savanna woodlands, they rely largely on the trees. Early hominid remains are located largely in savanna regions – but how much of the savanna were they able to use? I think the early hominids could use the savanna itself and that this represented an important change from their ape-like ancestors. I shall try to show (in Chapter 7) how they came to be able to do so. The other part of the question is: How dependent on trees did the transitional population and the earliest hominids continue to be? Quite dependent, I think, for both shelter and fruit, not disregarding their new ability to find food on the savanna itself.

Third, even though chimpanzees are very sociable creatures and have a relatively complex communication system and a flexible, multipatterned social organization, there appears to be a rough limit to chimpanzee community size. Chimpanzee communities, whatever the environmental context, are only known to vary from about 15 to 85 animals. This limited size is probably related both to patterns of resource utilization and to social and cultural constraints. Communicatory, cultural, and technological limits keep their communities small; chimpanzees have neither language and culturally patterned social organization nor sufficient expertise in tool con-

[4] Boaz (1979) estimates that the early hominid population on the savannas near Omo, Ethiopia, about 2.8 Mya to 1.9 Mya, did not densely populate that region (see Chapter 7, footnote 3).

struction and use to collect abundant food. The interesting question with regard to human evolution is: When did communities begin to enlarge? Certainly not yet for the earliest hominids – and probably not for most of human evolution. Clearly, with brains only a little larger than those of chimpanzees, the early hominids' communication system would not be adequate to the task of coordinating social activities in communities much larger or more complexly organized than chimpanzee communities. Similarly, with only the crudest of organic and, later, stone tools,[5] early hominid food gathering techniques could not support large communities. But even more important, small, very flexible and mobile living groups are utilized by human gatherer-hunters today. Dobe !Kung San camps range in size from only about 4 to 34 individuals (Lee, 1979). Perhaps small communities were utilized not only by our ape, transitional, and early human ancestors but also by most humans prior to the invention of horticulture and agriculture.

Sociability

Chimpanzees, as most "higher" primates, live in groups of both sexes and all ages. Friendly and relaxed interaction and the formation of persisting social bonds have their roots in the mother–infant relationship. Primates are nearly helpless at birth, and young chimpanzees remain dependent on their mothers for several years. Deep affectional ties appear to form during this long period (Figure 5:1). The extended association between mother and infant promotes subsequent formation of bonds with siblings and forms the basis for lifelong interaction with others.

Physical contact appears to have a calming effect on chimpanzees, as it does for other primates. The close physical contact between mother and offspring over a number of years is the context in which tactile communication originates and develops. Among chimpanzees, social "closeness" often is expressed by grooming – not only a practical means of keeping hair and skin in good condition but also an often exercised mode of tactile social contact. Grooming is frequent: 135 instances were observed by Sugiyama (1969) in the total observation time of 290 hours as contrasted to only 30 agonistic ("aggressive") interactions during the same half-year study period (Figure 5:2).

[5] The earliest established bipedal hominid fossil skeleton dates from somewhat less than 3 Mya in the Hadar Formation, Afar, Ethiopia (Johanson and Taieb, 1976; Johanson et al., 1976), but stone tools do not appear in the archeological record until almost a million years later. The first known stone tools appear in the Shungura Formation at Omo, Ethiopia, which has been dated 2.2 Mya to 2 Mya (Howell, 1976; Chavaillon, 1976; Merrick and Merrick, 1976; Isaac, 1978).

Friendly behavior also takes the form of a variety of gestural and vocal greetings. Social communication includes embracing, kissing, handshaking, body patting, grooming, presenting, mounting, genital gripping or inspection, crouching, "bowing," bobbing, "grinning," "pouting," and a wide variety of other facial expressions, beating on a tree trunk, loud cries, low groans, whimpering, hooting, high-pitched calls, shrieking, squawking, screaming, and panting (Goodall, 1968b; Sugiyama, 1969). Males and females both greet others of either sex. Of all social categories, mature female chimpanzees receive and give the most greetings (Good-

FIGURE 5:1. A grieving chimpanzee mother holds her dead infant and stares fixedly at her hands.

all, 1968b). This expresses their obvious sociability and, quite likely, is also a reflection of the substantial part they play in chimpanzee social life.

Among primates, adult females are usually quite gregarious.[6] This is hardly surprising, given their close and extended ties with offspring. Female chimpanzee sociability is not, however, limited to close kin, small parties, or even to the other members of a regional population. Chimpanzee females are known to sometimes change communities, either temporarily or permanently, at Mahali as well as at Gombe (Kawanaka and Nishida, 1974). Further, except for the few instances of pairs (e.g., gibbons and some South American monkeys), more than one female ordinarily lives in a primate social group. What vary most are the frequency and kind of interaction between males. In many primate species, there is only one male per group, or the males in the group are age-graded males, such as in gorillas; multimale groups exist but are not common for many species of primates. Chimpanzee males are quite sociable among primate males.

[6] This is not to imply that they cannot also be aggressive or destructive. At Gombe, one female, Passion, and her daughter Pom have been observed killing and eating three infants, the offspring of two partially paralyzed females (Goodall, 1977).

FIGURE 5:2. Chimpanzee sociability: grooming.

They exhibit much friendly behavior with each other and with females and young. Elaborate greetings characterize male–male chimpanzee interactions (Nishida, 1970). Males do not often fight, and most relations – even interactions in conflict situations – are mediated by facial expressions, vocalization, erection of the hair, and gestural or postural communication. And there have now been males, as well as females, that have been observed changing groups (Sugiyama and Koman, 1979).

Genealogical ties and maternal "investment"

The long period of infant dependency among chimpanzees not only promotes close, and extended, mother–offspring interaction but also makes possible relationships based on genealogical ties through the mother, including brother–brother as well as sister–sister and sister–brother friendships. Mother–offspring contact is frequent even past puberty, despite the fact that the young travel on their own fairly often. Sibling ties may also persist (Goodall, 1967a).

High quality maternal care is essential in the survival of chimpanzee offspring. Because the newborn are very weak, they need considerable physical support and protection, especially during the first three months. Mothers also guard their infants. Although other females and youngsters may be allowed to inspect an infant, mothers may move away when adult males approach. "In defense of her infant or older offspring a mother may threaten or attack the aggressor. One normally timid female actually hurled herself at the alpha male when he seized her infant during a charging display" (Goodall, 1975a:119). Mother–offspring affinity is expressed in play, grooming, sleeping in the same nest, affectionate behavior, and sharing patterns (Goodall, 1967a; Riss and Goodall, 1976).

Infants beg for and receive food (Goodall, 1968a; McGrew, 1975; Silk, 1978). Perhaps even more often, the offspring simply comes close to the mother and eats or carries away part of whatever food the mother has (Nishida, 1970). *Infants begin to solicit food from their mothers when only a few months old, and mothers continue to share quite regularly until the offspring is about four years old, about the age of weaning* (C. Clark, 1977; Silk, 1978). Silk (1978) has listed 14 foods that mothers at Gombe were observed to share with their offspring. Fruits, the most commonly eaten foods, are also the most frequently shared. Silk's list also includes insects, nuts, leaves, provisioned bananas, and meat. Other researchers have also noted mothers sharing; the foods mentioned include premasticated figs (Sugiyama, 1972), grapefruit (Albrecht and Dunnett, 1971), stems (Hladik, 1973), meat (Teleki, 1973a), and provisioned bananas (Goodall, 1968a).

Young chimpanzees are not weaned from the breast until they are around four or five years old, about when the mother becomes pregnant again. A youngster continues to be carried dorsally and to

FIGURE 5:3. A chimpanzee mother and her infant.

sleep in its mother's nest until the birth of a younger sibling (Goodall, 1975a). The chimpanzee mother–infant relationship is one of

great duration and intensity . . . The young chimpanzee . . . remains with the mother for nine to twelve years . . . the Gombe chimpanzee infant has no younger sibling until at least four, more often five, years of age, and suckles to within a few months of the next birth. This is an extremely long duration of parental investment on the part of the chimpanzee mother.   [C. Clark, 1977:235]

Even after a new infant arrives, the older offspring, now between four and five years old, continues to be dependent on its mother and spends its time in close contact with her. The mother grooms her offspring frequently. "Grooming enables the infant to maintain contact with the mother, and she with it, as suckling ends; this contact behavior endures throughout their lives" (C. Clark, 1977:254).

Noticeable infant depression, lasting from a few months to as long as a year, may occur during weaning. Infant mortality is high when the mother dies, even for offspring who appear to be sufficiently mature physically (three years) to survive on their own (Teleki et al., 1976). "Adoption" by an older sibling – of either sex – may occur, and perhaps this increases chances of survival, although depression and death may nonetheless result (Goodall, 1971; Teleki et al., 1976).

Within groups, the mother–offspring association is the basic social dyad; it is the most stable, long term social unit. The individuality so common in all other aspects of chimpanzee social interaction characterizes "mothering" and sibling relationships as well (Goodall, 1975a). Some chimpanzee females appear to be more effective mothers than others, and some "families" may be closer than other ones. Large genealogical units based on a combination of mother–offspring and sibling ties can include up to three generations: The famed Flo family at Gombe, for example, comprised an old female, Flo, her own offspring, Faben, Figan, Fifi, Flint, and Flame, and, later, Fifi's offspring, Freud (Goodall, 1971, 1973a). Flo was a high-ranking female. She was most often seen with Flint, her youngest living offspring. (Flame, born after Flint, lived only a short time.) Fifi also frequently associated with Flo and Flint, and Flo's two adult sons were also seen, though less often, with their mother or sister (Figure 5:4).

Sibling ties form during development. On the one hand, a newborn infant is generally an attraction to its older siblings. Also, as the mother's attention focuses on the new infant, her juvenile offspring increases its interaction with older siblings. These types of close interaction during development form the bases for sibling recognition and frequent association and interaction throughout life. Play is an important aspect of chimpanzee development, but because of variable composition and the generally small size of groups in chimpanzee society, young chimpanzees do not always have peers readily available for play and so partially rely on their mothers and older or younger siblings. This playful interaction no doubt also reinforces genealogical ties (see Figure 5:5).

Adults who associate frequently may be siblings. Male "friends" who associate regularly are in some cases known to be brothers. Faben and Figan at Gombe were such friends. Adult females who were often seen together, such as Flo and Ollie, may well have been siblings, though records do not go back far enough to document this. Sibling ties provide emotional support throughout life and, should the mother die, individuals have not lost their only close social tie. Even late in life such ties may persist; Goodall (1971) felt reasonably sure that Humphrey, the only chimpanzee to associate with Mr. McGregor during his final illness (probably polio), was his brother. Genealogical ties, first (and closest) between mother and offspring and subsequently between siblings, provide long term bonds and form a basis for building a wider network of relations. In those instances when young adult females (about eight years old) change

FIGURE 5:4. Flo, a chimpanzee mother, supports her youngest son, Flint, while her oldest daughter, Fifi, watches.

communities, such contacts with siblings would presumably be at least temporarily interrupted. But if such females remain in the new community and bear young there, a new matricentric network would begin to grow around them.

For humans, prior to the industrial revolution and the formation of large nation-states, kinship systems provided an extremely important – probably the most important – means of ordering and structuring communities. Fossils and stone tools do not tell us how early in human evolution symbolically structured kinship systems became important. However, if our early hominid ancestors had at least as extended a period of contact between mothers and offspring and among siblings as is the case for chimpanzees, there was a potential social framework to build upon.

For chimpanzees, the extended period of dependence on the mother provides sufficient time for the young to develop motor skills, to master modes of dealing with the external environment (such as when and how to locate dispersed foods), and to learn patterns of social interaction. Learning occurs in a social context from those with whom there are emotional ties; both technical and relational skills are so acquired. Much learning occurs by watching the mother or an older sibling, imitating that individual and practicing the skill (Goodall, 1973b). In learning to modify objects and use them as tools, for example, chimpanzees first manipulate objects in play (Goodall, 1970; McGrew, 1977). Only later are practical applications

FIGURE 5:5. A male chimpanzee at Gombe plays with his infant brother.

learned or developed – as in nest making or in finding and preparing suitable objects for "drinking" or termiting and obtaining ants.

Among chimpanzees, behavioral complexes – including object modification, tool use, and food preference – appear to be passed on from generation to generation, from mother to offspring. Similarly, although predatory behavior is frequently a male rather than a female activity at Gombe, on several occasions a mother and her two daughters (juvenile and adolescent) were observed catching and killing small animals and eating the meat. Goodall (1973b:173) suggests that "if it [predatory behavior] is maintained by both her daughters, [it] might eventually have a considerable influence on the role of females in hunting at Gombe."

Sexual interactions

Chimpanzee females, like other apes, Old World monkeys, and *Homo sapiens,* have a menstrual cycle, which for chimpanzees generally begins at about eight or nine and up to eleven years of age (Goodall, 1969; Hafez, 1971). In addition, most apes and Old World monkeys have "estrous" changes that are synchronized with ovulation, but humans do not. Frequency of mating is related to estrus but is more variable in primates than was once thought (Hafez, 1971). During estrus, female primates show physio-

FIGURE 5:6. A male checks a female's genital swelling for sexual "readiness." The infant remains clinging to its mother, as often occurs during sexual interaction.

logical changes in the genital tract, changes in hormone levels, and behavioral changes. Some species, such as chimpanzees, exhibit external morphological changes—for example, "sexual swellings," which consist of a gradual increase in size and change in color of swellings in the anogenital region culminating at midcycle. These obvious morphological changes during estrus in chimpanzee females, and also their behavioral (and possibly olfactory) ones, serve as sexual cues to males (Figure 5:6).

Most copulations among chimpanzees in the wild take place during estrus, when a female is not pregnant or lactating. Goodall (1969) reports, however, that copulations have been observed during the first three or four months of pregnancy when females still may have periodic sexual swellings and are willing to mate, even though they cannot become pregnant. In addition, and especially interesting, she noted occasional copulations when females had no sexual swellings. The old stereotype that all female primates (except humans) copulate only when in estrus is belied by the evidence.

Findings for captive chimpanzees are comparable (Lemmon and Allen, 1978). The sexual cycles and copulatory times for each of a group of 13 captive female chimpanzees were studied over a five-year period. By far the most copulations occurred during periods of maximal sexual swelling. At other times in the sexual cycle there were some copulations. In these instances, the stage of the cycle—whether there was no swelling or whether it was on the increase or decrease—seemed to make little difference. Only very few copulations took place during lactation. Chimpanzees, then, can and do copulate at any time; but frequencies differ greatly, with the most copulations occurring when the sexual skin is enlarged and the female can become pregnant, and the fewest when she is still nursing a dependent infant.

Male and female chimpanzees ordinarily copulate with many individuals, and mating may be initiated by either sex. Females approach and present to a male for copulation. Alternatively, a male may attract the attention of an estrous female by staring intensely, positioning himself so as to display his erect penis, beckoning, or moving vigorously in activities such as tree leaping or branch shaking (Goodall, 1968a). Often, a male simply follows an estrous female around until she copulates with him. Females may ignore willing males, and males may ignore female approaches. Some estrous females have been noted to run screeching from approaching males. The copulatory position requires female cooperation; in the common position, females remain crouched, while the male inserts from the rear. There are records of females terminating intercourse during a male's ejaculation (Goodall, 1968a).

Seventy percent of copulatory behavior observed by Goodall (1968a) occurred during social excitement, as when two groups met or when the animals arrived at a much liked food source. Goodall notes that, when several males are present, an estrous female may be mounted successively by each of the males in the group. One female copulated with eight different males, each within two minutes of another. Generally, there is little sign of jealousy or aggression. Males usually wait their turns and do not interrupt the sexual activity of others.

However, possessive behavior—in both sexes and at all ages—also has been noted at Gombe (Goodall, 1975a). An infant will typically try to interfere when a male is copulating with its mother (Figure 5:7). Similarly, mothers and adolescent daughters may try to interfere with each other's sexual activity. For example, when "Flo and Fifi were receptive at the same time, the mother would push at males copulating with her daughter and vice versa" (Goodall, 1975a:124). Males sometimes follow a female persistently; one slept all night in the rain at the foot of a tree in which an estrous female was nesting (Goodall, 1975a).

In addition, some males at Gombe occasionally try to "force" estrous females to follow them—apparently to keep the female away from other males. At the Gombe feeding station during daily observations over two and

a half years, 40 such male attempts to force females to follow were observed (McGinnis, 1979). In these instances a male first engaged in a "courtship-like display" that attracted the female's attention. When she moved toward him, he turned and moved off. If she did not follow, the intensity of his display increased and alternated with attacks on her. These displays and attacks ceased when the female followed

FIGURE 5:7. This is a common copulatory position for adult chimpanzees. Note the infant's presence.

the male. Of these 40 forced departures in two and a half years, there were 12 instances in which the male and female were both absent from the feeding station for four days or more and were presumed to be traveling together, apart from others, in a "consort" relationship. Attempts by the researchers to follow were not successful except in one case in which the female stopped, and vocalized, so frequently that the human researchers were able to keep up. In another situation, a "male tried to force two females to accompany him: when he attacked one for not responding fast enough the other escaped, and whilst he searched for her the first also escaped" (Goodall, 1975a:123).

Indeed, the effectiveness and "maintenance of both possessive and consort behavior depends on the female's cooperation" (Tutin, 1975:447). Not all "consortships" involve force. "The young female, Pooch, was often seen to follow the young male, Figan, with little or no coercion when the female was in maximal swelling" (McGinnis, 1979:435). Tutin's study clarifies the matter further:

Frequencies of male involvement in possessive and consort behavior do not correlate with age, dominance or the amount of agonistic behavior males directed at females. However, the amount of time males spent grooming tumescent females in group situations does correlate positively with the frequencies of possessive and consort behavior . . . There is also a positive relationship between the amount of time males spent grooming females and their generosity to females in food-sharing situations. (McGrew, pers. com.).

As previously mentioned, female cooperation is essential for the maintenance of these special relationships and they thus present an opportunity for females to exercise choice. If female choice is involved, it is of interest to note that the selection criteria appear to be social and caretaking abilities of the males and not their dominance status.

[Tutin, 1975:448]

At Gombe, courtship, courtship-like behavior, and other displays are fairly frequent at the banana provisioning station in the general context of excitement there. Females, however, are often initially frightened by these types of behavior. Males of the ancestral population, when excited, also may have exhibited behavior that similarly confused or frightened the females. In the transition from ancestral ape to early hominid, selection for greater intelligence may well have allowed males to discriminate more effectively during sexual interaction. First, transitional hominid males were probably learning how to ascertain female sexual interest and "receptivity" from a variety of cues (no longer only estrus-related cues). Second, increased intelligence (used in social contexts) could assist transitional population males in determining when to display and when to groom and share food. That is, transitional males may have become more effective than the ape ancestors in distinguishing and selecting behavior that would be sexually attractive to females.

In the wild, as previously noted, female chimpanzees sometimes leave their local community during estrus and go to neighboring ones; they may return later or remain in other communities permanently. This reduces the likelihood of mating with a sibling or familiar chimpanzee and suggests a possible preference for new males. The openness of chimpanzee groups, with females sometimes changing communities during estrus, suggests a long history of gene flow between neighboring populations of chimpanzees through much of equatorial Africa (Goodall, 1975a).

Females show considerable sexual individuality. And males may respond in various ways to females. Which animal initiates, how the other reacts, and the frequency of copulation vary with individual chimpanzees, and behavior may change with age and experience. Females solicit, accept, or avoid copulation. In 19 copulations observed by Sugiyama (1969, 1973b) among free ranging, unprovisioned chimpanzees in the Budongo Forest, 14 were initiated by females. Whether this is the usual pattern in free-ranging, unprovisioned chimpanzees is not yet clear from available information. Such frequent female initiation of sexual activities would be consistent with the degree of "investment" of mothers in their offspring before birth, in infancy, and during development. The hints of chimpanzee female selectivity in sexual interaction indicated by Tutin's study (1975) are also not surprising, given the correlation between parental investment and choice of mates noted for some species (Trivers, 1972).

"Rank" and "leadership"

Chimpanzees' flexible social organization is an integral aspect of their ecological adaptation. The composition of parties is not stable; and survival does not depend upon chimpanzees staying together all the time. The absence of a rigid social hierarchy of individuals from the most to the least "dominant" is consistent with their shifting associations (Mason, 1970; Nishida, 1970). However, in interactions at the feeding station at Gombe, where animals tend to become excited and competitive over provisioned bananas, one or more individuals of each sex has generally stood out as most aggressive and dominant (Riss and Goodall, 1976).

Overall, the concept of dominance as applied to chimpanzees is problematic. The concept does not sufficiently allow for the great amount of individuality, variability, and social group flexibility found in chimpanzee communities. "It is impossible to use the 'peanut test' (Itani, 1954) to decide dominance rank between two chimpanzees; the author has determined dominance relationships by observing which individual makes submissive expressions in an agonistic interaction . . . the dominance concept must be reexamined" (Nishida, 1970:73,74).[7]

Attempts to correlate chimpanzees' access to food with dominance or aggression produce ambiguous results both in the laboratory (Reynolds and Luscombe, 1969) and in the wild. At Gombe, the most aggressive male or female in the community generally does have some priority of access to food or locations (Goodall, 1975a). In addition, however, age, genealogical relationship, "friendship," and activity level (e.g., as in estrus) appear to relate to patterns of food distribution, rather than its being strictly regulated by a "dominance order."

Most displays and threats relating to food seem to occur in contexts where food is highly concentrated—for example, at the provisioning station or over freshly killed prey. In the latter situation the threats and displays observed are generally either expressions of frustration from animals without meat or objections to advances for meat portions (Teleki, 1973b). Teleki found no direct combat over meat. Rather than the strongest obtaining the most plants or meat from others, the reverse seems to hold. Many

---

[7] The peanut test is a standard procedure used on Japanese monkeys to determine relative dominance.

kinds of food are frequently passed from mother to offspring, and meat often is passed from males to females.

Similarly, age, dominance, or frequency of "aggressive" displays do not necessarily give a male priority in terms of access to females (Tutin, 1975). Estrous females generally move about freely and copulate with many males, often in succession (Goodall 1968a, 1969, 1975a). Sugiyama (1973a) reports an interesting instance of an estrous female who was grooming a big adult male and who paused briefly, approached a young adult male nearby, had sex with him, then returned to the former male to continue grooming him.

Initiation of activities depends upon individual experience, knowledge, and social ties, and it is relative to a particular situation. "Social rank" (as inferred from degrees of agonistic and "deferential" behavior) and "leading" others vary independently; they may even be inversely correlated when food is involved. In Menzel's experiments (1973a, 1974, 1975) food was hidden in a one acre enclosure and shown (or clues given about its location) to one member in a group of eight juvenile chimpanzees, who then led the rest to the food.[8] The chimpanzees preferred to follow Bell, a low-ranking female who was willing to share the spoils, and least liked to follow Rock, the most aggressive male.

How aggressive are chimpanzees?

The relative aggressiveness of chimpanzees poses a pertinent question but one that is difficult to answer satisfactorily. Reports from various observers give different overall impressions. Doubtless, observer selectivity contributes to confusion. At least as significant, the degree of agonistic interaction is influenced by characteristics of the particular population under study: whether or not the population is artificially provisioned, whether provisioned food is highly concentrated or spread out (Wrangham, 1974; Goodall, 1975a), whether the community is experiencing population pressure or is under stress in other respects.[9]

[8] This experiment was performed with each of five chimpanzees who were sufficiently independent to go off with the experimenter and leave the others.
[9] The behavior of different populations in a primate species may vary widely, depending on the degree of stress the population is experiencing. Among Indian langurs, for example, the degree of fighting and of infant mortality contrasts vividly between undisturbed forest living langurs and those that live under very crowded conditions and are exposed to frequent human harassment (Curtin and Dolhinow, 1978). At one end of the spectrum are relaxed behavior and general absence of fighting; at the other end are frequent and vicious aggression and an infant mortality rate that rose to 83 percent in one area. Curtin and Dolhinow conclude that such new behaviors "demonstrate the disturbing results whenever a remarkably adaptable species is pushed beyond the range of its flexibility" (1978:475).

In general, relationships between the different chimpanzees of the community are remarkably relaxed and peaceful so that it is often possible to follow an association through the forest for hours without witnessing a single aggressive act. Chimpanzees are, however, easily roused to displays of quite violent aggression which are seldom of long duration and which seldom result in discernable injury to the individuals concerned.

[Goodall, 1975a:114]

FIGURE 5:8. This male chimpanzee looks much larger than he is because his hair is standing on end (piloerection).

The individual and social variability exhibited by chimpanzees in so many other respects applies here too. "Aggressive" behavior is heavily dependent upon context and can take many forms: threatening glances, postures, or gestures; piloerection, charges, and chasing; displays (including waving the arms or throwing objects); and, at the extreme, fights involving body contact. These behaviors can be directed at other species or at other chimpanzees.

When aggressive acts are directed at other species, both male and female chimpanzees may display, chase, or attack. At Gombe, where the artificial concentration of provisioned bananas brings chimpanzees and baboons into frequent contact, chimpanzees stand up, wave their arms, attack, or chase baboons competing for provisioned food (Goodall, 1968b). Likewise, potential predators may be objects of aggressive action, as was suggested by experiments with stuffed leopards where both male and female chimpanzees directed displays, threw objects, and charged at the apparently threatening predator (Albrecht and Dunnett, 1971).

Male chimpanzees more frequently display or threaten (with either facial expression or body posture) other chimpanzees than do females. Yet females are capable of intense aggressive behavior—as when their young are threatened or when they are appropriating meat from baboons. In Kortlandt's (1967) experiments with a stuffed leopard that was "holding" a "baby" chimpanzee doll, the chimpanzee mothers were more fierce than

FIGURE 5:9. Chimpanzees sometimes stand upright during displays to threaten baboons away from provisioned food. Here, at Gombe National Park, Tanzania, a fearful "David" cowers behind a protective "Goliath."

either the chimpanzee females without offspring or the male chimpanzees (see Figure 7:7). Nonetheless, Bygott (1979) reports that about 90 percent of agonistic acts at Gombe involved males, even though males and females visited the provisioning station more or less equally. It would be interesting to investigate whether female chimpanzees are more selective than males in their aggressive behavior.

Chimpanzees have a diversified behavioral repertoire for expressing or responding to threats. There are, for example, numerous "friendly," "submissive," or "respectful" signals that a frightened or threatened individual can employ as an alternative to escape or fighting (Nishida, 1970). In fact, displays themselves may be viewed as a form of aggressive communication, and one that does not ordinarily necessitate a direct fight. Chimpanzees are able to communicate through various modes so that actual fighting—which might cause injuries—often can be avoided. A display between two males who have just met after a separation of some hours may be followed by an embrace and grasping of the scrotum (Sugiyama, 1969).

FIGURE 5:10. A new mother (*right*), holding her first baby, elicits a gesture of reassurance from a male chimpanzee who often bullies others.

Conditions of heightened excitement increase the intensity of social interaction, including display behavior. When more than half a dozen individuals are together—for example, near the feeding station—there is increased leaping and swinging through branches, sexual interaction, vocalization, and agonistic behavior (Goodall, 1968a). When Figan, an adult male at Gombe, was followed for 50 days, observers noted he engaged in three times as many displays in the camp area (near the provisioning station) as elsewhere (Riss and Busse, 1977). Such intensification may also occur during stress. After the death of a familiar chimpanzee, for instance, displays, vocalizing, and grooming increased among the chimpanzees present (Teleki, 1973c).

In 300 hours of observation of free-ranging, unprovisioned chimpanzees in the Budongo Forest in Uganda, Reynolds and Reynolds (1965) counted only 17 instances of agonistic behavior. None lasted more than a few seconds, and only a few of these encounters involved body contact. In a half year of observation in the Budongo Forest, Sugiyama (1969) noted 31 agonistic interactions and no fights (although he deduced that some occurred because injuries were noted). In contrast, at Gombe Stream Reserve, 284 attacks were observed in one year. At least two thirds of these Gombe attacks were associated with the artificially heightened excitement and greater concentration of chimpanzees occasioned by banana provisioning (Goodall, 1968a).

Subsequently, at Gombe, the degree of agonistic behavior seems to have intensified. There have been attacks on members of other communities that were so severe as to result in death (Goodall, 1977, 1979). Similarly, predation on infant chimpanzees has been observed (in most, but not all, cases the infants' mothers were not members of the community). This apparent increase in the frequency of severe and damaging aggressive interaction at Gombe has proved alarming to researchers there (Goodall, 1977). It is, however, also a very interesting phenomenon. It allows us to ask: What is the context in which the more extreme forms of aggressive behavior seem to have increased at Gombe?

First, long-term provisioning and habituation to humans may have generally "disturbed" the population to some extent. Second, because agonistic displays are quite common when chimpanzees are excited, and because such exciting instances have occurred very regularly due to provisioning over many years (rather than sporadically as ordinarily would have been the case under undisturbed conditions), it seems likely that young chimpanzees observing their elders' more frequent displays may have learned to act "more aggressive." Third, and perhaps most significant,

In the past few years there has been a gradually increasing area of land under agriculture outside the boundaries of the Gombe National Park. A large community of chimpanzees has repeatedly been seen and heard in an area formerly utilized almost exclusively by the small community to the south of the main Kasakela community. It is possible that this large community may have moved into the Park from outside and that the density of chimpanzees within the Park has, therefore, increased.

[Goodall, 1977:272]

The study community at Gombe is, therefore, currently encountering both spatial restrictions and pressure from what appears to be a chimpanzee community recently displaced by humans. Gombe chimpanzees, in short, may be experiencing serious population pressure and range restrictions. This is occurring in a community where young chimpanzees have had increased opportunity, due to provisioning over an extended period, to observe and learn aggressive behavior.

How much variability by sex?

The major behavioral differences between the sexes are, of course, those associated with the act of copulation and its consequences for females – pregnancy, birth, lactation, and "mothering." Other differences are not marked in chimpanzees, as is the case for some species. Overall, for mammals, the extent of behavioral difference by sex generally relates to degree of physical dimorphism (e.g., differences in body size and/or in sizes of canine teeth, horns, or other like structures between males and females). Typically, in mammalian species where there is considerable sexual dimorphism, behavioral differences between the sexes (either in frequency or in kind) may be marked. By contrast, chimpanzees and humans have very little sexual dimorphism (see Figure 3:11). On the average, for both chimpanzees and humans, females weigh roughly 83 to 86 percent as much as males, with considerable individual overlap (Lyght et al., 1966; de Benedictis, pers. com.). Similarly, for both trunk and length comparisons, female chimpanzees are about 92 percent as long as males, and human females some 94 to 95 percent as tall as males (Schultz, 1931, 1960; Napier and Napier, 1967; de Benedictis, pers. com.). In contrast, however, common chimpanzee males' canine (or "fighting") teeth are 40 percent larger than females; for humans the difference in canine teeth is only 6 percent (Garn et al., 1966). The small degree of chimpanzee sexual dimorphism in body size correlates with the absence of marked differences in types of behaviors between the sexes, even though some differences in frequencies do exist. For humans, with regard to canine tooth size, physical sexual dimorphism is less than among common chimpanzees (see Figure 9:4).

Male chimpanzees, because of their slightly larger body size and longer, heavier canines, are generally somewhat higher ranking than females of the same age, but this is not always the case (Nishida, 1970). Older females, in particular, may also have a high rank within the larger group.

Adult males are not always dominant over adult females. In reality some adult females were seen to be dominant over two adult males. Since much depends upon the personality and combination of the individuals concerned, male–female relationships among chimpanzees are so variable that they cannot be generalized by a simple formula.

[Nishida, 1970:73]

Males have been observed sharing sugarcane and bananas (Goodall, 1968a; Nishida, 1970) with adult females and also sharing meat (which males obtain more often) with males, females, and young – presumably friends or relatives who are nearby (Teleki, 1973a, b). Females share many wild fruits, provisioned bananas, premasticated fig wads, leaves and stems, split pods, insects, and meat with their infant, juvenile, and adolescent offspring.

Although further data are needed, there is some evidence that unprovisioned, free-ranging females may initiate sexual behavior more frequently than males (Sugiyama, 1969, 1973b). This is consistent with the extent of maternal "investment" in their infants (e.g., sharing food and sleeping nests, carrying and grooming, as well as pregnancy and lactation). Adolescent females (in estrus) and females with young sometimes change com-

FIGURE 5:11. A chimpanzee mother gazes hopefully at bananas being eaten by a male.

munities and so obtain a new cluster of sex partners (Nishida and Kawanaka, 1972; Sugiyama, 1973a; Goodall, 1973a; 1975a).[10]

Adult females give and receive greetings more often than males and rarely display at other chimpanzees. Adult males display more often than females and are more frequently involved in agonistic interactions. They tend to display on first meeting with chimpanzees away from Gombe camp (Bygott, 1979) but possess some greeting behaviors not noted for females, for instance, touching a male's genitals (Sugiyama, 1969). Because their very appearance (more prominent canines and larger size) can denote threat, male chimpanzees, unlike females, may have to demonstrate more convincingly through gestures and other nonverbal forms of communication a sociable, nonthreatening intent. They can do so through various

[10] Most accounts describing "stranger males" (Reynolds and Reynolds, 1965; Sugiyama, 1968, 1969, 1972, 1973a; Bygott, 1979) may refer to the meetings of males from different parties within the same community. This can be deduced from (1) the fact that, when the home ranges of two or more communities are mapped and all members of each community identified (Reynolds and Reynolds, 1965; Nishida and Kawanaka, 1972), only females have been noted for certain to change communities; and from (2) observations of males from different communities avoiding, chasing, or even attacking each other in areas of range overlap (Nishida and Kawanaka, 1972; Goodall, 1975a; Bygott, 1979; Goodall et al., 1979).

Sugiyama and Koman (1979) did, however, identify two males from another group that briefly joined a chimpanzee group at Bossou, Guinea, that was observed without provisioning (for six months) and the adults identified. This means that chimpanzee males exhibit an extremely wide range of behavior when stranger males meet—from ignoring each other and peaceable interaction to vicious fighting that can result in death (Goodall, 1977).

FIGURE 5:12. Chimpanzee and Dorothy Lamour on 1938 movie set of "Her Jungle Love." Humans and chimpanzees share many postures and expressions — sometimes to an almost uncanny extent.

friendly behaviors, described earlier, that can serve to reduce aggression, ease tension, and facilitate social relations.

Among chimpanzees, as among humans, most social differences between the sexes are matters of relative frequencies. Individuals exhibit a very wide behavioral range, not markedly delineated by sex. Nonetheless, the frequency differences are intriguing.

Summary: social interactions

Both adult females and males are very sociable and form enduring attachments. They travel together, groom each other, sit or feed together, share food, and may support each other in agonistic interactions. Adult "friends" who frequently associate may be siblings, mother and daughter, or mother and son. Individual preferences and personality traits probably also figure in the formation of friendships.

In the context of the temporary nature of chimpanzee groups and their loose social structure, patterns of communication in fact define relations between and among individuals and reinforce and maintain social bonds. Friendly behaviors such as kissing, embracing, grooming, and, for males, touching genitals are elaborate (Goodall, 1968b; Nishida, 1970). Such gestures appear to reflect situational factors and individual expression rather than to strictly define dominance–subordinance relations, as many gestural interactions have been interpreted to function for other primate groups.

Chimpanzees exhibit social patterns that remind us of human gestures: "begging" and sharing, a variety of greetings, "reassurance" gestures, and sometimes postures uncannily like our own (Figure 5:12). Social ties also are expressed in the meeting of two outstretched hands, touching in a way resembling handshaking (Sugiyama, 1969). Through gestures and facial expressions, chimpanzees communicate a wide variety of subtle social information. The more flexible and multipatterned the social organization, the more elaborate communication must be for accommodating and inter-relating a large number of individuals – for chimpanzees a community of up to 80 or 85 individuals in some areas, some of whom are infrequently seen.

SIX

Chimpanzees as a model of the ancestral population: mental capacities, communication, and sociation – bases for the evolution of the capacity for culture

THERE is no such thing as a human nature independent of culture . . . As our central nervous system – and most particularly its crowning curse and glory, the neocortex – grew up in part in interaction with culture, it is incapable of directing our behavior or organizing our experience without the guidance provided by systems of significant symbols.

Clifford Geertz, 1966

THE concept of culture, as used by myself and other anthropologists, does not refer merely to an interesting set of customs (such as the quaint beliefs of one's great-grandparents or the lifeways of a tribal society halfway around the globe). Rather, culture *is* the human adaptation. During the process of human evolution our capacity for learning and symbolizing increased radically, so radically that we depend on what we learn – the particular culture we grow up in for the most part – to inform us of the range of action available to us. Any specific culture is made up of systems of significant symbols. These sets of meaningful symbols are learned by infants and children in close affective interaction with other humans, initially and most intimately with their mothers. Such symbol systems, in turn, are used throughout human life in perception, communication, technological innovation and utilization, and social action.

In seeking a model of the ancestral population, a prime question, therefore, concerns identification of the sorts of mental, communicatory, and social capacities that may have existed in an ancestral ape population in order to provide a basis for the evolution of the human capacity for culture. Here, again, the conservative chimpanzees provide a useful model in the attempt to reconstruct characteristics of the population ancestral to both the human line and the closely related African apes – the gorilla and the common and pygmy chimpanzees.

Experiments with common chimpanzees in the laboratory and observations in the wild show that: They can make fine differentiations, generalize, and cognitively "map" the objects in an area; they can recognize, interpret, and respond to a wide range of signals; and they can "think." Even more important, and rather startling, laboratory studies have demonstrated that chimpanzees possess cognitive and affective capacities necessary for learning and using the rudiments of a symbolic communication system (a "language") similar to our own. And, significantly, there is evidence from observations in the wild that social traditions regarding foods eaten and tools utilized to obtain food differ from one chimpanzee community to another (Nishida, 1973; McGrew, 1979). Although some of these differences appear to have resulted from direct environmental influences, it is difficult to regard other differences as anything but "custom" – arbitrary and socially transmitted. The many types of data available on common chimpanzees' cognition and communication, combined with information on the use of gestural communication during pygmy chimpanzee sexual interaction (Savage-Rumbaugh et al., 1977; Savage and Bakeman, 1978), and on the intelligence of gorillas (Rumbaugh, 1970; Patterson, 1978a, b), together strongly support the idea that relatively sophisticated cognitive and communicatory capacities already existed in the ape population ancestral to the living African apes and to humans.

For contemporary humans, cultures differ widely from one society to another. What does not differ is that every human society has a culture, with a communication system that includes a spoken language. The communication system of each society is, as it were, one subset of that society's overall cultural system. Studies of chimpanzee communication, and chimpanzee capacities to learn aspects of human linguistic communication, therefore prove particularly interesting. Not only are they relevant for an inquiry into the evolution of the human communication system (including human speech and language), but they also provide a basis for inquiry into what Clifford Geertz has called "the growth of culture and the evolution of mind" (1962, as reprinted 1973:55).

Chimpanzee communication and cognition

Attempts to develop an adequate theory of the origin and evolution of the human capacity for speech and language have typically been hampered by dualistic concepts characteristic of Western languages and cultures. In particular, the polarities generally implied or assumed between "emotional" and "rational," "nonverbal" and "verbal," or "relational" and "referential" communication make it very difficult indeed to understand how a chimpanzee-like, nonverbal, "expressive" communication system could provide an evolutionary base for the development of human lan-

guage. Ironically, these polar concepts, which are so much a part of Western thought, also complicate the effort to comprehend why chimpanzees
(and other apes) are able to learn elements of human language under
experimental conditions. I will first point out important features of chimpanzee communication in the wild, then review some significant experimental results, and finally return to these two questions.

Mammalian communication systems may utilize most of the senses –
visual, olfactory, auditory, tactile – but one or two of these modes are
usually emphasized in a particular species. In nonhuman primate communication the visual mode is primary and is accompanied by the vocal–
auditory mode. Postures, gestures, and facial expressions (that is, body
movements that can be seen), combined with some vocalizing, are the
major means of signaling (Marler and Tenaza, 1977; Marler, 1977).
There is also considerable reliance on tactile communication, through
many forms of physical contact – grooming, touching, sitting next to one
another, or, for the young, clinging to and being embraced by the
mother. Humans also utilize these modes, but the vocal–auditory mode
is primary in human speech. Visual and tactile modes are utilized in our
nonverbal communication.

Chimpanzees exhibit a rich repertoire of nonverbal communication
modes. As can be seen in Figure 6:1, for example, chimpanzees have
extraordinarily expressive faces. Human researchers have been able to
form hypotheses about some chimpanzee expressions based on the social
context in which they are utilized and upon similarities to human expressions. Examples of a few of these expressions and probable "meanings" include: (1) "glare," anger; (2) "pout face," desiring-frustration; (3) "whim-
per face," frustration-sadness; (4) "hoot face," excitement-affection; and
(5) "play face," playfulness (Goodall, 1968b, 1971; Chevalier-Skolnikoff,
1973).

Although chimpanzee facial expressions are rich and various, those of
humans are even more so – particularly in the region around the mouth.
"Should it be found that these different facial expressions have subtle
functional differences, this would suggest that the continued muscle differentiation about the mouth in man might possibly have been selected for
emotional expression as well as for speech" (Chevalier-Skolnikoff,
1973:80). An impressive mental capacity interrelates with chimpanzees'
nonverbal communicatory capabilities to mediate their frequent interactions and fluid social organization.

Darwin (1871) pointed out the significance of language for expressing
the wishes of individuals and groups and, therefore, for mediating social
behavior. It is evident, however, from the rich nonverbal repertoire of

chimpanzees that many social interactions can be mediated without the use of language per se or even of vocal communication. These social communications are more elaborate and complex and are more specifically interanimal in nature (i.e., truly communicatory) than would be expected if they were mere expressions of somatic or motivational states, such as fear, anxiety, anger, or excitement.

Chimpanzees show an awareness of what is being communicated by responding in a variety of ways to subtle signals (Figure 6:2). For example, when one animal "begs," hand outstretched, palm up, while looking intently into the face of an individual who has a preferred object, the other's response may be to share with the begging animal, to threaten, to pull away, or to turn its back on the other individual and, by implication, on the request itself.

As already mentioned, the many expressions of "reassurance" that involve some form of physical contact also are characteristic; patting, em-

FIGURE 6:1. Chimpanzees have expressive faces: see above and on facing page.

bracing or hugging, and kissing may occur in contexts that involve animals that have been frightened, attacked, or excited (Goodall, 1968b). One animal may "comfort" another by putting an arm around that individual, or an adult may pat a young animal on the head or another on the back in a manner we find familiar (Goodall 1968b, 1976; Goodall and Hamburg, 1975). Similarly, there is a range of conciliatory gestures, such as bowing, bobbing, crouching, kissing, presenting, and grinning, that may be used instead of escape or fighting in response to another's agonistic behavior. Such behavioral and communicatory choices would seem to indicate an ability not only to observe but to evaluate the danger in the other chimpanzee's behavior. This sort of mental capacity, combined with the wealth of communicatory postures, gestures, and facial expressions, could be significant in the relatively low frequency of aggression reported among unprovisioned chimpanzees in the wild.

Underlying chimpanzee social interaction and communication appears to be some sense of "other." This is inferred from observations that chimpanzees recognize and greet other chimpanzees, prefer the company of some

over others, show awareness of the state (and even of the degree of intensity of feeling) of the other animals and have an appropriate behavioral response, and – for pygmy chimpanzees – can even gesture what position one would like the other to take for copulation (see Figure 6:5). The interactional or social aspects of chimpanzee communication are based on relatively sophisticated mental processes that form the basis for their complex communication. Chimpanzees interpret what they observe in their social environment. Their social interactions are communicatory in nature and, conversely, much of their communication is social.

Communication and the environment

FIGURE 6:2. A chimpanzee holds out its hand to another chimpanzee who has meat, in a human-like "begging" gesture.

As remarkable as is their complex relational communication, chimpanzees can also transmit information about the physical environment. This capacity for referential communication, like some of their social communication, goes beyond that common to mammals and is extremely suggestive regarding ancestral ape cognitive and communicatory capacities.

From extensive experiments and observations on several chimpanzees in a one acre enclosure, Menzel and his associates have demonstrated that chimpanzees are more aware of their environment, spend more time in the center of an area, cover an area more systematically, and notice and investigate more kinds of objects than do monkeys (Menzel, 1969). These chimpanzees rapidly learned and systematized information about their environment. They are able to, in some sense, cognitively "map" their experimental one acre environment. They further have demonstrated the capacity to communicate features of the environment to each other using nonverbal signals (Menzel, 1971a, 1974, 1975; Menzel and Halperin, 1975). For example, in experiments in which an object was shown to one chimpanzee, when that chimpanzee and the others were subsequently released, the behavioral response of the others differed—not only depending on characteristics of the "leader" (as discussed previously) but also depending on the nature of the object. For a fear object (e.g., a snake), they followed far behind. In contrast, for a much liked food, the other chimpanzees rushed ahead in an effort to find the food first. Although the mode of communication of the chimpanzee "leader" (who had been shown the experimental object) may partially have been "expressive" (e.g., excitement or fear), it clearly had a referential function. Further, in those cases where others succeeded in getting to the object before the leader, the others must have "read" other behaviors—such as rate and direction of movement—as well.

Experimental results such as these argue for further research on communication in the wild. There are many specialized questions to investigate. Does drumming behavior, for example, have anything to do with signaling about food sources, as some of the observations by Reynolds and Reynolds (1965) would seem to suggest? Even more to the point, what are the implications of their curiosity and investigative behavior, combined with their extraordinary capacity to communicate information about the environment (as demonstrated experimentally) for chimpanzee group movements and food finding in the wild?

Mental capacities: on the interpretation of laboratory studies

The data on social communication in the wild plus Menzel's experiments on communication of information about the environment (within a chimpanzee group in a one acre enclosure) support the idea that chimpanzees and humans share some of the basic mental capacities requisite to human communication, including language. Laboratory studies further strengthen this conclusion.

Chimpanzees, in common with some of the other primates, have the intellectual capacity to abstract and exchange information between different sensory modalities, specifically between vision and touch (Davenport and Rogers, 1970; Davenport et al., 1973, 1975; Cowey and Weiskrantz, 1975; Davenport, 1976; Jarvis and Ettlinger, 1978). This capacity, known as cross-modal perception, previously was thought to be an exclusively human trait. Cross-modal transfers are a necessary, although not sufficient, basis for language as we know it (Geschwind, 1970a). This is so because the ability to name objects, a fundamental aspect of human language, depends on the capacity to make these transfers. It is, in other words, not an ability limited to a specific sensory modality but one that enables us to make connections, transfers, and transformations among the senses. More basic, this ability lies at the root of conceptualization, which is fundamental to symbolization. And without symbolization, human culture would be impossible.

Further, Gallup (1970) has shown that chimpanzees, but not monkeys, have a concept of self-recognition. After chimpanzees were exposed to mirrors for two days (16 hours), behavior directed toward the self in the form of self-grooming to parts of the body visually inaccessible without the mirror increased, whereas social responses directed to the mirror image (as if it were another chimpanzee) decreased. As further experimental evidence, an eyebrow ridge and top of the opposite ear were marked with red dye on four chimpanzees. Mark-directed responses dramatically increased as they visually inspected the dyed areas in the mirror. In contrast, six macaque monkeys were exposed to mirrors, but even after three weeks they continued to respond to the mirror as if it were another monkey. The capacity of chimpanzees for self-recognition and self-directed behavior with mirrors again indicates their high level of cognitive ability. In view of the indirect evidence from field studies for the perception of "other" among chimpanzees, this laboratory evidence for awareness of "self" proves particularly intriguing.

But all this very important evidence on chimpanzee mental and communicatory capacities almost pales into insignificance when placed alongside the many experimental studies on chimpanzee abilities in which the chimpanzee learned aspects of human linguistic codes (Fouts and Rigby, 1977; Rumbaugh, 1977b, c, 1978). Chimpanzee "language-learning" experimentation began in 1947 with the Hayses' six year attempt to teach speech to their home-reared chimpanzee, Viki. Researchers, chimpanzees, and methods have changed, but chimpanzee "language-teaching" projects continue to the present. The major types of studies will be reviewed, compared, and their results assessed in the perspective of what is known from field studies about chimpanzee communication. A major impact of the experimental work is to highlight the need for further research into communication in the wild. Even more important, for my purposes here, it is now feasible to suggest what significance these experimental results on chimpanzee language learning might have for reconstructing bases for the evolution of the capacity for culture.

Chimpanzee "language-learning" experiments

Viki, the Hayeses' chimpanzee, never learned to speak,[1] but she did communicate effectively with the Hayeses on many occasions, often using gestures.

Like all chimpanzees, Viki used gestures spontaneously to a certain extent . . . At times her gestures became very explicit. Watching bread being kneaded, she begged for a sample of dough by going through the kneading motions . . . and then holding out her hand, palm up, moving her fingers in the gesture that means "give me" to both her species and ours . . .

The key that locked her enclosed bed . . . was kept in the left-hand corner of a certain drawer; in the right-hand corner was the key that locked . . . the house. She early developed the habit of putting our hand to the right-hand knob as a sign she wanted to go out for a ride, and to the left knob when she was sleepy.   [Hayes and Nissen, 1971:106]

In the well known longitudinal study started about 1966 by the Gardners (1969, 1971, 1972, 1975a, b), a young female chimpanzee, Washoe, was taught simplified gestural signs taken from American Sign Language for the deaf (Ameslan or ASL). She learned to make combinations of these signs that were meaningful to her tester-trainers. The Gardners, like the Hayeses before them, succeeded in establishing a close social relationship with Washoe. They taught simplified ASL to Washoe in a stimulus-rich environment. Of particular interest was the two-way nature of the ASL communication between Washoe and her human tester-trainers, the apparent meaningfulness of their ASL "conversations," and the contextual appropriateness of Washoe's spontaneous use of ASL signs. As an informal test of contextual appropriateness of Washoe's spontaneous use of ASL signs, a research assistant, Susan Nichols, stepped on one of Washoe's rubber dolls.

The doll test was performed on four occasions during a 2-week period, and each time there were several repetitions . . . Washoe's different phrases were: *up Susan, Susan up, mine please up, gimme baby, please shoe, more mine, up please, please up, more up, baby down, shoe up, baby up, please more up,* and *you up.* [Gardner and Gardner, 1971:167]

One of the advantages of the Gardners' choice of ASL as the medium of instruction is that it is a "real" human language in actual use among deaf

[1] Viki did learn to reproduce voiceless approximations of *mama, papa, cup,* and *up* (Fouts and Rigby, 1977; Rumbaugh, 1977b).

Lucy signs "hat"

Washoe signing "flower" with Roger Fouts

FIGURE 6:3. Lucy and Washoe, two female chimpanzees, were taught signs from Ameslan (American Sign Language) and learned to use these signs meaningfully.

human beings. Moreover, it is a language that utilizes gesture. Whereas chimpanzees appear to lack some of the vocal apparatus needed for learning speech, gesture is an important component of their own communication. On the problematic side, a gestural language such as ASL does not lend itself to ready testing of chimpanzee achievement or to ease in recording competence changes. Perhaps in partial response to these limitations, other experimenters have devised artificial "languages," as well as other methods of teaching and recording these types of "language use." These methods range from the counting of correct usage of plastic chips that have been assigned meanings to machine recording of use of symbols on keys attached to computers. As Fouts and Rigby point out, however, such refinements can also prove limiting. "For example, the computer is not programmed to accept novel or innovative uses of the language . . . the artificial language approaches are limited to examining only behavior conceived of by the experimenters and not responses created by the chimpanzees" (Fouts and Rigby, 1977:1051).

The type of work pioneered by the Gardners—teaching a human sign language (ASL) to chimpanzees—has been continued by a number of researchers with several additional chimpanzees (see review article by Fouts and Rigby, 1977). Individual differences in ASL acquisition have been explored, emphasis has been placed on teaching syntax, and research has begun on intraspecific communication between chimpanzees using ASL (Fouts, 1975; Fouts and Couch, 1976).

Premack, working about the same time with the chimpanzee Sarah, devised a method of teaching aspects of "language" that was somewhat more amenable to formal testing and verification than the work with ASL (Premack, 1970, 1971a, b, 1976a, b, 1978; Premack and Premack, 1972). Premack used plastic chips of different shapes and colors. Each plastic chip was assigned a meaning—some represent an English noun or verb, and some stand for a grammatical category such as the interrogative or conditional. In test situations, Sarah learned to recognize and respond to about 130 of these plastic chips with 75 to 80 percent reliability.

Subsequently, computer technology was utilized in the Lana project (Rumbaugh et al., 1973; Rumbaugh, 1977a, b, c) in an effort to further objectify observations and to develop a system that was operational around the clock. For this project, an artificial language called Yerkish was devised. Yerkish signs are made up of nine arbitrary design elements (e.g., triangle, box, wavy line) superimposed on each other in a variety of patterns. Each pattern stands for an English word. The Yerkish "words" were superimposed on keys attached to a computer. Initially Lana was taught a few stock sentence beginnings, such as *Please machine give,* and signs for a number of desirable items (*juice, banana,* etc.). She mastered these quite rapidly and went on to learn a more varied repertoire. After slightly over a year of formal training, Lana, on her own initiative, instituted a conversation with Timothy Gill by requesting a drink of his coke (Rumbaugh and Gill, 1977).

Subsequently, Timothy Gill (1977 a, b) devised a means of regularly enticing Lana into "conversations" by changing aspects of her feeding schedule and/or "lying" to her. Gill describes several conversations that were generated under these circumstances. In one instance he had substituted water for monkey chow.

FIGURE 6:4. Young chimpanzee using computer keyboard to communicate in "Yerkish" with researchers. Notice the complex and detailed symbols (shown here above keyboard) that the young chimpanzee has learned to use.

"Lana responded as follows: *?You move water out-of-machine.* I responded *Yes,* and removed the water. Lana then asked, *?You put chow in machine,* to which I again responded *Yes,* and the conversation ended with chow being placed in the machine" (Gill, 1977b:130).

Savage-Rumbaugh and Rumbaugh (1978) later went on to use Yerkish and a similar technology in experiments with four young chimpanzees. By using very stringent performance criteria, combined with the constant monitoring made possible by the computer hookup, they have been able to discern successive "levels" of "word learning." Because of the results of their experiments, they state:

> The fact that an animal can come to use a set of signals of any sort to satisfactorily diminish its desires is not equivalent to the use of those same signals as true symbols . . . Thus, contrary to the findings of Premack (1976[a]), errorless trials . . . do not lead to symbolic learning even in simple tasks such as food names.
>
> [Savage-Rumbaugh and Rumbaugh, 1978:283]

They do conclude, however, that, with appropriate training, it is possible for chimpanzees to learn to use Yerkish "lexigrams" as true symbols. After reaching this level, the chimpanzees were able to make spontaneous use of lexigrams.

When symbols were left lying about their room, they spontaneously picked them up and brought them to the human companions to indicate desires for foods and drinks which the companions were holding; or if none were visible, they brought symbols in front of the humans and pointed to them repeatedly. If they were asked in Yerkish (on the computer hook-up) "?GIVE M & M" (or another favored food) they always responded with food barks and hugs. If asked "?YOU WANT CHOW" (*chow* is a commercial food for primates) they frequently ignored the question, erased it, and asked "GIVE M & M?" (or banana or orange).

[Savage-Rumbaugh and Rumbaugh, 1978:298]

These studies are significant because they demonstrate (1) that chimpanzees think in a manner humans consider to be intelligent and (2) that chimpanzees can learn to use aspects of human language in two-way communication with humans. We understand their abilities in our terms — conceptualization, referential communication, symbol using. They can do things that, when we do them, we describe in these terms. The simplest explanation for their behavior is that they do think and that they are capable of learning rudiments of linguistic systems devised by humans. If not, then a very complex explanation is necessary.

In addition, the experimental studies, as well as the field studies, illustrate the critical importance of affective ties and social interaction for chimpanzees — as for humans — in learning a complex communication system. As Fouts has pointed out: "If there is no relationship there is no language, since there is obviously no one to talk with" (1977:118). Savage-Rumbaugh's and Rumbaugh's (1978) attempts to teach Yerkish to four young chimpanzees has poignantly illustrated the importance of the mother—offspring bond in learning. Sherman, who had been left with his mother the longest, appeared highly observant of his social and physical world and learned some aspects of Yerkish much more rapidly than the other three chimpanzees. In contrast, Kenton, who had been removed at birth from his mother (and had thus experienced the most severe maternal deprivation in the group) had difficulties with many learning tasks.

It became necessary to keep someone with him throughout the entire day, carrying and holding him, and gesturing toward all aspects of the environment in order to get him involved enough to show the proper symbol-referent connections . . . In other words, it was necessary to provide him with the stability and affiliations of an attachment figure before he displayed symbolic learning and associated skills.

[Savage-Rumbaugh and Rumbaugh, 1978:288]

This point had been noted earlier by Menzel, Davenport, and Rogers in comparing the responses of 19 juvenile chimpanzees to novel objects. They observe that

Juvenile chimpanzees that have been raised in "normal" fashion for the first year or so of life – i.e., mother-reared and wild chimpanzees – never do show the strong and pervasive fear of novelty (at least in laboratory settings) that is characteristic of "cultureless" mother-deprived and restriction-raised infants.   [1972:167]

Clearly, emotional and attachment needs must be met in order for the young chimpanzee to have the confidence to deal with novelty and to adequately focus on the external environment. But, for a theoretical understanding of the evolution of symbolic capacities, there is something of even greater significance. Chimpanzee communication in the wild is largely social, and it is in social contexts that the communicatory abilities revealed in laboratory studies are ordinarily utilized. Therefore, affective interaction and social communication are prerequisites to successful learning of (and for communicating with) human symbols in laboratory settings. This interaction between the social, the affective, and the intellectual was doubtless enhanced in human evolution. It may, indeed, have been critical to the development of the human capacity for symbolization, language, and culture.

The use of quite complex nonverbal communication "about something" in highly social settings has been illustrated by laboratory observations of sexual interaction among three pygmy chimpanzees (Savage-Rumbaugh et al., 1977). Eye contact and facial expression are used to indicate interest in sexual engagement. Further, many body movements and gestures precede copulation. Pygmy chimpanzees use a wide variety of positions for copulation, and some mutual agreement as to position must be reached if they are to actually engage in sex. Many of their movements and nearly all the gestures observed by these pygmy chimpanzees prior to intercourse seem to concern copulatory position (Figure 6:5). Especially interesting is the fact that the movements and gestures used in these sociosexual contexts range from very explicit ones, such as one animal trying to turn the other around or the other actually moving to her preferred position, to purely iconic gestures in which a desired or agreed on position is simply indicated gesturally. Here then, in these sociosexual contexts, an integration of a variety of communicatory modes is exhibited – eye contact, facial expression, body movement and position, and hand gestures. Included are gestures that are iconic, and that can perhaps be considered "presymbolic" forms of communication. These observations of pygmy chimpanzees' sociosexual communication provide a particularly clear-cut example of the sort of integrated communicatory capacities that, if they existed in the ancestral population, would have provided a firm foundation for the evolution of the human communicatory system.

Anatomical basis — chimpanzee brains

If we assume that chimpanzees think, this does not imply that their mental and communicatory capacities have a neurological base identical to our own. They can learn to have appropriate responses and even to generate meaningful new "terms" or engage in simple "conversations" when taught rudiments of human linguistic codes; but their neurological capacities may not be adequate for the full development of language. Chimpanzee brains and communication, as compared to our own, likely parallel the situation with regard to structure and behavior in the locomotor realm. Although they have the ability to stand and walk bipedally, they do not possess the structural specialization for bipedalism as their primary means of locomotion. Their hip, knee, and ankle joints, as well as the form and function of their feet, are those of a climbing animal (Zihlman, 1967).

Similarly, their behavior evinces complex mental abilities, but there are differences between chimpanzee and human brains. Humans have three times the neocortex size expected for a primate of our body size (Passingham, 1973); further, humans have more association cortex than would be anticipated for a primate, even one with such a developed neocortex. The association area in the angular gyrus region in humans receives input from all cortical sensory areas, thus connecting visual and auditory, tactile and visual, and tactile and auditory; it is thought to be a necessary anatomical base for cross-modal perception and human language (Geschwind, 1965).

An important feature of the human brain, not related to its size, is its asymmetry. This is expressed not in its gross anatomy but in the structure itself (Geschwind and Levitsky, 1968; Geschwind, 1970b; Passingham, 1973). Asymmetry may relate to the functional specialization necessary for symbolizing and, therefore, may well be a prerequisite for language. The chimpanzee brain also appears to be somewhat asymmetrical (LeMay and Geschwind, 1975; Yeni-Komshian and Benson, 1976; LeMay, 1976; Galaburda et al., 1978). This might indicate that an anatomical basis exists in chimpanzee brain structure for the striking symbolic behavior documented among laboratory chimpanzees. The complexity of chimpanzee communicatory abilities in the wild, combined with laboratory data, makes the question of structural similarities between the great apes and humans with regard to brain asymmetry particularly pertinent. It appears that this brain feature is already characteristic of (although perhaps elemental in) chimpanzees and some of the other great apes (Galaburda et al., 1978). It is not, however, found in rhesus monkeys (Yeni-Komshian and Benson, 1976; Warren and Noneman, 1976).

A pygmy chimpanzee female, Lokelema, aged about 25 to 35 years, and a young male, Bosondjo, about 5½ to 7½ years, engage in mutual eye contact.

Bosondjo then touches Lokelema gently on her shoulder and pushes her upper body away from himself — a gesture generally used to induce the recipient to turn around for dorsoventral copulations. She does not turn around. However, she displays a lips-back facial expression, often a signal of copulatory intent.

She continues to ignore his gestural requests; he moves behind her and attempts to push her into position for dorsoventral copulation. They maintain eye contact with each other, even though he is now nearly directly behind her.

FIGURE 6:5. Communication during the choice of sexual position in sociosexual interaction between two pygmy chimpanzees.

*Social communication and mental capacities—the use of intelligence
in experiments and the wild*

An especially important question concerns the ways chimpanzees in their
natural habitats apply the mental abilities they have so remarkably demonstrated in laboratory and experimental conditions. Cognitive mapping of
food sources (demonstrated in Menzel's enclosure but doubtless exercised
in the wild as well), foresight in tool use, and many types of social interactions serve to illustrate how these capacities are ordinarily exercised.

In one of his experiments, Menzel (1973c) has shown that chimpanzees
may find and eat food selectively. Preferred foods (fruits) and other foods
(vegetables) were hidden randomly around an enclosure; a chimpanzee
was carried and shown where each piece of food was hidden. When
released, the animal found and ate the preferred food first, obtained by a
least-distance strategy, then located and ate the other food. As Menzel has
suggested, this indicates a cognitive mapping ability; that is, chimpanzees
can selectively organize information about the environment and utilize it
efficiently. In the wild, of course, their foods are widely scattered and
available in specific areas at certain times of the year. The ability to organize environmental information in such a sophisticated way is probably
what enables them to discriminate preferred food in different areas. This
suggests that additional resources likely are available to them and may be
used at times when preferred foods are scarce. The cognitive ability
evinced in how chimpanzees utilize space and their capacity to communicate about objects in their environment as evinced in experiments obviously would seem to facilitate their dietary and food-getting behavior in the
wild.

Another example of chimpanzee mental abilities appears in what might
be considered "foresight." Chimpanzees possess concepts that enable
them to utilize aspects of their environment in novel ways: They select,
prepare, and carry grasses and twigs to a site for use in termiting; a new
probe replaces the old bent one that is no longer usable (Goodall, 1970).

Similarly, chimpanzees' utilization of environmental information is not
unlike that in interactional contexts such as begging and food sharing or
aggression/submission, where social information is discriminated and responded to in a number of ways. Social memory—for example, recognition
of large numbers of individuals—and environmental memory are both impressive and probably depend upon the same basic set of mental capacities. In investigating chimpanzee communication and mental capabilities
in the wild, it is far more fruitful to focus on the complexity and sophistication of their responses to each other and to the environment than to restrict

attention to their expression of motivation states. Examining chimpanzees' mental capacities and social and environmental communication in the light of a broader perspective gives important clues as to the bases for evolutionary change. Not only can we hypothesize that the ancestral population possessed relatively sophisticated mental capacities and communicatory abilities, but we can also begin to comprehend the nature of the capabilities and behaviors that were to later prove fundamental to the capacity for culture.

Viewing communication as an evolving behavioral system: cognition and emotion

The delineation of processes involved in the evolution of the capacity for language – perhaps more than in the evolution of any other behavior – has stubbornly eluded solution. Considerable discussion has centered on the question of whether a gestural language or a vocal language evolved first. The proponents of a gestural language note that considerable nonvocal communication occurs among apes (Hewes, 1973a, b), and experiments indicate that chimpanzees can be taught elements of human sign language (Gardner and Gardner, 1972) but not to speak (Hayes, 1951; Hayes and Nissen, 1971). On the other side, Washburn and Strum (1972) and Washburn (1973) have pointed out that the essential character of human vocally based language is that it is a system whereby, through the recombination of a limited number of arbitrary elements (phonemes), it is possible to produce vocal signs for a potentially endless variety of meanings. Both arguments are valid, and it is only because the discussion has been phrased in terms of (1) language rather than communication and (2) gestural language versus vocal language that there appears to be a controversy. An integrated communicatory system, including a wide range of nonverbal communication modes with speech, is what has evolved in the human instance.

Early anthropologists were fascinated with the relationships of language and culture – of symbol system to symbol system (Boas, 1911; Sapir, 1931; Whorf, 1956). Later the importance of studying symbols in action was stressed, and a new subdiscipline developed that dealt with the use of speech in society (Goodenough, 1971; Gumperz and Hymes, 1972; Pride and Holmes, 1972). With the appearance of studies on kinesics, paralanguage, and nonverbal communication, the full range of elements that enter into human communication has become apparent (Hall, 1959; Goffman 1963, 1969; Birdwhistell, 1970; Chapple, 1970). For example, work on both verbal and nonverbal communication among Black Americans has illustrated how the total communicatory system of Black Americans differs from that of members of the white subculture (Kochman, 1972). In order to understand the evolution of human communicatory behavior and capacities, the total system (of which the evolution of speech is but one part) must be dealt with. Just as language and culture was too limiting a framework, so also is speech and society. Darwin, in *The Expression of the Emotions in Man and Animals* (1872), pinpointed an area that we too must investigate.

The relevant question is: How did the somatic, expressive communication already present in the ancestral population mediate the development of the more arbitrary, symbolic, and referential aspects of the fully human communicatory system? Data on chimpanzee communication and mental capacities are immensely significant for they enable us to hypothesize the probable nature of the ancestral population's communication system – the system that formed the base from which the hominid system evolved. Communicating about the environment, decoding complex social and/or environmental messages, and responding appropriately were the sorts of adaptive activities on which natural selection acted.

What must be stressed regarding chimpanzee communication is that, although the mode is expressive, information about the environment is both sent and decoded. There is therefore reason to assume that the ancestral population already possessed some of the underlying mental capacities necessary for further communicatory development, particularly with regard to the referential function. This is crucial; in evolution no capacity or structure appears *de novo* without a behavioral precursor.

Nonetheless, it is not surprising that early works on primate communication and on the evolution of human communication did not delineate the behavioral base from which human communication evolved. Relatively detailed information on chimpanzee communication in the wild has just begun to appear (Reynolds and Reynolds, 1965; Goodall, 1968b; Nishida, 1970). Moreover, much remains to be done in order to integrate research on human kinesic and paralinguistic communication with theories of evolutionary development.

Not so very long ago it was still intellectually feasible to claim that "it is the communication of thought, rather than the thought itself, that is unique to man, makes human culture possible, and that is the primary factor in separating man from beast" (Washburn and Strum, 1972:477). Today, it must be acknowledged that humans are no more unique in this respect, as compared with chimpanzees, than in tool using and making (Tanner and Zihlman, 1976b). Interanimal referential communication in experiments (and probably in the wild as well) illustrates that more than the expression of motivational states is involved. Chimpanzees have the ability to transfer information external to themselves to other animals. They are, in other words, able to communicate *about* something – even though they must do it in an "expressive" mode (unless they have been provided with and taught the meaning of symbols by humans). The earlier dichotomy between animal tool using and human tool making can no longer stand when in fact selection of materials and modification of objects by chimpanzees occur regularly. Likewise, the communication of chimpanzee thought, in an elemental way, occurs.

At an early stage it was important to set up a dichotomy, as Washburn and Strum (1972) did, in order to highlight the issues. Now, with more data and in the context of a sequential model, the nature of the ancestral population's communication system can be hypothesized. With this base, it is hoped that it will eventually be possible to envision the steps intermediate to development of the fully human communication system, which includes language as an integral part.

Previously Lancaster, as Washburn and Strum, believed that primate communication systems "are not steps toward language" and focused her attention on the "major gap that separates language from nonhuman communication" (Lancaster, 1968b:439). The present challenge is rather to hypothesize how the cognitive and affective-social capacities underlying the nonverbal communication system of the ancestral apes could provide a base from which the human capacity for symbolic thought, language, and culture could evolve.

Menzel's work in experimental psychology with a group of common chimpanzees in a one-half-acre to one-acre enclosure (Menzel, 1974, 1975, 1978; Menzel et al., 1978) and the observations of Savage-Rumbaugh, Wilkerson, and Bakeman (1977) of sociosexual interaction among three pygmy chimpanzees in the laboratory are perhaps the most significant research to date on common and pygmy chimpanzee mental capacities and on their communicatory abilities and processes. Menzel's data on "natural" nonverbal communication about the external environment make it possible to link experimental work in the chimpanzee "language-learning" projects with field studies and to interpret both more satisfactorily. Similarly, Savage-Rumbaugh's, Wilkerson's, and Bakeman's observations of pygmy chimpanzee sociosexual interaction illustrate the interaction of many communicatory modes, including the impressive "presymbolic" iconic gestures. But all of their work cries out for field studies to further explore how the abilities they have unearthed are used in the wild.

Many investigators have overstressed vocalization per se in primate communication – apparently because of their interest in the evolution of the unique human ability for speech. Primates communicate, Lancaster (1968b) emphasizes, by utilizing a complex constellation of many modes – postural, gestural, vocal, facial expression, movement – within a social context. But this is also true of human communication. Social context, body movements, facial expression, stylized gestures, and paralinguistic vocal qualities such as breathlessness, tone of voice, and speech speed are all exceedingly important in human communication and are essential to our evaluation of linguistic utterances. Indeed, these cues are critical to decoding meaning: Is the person telling the truth? How important is the information? What sorts of things are being left unsaid?

Just as students of primate communication formerly overemphasized voc- alization, so also in the past students of human communication focused far too exclusively on formal language – phonetic and phonemic structure and semantic categories. To compare human language in its narrower sense with an overly simple account of nonhuman primate communication – that is, seen as strictly limited to the expression of motivational states – can highlight what has been added during the course of human evolution. Such a frame- work, however, makes it impossible to understand how human communica- tory behavior and structures could have developed. The relevant compari- son, in fact, is between human communication in its entirety and primate communication in its full complexity and sophistication.

Implications of chimpanzee behavior for reconstructing hominid origins: a basis for the evolution of the capacity for culture as the human adaptation

Patterns of behavior in the ancestral ape population similar to those ob- served among living chimpanzees could have provided an important basis for elaboration in the course of the hominid divergence. Previously, walk- ing upright on two legs, making and using tools, killing animals and eating meat, sexual activity outside estrus, and complex communicatory and cog- nitive abilities were thought to be unique to the human primate. However, evidence from long-term and numerous field and laboratory studies on chimpanzees demonstrates that this is not the case. Chimpanzees do many things – albeit often only occasionally or in a rather rudimentary manner – once thought to be distinctively human. Two interrelated dimensions of chimpanzee behavior are particularly impressive: those associated with the external environment, such as object modification and manipulation, the range of foods eaten and patterns of food getting, and modes of defense from potential predators, on the one hand; and on the other, chimpanzee social patterns, that is, interactions within communities of from about 15 to some 85 or so individuals (depending on environment and other circumstances), which encompass shifting subgroups of variable composition. Environmental and social patterns are intimately related through the communication system by which both social and environmental skills are learned and information is transmitted.

A generalized capacity for innovation with objects, for modifying and using them as tools, is present, and chimpanzees' flexible, complex social structure is mediated effectively through their communicatory capabilities. Facial expression, posture, gesture, and other forms of nonverbal communication are impressive both in the wild and in experimental contexts. Chimpanzee mental abilities (demonstrated in both laboratory and field situations), combined with their social communication and communication about the environment, are extraordinary. Cognitive and communicatory capacities such as these may be regarded as among the most critical "prospective adaptations" of the ancestral population. It is such abilities, combined with a long period of infant dependence on the mother (i.e., time to learn, in a context facilitating learning) and social structural flexibility, that probably formed the base for later evolution of the human capacity for culture. Given an ancestral population with behaviors similar to living chimpanzees, it is possible to suggest the characteristics of the transitional population and to explore how a population with these features could begin to exploit a new habitat and eventually speciate.

SEVEN

The transition to Australopithecus: natural and sexual selection in human origins

THE genetic equipment of the human species is not like a watch which arose by the accidental coming together of disjointed parts of the mechanism, nor is it like a poem accidentally typed out by a monkey pounding the keys of a typewriter . . . natural selection introduces an antichance quality in evolution. The bodies of our animal ancestors were going concerns and not merely human bodies under construction; these animals were as fit to live in their environments as we are in ours.

Theodosius Dobzhansky, 1958

IN thinking about the transition to *Australopithecus,* the first hominid genus, let us begin by hypothesizing an ancestral population of chimpanzee-like creatures living in the forests and at the forest fringes in Africa at the end of the Miocene or beginning of the Pliocene some 8 million to 4 or so million years ago and beginning to utilize the vast, comparatively open savannas of eastern Africa in what are now Ethiopia, Kenya, and Tanzania. The hominid divergence becomes explicable if we assume that a particular behavioral innovation — gathering with tools, used preeminently for plant foods — marked off this transitional population from the ancestral apes (Tanner and Zihlman, 1976a; Zihlman and Tanner, 1979). The generally recognized changes in behavior and anatomy that differentiate the hominids from apes can be understood in terms of the gathering innovation. In this context, I describe the general processes usually thought to be involved in speciation. I then go on to explore in some detail the operation of specific selective processes that may account for the divergence of the hominid line.

Over the years scholars have suggested times of divergence for the hominid line from some 30 million to only 2 million years ago. If the divergence were early, we could expect to find a sequence of fossil forms to substantiate this As yet, this fossil sequence is not apparent. In the absence of such a sequence but in the presence of (1) a well-documented and dated hominid fossil record in East Africa extending back over 3 million years with

133

further fragmentary hominid-like fossils to about 4 million years ago, (2) the extensive biochemical similarities between humans and African apes, and (3) anatomical and molecular evidence placing the divergence of Asian apes earlier than that of African apes *and* hominids, perhaps some 11 million to 7 million years ago, it is reasonable to assume a Mio-Pliocene divergence between the newly established hominid line and the ape ancestral population some 8 million to 4 million years ago. If the divergence is this recent, the many similarities in structure and behavior of humans and African apes, particularly humans and chimpanzees, are due to inheritance from a common ancestor and did not rise independently.

During the transition from an ancestral population to *Australopithecus* critical changes occurred.[1] There was a move into a new habitat, the African savanna, where the earliest hominid fossils are found. A new locomotor adaptation, bipedalism, was evolving in a feedback relationship with the use of tools and hands to obtain food over a wide range. The omnivorous aspects of the diet were enhanced, and new kinds of plant and animal foods became increasingly important.

The eastern African savanna: an available niche

Today, eastern and southern Africa contain vast regions of mixed grasslands and forests called savannas. Although the term can refer to many different combinations of vegetation in various parts of the world, all savannas contrast in important ways with the rain forests in central and western Africa. Bourlière and Hadley review the nature of tropical savannas: "*Savanna* is used in its broad sense to refer to a tropical formation where the grass stratum is continuous and important occasionally interrupted by trees and shrubs . . . the main growth patterns are closely associated with alternating wet and dry seasons" (1970:125,126). About half the surface of Africa is covered by dry savanna and grass steppe or by open woodland and mixed savanna.

These areas are a mosaic landscape that includes open grasslands, scattered tree clumps, riverine forests, gallery forests, and marshy areas. Vegetation ranges from open grasslands interspersed with groups of trees to relatively dense forest. High trees with grassy floors or lower vegetation and dense undergrowth may be found adjacent to or surrounded by open

---

[1] No certain knowledge is possible, of course, as to what happened during this critical transition. Only minimal fossil evidence for this period exists, and it is discussed in the next chapter. This chapter deals with my hypotheses about the important changes that may have occurred – and why – during the transition from an ape ancestor to the earliest hominids. For smoothness in writing, I have eliminated many of the implicit *ifs, maybes,* and *could have beens* and often use the assertive mode.

grasslands. Density and distribution of vegetation are influenced by variation in amount of rainfall each year and by its seasonality. In tropical regions, because there is an absence of marked changes in day length and temperature, most seasonal events are associated directly or indirectly with fluctuations in rainfall (Bourlière and Hadley, 1970).

Diversity of vegetation and landscape characterizes savanna; this is reflected in the number and density of both plant and animal species. Within these areas are many habitats for species that can utilize the rich variety of resources. This is true for eastern Africa today and was also the case in southern Africa prior to the decimation of fauna that followed European settlement. The eastern and south-central African savannas have exceptionally high carrying capacities for large mammalian species (Bourlière,1963; Butzer, 1971). The adaptation of several species of ungulates — all eat grasses, but each species may consume a different part of the plant (Gwynne and Bell, 1968) — illustrates how this is possible. Human populations can also exist comfortably in bush country, which, to a casual Western observer, appears to have minimal resources. The San-speaking "bush people" of the Kalahari Desert, in the southern part of Africa, know how to exploit this marginal environment. For example, the !Kung San of the Dobe area in the northern Kalahari, who live in a region that includes woodlands with a concentration of mongongo nut trees, expend only two to three and a half days per adult a week to provide themselves and dependents with a sufficient diet of gathered plant food plus some meat (Lee, 1968, 1969, 1972, 1979).[2] This means that, among this group of !Kung, each productive individual finds food for herself or himself and dependents and still has about three and a half to five days for other activities. The ≠Kade San, who also live in the Kalahari but in an even more marginal environment, where mongongo nuts are unavailable, spend about 4.5 hours per day getting food, or approximately 32.5 hours weekly (Tanaka, 1976).

Many parts of plants, such as the seasonally variable seeds, fruits, nuts,

[2] Williams (1977) has suggested that this represents an unrealistically low figure, because Richard Lee, in his dissertation (1965), noted that about two thirds of the population of the Dobe region had been moved from there in a resettlement program some two or three years before he did his first field work. The questions here, of course, are: (1) how long has there been a human "population problem," and (2) how long has it been necessary for gatherer-hunters to live in relatively marginal areas such as the Kalahari Desert? My answer to both questions, in evolutionary terms, is not very long. The depleted population studied by Lee, which lived in a somewhat less marginal region than some of the other San bush people, is probably *more* representative of early gathering and hunting populations than are overpopulated groups living in marginal areas. Prior to the inventions of horticulture and agriculture — only several thousand years ago — gathering-hunting populations had their choice of the whole globe. An overpopulated globe appears to be a very recent phenomenon.

and berries, are available for on-the-spot consumption; roots and tubers growing underground can be dug up; insects such as termites, ants, grubs, and grasshoppers are also available; the honey guide, an African bird that feeds on beeswax, leads humans and other species to honey. Also common on the savanna are lizards, snakes, small vertebrates, birds, and birds' eggs; the young of over 20 species of ungulates; burrowing animals such as rodents, aardvarks, and warthogs; hares and rock rabbits; and baboons and other monkeys. The many species of antelope range in size from the tiny dik-dik to the eland, weighing over a ton; elephant and hippo are numerous. Rivers and lakes make water available and also house a range of plant and animal life, either temporarily (hippo) or permanently (crocodiles). Along with the richness of primary fauna – the prey species – varied predator species are also found. In the Serengeti plains, for example, Schaller (1972) describes lions, hunting dogs, leopards, cheetahs, hyenas, and vultures. The richness of the savanna is evident in the range of plant species, birds, and mammals (including carnivores) that make up the food chain.

Environment of the Mio-Pliocene

How long has this characteristic savanna mosaic of grasslands, shrubs, and forested areas been in existence? Recent pollen studies indicate that grasslands have existed in Ethiopia for over 2.5 million years (Bonnefille, 1976a). This suggests that, contrary to common assumptions, eastern African grasslands are not necessarily recent or entirely the result of human burning activities. Even prior to these new data, the relative antiquity of savannas in Africa should have been obvious from the range of fauna primarily adapted to such grasslands. Mio-Pliocene deposits further indicate that the mosaic quality of this area was present at that time (Butzer, 1978).

Between 8 million and 4 million years ago is a reasonable time of divergence, given ape–human molecular similarities and rates of substitution. Early hominid fossils have been found in both eastern and southern Africa but have been dated only for eastern Africa, where hominid fossils exist that are probably over 3.5 million years old. What were these areas like about 5 million or 4 million years ago? In southern Africa, the climate and topography were probably very much like today, although possibly somewhat more arid. There was no volcanic activity and there were no major topographical changes (Bond, 1963). By contrast, in eastern Africa volcanic activity was occurring sporadically from about the middle Miocene, or somewhat earlier, through much of the Pliocene and even into the Pleistocene. Therefore, topography was changing immediately prior to and during the period in which the earliest known hominid fossils appear (Baker and Wohlenberg, 1971; Baker et al., 1971; King and Chapman, 1972). Lakes and rivers developed and dried up. Throughout the Pliocene and Pleistocene rainfall varied. This variation, combined with topographical changes—uplifting and volcanic action—and consequent shifts in drainage patterns, no doubt altered the size and distribution of grasslands and wooded areas, in eastern Africa in particular. It is therefore likely that the initial isolation critical to speciation occurred in the eastern rather than the southern African savannas.

Moving into a new habitat

When a group begins moving into and exploiting a new zone, thereby initiating a new adaptation, three types of access are involved: physical, evolutionary, and ecological (Simpson, 1953). Physical access refers to the geographic region the group already occupies or where it can and does reach by dispersal. Evolutionary access means that the group must have at least minimal prospective adaptations for the new zone. Ecological access implies that the particular adaptive zone or niche must either be empty or be occupied by organisms that will not interfere with the entering group.

As the generalized ape stem population in equatorial Africa differentiated and radiated, gorillas evolved and adapted to rain forests, chimpanzees to less dense forests, and hominids to the savanna. Today some chimpanzee populations live in woodland savannas containing both riverine forests and grasslands, and they utilize the scattered, varying vegetation within this habitat (Figure 7:1). The immediate ancestors of the hominids, like some contemporary chimpanzees, probably lived in this type of varied habitat about 5 million years ago. If so, *physical access* to the mosaic savanna environment existed.

The ancestral population was sufficiently generalized and adaptable so that the potential for moving into a wide range of habitats was present. There was adequate *evolutionary access* or prospective adaptation for this new niche on the savanna. In fact, to all indications, the ancestral chimpanzee-like population of about 5 million years ago possessed behavioral and anatomical elements basic to the development of a gathering adaptation in which a wide range of savanna plant foods could be exploited with tools. It was extensive plant gathering combined with some predation on small and young animals that provided, I suggest, a substantial omnivorous diet for this transitional population as it was moving into the mosaic savanna.

The behavior of the ancestral population was complex. As among living chimpanzees, there was emphasis on coordination of eyes and hands in

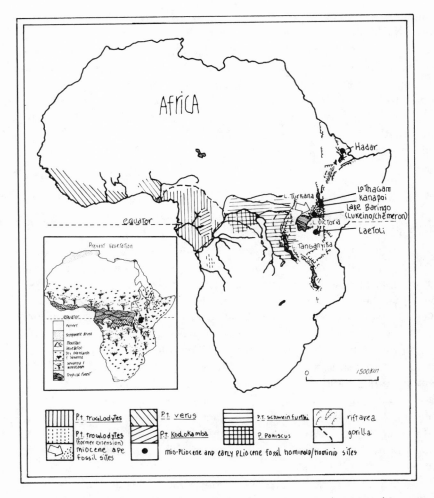

FIGURE 7:1. Contemporary African apes—the common and pygmy chimpanzees and the gorillas—live in western, central, and eastern Africa. Although most live in forest habitats, the ranges of some common chimpanzees extend into eastern African savanna woodlands. The ancestral population may have utilized a similar range of habitats.

motor tasks and on both social and visual memory. Further, elements that presumably already existed in the ancestral population included ability to stand up on the rear legs and occasionally to walk bipedally; ability to carry objects; ability to find and modify objects for use as tools; flexible social organization; food sharing; long and intense patterns of socialization that provided the context for learning a broad spectrum of skills; a developing potential for generalization and conceptualization; a well developed nonverbal communication and decoding system capable of transmitting limited referential information; and an omnivorous diet that utilized a wide range of plant and animal species.

In terms of *ecological access* to the savanna, the niche for a day-living omnivore was available in the late Miocene or early Pliocene. There is no evidence to suggest that any large omnivores exploited these areas prior to the beginning of the hominid line 4 million or 5 million years ago. *Homo sapiens sapiens* is the only large omnivore that does so today. During the initial transition from a forest-living omnivore (which, like chimpanzees, probably relied heavily but not exclusively on fruit and leafy foods) to a forest-fringe and, later, savanna-living omnivore, the diet probably expanded to include more types of plant food and a somewhat larger percentage of protein.[3] This is not to imply a hunting adaptation among the transitional hominids. Insect collecting continued. So, too, did occasional predation without tools on small animals in chimpanzee fashion. But neither was primary. It was the diurnal omnivorous niche that was available to a population transitional between ancestral apes and early hominids. They found the key to exploit it successfully.

Gathering as the critical innovation

Gathering—a new way of exploiting plant food with tools—emerged as the basis for the hominid divergence. This innovative food-getting pattern enabled the transitional population to move into a new habitat away from the

[3] These transitional hominid omnivores and the early hominid omnivores that succeeded them—as some populations of their ape-like ancestors and of chimpanzees today—did not densely populate the regions in which they lived (see Chapter 5). Boaz (1979), in extrapolations from comparative fossil frequencies at five sites at Omo, Ethiopia, 2.8 Mya to 1.9 Mya, estimates early hominid densities per square kilometer at only 0.006, 0.008, 0, 0.016, and 0.006, respectively, low densities fairly similar to savanna-living carnivores. The low density of the common chimpanzee today, in the Tano Nimri Forest, Ghana, at 0.09 individuals/km^2, or at 0.07 to 0.08 head/km^2 in an arid savanna woodlands region in Ugalla, Tanzania, is also similar to early hominids at Omo (Boaz, 1979; Itani, 1979). Early hominid omnivores, as probably the transitional hominid omnivores before them, apparently maintained a low density similar to some of the ape-like ancestors in the move from the forest fringe to the savanna, or even reduced somewhat in density. (Chimpanzee population density and the range covered by a chimpanzee community vary considerably from tropical forest to arid savanna woodlands, with the latter much lower [see Chapter 5].)

The diet of the transitional and early hominid omnivores was probably quite different from that of either the herbivores or carnivores that already lived on the savanna. It was by establishing a diurnal omnivorous adaptation that they found an effective savanna niche. Although initially providing the base for only a modest population, this omnivorousness some millions of years later—with the invention of agriculture and domestication of animals—was to provide the foundation for enormous population growth.

tropical forest. It differed fundamentally from the foraging pattern of the ancestral population that is still characteristic of other primates today. Foraging is on-the-spot collection and consumption of plant food and presumes that, after weaning, the young individual is on its own. In contrast, gathering involves collecting and carrying quantities for later consumption by more than one individual; it is compatible with extended dependence of the young.

There are a number of patterns relative to food exploitation present in chimpanzees, which the postulated ancestral population can reasonably be assumed to have applied in the savanna context. These behaviors, in turn, provided a foundation for the development of gathering. They include carrying food to a protected spot for later consumption, for example, carrying nuts to a nearby spot for cracking them open and carrying fruit and animal food to nearby trees to consume there (Goodall, 1965; Albrecht and Dunnett, 1971). A logical extension from earlier behavior would be carrying food from the comparatively open areas to the more protected trees to eat. And because trees are usually located near water sources, this would be doubly useful as food with less water content (e.g., dry fruits, berries, nuts, seeds, tubers) and food for which more water is needed to metabolize (e.g., high protein foods such as nuts, seeds, insects, meat) became increasingly important. Chimpanzees eat both dry fruit and hard seeds in savanna woodlands during the dry season (Suzuki, 1969), and it is likely that such foods were also used by the transitional population. Furthermore, the concepts of unseen food that can be found at a particular time (e.g., seasonal fruits) or in a particular place (e.g., termites) could be generalized and applied to vegetable food under the ground (Figure 7:2). Chimpanzees occasionally employ sticks as levers at Gombe (Goodall, 1970) and in laboratory studies use sticks as digging implements (Köhler, 1927).

It is not difficult to imagine transitional hominids obtaining underground food by utilizing a short wooden or stone implement to dig and pry up roots and tubers when the ground was soft. At first, whatever appropriate object was at hand would be used, with or without modification; later, one selected and/or modified for that specific purpose could be carried along during the food quest.

The role of females in gathering ventures is emphasized because, first, childbearing and lactation cause additional nutritional stress on women (Figure 7:3). The effective gatherer would be most likely to bear a healthy infant. Second, it is likely that mothers were the ones who began to share plant food regularly with their young (Figure 7:4). Initially, readily available plant foods could be premasticated and shared with relatively young

FIGURE 7:2. Chimpanzees occasionally use sticks as digging implements. Here, a chimpanzee in the Barcelona Zoo grasps and pokes a stick into the ground, as Sabater Pí also observed in a natural setting in the Republic of Equatorial Guinea.

offspring or broken and shared with somewhat older offspring. Such foods would also supplement nursing. Subsequently, as the transitional hominid treks extended further out from the forest and they made more consistent use of the mosaic savanna, where edible plant foods were widely dispersed and less immediately available, mothers would begin to exercise foresight in gathering sufficient plant food to share with their young. It was the mothers who had reason to collect, carry, and share plant food; at this time, males were likely still foragers, eating available food as they went.

Many foods available on the savanna were no doubt familiar to the ancestral population and continued to be used by the transitional hominids. A change in proportions rather than in kinds of food occurred in the initial stages of hominization. The diet of the transitional hominids doubtless included not only fruits and berries but also seeds, nuts, tubers, roots, insects, eggs, lizards, and small mammals such as rodents, hares, young ungulates, and primate infants. Adaptability in diet is characteristic of chimpanzee and gorilla populations; both show variability in different geographic regions. This is also true of baboons and other monkeys. By analogy with chimpanzees, who are able to find different species of fruit in different locations at

FIGURE 7:3. A mother from a southern African gathering-hunting society nurses an older child.

different parts of the year, I think the ancestral population already possessed a highly developed memory for finding many types of food in the appropriate locales during the right seasons. Considerable traveling over a large range provided further reason for expanding the diet to include greater quantities of those berries, nuts, and other seeds plus tubers and roots commonly found on the grasslands separating tree clumps. The transitional hominids' ability to generalize information enabled them to expand their resource base from familiar foods eaten in the forest to include new foods. Gathering-hunting peoples who inhabit the African savannas today eat a variety of plant and other foods, many of which are similar to what chimpanzees eat, although differing in frequency and relative amounts (Suzuki, 1966, 1969; Teleki, 1975). Although the transitional population was extending its dietary repertoire, it continued to eat many of the foods the ancestral population ate: There was a degree of dietary continuity through the transitional hominids. The gathering innovation was successful. Savanna plant foods were obtained effectively, and there was little

FIGURE 7:4. A chimpanzee mother (*right*) allows an older offspring to take food from her mouth.

competition with other species. Rapid selection for making the behavior more efficient therefore occurred.

Gathering and bipedalism

Walking long distances while carrying is essential to this food pattern. A long-range gathering and foraging strategy was what was developing during the transition to *Australopithecus*. Mobility over large expanses for both females and males, and effective carrying, was made feasible by the development of a system of upright, two-legged locomotion. There was much to be carried by the gathering mothers—their infants, their tools, and the gathered food. Selection operated on the bipedal behavior present in the ancestral population; as the transitional population began to exploit the new niche, the new locomotor pattern rapidly became an integral part of it (see Figure 7:6). Bipedalism freed the arms and hands from locomotor functions and body support. The change from four limbs of support to but two created problems of balance and stability that were met by anatomical modifications of the pelvis, limbs, and feet. The muscles and joints of the pelvis and lower limb changed; the legs became longer and massive and the ankle and foot developed for support rather than mobility; the first toe lost its ability to oppose other toes as the foot developed for support. The upper limbs and trunk were reduced in mass and length. Concurrently, the motor skills of the hands were developing for manipulation of objects in many contexts, especially in relation to collecting food.

Gathering and tools

Plant food probably accounted minimally for 80 to 90 percent of the diet of the transitional population; this figure is intermediate between that of

FIGURE 7:5. A !Kung San mother cracking nuts she has gathered. She is accompanied by three of her children. Note the ease with which the children help themselves to the nuts.

South African bush people, about 70 percent, and chimpanzees, 90 to 99 percent (Lee, 1979; Riss and Busse, 1977). Obtaining and preparing plants is therefore the most obvious context in which to begin hypothesizing about tool use. Making and using tools must have been integral to the gathering adaptation. Initially, most of these tools, as among chimpanzees, would have been organic. Tools for digging (and possibly for carrying) were likely to be the initial additions to the tools already used by the ancestral population.

Savanna roots and tubers may well have been important new foods. Initially, they could have been obtained by digging with the fingers in loose, moist earth during the rainy season. Later, pointed sticks or sharp rocks could be used to pry up roots and tubers growing close to the surface even when the ground was dry and hard. These roots and tubers were relatively tough and fibrous but large enough to be divided; sharp-edged rocks were probably used to scrape off dirt and to cut them up for sharing. Long sticks could knock fruits and nuts from trees. Rocks were likely used to crack open and halve nuts or large fruits with tough rinds. At this stage objects that could be used as implements were found, modified slightly, and occasionally formed, but tools were not "made" in any sense that would be recognizable in the archeological record. Females would more frequently use objects as tools to obtain, open, and divide plant food, as they habitually shared with offspring. Conceivably, they may also have begun to develop very elementary containers for carrying some of the food they collected.

Gathering and the hominid adaptation

As the period of physical dependence lengthened (a biological side effect of selection for greater intelligence and more extended social learning), offspring with mothers intelligent enough to find, gather, premasticate, and share sufficient food with them had the selective advantage. The quality of maternal care became critical for these dependent and vulnerable young. Similarly, a mother's gathering effectiveness improved her own nutrition and thereby increased her life expectancy and fertility. Although males certainly foraged and perhaps occasionally gathered, it would have been primarily for themselves rather than for a dependent individual. They too perhaps sometimes shared food, but not regularly with a child whose survival chances depended on it. Similarly, males doubtless also used tools on occasion to obtain plant food, but such sporadic tool use made less difference for them than for females.

FIGURE 7:6. This chimpanzee is walking bipedally while carrying bananas. It is hypothesized here that bipedal carrying-behavior occurred and was selected for among the transitional population.

As the population was able to increasingly utilize forest fringes and areas away from forests, gathering for offspring became necessary. Food, though plentiful, was less readily accessible, required tool use to obtain in many instances, was acquired in areas where the hominids were more vulnerable, often was not immediately visible, and was more widely dispersed. Concurrently, the physical dependency of the young was lengthening because of the development of bipedalism and the need to learn skill in tool making and tool use to obtain food. Bipedalism, tool use for food and defense, an enhanced communicatory range and developing cognitive potential, elaboration of long-term social ties—with mothers carrying their offspring and caring for them for a longer time— were all linked to gathering plant food with tools in the new habitat.

Protein sources

The transitional hominids were capable of obtaining protein by gathering seeds and nuts, collecting termites and ants with sticks and grass stems like chimpanzees, collecting birds' eggs, and chasing, catching, and killing small animals. On the savanna they might seek out ostrich eggs as contemporary gatherer-hunters do. Like chimpanzees, the transitional population doubtless used modified stems and other organic material as tools for obtaining insects. They perhaps were especially drawn to the large termite hills found on the African savanna. Termite hills might have become important markers of the terrain as well.

Because of the abundance of small animals on the savanna, the amount of daytime predatory activity perhaps increased somewhat. Prey might have included lizards, hares, baboons, young bushpigs, and young ungulates: Weight probably did not exceed 9 kilograms, with the more usual range considerably smaller. Again, like chimpanzees, the transitional hominids caught defenseless, small, or young animals with their hands. Because suitable prey are present in both forest and savannas, initially there would be little need to find new prey animals as they began to move out of the forest and utilize open areas for food getting. Later, after they were thoroughly familiar with the savanna, they probably learned to find the young of additional species—for example, of ungulates, perhaps particularly those species whose mothers leave their young alone, hidden in the tall grass.

Both males and females caught and killed animals. However, a female carrying an offspring or with a small one walking beside her doubtless preferred activities that resulted in reliable sources of protein, such as egg and seed collecting, termiting, or ant dipping. She focused on providing for her and her offspring's needs by seeking out foods not likely to escape: a wide variety of plants and plant parts, eggs, honey, insects. Because the survival of her offspring depended upon her efforts, she had to ensure a regular food supply. Females without offspring obtained small animals for food, and mothers whose offspring were nearing independence probably taught them how to catch prey, as Jane Goodall (1973b, 1979) describes for a Gombe chimpanzee mother and her daughters.

It is highly unlikely that tools were used for killing animals at this time. The prey was small and defenseless and could be caught and killed with the hands. Predatory behavior, therefore, was not hunting: It was accomplished without tools and with the hands or, occasionally, the teeth. For the transitional population, like chimpanzees today, there is no reason to suppose that predation was organized, planned, regular, or even a particularly significant source of food.

Throwing with power and precision—as is necessary in hunting—is dependent on anatomical and neurological features that, at this early date, would have not yet developed (Goodall, 1970). The Mio-Pliocene transitional hominids were not physically equipped for effective hunting with tools. Anatomical and neurological correlates for throwing with precision and power include fine motor control of the hand, particularly the thumb, hand-trunk-arm and eye coordination; and pelvic rotation and trunk stability over the feet (Zihlman, 1967, 1978c). There is no evidence that any of these anatomical specializations were characteristic of the transitional population.

The transitional hominids were also learning what displays and objects were effective in intimidating and frightening away potentially dangerous animals. They probably tossed grass, foliage, branches, rocks, and dirt in the general direction of dangerous animals in order to disperse them. But this did *not* constitute hunting with tools. They were trying to get rid of such carnivores, not obtain them; and they could not hit the animals consistently or kill them with the objects they used. Defense involved dispersion of big carnivores by antagonistic displays and throwing objects. In contrast, the predatory behavior of these transitional hominids, as among chimpanzees, was a matter of capturing small, relatively weak and helpless animals and then killing them without the use of tools. Using objects and motor patterns for defense, that is, to disperse animals, is a very different process from that operating later in the Pleistocene when tools, motor patterns, and social organization came to be used to obtain large animals for food.

Patterns of social interaction

As the transitional hominids moved into the savanna, they took with them flexible habits of association – the potential to form groups of various sizes and composition under differing circumstances. This advantageous capacity also is characteristic of both chimpanzees and human gatherer-hunters (Lee, 1972, 1976, 1979; Silberbauer, 1972; Yellen and Harpending, 1972; Marshall, 1976; Jochim, 1976). The flexibility of the transitional hominid's chimpanzee-like social organization, in contrast to a rigidly structured organizational form such as that of baboon troops, facilitated the exploitation of savanna resources. Small groups of individuals could gather termites, fruits, roots, nuts, and other seeds in a variety of nearby spots while others ranged farther for longer periods of time to find edible fauna and flora in more distant locales. Groups could vary in size, composition, and organizational complexity because the ability to recognize and communicate with a large number of individuals and thereby have structured, ordered social relations with them was present. In this respect, the adaptation of the transitional hominids was similar to contemporary gatherer-hunters where social organization, as we would expect, is also flexible. A flexible structure is nonetheless a structure; it is a sophisticated organizational form that relies on effective communication and knowledge of the environment.

What were the basic organizing principles of transitional hominid groups? The mother–offspring tie was primary; this was the elemental social unit for them as it is for other primates. Among contemporary human groups this unit remains important. It is incorporated into all known social organizations; in every society it is the basic organizational form that is relied upon when other more complex or extended structures break down or do not function effectively; and in some societies it is elaborated upon in such a way that the mother–offspring dyad is the fundamental building block of kinship organization and is also central in terms of social values and human affect (Tanner, 1974).

More extended genealogical relations, particularly those linking siblings, were probably also important, and especially so in the event of the mother's death. Sibling ties have their basis in the relatively long mutual association with the mother, doubtless continued into adulthood. This social continuity provided a basis for building larger networks of individuals who might come together from time to time over long periods. Such groupings likely would include several adult females, perhaps sisters or females whose mothers were sisters, their offspring, and often their female offspring's offspring as well, plus a number of adult males. Many of the adult males would be brothers and sons of the senior females. A few might be the senior females' preferred sexual partners or friends. Females necessarily formed the central core of this larger group, because the mothers did most of the socialization of the young. Mother–offspring and sibling bonds were fundamental; sibling ties continued into adulthood as sister friendships, brother friendships, and brother–sister friendships, with offspring of sisters probably also in frequent association. Individual choice of friends and traveling companions based on personal features would also be developing.

Socialization of the young for savanna living was accomplished within the genealogical unit. Mother and sisters acted as the focus for offspring and young siblings of both sexes to learn about gathering. Mature males – brothers, older sons, and friends of senior females – and older females with nearly independent offspring were a focus for young males and females to learn and practice predatory behavior. Each sex learned to obtain both plant and animal food, but during the life cycle intensity and frequency varied. There was much to learn about the savanna way of life; this necessitated a longer period of social dependency. Females passed on innovations, skills, and environmental information to both male and female offspring. The complex social patterns of individual recognition and greetings, environmental information concerning the distribution of food sources and raw materials for tools over a large range, and appropriate motor patterns for making and using gathering tools, for digging, knocking down, scraping, opening, or dividing food, for carrying implements, food, and babies, and for defense from predators all had to be learned.

Innovations spread rapidly from one individual to others because these transitional hominids, like the nonhuman primates of today, had the capacity for rapid learning and effective communication (Köhler, 1927; Itani, 1965; Menzel et al., 1972). Mothers, as the socializers, were the carriers of group tradition; the social and technical inventions of the females were passed on to their offspring during the socialization process and eventually became part of the behavioral repertoire of the transitional population as a whole. The mother–offspring relationship is of fundamental importance to the transmission of technical innovations and environmental information necessary to the establishment of gathering as a basic form of ecological adaptation.

Cooperation

For the transitional population, cooperation in the sense of planned, coordinated, and goal-directed interaction can hardly be expected. This is not to say, however, that there might not be several individuals involved in gathering, predation, or defense. But such involvement would simply be a result of chance association as friends or kin. In obtaining food or dealing with potential predators, the presence of a number of individuals could increase the effectiveness of the activity even though it was not cooperation in the full sense. ,

Differing behavior frequencies

There was no division of labor per se, but frequency differences necessarily occurred. These were sex linked but not sex specific. Particularly for females they varied with situation and over the life cycle. Females with dependent offspring were frequently occupied with gathering the plants that were the most regular foods and supplied most of the caloric intake for themselves and their young. Males, nulliparous females (mostly adolescents), or females whose offspring had died or were already self-sufficient gathered or foraged plant and other foods for themselves and occasionally caught and killed small animals, which were widely shared. Sharing gathered food, mostly plants, served to further intensify and reinforce the genealogical bonds between mothers and offspring and among siblings. Meat, although only sporadically available, was probably shared quite widely among those present at the time, as it also is among chimpanzees.

Males could perhaps enhance and strengthen their relationships with those with whom they were traveling or resting through such sharing.

Predator avoidance, defense, and social organization

Predators posed a problem for this diurnal omnivorous primate, which was now obtaining a large proportion of its food in the relatively open African savanna where predator pressure was high. Their upright posture and developing bipedal locomotor pattern meant that the transitional hominids were more visible to predators. Furthermore, their wide-ranging activities could mean trees were not always nearby and, because of their changing foot structure and new food-carrying pattern, not a particularly convenient place for quick daytime retreat in any case. Climbing trees would be less efficient than for the ancestral population. Nonetheless, as all of us can recall from childhood escapades, the ability to climb trees has hardly been lost—even for contemporary humans. The transitional hominids probably still regularly utilized trees for protection when resting and at night. Gathered food could also be shared in leisure back in the protection of trees, away from exposure to carnivores roaming in open country. Because mothers carried their young and gathered for them, infants were less exposed to predators than would be the case if the young had to forage for themselves.

In open country, infants and probably older offspring up to four or even five years of age or older were carried at least part of the time by gathering mothers. Regular campsites probably did not yet exist. This meant that the young could not be left back at camp and for safety would necessarily have to be carried longer than among contemporary gatherer-hunters.[4] This, in turn, implies that mothers probably did not gather as intensely—for as many hours at a time, over as extensive a region, or in quest of such large quantities—as is the case for human gatherers today. Toddlers could safely romp and play on the ground and in trees only back at the resting spots that were comparatively free from danger—and even there only when adults were alert to danger from predators. Such resting spots were not yet, strictly speaking, campsites but did have some of the same functions. Because of their extensive knowledge of the terrain, the transitional hominids knew where to find trees and water sources, and could program their gathering excursions so that trees would be available when they took rest during the day and at nightfall.

[4] Bush women in the Kalahari carry their children as long as they are nursing, up to about three years of age. After that they usually leave them in camp because if they take them gathering the mothers must carry water for them or pick them up and carry them if they get too tired (Draper, 1976).

The hominid pattern of dealing with predators was basically one of intelligent avoidance supplemented by intimidation. For the transitional population defense consisted, first of all, in being able to see predators better because of walking upright. Secondly, they learned about the behavior of carnivores and so could usually avoid them. Sleeping in protected spots, probably usually in fairly large groups (which provided a choice of sleeping partners), was important because savanna carnivores primarily prey at night. Standing and walking bipedally would also contribute to the effectiveness of defensive displays, as observed for chimpanzees. Transitional hominids, when displaying bipedally, would appear large, their arms could be waved while they vocalized, and sticks and rocks could be thrown (Figure 7:7). As intimidation this would be quite effective.

This pattern of avoidance and intimidation is very different from that of each of several monkey species that live in relatively open country. Speed, for example, combined with lookout and diversionary tactics, plus hiding and concealment, is typical of patas monkeys (Hall, 1965a). An exceptional interaction occurred during the height of the dry season, when animals congregate around water holes; Struhsaker and Gartlan (1970) observed one instance in which three patas males chased a jackal that had made off with an infant. The jackal dropped the infant, which was retrieved by a female. The patas's adaptation for speed allows groups to be small, and ordinarily there is only one adult male in the group. Vervet monkeys, on the other hand, have evolved an elaborate alarm call system whereby the members of the social group provide each other with specific predator information so that each can respond appropriately — climbing up into the closest trees to avoid a terrestrial predator or dropping down from the forest canopy should an aerial predator threaten (Struhsaker, 1967). For both patas and vervet monkeys, each member most frequently responds on its own. In contrast, savanna-living baboons live in multimale/multifemale groups, and adult males — which are nearly twice the size of females and have large canine teeth — are anatomically and behaviorally equipped to protect females and young (Washburn and DeVore, 1961b; DeVore, 1963; Hall, 1965b; Struhsaker, 1967). The sexually dimorphic and stratified baboon social structure protects all individuals, but members must always stay together. Such baboon-like social rigidity was not necessary for the viability of the transitional population. During peak danger times from night-roaming carnivores, transitional hominids probably did sleep together in fairly compact groups. During the daytime, however, the means of intimidation were sufficient to make attack unlikely, even on lone adults. Because the transitional hominids were so social, individual isolation for long periods was unlikely but

FIGURE 7:7. Transitional hominid females undoubtedly could defend themselves and their offspring with tools. Here, in an experiment carried out by Adriaan Kortlandt in the early 1960s in Zaire (then the Congo), a wild chimpanzee mother with an infant on her back is brandishing and throwing a stick at a stuffed leopard with a baby chimpanzee doll in its paws.

could and perhaps did occur on occasion. More significant, safety during the food quest did not necessitate fixed, rigid, stratified, or compact association.

Sexuality and social interaction

For primates, most (but not all) sexual activity takes place during estrus when bodily changes in the female signal her active interest in copulation. Which males actually participate and during what part of the female's estrous cycle depends upon the nature of the social organization. In hama-dryas baboons, for example, the senior male regularly copulates with the adult females who associate with him. By attacking these females when they copulate with others, he tries to prevent the females from sexual interaction with other males, particularly the younger ones (Kummer, 1968). As for savanna baboons, Hall and DeVore (1965) think that domi-nant males mate most frequently with the females in the peak of estrus when there is maximal swelling. Among gibbons, who live in pairs, copu-lation is between a single male and a single female (Carpenter, 1940; Ellefson, 1968). In contrast, among chimpanzees—the apes most like the ancestral population—a single female may mate with several males in succession. These males do not ordinarily interfere with each other, and they in turn may mate with several females.

There are several aspects of estrus: the hormonal, which determines the timing of fertility for the female; changes in female behavior (i.e., their activity level tends to be higher and they more frequently initiate or allow copulation); morphological changes, such as the swelling and reddening of the female genital area, which provide a visual sign to males; and the pheromones, which act as an olfactory signal. The evolution of sexual behavior has included changes in all of these components.

In humans, there are cyclic hormonal and physiological changes in the reproductive tract. However, sexual signaling by means of the swelling and reddening of the genital area does not occur. There is no apparent change in behavior at time of ovulation except, perhaps, a slightly greater activity level. And if in fact women are more desirous of having sexual intercourse around the time of ovulation, as some suggest, this would be difficult to measure because cultural factors are so important in human sexual interaction.

For the transitional hominids, the issue is really not whether estrus was "lost" or not, but rather how the role of each of the components—hor-monal, morphological, pheromonal, behavioral—was modified (in com-parison to ancestral apes) and how this interaction of components affected the outcome of sexual behavior. A monthly hormonal cycle and associated physiological changes, as in living Old World monkeys, apes, and hu-mans, were doubtless also characteristic of the transitional hominids.[5] But

---

[5] Female monkeys and apes may, on occasion, also engage in sexual activity when not in estrus or when already pregnant (Goodall, 1968a; Loy, 1971; Chalmers and Rowell, 1971; Hafez, 1971; Lemmon and Allen, 1978), so that for nonhuman primates as well as humans there is some flexibility in sexual activity. Not all copulation is directly tied to hormones and estrus or therefore to ovulation and pregnancy. A study group of pygmy chimpanzees, in particular, has continued to copulate throughout all phases of the female's cycle (Savage-

as they began to travel more frequently bipedally, the swelling and reddening of the sexual skin (which, in other primates, reach their maximum at the time of ovulation) were probably diminishing. In a bipedal hominid the genital area is below the trunk and between the legs rather than at the rear; sexual swelling therefore would not be easily visible and so could not serve as an effective visual signal. Pheromones would also be less effective as olfactory signals of sexual state because males could not readily sniff the genital region of bipedal females.

In terms of behavior, important changes were beginning. The old argument is that with loss of estrus females became receptive at any and all times. This would appear to be more in the realm of wishful thinking than a description of actual sexual interaction in any known society. There is therefore little reason to hypothesize a type of interaction for the transitional population that neither was probable for the preceding ancestral population nor accurately characterizes human sexual interaction today. What *is* evident, however, is that transitional hominid males now had less information by which to judge whether the females were ready for sexual intercourse. In the absence of sexual swellings, males conceivably might try to continue to sniff the genitals frequently — despite the physical contortions that would be involved when walking upright — in order to gain olfactory clues on possible mating times.

A more likely alternative is that females did more and more direct initiation of sexual activity — by overtly soliciting intercourse and by nonverbally signaling receptivity (Figure 7:8). Morphological changes were replaced with other forms of communication where females through degree of physical spacing and type of gesture, facial expression, eye contact, posture, vocalization, and other nonverbal behavior signaled to males that they were willing — or unwilling — to engage in sexual intercourse. The loss of estrus then can mean that a female can initiate sex with males at any time. But it can also mean that she may choose not to mate, even when her hormones are such that she could become pregnant.

Rumbaugh and Wilkerson, 1978). This contrasts with the situation for common chimpanzees which, both in captivity and in the wild, tend to copulate primarily when the female is in estrus (Savage-Rumbaugh and Wilkerson, 1978). In a study situation, where captive pygmy and common chimpanzees were housed adjacent to one another, Savage-Rumbaugh and Wilkerson observed that "Just as the male *P. paniscus* [pygmy chimpanzee] copulated with females of his own species throughout their cycles, he likewise copulated with the *P. troglodytes* [common chimpanzee] females throughout their cycles. They responded to his soliciting gestures by pressing their genitals close to the wire. This suggests that, at least among *P. troglodytes*, copulation may tend to be limited to the maximal swelling phase [of estrus] because of the [common chimpanzee] male's lack of interest during other phases of the cycle and not because of the female's unwillingness" (Savage-Rumbaugh and Wilkerson, 1978:333).

FIGURE 7:8. The female chimpanzee on the right approaches a male and presses her genitals against his back, apparently in an attempt to initiate sexual interaction. The male is eating a banana while copulating with the female on the left.

Communication, mental activity, and the brain as the integrating structure

Communication about the environment and communication that mediates a complicated variety of social interactions presuppose an evolving brain — a brain that can both send and receive messages. The brain makes possible the recombination of elements for the expression of complex messages. It is also the brain that interprets, decodes, or "reads" the behavioral messages of others. Recall that Menzel (1971a, 1979) and Menzel and Halperin (1975) — in key experiments for unraveling evolutionary trends in communication and, in particular, for comprehending the nature of the human communication system and how it evolved — have shown that chimpanzees can communicate to each other information about the environment through postures, direction of movement, gestures, vocalizations, and facial expressions that had heretofore been regarded as merely expressing emotional states (Tanner and Zihlman, 1976b).

For the transitional hominids, the communication system would be evolving to express more complicated messages. As communication became the medium of more variable and complex social relations, including sexual behavior, the brain's capacity for social communication would necessarily develop in order to both accommodate and facilitate these interactions. In addition, selection would be for increasing effectiveness in communication about the environment. At first this would be effected by recombining and utilizing nonverbal elements such as direction and rate of locomotion, postures, facial expressions, and gestures, with some vocalization to convey information about food sources, water, predators, possible resting or sleeping spots, and other aspects of the environment. Thus a gesture such as pointing—toward a berry patch or a lion—could be combined with facial expressions, bodily movements, and sounds indicating either excited anticipation or fear and agitation to "say" two very different things. Social and physical context also affect the meaning of messages. A chimpanzee's outstretched hand may elicit food from another chimpanzee, in which case it has been referred to as "begging." Alternatively, it may evoke a tactile social response that we would describe as "comforting"; in the latter instance the outstretched hand has been described as indicating a request for "reassurance" (Goodall, 1972). Among the transitional population it is reasonable to suppose that a wide repertoire of nonverbal communicatory elements, including context, was used; selection would be for a communication system in which a more complex brain made it possible for various in-context combinations of body movements plus some vocal components to convey more complicated social and environmental information than could the ancestral population. It is therefore possible that some of the requisite mental abilities for the later development of speech as we know it were already evolving at the time of the transitional hominids.

The brain also plays important roles both in social memory and in remembering information about the environment—in the foresight involved in getting food; in the invention and manipulation of tools; in overall body coordination; and in general sociability through appropriate modulation of affect in social interactions. All would be selected for and all relate to somewhat increased cortical control (and so less hormonal control) of action, including aggression and sex. The basis for choice of all kinds—to grimace or fight, where to go and what to eat, sexual choices, with whom and when to travel, friendships based on personality preferences—all involve a degree of neural development and control. Even at this early stage it seems likely that changes in the brain occurred to accommodate, facilitate, and make possible such behaviors.

The interrelations and the feedback dynamics of social learning, increasing cranial capacity, and intelligence become obvious when viewed in relation to the new locomotor pattern and how it prolongs infant dependency. With bipedal locomotion evolving, learning to walk required more time to develop motor coordination prior to independence with regard to locomotion than was true for the quadrupedal ancestral population. This meant that the mother—or older sibling, mother's sibling, or mother's friend—had to carry a child that could no longer cling as effectively because the changed anatomy of bipedalism required loss of the foot's

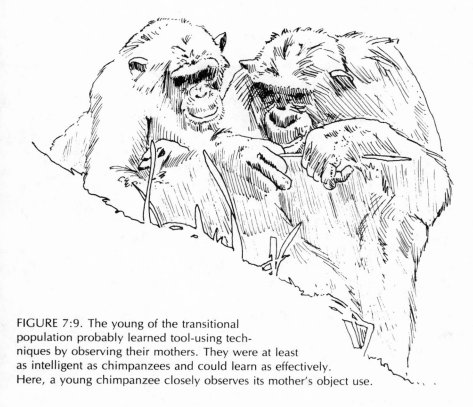

FIGURE 7:9. The young of the transitional
population probably learned tool-using techniques by observing their mothers. They were at least
as intelligent as chimpanzees and could learn as effectively.
Here, a young chimpanzee closely observes its mother's object use.

ability to grasp the mother. Even young who were already able to walk
would have to be carried frequently and often, because they would tire.
Bipedalism was an effective adaptation for savanna-living adults, but for
the two-year-old or three-year-old toddler it was not so great. The young
had to be physically cared for over an extended period because of the time
required for motor development: The social implications of this fact must
have been far-reaching. Social bonds between mother and offspring had to
be close and intense so she would give her infant and child the care
necessary to its survival. This long-term contact with adults in turn offers
the young increased opportunity to watch adult activity at close hand and
to learn about the environment, where to find food, how to use tools
effectively in a variety of ways, how to make tools, and where to find the
raw materials (Figure 7:9).

With effective baby and child care, the young can be born more physically immature—which was certainly fortunate, for this was becoming necessary due to changes in the pelvis for bipedalism. Because infants and
young must in any case be cared for already, increased immaturity at birth

would not be selected against. So, with bipedalism came prolonged dependency. This in turn became adaptive in another context: It allowed for intensive, extended learning about the social and ecological environment and gave a distinct selective advantage to individuals who could benefit most from this opportunity to learn.

Once a young individual was no longer economically dependent on its mother, it was really on its own. This was especially true when the gathering adaptation was just developing and the transitional hominids still resembled the ancestral population in many respects. Selection would intensely favor the more intelligent young who could effectively execute the new behaviors. This is why, as Holloway (1976a) suggests, the hominid brain could be reorganized early in evolution. Reorganization could have happened quite rapidly: Young who did not make it and died before reproductive age did not pass on their genes. Selection would favor young who were curious, playful, and cued into the behavior of other group members, imitating tool-using skills and environmental know-how, learning to recognize many individuals and to interact within a wide and diverse social network, a group nonetheless even though not together all the time. Selection was operating for successful behaviors at all levels – the population, the immediate social network, within a genealogy for helping each other survive, and at the individual level, particularly for the young. Bipedalism, hand-eye coordination, and changes in the brain were the initial anatomic/behavioral changes that were intimately linked to and interrelated with all other aspects of behavior: bipedal displays for predator protection, bipedalism for carrying young and gathered food, endurance for walking long distances, hand-eye coordination and manipulative functions in tool making and gathering, and the increasing intelligence and more effective communication that made it possible for the young to learn what they would need to know to survive while they were still being cared for physically. Expanded awareness, increased reaction potential, enhanced social relations – all relate to the brain, memory, and more choices in all realms.

Selection and the origin of the hominid line: the role of females in speciation

Initially the transitional hominids were spatially and genetically continuous with the ancestral population. They began expanding away from the tropical rain forest, where the chimpanzees and gorillas were diversifying, into the forest fringes, and gradually into more open areas. Probably there was little to impede population movement between these ecological zones at first. However, a period of less rainfall, pronounced volcanic activity, the origin of a lake, changes in a river's course, or other such events can readily break up areas of continuous vegetation. Geographical barriers can create isolated pockets impeding gene flow. Topographical changes can thereby contribute to speciation. The transitional hominids, who at this time were only racial or subspecific apes, could have become isolated from the parental population and then have begun to rapidly change from it.

In eastern Africa during the Mio-Pliocene volcanic action, changing topography and drainage patterns meant frequent shifts in vegetation. Isolation was therefore more probable on the savannas of eastern Africa than farther to the south. The hypothesis that speciation began in eastern Africa during this period is consistent with what was going on there environmentally, for this was a time of change (Andrews and J. A. H. Van Couvering, 1975). Also, if in fact the savannas of southern Africa were more arid, that region would have been less propitious for the origin of the hominid line but suitable for the spread of hominids after their adaptation was established. The absence of living apes in southern Africa and the absence of an ape fossil record there, despite the probability that conditions favorable to fossilization may have existed, lend further support to the idea that the hominid–ape divergence took place in eastern Africa.

Major topographical changes occurred during the relevant time period, and the eastern African savannas are adjacent to areas inhabited by the living great apes most closely related to the hominids. The forest fringes of eastern Africa were the most likely locale for initial speciation. Specifically, within this large region, the earliest hominid fossils are all found within the eastern rift valley system (see Chapter 8). In this area changing patterns of the mosaic made isolation highly probable. Given spatial isolation, genetic reconstruction occurs (Mayr, 1970). As the population began to use regions within the comparatively open areas more and more intensely, elements present in the ancestral population were elaborated and integrated genetically to form a new pattern. Because of the significance of regulatory genes in determining phenotype, relatively few mutations were necessary; evolution could therefore proceed very rapidly.

Gene flow is impeded where there is variation in niche requirements even without total isolation. Even with only partial separation between the ranges of two populations, a marked degree of difference can develop. For example, hamadryas and savanna baboons have long been considered separate species; yet, where their ranges overlap, interbreeding takes place and produces a hybrid population (Kummer et al., 1970; Nagel, 1973). It is probable that in the initial stages of speciation – before geographical separation or reproductive isolation were complete – a comparable situation existed for the transitional hominid population. In other words, there may well have been a directly ancestral population of apes, living some 6 million to 5 million years ago in the forest fringes of eastern Africa and beginning to exploit resources away from trees, which already differed in gene frequencies as compared to the rest of the parental stock.

Speciation and therefore the shift into a new niche or adaptive zone almost without exception begin with a change in behavior. Behavior is "the most important evolutionary determinant, particularly in the initiation of new evolutionary trends" (Mayr, 1970:363). Anatomical adaptations to the new niche are acquired subsequently. Behavioral reorganization is often an initial step. Elements present in the ancestral population can be rearranged so as to have the same, or similar, function but in a new context or, alternatively, a different function in the same context. Dietary and habitat preferences are behavioral phenomena. They both play a major role in the shift to a new adaptive zone. The conspicuous termite hills several feet high that are a common feature in open savanna country could have been one kind of tantalizing food source that drew the transitional population (which I assume was a curious and exploratory one) ever further into the savanna.

New behaviors by transitional hominids almost certainly included: looking for food in a different ecological region, the forest fringe and mosaic savanna as opposed to denser forests; using tools with increasing regularity to acquire food; more frequent bipedalism to carry food, objects, and infants; walking longer and longer distances daily during foraging and gathering; and upright posture to check on possible predators, for protective display, and to locate food sources. The underlying anatomical bases for increasing the effectiveness of these behaviors were to follow shortly— grinding molars to chew savanna plant foods, loss of the grasping toe for a better bipedal support base, and changes in the pelvis, hand, and brain.

If the selection pressures were intense for integrating these behavioral patterns and providing an appropriate anatomical base to enhance their effectiveness, even a small degree of spatial isolation may have been sufficient for speciation to begin. An individual as a whole—representing the total genotype expressed as the phenotype—and not individual genes is the target of selection.

What particular effect a particular gene will have depends to a very large extent on its genetic milieu, that is, on the specificity of the other genes with which it is associated in the genotype. This universal interaction has been described in deliberately exaggerated form in this statement: *Every character of an organism is affected by all genes and every gene affects all characters.*   [Mayr, 1970:164]

It is the integration of all genes to produce a base for successful behaviors that is important in the evolutionary process. As the new pattern of behavior emerged in initial speciation, the heightened effectiveness of this population's use of the savanna lessened competition with neighboring populations.

Full spatial isolation of the transitional population almost certainly could not have lasted very long, given both the changing savanna mosaic and the population's omnivorous diet. We must assume, then, that – after an initial period of isolation sufficient to give the new adaptation a start and to allow time for selection of an appropriate underlying genetic complex – the transitional population and the parental population overlapped geographically from time to time. It is therefore necessary to hypothesize that both sexual and natural selection were essential to establish a separate line and that both served the same ends, that is, selection for one basic adaptation that was distinctively hominid. Essentially the same behavioral complex was being selected for both males and females: grinding molars, bipedalism, tool use – all of which were related to obtaining plant food as the primary feeding adaptation – plus generalized sociability, enhanced communicatory capabilities, and feeding and protection of the young.

Natural selection

The measure of natural selection is reproductive success (Dobzhansky, 1970). The crux of the matter is how many offspring survive for any given female or male, rather than the number of copulations or number of infants born per se. Transitional hominid fathers, like the ancestral population before them, would not know their young and so could not effect the specific survival chances of their own progeny as differentiated from other young of the community. In contrast, mothers directly influenced the survival of their own offspring. Those mothers whose offspring most often survived must have been sufficiently intelligent to find ways to support their relatively helpless infants – for example, by foresight and innovativeness in food collecting and willingness to share appropriate food with them.

A female's effectiveness as a gatherer not only would aid the survival of her offspring but also might increase the number of children she bore in her lifetime. Adequacy of maternal nutrition, length of nursing, whether nursing is a primary or supplemental food source past infancy – all may be directly related to fertility (Frisch, 1978). Effective gatherers would be better fed themselves, live longer, bear more children, and their children would have a higher survival rate. For gathering females, natural selection for bipedalism and tool use in the food quest was intense: Female bipedalism, tool use, and intelligence were inextricably linked with reproductive success.

Much has been written about the evolution of altruism (Hamilton, 1963, 1964, 1971; Trivers, 1971) and its role in species survival. It is unnecessary to detail that discussion here, but it should be pointed out that the human potential for at least limited altruism – in the sense of mothers consistently sharing food with young – must have been strongly selected for during this period of transition to humanity. Similarly, offspring of mothers who found tactile pleasure in holding and nursing their infants had a survival advantage. In addition, generally relaxed and friendly interactions with others on the part of mothers was adaptive for survival of the young because maternal sociability would facilitate obtaining food. For example, if mothers gathered in areas already utilized by others, friendly interaction could lead to opportunities for food sharing with other adults. Mothers probably sometimes solicited meat and large or scarce plant foods from other females and from males. Maternal sociability might further minimize mother–offspring isolation by increasing group size, which could indirectly serve to better protect the young from predators.

For males it was primarily their individual survival that was at issue in terms of natural selection. Bipedalism had value in keeping up with gathering females traversing a wide range on the savanna and in defensive displays but provided no particular advantage in predation at this initial period in the transition from an ancestral ape to an early hominid. Bipedalism, tool use, and intelligence were marginally more adaptive for foraging males. However, their plant foraging efficacy would not appear to affect their reproductive success.

"Kin selection"

One special instance of natural selection has been termed "kin selection," or selection that favors certain clusters of kin and therefore their genetic potential over other kin clusters (Wilson, 1975). Because of the lengthening dependence of the young, the mother–offspring relationship became ever more central to the social life of the transitional hominids. Even after the young were essentially independent – able to walk bipedally and to use tools skillfully to obtain food – mothers doubtless continued to share with them on occasion. Affective ties developed during the long, close association of infancy and youth. Mother and adult offspring recognized each other and continued to associate frequently. In the context of this long-term mother–offspring association, ties among children of the same mother developed. These continuing mother–offspring and sibling relationships made kin selection possible. Mothers and offspring share many of the genes that are ordinarily in free variation in a population, and siblings with different fathers – as would ordinarily be the case – also share some of these genes, although not as many as mothers and their young.[6] Therefore, behavior among kin that favors mutual survival serves to pass on shared genes. An older sibling, for example, might carry, groom, share food with, play with, or teach skills to a younger sibling, and this might help the sibling to survive. Furthermore, in a small group, any adult male who did likewise for the young of the group might inadvertently assist in the survival of young that he fathered.

In kin selection male and female siblings would have an equal opportunity to pass on their genes through care of younger siblings. Whatever input – in terms of time, energy, and shared food – they had into their younger siblings' survival also lessened the energy expenditure of their mother, thereby tending to increase her fertility. If some mothers encouraged their young to behave in ways that enhanced the development of affective ties, mutuality, and sharing among their children more than did other mothers, kin selection would favor those maternal lines more than others.

Parental "investment"

Parental "investment" has been defined as "any investment by the parent in an individual offspring that increases the offspring's chance of surviving (and hence reproductive success) at the cost of the parent's ability to invest in other offspring" (Trivers, 1972:139). Parental investment is directly proportional to degree of dependence. Because of increased bipedalism and tool using in food collecting, the transitional hominid offspring were much more dependent than the young of the ancestral apes. At this stage males had very little direct investment in their offspring. Females had the biological investment of internal gestation, birth, and nursing and were providing most of the physical care *and* food, as well as much of the protection for their infants. Although some food and protection were supplied by males, sexual partners were only occasionally and irregularly involved; brothers and sons who frequently associated with mothers and sisters probably were the males who most regularly contributed animal protein and protection.

Sexual selection

Sexual selection is a special case of natural selection (Simpson, 1972). It can be intimately interrelated with the phenomenon of parental investment. Among many species of birds and insects, Trivers (1972) has shown that degree of parental investment correlates with sexual choice. In other

---

[6] A population shares many genes, of course; as do closely related species. In terms of kin selection, it is only those genes that vary within a population but may be shared by kin that are relevant.

words, the partner investing most in offspring appears also to be the one who exercises sexual selectivity. For the transitional hominids, infant survival depended upon maternal effectiveness. Parental investment essentially was maternal investment. If the correlation found by Trivers holds for mammals, including the higher primates, the transitional hominid females were sexually initiating and selective – a hypothesis that is not inconsistent with the reconstruction of sexual behavior in the ancestral population.

The more intelligent transitional female (remember, it is her offspring who will be most likely to survive) could use her intelligence to select males for copulation. In other words, increases in intelligence and a richer, more sophisticated communicatory repertoire mean the mating system itself could become more complex. I hypothesize that the mating system was changing so as regularly to include female discrimination and choice of sex partners in terms of a number of characteristics. Females probably had sex more frequently with those males who were around often, playing with offspring, helping in protection, occasionally sharing meat and foraged plants, and who were generally friendly. With females choosing the less disruptive males, there also would be less likelihood that males having sex with mothers might accidentally injure offspring. To the extent that the ability to learn to be more sociable has been enhanced by genetic changes that have augmented our human potential – and this is a subject about which little is known – sexual selection in the hominid divergence also could have increased the capacity of males for relaxed social interaction.

Selective pressure for speciation (of this transitional population from the ancestral apes) was likely intensified by females who more frequently chose males who differed most in certain respects from males of the ancestral ape population.[7] Males who sometimes shared food were doubtless

---

[7]   The question of to what extent partner preferences were exhibited is an interesting one. At Gombe, some "consort" relationships form among chimpanzees (Tutin, 1975; McGinnis, 1979). Two aspects of this occasional pairing, despite the overall sexual gregariousness and "tolerance" of chimpanzees, are of particular interest from an evolutionary perspective: (1) the temporary "disappearance" of a consort pair from chimpanzee aggregations and (2) the variety and individuality of behavior – for females, from willing pairing to disinterest or active unwillingness, and for males, from "friendly" actions to attacks.

In sexual interaction on the savanna among the population transitional between ancestral apes and the earliest hominids, behavior closer to the sexually gregarious and tolerant chimpanzee norm would likely predominate. Because of danger from predators, a male and female would be unlikely to go off alone at night on the savanna. Opportunities for sexual gregariousness would therefore exist at night when the savanna-living transitional population would tend to aggregate in safe sleeping spots. Nonetheless, even in transitional population nighttime sleeping groups, females and males might exercise some sleeping partner preferences. Chimpanzees in the wild ordinarily build their own nests and sleep alone; only mothers share their treetop nests with dependent offspring. In captivity, however, four female and two male chimpanzees housed at Stanford University demonstrated definite sleep-

preferable to more selfish individuals. Similarly, females would have reason to choose friendly males who, like themselves, only rarely (and selectively) engaged in displays against other transitional hominids but who nonetheless were skilled in defense and protection against predator species by intimidation displays and by throwing objects. This could have interesting implications for understanding conflict and aggression and how they relate to our human nature. What may have been selected for among the transitional hominid males was the capacity to be extremely social but yet sufficiently aggressive when required and an ability to make fine discriminations as to situational necessity. Thus, the males of the transitional population would come to more closely resemble the females than had the males of the ancestral population.

As Trivers has pointed out, when two recently speciated populations come together,

selection may favor females who prefer the appropriate extreme of an available sample, since such a mechanism would minimize mating mistakes. The natural selection of females with such a mechanism of choice would then initiate sexual selection in the same direction, which in the absence of countervailing selection would move the two male phenotypes further apart than necessary to avoid mating error.   [1972:166]

And so, as Darwin noted (1871), in sexual selection the male is more strongly modified away from the ancestral population male. In the hominid divergence some aspects of this modification appear to have been toward the same general line of development as the transitional female.

Much of the selection pressure engendered by female choice of sexual partners was directed toward male social and communicatory behavior, reinforcing the potential and capacity for sociability, social learning, and intelligence. Sexual selection also increased the contribution of genes from males who exhibited frequent bipedalism. A male's contribution to the gene pool necessitated his keeping up with the gathering females as they covered large expanses searching for food. Further, obvious visual cues such as a *bipedal* male's erect penis could have attracted female attention and action.[8] Such an image might appear amusing and improbable, but let

---

ing preferences based on long-term peer association and, especially during estrus, apparent sexual interest (Riss and Goodall,1976). Similarly, at Gombe, some consortships repeatedly involved the same individuals (Goodall, 1975a; McGinnis, 1979). Wild chimpanzees' nests in trees probably cannot support more than one adult; however, captive chimpanzees caged without trees, and often without nest-building materials, frequently choose to sleep in physical contact with one or more others.

[8] Even more directly, in the above context, sexual selection may have contributed to growth in the size of the males' penises. *Homo sapiens sapiens* males are quite well endowed.

us remember that these ancient forebears living in the warm African savannas had not yet invented clothing. As the female hormonal cycle and ovulation came to contribute less to timing of her arousal, it is not illogical that visual cues could become increasingly significant. If so, sexual selection for bipedalism would be yet another instance of natural and sexual selection together advancing the species' adaptation farther along the same path for both females and males.

After Darwin, evolutionists focused on natural selection. Sexual selection was almost ignored until quite recently (Campbell, 1972c); or, when not ignored, sexual selection has been noted primarily in those instances where the male has come to have some unusual characteristic, for example, the male peacock tail. Moreover, sexual selection often has been assumed to refer only to male-male competition.[9] Most writers have either ignored female choice or considered it trivial. Generally, female choice is treated as important only in the most obvious ways—that females merely select a potential partner of the right species, the right sex, or one who is sexually mature. But Trivers demonstrates that female choice can be of adaptive value in making fine discriminations among broadly appropriate males (1972). This ability to discriminate is not necessarily exclusively a matter of conscious cognition, as illustrated for fruit flies, among which the female has the ability to pick the genetically rare male for mating (Ehrman, 1972). Among transitional hominids, however, in addition to any unconscious mechanisms operating, female choice was probably also beginning to come into the conscious realm.

For the transitional population, the evolutionary implication of maternal investment combined with sexual selection is that the females—through their choice of males with whom to interact sexually—influenced which males contributed genes to the next generation. Over time, sexual selection changed gene frequencies in the transitional population. Selective pressures during speciation were intensified because females more frequently chose males who differed most in certain features from males of the parental population.

Overall, selection was for the integration of a genotype to produce a phenotype for interrelating certain activities—gathering food, carrying, covering large ranges on the savannas, using tools in food collecting and in protection—and for development of the capacity to elaborate social skills, including communication. Moreover, selection was for sexual activity that

[9] Leutenegger, for example, hypothesizes a "strong relationship between polygyny and positive allometry or sexual dimorphism in body size" (1978:610). To rephrase his hypothesis somewhat: Strong male-male sexual competition is assumed to be correlated with sexual dimorphism.

did not break up the genetic complexes underlying these behavioral patterns. Natural, kin, and sexual selection were complementary and reinforcing processes in the divergence of the hominid line. Natural selection worked intensively on females' genes through differing rates of reproductive success. The genetic capacities for the advantageous behavioral adaptations of certain mothers were selected through higher ratios of infant survival along particular maternal lines. Children of bipedal, intelligent, sharing gatherers fared well. Sexual selection, in contrast, more directly affected the males through differential opportunity to contribute to the gene pool because of nonrandom female choice. Female preferential copulatory behavior pushed the divergence in the same overall direction as natural selection—for bipedalism, intelligence, and sociability. Kin selection works on both females and males as genealogically related individuals of both sexes engage in behaviors that enhance the survival of young individuals—siblings as well as offspring—with whom they share genes.

For the transitional hominids, natural selection resulted in increasing maternal investment in offspring because (1) mothers gathered plants and shared them with offspring and (2) offspring were dependent on mothers while learning to walk and to collect food with tools. Heightened maternal investment resulted, in turn, in increased sexual selection by females. Natural and sexual selection reinforced each other during the transition. Selective pressures were intense, and evolutionary change may well have been extraordinarily rapid.

The topics of the "descent of man" and "selection in relation to sex" are more closely related than Darwin (1871) ever realized. He juxtaposed the correct questions and looked to the appropriate types of information for answers. The two parts of his book, sometimes viewed by others as two books—"man's descent" and "sexual selection"—Darwin considered as one, though interestingly he never fully related the two parts. He was prevented from harvesting all the fruits of his fertile imagination because he did not follow through with the logic of his own argument—to discover how female choice influenced the origin of the hominids; that is, to show how sexual selection was important at the very onset of human evolution. Because of an unfortunate blind spot engendered by his own cultural background, Darwin was unable to explicate the necessary interrelationships and carry his work on to its more logical conclusion.

EIGHT

Evidence on the transition: what can the earliest hominid fossils reveal about the ancestral population and the transition?

Are there transitional fossils?

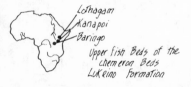

ATTEMPTS to verify the existence of hominids earlier than 4 million years ago have proved frustrating. Possible candidates include finds from Baringo, Lothagam, and Kanapoi in eastern Africa. All of these sites are in Kenya to the west and south of Lake Turkana (formerly known as Lake Rudolf). These very scanty but somewhat hominid-like and therefore suggestive fossils, mostly dental remains except for an arm bone and a piece from the side of the skull, all date from the Late Miocene or the Pliocene from about 6.5 million to 4 million years ago. The relative sequences of these early sites can be determined from faunal correlations (White and Harris, 1977). These sequences (Figure 8:1) are consistent with paleomagnetic evidence and the available absolute dates (Cooke, 1978).

By this period, at the end of the Miocene and during the Pliocene, the eastern African Rift System was well established (see Figure 3:5). Conceivably, the ridges and depressions of the rift system itself and the dry expanses that formed in its rain shadow, along with the lakes and rivers of the region, constituted geographic barriers that resulted in geographic isolation for a population of ancestral apes (Kortlandt, 1978). Genetic changes may have occurred in a spatially isolated transitional population; this in turn may have led to reproductive isolation. During this period, the Mio-Pliocene of about 6 million to 4 million years ago (from which the early hominid-like fossils date), woodlands may still have been fairly widespread in eastern Africa, with savannas not becoming extensive until toward the end of the period, about Plio-Pleistocene times (J. A. H. Van Couvering, 1975; Butzer, 1978).

169

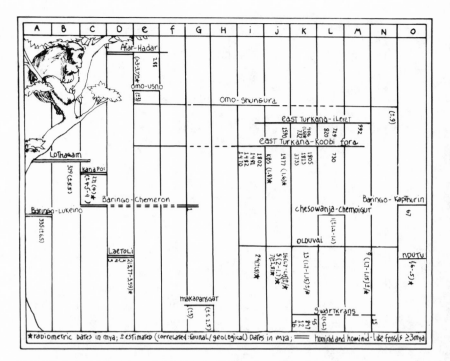

FIGURE 8:1. African hominid sites (with numbers of selected specimens) ordered and correlated according to fossil suid ("pig") phylogenetic sequences (*A* through *O*). Very early sites, 3 Mya or older, are indicated by double lines whereas later sites have single lines. Dashed lines indicate periods for which suid fossils are absent. Available dates are in parentheses.

An early hominid-like find is the crown of one lower molar tooth from the Lukeino Formation in the Baringo area, currently dated about 6.5 million years ago (Pickford, 1975). The site was probably a lake margin setting. The setting, given the period and the site's closeness to water, may have been wooded. The tooth (KNM LU335) is a left lower molar, somewhat water rolled, with roots missing. The tooth enamel is very thick, often thought to be an adaptation for heavy chewing; it shares this feature both with the ramapithecids (see Chapter 3) and with australopithecines, the early hominids. The tooth is considerably smaller than that of later australopithecine fossils. It is most similar to chimpanzee molars in size. The surface grooves on the top of the tooth have a dryopithecine (i.e., Miocene "ape") Y configuration. Cusp proportions are very similar to modern chimpanzees' (McHenry and Corruccini, 1980). Although there are also some resemblances to hominid teeth in this molar's shape, McHenry and Corruccini's recent study demonstrates that these resemblances are simply shared primitive features, not derived hominid traits. This molar tooth bears most resemblance to those of pongids.

Slightly more data are available at Lothagam Hill. This is a riverine setting. Remains of a diverse fauna indicate considerable environmental diversity (Howell, 1978a). Here, part of a hominid-like mandible with one molar tooth and roots of other molars were found by Patterson in 1966. It does not have a secure date, but a reasonable date of about 5.5 million years ago has been suggested. Initially the fossil was provisionally classified as *Australopithecus* sp. cf. *A. africanus* (Patterson et al., 1970), in other words, as an early gracile hominid. Since then, measurements from the Lothagam mandible fragment and tooth have been compared with those from living apes. According to Eckhardt (1977:356) "16 repeatable measurements taken on a cast of the Lothagam specimen all fall within the range of a small sample (N = 75) of living chimpanzees and gorillas." Eckhardt also states that the mandible articulates closely with the palate of a Miocene fossil ape — a large dryopithecine, UPM26-11, from Moroto, Uganda. This information does not, therefore, support an interpretation of the Lothagam jaw fragment as an early hominid. McHenry and Corruccini's recent measurements, however, put the "Lothagam Hill specimen . . . intermediate between *Pan* and the earliest australopithecine . . . *A. afarensis* . . . The Lothagam fossil . . . does share some derived traits unique to known early members of Hominidae" (1980:398). It seems quite possible, then, that this fossil could represent either the ancestral ape line *or* be a remnant of the transitional population.

Part of what could well be an early hominid upper arm bone (humerus) was found at Kanapoi associated with the remains of a number of other animals (Patterson and Howells, 1967); all are dated about 4 million years ago (Behrensmeyer, 1976).[1] Unfortunately, an upper arm bone is not very informative because the arms of the early hominids remained far more conservative than the pelvis, lower limbs, and foot. This piece of humerus could be an early hominid upper arm bone, but it is hard to tell for sure because this is a part of the skeleton that changed little in the ape–human divergence.

A fragment from the side of the skull (a temporal bone) was found in the Upper Fish Beds of the Chemeron Beds at Baringo; it probably dates from

[1] Initially, dating at Kanapoi was problematic: Faunal evidence suggested a date of 4.5 Mya to 4 Mya whereas the basalt cap above the fossil deposits had originally been dated at less than 3 Mya, a date that seemed too recent for the associated fauna (Patterson et al., 1970). A redating of the Kanapoi basalt has now yielded a date of about 4 Mya, which is compatible with the faunal evidence (Behrensmeyer, 1976).

Date (Mya)	Sites in eastern Africa	Remains found
4 or less (estimated)	Baringo, Chemeron Beds (Upper Fish)	Skull fragment (temporal bor
4.5–4 (faunal and K/Ar dates)	Kanapoi	Upper arm fragment (humeru
5.5 (estimated)	Lothagam	Jaw fragment (mandible) anc tooth
6.5 (estimated)	Baringo, Lukeino Formation	One lower molar tooth

less than 4 million years ago. In a number of respects it resembles early gracile australopithecines, although some ape-like features are still apparent (Martyn and Tobias, 1967).

In sum, a few eastern African fossils dating from before 4 million years ago have been identified as possible hominids by some investigators. They are all candidates for transitional status. Faunal correlations and absolute dates make it feasible to depict the relative time sequence of these early sites. The earliest is a 6.5 million-year-old tooth from Baringo that is quite ape-like. Next is part of an upper jaw and a tooth at Lothagam that is about 5.5 million years old. It has now been shown to be very similar in both shape and measurements to those of apes but also to show important resemblances with early hominids. It could be a late ape, or a member of the transitional population, beginning to show some of the changes that would occur in the origin of the hominid line. A humerus fragment at Kanapoi from about 4 million years ago might or might not be hominid; so too for a piece from the side of the head at Baringo (probably dating from 4 million years ago or less).

The location of these few Mio-Pliocene remains discovered at Lothagam, Kanapoi, and Baringo-Lukeino that date from before 4 million years ago, as well as of the much more plentiful finds from Laetoli and the Afar Depression (Hadar Formation), discussed below, dating between about 3.7

Current classification	Comments
Uncertain	Transitional/early gracile hominid? Australopithe-cine-like, but not robust
Uncertain	Transitional/early gracile hominid? Quite hominid-like; large, but different from robust forms
Uncertain, possibly *Homin-dae indet*	Transitional population? Many ape, as well as significant hominid, features
Uncertain, probably *Homin-oidea indet*	Ancestral population? Many pongid features

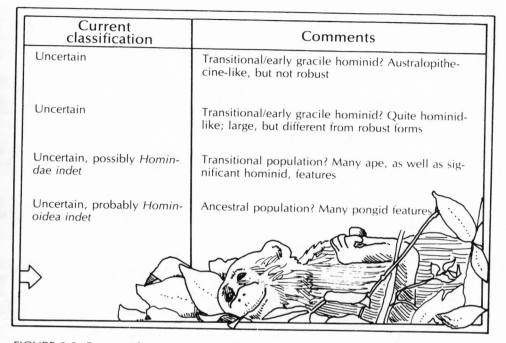

FIGURE 8:2. Eastern Africa: early hominid-like remains before 4 Mya. At present, these are the only available fossil candidates for possible transitional status.

million and 3 million years ago, is of real interest. All these early remains were found just east of the central African tropical forests, in the eastern rift valley system. This is very close to where early Miocene ape fossils have been found. Today, African apes are spread throughout the lowland tropical forest belt to the west of the sites; and chimpanzee ranges extend somewhat eastward into savanna woodlands not very far from the sites of the early hominid-like fossils (see Figure 8:3).

There are, in short, two things that are significant concerning these meager Mio-Pliocene finds—possibly late ancestral ape, possibly transitional, possibly very early hominid remains. First, they are located in the same general area as much earlier Miocene ape fossils and immediately to the east of the range of today's African apes. Second, they resemble both subsequent hominid fossils and the African apes.

Footprints at Laetoli: bipedalism—the mark of hominid status

Footprints, preserved in volcanic ash, and fossil hominid remains were unearthed at Laetoli in the Laetolil Formation near the Garusi River south-

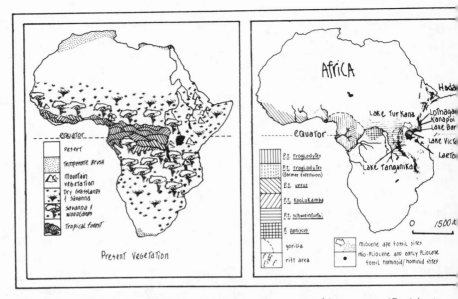

FIGURE 8:3. Ranges of various species of contemporary chimpanzees (*Pan*) juxtaposed with the sites where Miocene "ape" remains and early hominid and hominid-like fossils have been found. Some chimpanzees live in a mosaic savanna-forest environment. If the ancestral population had a similar ecological range, physical access to the mosaic savanna of eastern Africa existed. This is where the earliest hominid-like and hominid fossils are found.

west of Olduvai Gorge in Tanzania. Of all known hominid remains, the Laetoli finds are the closest to what one might expect, at the end of the transition, for very early basal hominids (Figure 8:4). A number of potassium-argon dates have been obtained that define the lower and upper limits for the age of the deposits in which the remains were found; dates average 3.77 million years ago for the lower limit and 3.59 million years ago for the upper limit (M. D. Leakey et al., 1976; White, 1977).

The footprints—two similar sets close together plus one rather different set in a different place—tell a remarkable story. Let us consider the two adjacent sets of footprints first. These are the footprints of two fully upright, two-legged creatures striding along in a strikingly human manner (White, 1980). "The best preserved print . . . shows the raised arch, rounded heel, pronounced ball, and forward pointing big toe necessary for walking erect. Pressures exerted along the foot [as well as the length between the steps, compared to the creature's size] attest to the striding gait" (M. D. Leakey, 1979:452). It is this feature that determines their hominid status. The Laetoli finds—footprints and fossils—are the earliest remains that are fully established as hominids (Figure 8:5).

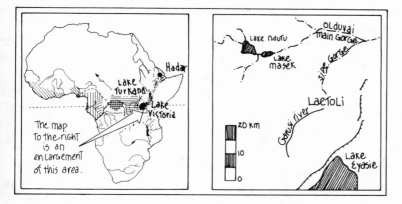

FIGURE 8:4. Laetoli and Afar (Hadar Formation). The basal hominid, *Australo-pithecus afarensis,* was discovered at these two sites. The basal hominid remains found at Laetoli date from about 3.77–3.59 Mya, and at Afar from some 3 Mya.

Important though this is, what is even more fascinating is that clues to social behavior are evident in these footprints. These clues are consistent with the behavior the model presented here predicts. The prints are of different size, the smaller possibly female, the larger perhaps male. The prints are very close together, too close for them to have traveled side by side (Figure 8:5). Furthermore, the smaller prints were made during or immediately after a light rain and therefore are sharp and clear. The larger prints apparently were made when most of the ground was dry but in one place slightly moist—thus, probably either a while after or a while before the rain. These latter larger prints are therefore somewhat blurred, save for the clear one made in one slightly moist space (M. D. Leakey, 1979).

Those are the facts. From them an artist drew a man (carrying a stick) walking immediately in front of a woman for Mary Leakey's article, "Footprints in the Ashes of Time," in the *National Geographic* (1979). Leakey's words in no way suggest this artistic imagery. Indeed, the evidence is quite to the contrary. The "woman" (smaller prints) seems to have traveled by herself, in or right after the rain, capable of walking alone on the savanna—just as the model for the transition presented in this book suggests was feasible due both to social structural flexibility and to early woman's ability to use tools to defend herself. The "man" (larger prints), who also walked along the same way, went at a somewhat different time—either before the rain or some time after it, when most of the ground was quite dry, with only one spot damp enough for one of his footprints to also be clear and distinct.

The third set of footprints is rather strange. Here too the great toe is situated as in the human foot (M. D. Leakey and Hay, 1979), rather than

Date (Mya)	Site in eastern Africa	Remains found
3.77–3.59, (K/Ar date)	Laetoli, near Garusi River, Tanzania; Laetolil Beds	Fragment of palate (maxi (1938–1939) 22 individuals: teeth and (maxilla and mandibles); fragments; ribs; hand, arr and leg bones (1974–pre Hominid footprints (1976–present)

opposed like a thumb, as is the ape great toe. But these footprints are much broader than the two other sets, in proportions almost resembling a hand more than a foot. Further, the gait was rather shambling and the steps much shorter than even those for the smaller ("female") hominid in the other trail (M. D. Leakey and Hay, 1979). This creature had a hominid-like toe, but it clearly was not striding along effectively like the other two. Is this third set the footprints of a remnant of the transitional population – one for whom bipedalism was not yet fully evolved? So little is known that it is almost too soon to even ask this question. Yet, should the answer prove to be yes, it could be that at Laetoli we have a glimpse of the end of the transition – of a population literally becoming human.

In this respect, it is relevant to recall what was happening at this time to

Current classification	Comments
Australopithecus afarensis (originally "*Meganthropus africanus*") *Australopithecus afarensis*	Early basal hominid; gracile; rather similar to *A. africanus*, but not identical; sexual dimorphism possibly greater than for later hominids; small molars; canines and incisors quite large; jaw protrudes
Australopithecus afarensis	Two sets of hominid footprints at one site; one set smaller (female?), the other set larger (male?): condition of prints indicates they traveled separately and at different times, the former when the ground was wet, the latter when it was drier; form of foot and stride are those of an upright, fully effective biped; great toe parallel to other toes

FIGURE 8:5. Eastern Africa: basal hominid remains at Laetoli, about 3.77–3.59 Mya. These are the earliest known hominids. They are clearly bipedal. with an However, their dentition retains important ape-like features. The jaw protrudes, and the incisors and canines are still quite large. Sexual dimorphism may also be greater than for later hominids.

the eastern African environment. Woodlands may have still been extensive in the Mio-Pliocene of approximately 6 million to 5 million years ago. But by the time hominid fossils appear at Laetoli, after 4 million years ago, this particular area, at least, was already savanna: The sediments are wind worked, and the associated animal bones are those adapted to dry savanna grasslands (Howell, 1978a). And by the Plio-Pleistocene of some 3.5 million to 1.5 million years ago, most of eastern Africa was already largely savanna (J. A. H. Van Couvering, 1975; Butzer, 1978).[2] From the available evidence, it is entirely feasible that a transitional ape/hominid population first became geographically and reproductively isolated from ancestral apes somewhere in the eastern African rift zone, then was subsequently exposed to a shifting environment, with increasing amounts of grasslands. Behavior (and subsequently anatomy) would then also change, as this late transitional/early hominid population began to learn how to traverse and utilize relatively open country (Figure 8:6). The first changes may well have been the development of gathering with tools and its anatomical correlate, bipedalism. Once bipedalism was fully developed, gathering could, of course, become more effective.

Thus, at Laetoli, we have very early hominids in the savanna. Some of them, at least, were fully effective bipeds. What else were they? To answer this, we must look at the fossils themselves.

Dental remains at Laetoli and Afar (Hadar): clues to a pongid ancestry and the new hominid adaptation

The first find was made in 1938–1939 when Kohl-Larson discovered a small fragment of an upper jaw, or maxilla.[3] Since 1974, fossil parts of 22 further individuals — teeth, mandibles and a maxilla, skull fragments, ribs, plus hand, arm, and leg bones — were discovered in the Laetolil Formation by Mary Leakey and associates. They initially termed this form *Homo*, that is our own genus. Presumably this was because of its comparatively small premolars and molars, (M. D. Leakey et al., 1976), which are smaller than those of many gracile and all robust australopithecines (Johanson and White, 1979). They did note, however, "some primitive traits concordant with its great age" (M. D. Leakey et al., 1976:464). These primitive traits are indeed primitive: a large, somewhat projecting,

---

[2] Savanna includes expanses of grassland, patches of bush, and woodlands, with gallery forests along rivers and around lakes. It is a mosaic environment.

[3] This maxillary fragment was originally called *Meganthropus africanus*. Robinson (1953) later forcefully pointed out similarities with the southern African gracile hominid now termed *Australopithecus africanus*. (Of the many early hominid fossils that have been discovered in Africa, most are currently assigned to the genus *Australopithecus*, and many are further classified into gracile or robust variants.) Some 25 years later, after many further fossil discoveries, a strong case was made for considering the finds at Laetoli, Tanzania, and those dating from a roughly similar period at another site, Hadar in the Afar Depression, Ethiopia, members of a distinct — and the earliest known — hominid lineage, *Australopithecus afarensis* (Johanson, White, and Coppens, 1978; Johanson and White, 1979). Although this early basal hominid lineage exhibits considerable variability, the case for its distinctiveness is quite convincing. A wide range of features fall *between* those previously thought to distinguish apes from the human line (Le Gros Clark, 1950; Johanson and White, 1979).

sharp canine; large, procumbent incisors; and generally protruding jaws (White, 1977; Johanson, White, and Coppens, 1978). *Such features are extremely reminiscent of ape dental configuration.* The relatively small size of the molars and premolars, although probably already showing significant expansion, is also still somewhat reminiscent of the undoubtedly even smaller molars and premolars of the ape ancestor.[4]

For a model that posits a comparatively recent divergence between apes and humans, the Laetoli finds are true gems. The dentition, in particular, still retains notable similarities to that of the apes. At Laetoli there is clear evidence that the sepa-

FIGURE 8:6. A chimpanzee standing upright, looking over tall grasses in the mixed forest-savanna of Gombe National Park, Tanzania. Over time the transitional population may have moved out from environments similar to this into eastern African savannas with a greater proportion of grasslands.

---

[4] The average premolar grinding surface ($P_3 + P_4$, combined upper and lower) for common chimpanzees is only 79 mm^2 and for pygmy chimpanzees only 58 mm^2, whereas it is 104 mm^2 for *A. afarensis*. For molars, the average grinding surface for common chimpanzees is 106 mm^2 (M_1, M_2, and M_3, upper and lower); for pygmy chimpanzees it is 87 mm^2 (M_1, M_2, and M_3, upper and lower); and for *A. afarensis* it is 178 mm^2 (M_1, M_2, and M_3, upper and lower) (Mahler, 1973; Johanson, 1974; Johanson and White, 1979). For the "gracile" *A. africanus*, the average premolar grinding surface ($P_3 + P_4$, upper and lower) is 114 mm^2 (Wolpoff, 1971). *A. africanus*'s average molar grinding surface (M_1, M_2, and M_3, upper and lower) is 199 mm^2 (Wolpoff, 1971). In sum, if the ape ancestor had premolar and molar grinding surfaces as small as common and/or pygmy chimpanzees, *A. afarensis* already shows considerable expansion of cheek teeth grinding surface — though still less than the subsequent *A. africanus*.

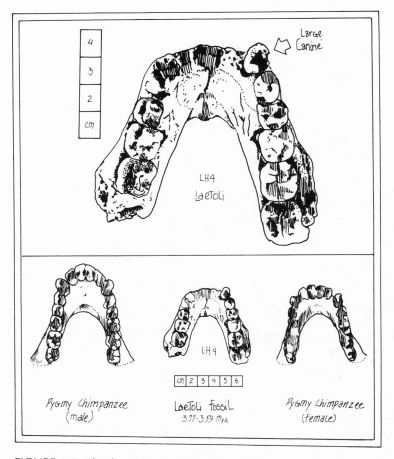

FIGURE 8:7. This basal hominid jaw (LH4) from Laetoli, Tanzania, has a fairly large canine. This jaw is among the earliest confirmed hominid fossils in Africa and dates from about 3.77–3.59 Mya. Note the striking similarities in canine teeth and in overall shape and size between this basal hominid jaw and the jaws of pygmy chimpanzees.

ration between ape and human had already occurred: The fossil footprints attest to that. But the dentition demonstrates significant pongid affinities (Johanson, White, and Coppens, 1978; Johanson and White, 1979).

The overall similarities of jaw and tooth proportions between the Laetoli fossils and pygmy chimpanzees, for example, are striking (Figure 8:7). The fossil canine of the Laetoli form is larger than that of living humans or later australopithecine fossils but smaller than the canines of most great apes. The canine size is, however, quite comparable to that of pygmy chimpanzees.

Nonetheless, the Laetoli fossil jaw and pygmy chimpanzee jaws do appear to differ in the somewhat greater prognathism of the pygmy chimpanzee. This somewhat more pronounced protrusion of the pygmy chimpanzee jaw as compared to the Laetoli jaw — despite the fact that the front part of the Laetoli fossil jaw protrudes further than for later hominids — is doubtless significant. It may well be related to distinct and fairly recent dietary differences of the newly speciated hominids from their ape ancestors. The chimpanzee jaw is adapted to a shearing motion for fruit eating. The relative proportions of the Laetoli fossil jaw, with the somewhat reduced prognathism, perhaps already show some initial adaptation for heavier cheek teeth (molar and premolar) usage for chewing tough savanna roots and seeds. The rather extreme chippage and wear on the canine tooth (M. D. Leakey et al., 1976) is, therefore, unsurprising. Although still bearing important resemblances to apes, these jaws were being used differently.

The Hadar Formation in the Afar Triangle or Depression, Ethiopia, is also very early (dating from at least 3 to some 3.7 million years ago) and has produced surprisingly complete and well-preserved hominid fossils (Aronson et al., 1977; Cooke, 1978b; Johanson and Edey, 1981). Parts of what is now the Afar Depression were once occupied by lakes, and there was apparently a fairly rapid but extremely gentle sedimentation process (Taieb et al., 1976). This accounts for the unusually complete fossils and interesting variability found there.

At its earlier end, the Hadar Formation overlaps the Laetolil Formation (see Figure 8:1) in terms of fossil suid ("pig") correlations (White and Harris, 1977). At its more recent end, fossil suids of the Hadar Formation appear to be contemporaries of those in the Usno and early Shungura formations at Omo (see Chapter 10). This is very significant information, for the remains at Hadar, like those at Laetoli, appear more "primitive" — closer to the transitional and ancestral populations — than those of most other (and more recent) australopithecines (Figure 8:8). All the Hadar (like the Laetoli) remains are now termed *A. afarensis* (Johanson, White, and Coppens, 1978; Johanson and White, 1979).[5] Of the many other australo-

---

[5] Before systematic comparison of the Laetoli and Hadar fossils and, in particular, before either were compared with apes to assess the possible ancestral qualities of these fossils, various fossils among them were tentatively identified (see Figure 8:8) as gracile australopithecines (*A. africanus*), as robust australopithecines, and as *Homo* on the basis of similarities with subsequent southern and eastern African fossils (Johanson and Taieb, 1976; Johanson et al., 1976; M. D. Leakey et al., 1976). This does speak to a certain variability among these early hominids. That these earlier, ancestral hominids (*A. afarensis*) should exhibit a range of similarities with various descendants is not, however, surprising.

Strata	Level/Date	Remains
KADA HADAR ★288 LUCY	Kada Hadar	"Lucy"—partial skeleton, including pelvic bones: AL288-1
★188 ★241 ★★★333,333 w ★★ 333x Denen DORA	Denen Dora	Right lower jaw fragment: AL188-1; left lower molar: AL241-14
		Several individuals— jaw parts, teeth, partial crania, postcranials: AL333, AL333W, AL333X
		Molar: AL161-40; mandible: AL207-13; molar: AL366-1; molar: AL388-1
★211 ★266 Sidi HAKOMA ★277 ★228 ★128,129,166 ★198,199,200 Below 10m. BASAL	Sidi Hakoma	Right leg (femoral) fragment: AL211-1
	Basalt layer At least 3 Mya to about 3.7 Mya	Part lower jaw: AL266-1
		Left lower jaw fragment with canine: AL277-1
		Leg (distal femur): AL228-1
		Skull side (temporal) fragment: AL166-9
		Postcranial material (femoral and tibial parts, ischium), mandible: AL128, 129
		Half lower jaw; 3 teeth: AL198
		Partial upper jaw (maxilla): AL199-1
		Complete upper jaw with teeth (maxilla): AL200-1; associated molar
		Distal humerus: AL137-48a; distal ulna: AL137-48b; mandible and teeth: AL145-35; mandible: AL311-1; distal humerus: AL322-1; mandible and tooth: AL400-1; mandible: AL411-1

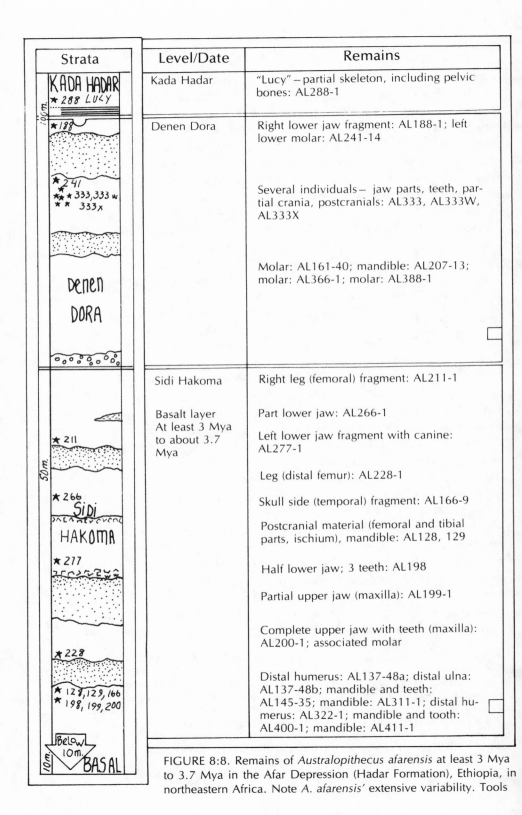

FIGURE 8:8. Remains of *Australopithecus afarensis* at least 3 Mya to 3.7 Mya in the Afar Depression (Hadar Formation), Ethiopia, in northeastern Africa. Note *A. afarensis'* extensive variability. Tools

Comments

Resembles Laetoli basal hominids; rather like gracile *A. africanus* from Sterkfontein but more primitive, particularly in aspects of mandible and pelvis

Molars heavily worn; resembles *A. africanus*

Children and adults, possibly of both sexes; they apparently died together, perhaps in a flash flood; previously called "*Homo* family"

No information available

$\Rightarrow$

Upper leg similar to other australopithecine remains

Front rounded, sides straight, then flare; resembles "*Homo*"

Heavy dental wear; canine worn flat; resembles "*Homo*"

Upper leg not large; smaller than AL129-1A

Skull side rather large

Very small; postcranial remains show striking similarities to AL288-1, "Lucy," 80m above; resembles, but more primitive than, later gracile *A. africanus*

Heavy wear on molars and a premolar

Large canines; broad incisors; protruding front teeth; similar to complete AL200-1 upper jaw but smaller

U-shaped upper jaw: slightly rounded front arc, tooth rows parallel; large canines; broad incisors; protruding front teeth; considerable tooth wear and chippage

No information available

$\Rightarrow$

have also been found in the Hadar Formation, in the upper part of the Kada Hadar Member, about a half million years younger than the more recent fossils.

pithecine remains known in eastern and southern Africa (to be discussed in Chapter 10), only the earliest remains at Omo (dating from about 3 million years ago) could conceivably also be classified as *A. afarensis* (Howell, pers. com.).

The most remarkable find is "Lucy," a small female only about 110 or 120 centimeters tall who died when she was about 20 years old (Figure 8:9). Some 40 percent of her skeleton is preserved (Johanson and White, 1979). Lucy's skeleton, like the footprints at Laetoli and other remains at Hadar, confirms the bipedalism of this early population (Johanson, Taieb, et al., 1978).

Clues to social behavior can also be discerned at Hadar. The remains of several individuals—children and at least five adults—have been found in one spot (Johanson, 1976; Howell, 1978a). They died together—suddenly, possibly in a flash flood—and therefore presumably associated when alive as well (Johanson, 1976). This group was living in eastern Africa some 3 million years ago, at a time when the environmental shift from woodlands and forest to savanna was probably already underway (J. A. H. Van Couvering, 1975; Butzer, 1978). The small size of this group is reminiscent of group size (15 to 40) for chimpanzees traveling together in a comparatively arid region in Ugalla, Tanzania (Itani, 1979; see Chapter 5). For those particular chimpanzees, the group size was somewhat smaller (with population density much smaller) and the area traversed for

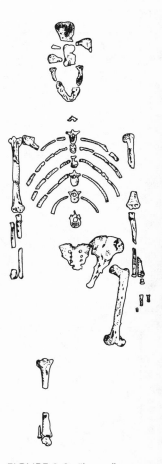

FIGURE 8:9. "Lucy," an exceptionally complete skeleton of a very early hominid (*A. afarensis*) from the Hadar Formation, Afar Depression, Ethiopia. Dated nearly 3 to about 3.5 Mya, this is the earliest known skeleton of *Australopithecus* (AL288).

food far more extensive than for chimpanzees living in the tropical forest. The Ugalla, Tanzania, environment is exceptionally arid for chimpanzees. But for early hominids such an environment may not have been particularly unusual. Small, flexible, and very wide-ranging groups (along with gathering and bipedalism) would be advantageous to early hominids adapting to an expanding savanna. Resources were scattered and not extensive. The new environment required cognitive mapping of food sources, collection of sufficient quantities to feed the young when food was not immediately available, a locomotor system that could traverse extensive areas, and groups that were not so large as to overburden food supplies.

With the dietary changes consequent to gathering on the savanna came changes in the dentition. In many important respects, similarities to the ancestral apes remained (see Figure 8:10). But indications that the teeth were already being used differently exist (Kimbel, 1979). There is also considerable variability in dental and other features—hints that this was a population undergoing change.

An almost full upper jaw (AL200) and a half upper jaw (AL199) are among the earliest remains at Hadar. These jaws evince pronounced ape-like characteristics. (AL200, because it is most complete, will be discussed in detail and is pictured in Figure 8:10. AL199 appears very similar but is significantly smaller.) For example, there still is a small space between the four front incisors and the canine teeth. Such a diastema, as it is called, usually provides space in ape jaws for the protruding canines from the lower jaw when the mouth is shut. Consistent with what can be inferred from the slight diastema, the upper jaw also shows rather substantial upper canines. In addition, the jaw itself protrudes considerably. Therefore, its shape resembles that of a long U (with rectangle-like dimensions), and in this respect it approaches ape jaw shapes instead of being rounded and short (with square-like dimensions) as human jaws are today (see Figure 8:10). The pronounced protrusion of this Afar (Hadar Formation) upper jaw (AL200) is ape-like. So too is the large upper canine and the fact that spacing of the upper teeth still appears adapted to a relatively large lower canine. The dental characteristics of AL200, in particular, suggest that the ape–human divergence may not have been very far in the past.

Similarly, cranial features of *A. afarensis* are more "primitive" than those of later australopithecines and exhibit many similarities with chimpanzees (Kimbel, 1979). Preliminary measurements of cranial capacity range from about 385 cubic centimeters to 450 cubic centimeters for adults—larger than for chimpanzees but at the lowest end of the range for subsequent australopithecines (Holloway, pers. com. to Kimbel, 1979).

When taken together, these [cranial and dental] features present a distinctive and highly generalized craniofacial pattern, one which is indicative of a considerable amount of anterior tooth use as well as the capability for producing enormous masticatory force at the molar row . . .

The morphology of the Hadar crania combines with the primitive nature of the teeth and mandibles to suggest that *A. afarensis* may bridge

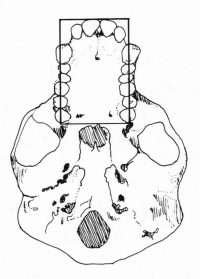

Chimpanzee
Pan Troglodytes Troglodytes

Hominid fossil
AL 200-Hadar (3-3.7 mya)

the gap between Miocene hominoids [Miocene "apes"] and other hominid species of the [later] Plio/Pleistocene. [Kimbel, 1979: 454]

Overall, craniodental features are markedly similar to those of both Miocene and contemporary apes but also show important resemblances to later hominids.

The Hadar canines — like those at Laetoli — are large and chipped (Johanson et al., 1976; Johanson and Taieb, 1976; Johanson, Taieb, et al., 1978). Apparently they interfered with effective grinding and chewing. Electron microscope study of the front teeth, including canines, shows some ribbonlike wear similar to what is seen in apes (Johanson, Taieb, et al., 1978; Ryan, 1979; Ryan, pers. com.). But more impressive are indications of important crushing and grinding activities (Ryan, 1979). Whereas chimpanzees use their procumbent front teeth primarily to grab and shear fruit, the front teeth of these basal hominids — although still physically resembling those of apes in important respects — were already involved in crushing and grinding. In other words, these very early hominids at about 3 million years ago might have done a lot of chewing and grinding of savanna vegetation, but without a fully effective dental apparatus. Remember, behavior changes before anatomy.

These properties invite an important question: Could these dental characteristics still be somewhat transitional in form — the teeth and jaws of a

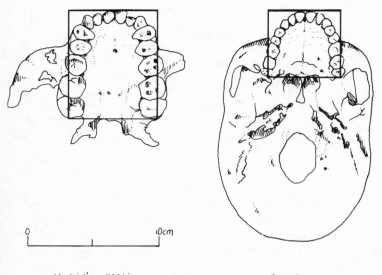

Hominid Fossil
Oh 5 "Zinj"- Olduvai (2.0-1.7mya)

Bantu
Homo sapiens sapiens

FIGURE 8:10. The basal hominid upper jaw found at Hadar in the Afar Triangle (AL200) still exhibits important ape-like features, especially in the large canine and the jaw's overall shape. A later robust australopithecine jaw found at Olduvai Gorge (OH5) has a more human-like shape but is much larger.

very early hominid, not yet completely adapted in terms of structure to chewing the gritty, tough vegetable food of the savannas?[6]

Evidence for pongid ancestors and the gathering hypothesis from ape and human saliva: evolutionary and dietary aspects of salivary proteins in primates

Humans and apes share a fascinating feature in, of all places, their saliva (Azen et al., 1978). This feature is a set of salivary proteins – the Pb proteins and related PPb (or post-Pb) protein. The Pb proteins are thought to make tooth enamel more resistant to decay caused by large amounts of plant carbohydrate and/or a high variety of texture in the diet (Azen et al.,

[6] The size of the robust temporal fragment, AL166–9 (Johanson et al., 1976), presumably from the same population, might indicate that jaw muscles were already beginning to enlarge. This must be considered a possibility only. The fragment also bears important resemblances to that part of the skull on chimpanzees (White, pers. com.). It will be some time before it is feasible to definitely sort out all the resemblances of *A. afarensis* to forms that may have evolved from it (e.g., later australopithecines), from those similarities to apes that, in turn, may resemble the ancestral ape-like population from which *A. afarensis,* itself, evolved.

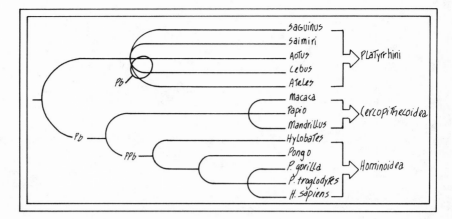

FIGURE 8:11. The Pb proteins in saliva may interact with tooth enamel to make it more resistant to dental caries caused by large amounts of plant carbohydrate and/or texture in the diet. The diagram illustrates the postulated evolution in ape and human saliva of the Pb proteins and related PPb protein (which their salivas share). The arrangement of species from top to bottom tends to follow a dietary gradient from predominantly insectivorous (*Saguinus* and *Saimiri*) to largely frugivorous-folivorous. The omnivorous humans are the only exceptions.

1978). In the course of primate evolution, there seems to have been a relationship between the evolution of the salivary Pb proteins (their increasing complexity) and related PPb protein (which may have arisen through Pb gene duplication), the reduction of dental cingula (enamel ridges at the bases of tooth crowns related to type of mastication and, therefore, diet), increasing body size, and the shift from a highly insectivorous to a predominantly frugivorous-folivorous diet. In other words, the complexity of the Pb proteins among primates follows a dietary gradient. So too do the reduction of dental cingula and increasing body size. The evolution of these salivary proteins along this gradient — predominantly insectivorous to predominantly frugivorous-folivorous — is illustrated in Figure 8:11. Apes and humans share relatively complex Pb proteins and the PPb protein. All the apes are predominantly frugivorous-folivorous, whereas humans are omnivorous. What this means is that certain aspects of the diet did not change sufficiently in the process of becoming human for there to be strong selection for a change in salivary proteins from that of the ape-like ancestors. Early humans shared with the apes saliva proteins useful in a diet having a great deal of plant carbohydrate and/or texture. This model suggests that the foods gathered by the early hominids had both. That human saliva proteins still resemble those of the apes is consistent with the

FIGURE 8:12. Possible types of early gathering. Here, one female uses a stick to dig for edible roots while another picks acacia-like pods.

strong probability that gathered plant food remained extremely important throughout human evolution.[7]

Models and data: a remarkable fit

A fairly recent ape-like ancestor has been hypothesized. Both the fossils before 4 million years ago and the exciting Laetoli and Afar (Hadar Formation) finds support this hypothesis. Primary reliance on plant food, with early tools invented by females for gathering, is a key feature of the model (Figure 8:12). The plant food reliance of apes and human gatherer-hunters is well documented. Salivary data, showing complex Pb proteins and the PPb protein for both humans and apes, support the inference of plant food primacy. The evidence is also clear regarding female chimpanzees' significantly more frequent preparation and use of tools in food getting (albeit, in the case of chimpanzees, for insect gathering). Male chimpanzees simply do not use tools as often to obtain food, a fact consistent with the lesser nutritional stress on males. Further, there is no question but what mother chimpanzees share food with their offspring. That tool-using, plant-gathering early hominid mothers would do likewise is extremely probable. Also of interest are data on sexual dimorphism. Several remains at Laetoli and Hadar exhibit notable size differences – for example, the footprints at Laetoli and the upper jaws AL200 and AL199 at Hadar. These differences in size can be interpreted as due to sexual dimorphism (Johanson and White, 1979). These size differences appear greater than those between the sexes for humans today. However, the canine teeth do not appear to exhibit as pronounced dimorphism as among most living primates (Johanson and White, 1979). Quite possibly, then, *A. afarensis* had already undergone some reduction of sexual dimorphism, and its descendants were to undergo even more. This is consistent with the selective processes hypothesized in Chapter 7: The gathering innovation led to increased maternal investment, which, in turn, was associated with preferential female sexual selection of males who, among other things, appeared less physically frightening or threatening to the females.

Thus, in brief, the characteristics of the basal hominid, *A. afarensis,* are consistent with the model's predictions. Because very few data on *A. afarensis* were available when work on this model was beginning (Zihlman and Tanner, 1974; Tanner, 1975; Tanner and Zihlman, 1976a), it has been especially exciting and gratifying to follow the course of research on these basal hominids.

[7] Predominantly frugivorous-folivorous primate species, as compared to those that are largely insectivorous (*Saguinus* and *Saimiri*), also have reduced dental cingula. This correlates with the differences in diet and salivary protein complexity (Azen et al., 1978). It would therefore be interesting to know how *A. afarensis*'s dental cingula compare as well.

NINE

Gathering and the australopithecine way of life

HOWEVER abundant they may be in the fossil record, man did not live by teeth alone, and those who would analyze the fossils must understand the behavior of those who left the bones.

Sherwood L. Washburn, 1968a

DATA never speak for themselves; a framework for analysis is always necessary. But in the reconstruction of the way of life of the early hominids—the australopithecines[1]—the limitations of the fossil and archeological record make a framework for the interpretation of available information particularly critical. Any framework must, however, be continually tested against existing data and, especially, new data as they appear. It is, indeed, in the intimate interplay between pattern making and nit-picking attention to detail that science moves forward. As Kuhn (1962) has pointed out, data that are anomalous in one formulation but fit another are particularly significant in model building.

The approach taken here emphasizes the interrelationships of evolving mental and anatomical capacities, patterns of communication, social organization, technology, and environment. It is important to look both to biol-

---

[1] I am here using the term *Australopithecus* to delineate the earliest hominids, undoubtedly more than one line, dated roughly between 3.5 Mya and 1.5 Mya: from earlier to later, *A. afarensis, A. africanus, A. robustus/boisei,* and *A.* or *H. habilis.* Taxonomically, two or more lines have been identified, and they have variously been considered two to several species or even two genera (*Homo* and *Australopithecus*). At this time, however, I refer to them collectively as the genus *Australopithecus* because (1) they shared a number of anatomical and behavioral characteristics as part of their adaptation to the African savanna during the Plio-Pleistocene, and (2) they are differentiated as a group from apes by bipedalism, larger grinding teeth, smaller canines, and larger brains, but (3) still have considerably smaller brains than our own genus *Homo.* Where, precisely, to differentiate generically one of the lines from the succeeding *Homo erectus* is the taxonomic question, and it will probably not be resolved fully until more data exist. Recently, for example, R. E. F. Leakey et al. (1978) termed some fossils *Australopithecus* that they had previously called *Homo* (and that are still classified *Homo* by many scholars).

ogy — where this type of interaction is called "adaptation" — and to cultural anthropology, where "cultural ecology" is the relevant concept. No term has been coined for the domain that applies to the early hominids: Culture as we know it today did not yet exist, but some reliance on social tradition must be presumed. Nonetheless, from comparative studies of mammalian and particularly primate adaptation and of the ecological patterns of living peoples, the approximate range of phenomena can be delineated. In mammalian adaptation, technological elements are rare and true symbols probably nonexistent; among contemporary humans, technology and symbol-reliant behavior are fundamental. For the early hominids, the interaction between organism and environment was mediated by social organization, in turn facilitated by their developing communicatory range and a nascent technology. Symbolic components, especially in communication and tool making and using, were doubtless becoming significant but were much less developed or important than for *Homo erectus* or for humans today.

This chapter presents a model of the early hominid way(s) of life; the next chapter discusses the fossil remains, site by site, and examines the question of variation. This sequence is an artifact of the necessity for clarity in presentation. In actuality, of course, there has been a continuous interaction between data and ideas. My primary objective in this chapter is to present an overall description of early hominid lifeways; however, the particulars of certain fossils from specific sites are brought into the discussion from time to time.

I refer to the early hominids who lived in eastern and southern Africa (Figure 9:1) from roughly 3.7 million years ago to about 1.5 million years ago as *Australopithecus,* making use of both morphological and chronological criteria for this classification (Campbell, 1972b, 1973, 1978).[2] As used here, all early hominids prior to *Homo erectus* are australopithecines (Wolpoff, 1978b). All of these early hominid fossils exhibit a roughly similar level of evolutionary organization, but four varieties seem apparent. First, the very early *A. afarensis,* found from roughly 3.7 to 3.0 million years ago at Laetoli, Hadar, and possibly Omo in eastern Africa, still exhibited many similarities with pongids; yet this form was already clearly, effectively, bipedal. Then came the early "gracile" australopithecines (*A. africanus*) from

[2] Hominid-like fossil fragments dating prior to the first confirmed hominids at Laetoli at about 3.77 Mya to 3.59 Mya may also be australopithecines or may be remains of transitional or ancestral populations or, in some instances, of closely related "ape" (or pre-ape) lineages (see Chapters 3 and 8). Although the first known *Homo erectus* fossils date from about 1.5 Mya, australopithecines persist for some time after that.

about 3 million to 2 million years ago.[3] Finally, starting somewhat before 2 million years ago, two rather different "advanced" australopithecine forms appeared—the very robust form (*A. robustus/boisei*) and an advanced, larger-brained, and more gracile form, *A. habilis* (often called *Homo habilis*). Despite considerable variation within *Australopithecus* over its 2 million year tenure, there are enough similarities among these two-legged, small-brained fossils to speak of a generic adaptation. The available evidence indicates that all the early hominids were relatively small in brain and body, were bipedal, used tools, and probably ate primarily plant food. The basis for the early hominid adaptation was, most likely, an innovation in food getting: using tools in gathering food (Linton [Slocum], 1971; M. Harris, 1972; Teleki, 1975; Tanner and Zihlman, 1976a; Zihlman and Tanner, 1979; McGrew, 1979).

Although others have mentioned that early hominids probably gathered much of their food, until quite recently the prevailing idea underlying reconstructions of social behavior has been that *Australopithecus* was primarily a hunter. There are, however, considerable data that are anomalous from a hunting perspective. For their small size, all australopithecines— even the early basal hominids and the so-called gracile line—had powerful chewing and grinding capacities. This kind of chewing apparatus is best understood as an adaptation to a diet including a high proportion of tough, uncooked plant food. Further, given their small size and still very simple technology, it is improbable that they pursued, captured, and killed large dangerous animals with tools. The data on size, tools, and teeth do not fit a hunting model but make a great deal of sense when viewed within a gathering context.

There has been a misemphasis on hunting—that is, using tools to stop and kill moving animals—at this early stage of hominid evolution. Along with the premature emphasis on hunting has come a plethora of dubious assumptions: for example, the supposition of male-male bonding, assumed to have been developed for cooperation in hunting and in defense; similarly, the belief that males provided meat for and protection to females

---

[3] The gracile lineage bears closer similarities to later hominids, including ourselves, than does the robust lineage in that the cheek teeth (premolars and molars) of the gracile australopithecines and the musculature working their jaws is of only moderate size. In contrast, the robust lineage has much larger cheek teeth and a very robust jaw musculature, with muscles reaching up to the sides of the face and the top of the head where they are attached to prominent bony protruberances at the sides and top of the skull (DuBrul, 1977).

Interestingly, now that the earlier *A. afarensis* has been identified, it seems apparent that the early "gracile" line (*A. africanus*) had already evolved considerably along the same direction as later robust australopithecines (Johanson and White, 1979).

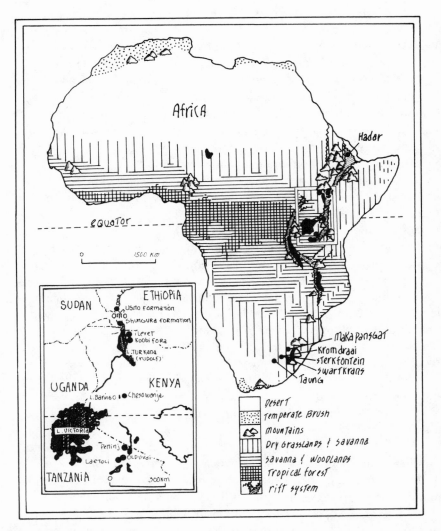

FIGURE 9:1. Australopithecine fossil sites in eastern and southern Africa. Evidence of the earliest confirmed bipedal hominids has been found at Laetoli, Tanzania, and Hadar, Afar Triangle, Ethiopia, in eastern Africa. These fossils date from roughly 3.5 Mya to 3 Mya. *Australopithecus* continues, spreads to southern Africa, and evolves. *Homo erectus* eventually appears about 1.5 Mya to 1 Mya at several sites in Africa.

with whom they had fathered offspring, and so to their own young. The presumption that females did not provide a significant degree of food or protection for themselves and their offspring apparently then followed. Reconstructions largely fail to make note of females in these contexts.

With the supposition that males were the providers of meat and were the defenders of females and young in the face of danger, the idea of a pair bond became intimately interwoven into the evolutionary saga, with our earliest hominid female forebears – much like American women of the 1940s and 1950s – relegated to a passive role in sexual, economic, techno-logical, protective, and even most social behaviors. Here is the evolution-ist version of the Adam and Eve story: a pair-bond mating system, with coterminous economic and mating units.

Male tool use related to hunting and protection frequently is referred to in popular and scholarly writing alike; female tool use has seldom been mentioned. Yet it seems highly probable that early hominid females made and used tools for digging up vegetable food, knocking down fruit and nuts, collecting insects and their products such as honey, and dividing plant and animal food. They also may have invented a simple container for carrying gathered food and a device for supporting infants. And it is very likely indeed that both sexes used tools for protection and eventually some butchering and that neither males nor females used tools in extensive big game hunting.

Here, in terms of the hunting model, is a case where popular writing has greatly exaggerated anything ever put forward by students of human evolu-tion. Yet, in terms of model building, it is a question of emphasis. The assumption of male tool use for hunting has – like the use of some of Darwin's phrases in Social Darwinism – become part of Western society's modern evolutionary "origin myth." For example, male hunting with tools has been seen as male killing with tools from very early in the human past and has been used to explain and, in a sense, legitimize male involvement in warfare. Warfare does indeed need study and explanation. The explana-tions will be far more complex, however, and warfare itself is probably quite a recent human invention – one that is associated with fairly large, organized human societies such as tribes and, in particular, nation-states. At any rate, we have here an example of one sort of modern evolutionary myth making that has been associated with a hunting model.

Tight social organization has been supposed necessary for protection on the "exposed" savanna. The argument that there is safety in numbers has had as its implicit corollary that males, and cooperation among them, were necessary for protection. But what about the surprise that upright hominid

FIGURE 9:2. Possible patterns of defense against leopards at Swartkrans. For experiments with chimpanzees and a stuffed leopard see Figure 7:7.

posture gave to predators and, especially, what about the use of tools for defense?[4]

If tools are used for defense—and such "tools" may be as simple as readily available sticks, branches, stones, and wads of grass—then both females and males can frighten away carnivores (Figure 9:2). At one australopithecine site, Swartkrans in southern Africa, there is evidence that the early hominids may have occasionally been killed and eaten by leopards

[4] Similarly, regarding gatherer-hunters today, Lee's (1979) important new book on the !Kung San of southern Africa stresses how flexible and shifting !Kung groups are. He argues for use of the term "camp" to describe their groupings—a term that translates their own—rather than the previously used "band," with its quite different connotations. Tight social organization is not characteristic of the !Kung.

(Brain, 1970, 1974a, 1978). There was, then, need for defense. If australopithecines were as intelligent as chimpanzees, and if females were as self-protective and protective of their infants as are chimpanzee females, then both female and male hominids would learn to use such tools for protection (see Figure 7:7). The group therefore did not always need to be large or to have an adult male accompanying females and young. Group flexibility could be maintained, with changes in both size and composition occurring in response to variable ecological conditions.

Intelligence usually has been discussed relative to hunting – in turn assumed to be a male activity. By implication, then, there is no selection pressure for female intelligence. The list could go on and on, but that is hardly necessary. The point is not to dwell on all the gaps in past reconstructions but to develop a model that corrects the imbalance. Even now, when a role for gathering is often acknowledged, the far-reaching implications of this major innovation are rarely explored.

The approach taken here obviously is not without assumptions: The perspective is evolutionary. From this it follows that selection operated on all ages and both sexes for effective behaviors. As a corollary, females as well as males were intelligent and active. They were not so encumbered by being pregnant or carrying a young child that they were prevented from tool making and using, thinking about where to find food, gathering it, or defending themselves and their children. Indeed, it is assumed that there was selection for all adult females to possess these capacities and consistently utilize their abilities. The children with the best survival chances were those whose mothers most effectively exercised such capabilities. Even among modern gatherer-hunters living long after the invention of hunting with tools, women still consistently provide a large proportion of the food and have an essential economic as well as social role in the group (Lee, 1968, 1979; Lee and DeVore, 1968, 1976; Gould, 1969).

Anatomy and the australopithecine adaptation

The earliest hominids developed an entirely new method of locomotion – upright posture and bipedalism. This new pattern differed fundamentally from that of the ape ancestors. Locomotion is the basis through which an animal exploits the resources in its environment; locomotion is the nearest thing to a total body activity. In hominids, bipedalism is an integral part of the activities that are hallmarks of the hominid line: tool using, carrying, throwing, walking long distances. *Australopithecus* was anatomically equipped for bipedalism (Lovejoy, 1978, 1979; Johanson, Taieb, et al., 1978; Zihlman, 1978c; M. D. Leakey and Hay, 1979; M. D. Leakey,

FIGURE 9:3. Australopithecine walking with baby on her back, holding a tool in her right hand.

1979; McHenry and Temerin, 1979; Zihlman and Brunker, 1979). The pelvis was broad and bowl shaped for extensive attachment of muscles important in locomotion; the foot had a well-developed great toe that could no longer grasp and an immobile arch to maintain support. As the adaptation evolved, the lower limbs increased in length and so made longer steps possible; this contributed to a more efficient gait because greater distance could be covered with each stride. Muscles and their attachments underwent changes to enable two limbs to perform the functions previously carried out by four—forward propulsion, braking, balance, and support.

Bipedalism, combined with arms and hands available for a variety of uses, had tremendous adaptive value (Figure 9:3). Hands and arms were freed to collect and carry plant food; to carry infants or partially support them with one hand if they were resting on a hip or in a sling, while the other hand was used to collect food; to carry raw materials for tools and implements of defense; to make tools; to hold and use digging implements; to skin animals; and for holding, aiming, and throwing objects to frighten away predators.[5]

Selection operated directly on this bipedal complex because the young most likely to survive were offspring of (1) women who had the physical abilities for long-distance walking to collect food and for carrying both food and infants and of (2) men who were as good at walking as the women and therefore were the ones available for sexual interaction during and after a day's far-ranging gathering. The locomotor pattern was intimately related to the other anatomy—action complexes through which the hominids utilized their environment.

Despite australopithecines' effective bipedalism, some of their arm, hand, and wrist bones still resembled those in apes. The shoulder was designed for rotation, and arm bones were longer than for humans today—features that, at the very least, indicate that effective brachiators had a place in the line ancestral to the australopithecines (Keith, 1923; Morton,

[5] More than the hand is involved in many of these behaviors. In throwing, for example, the hand holds the object, the arm is raised, and, at the same time, the trunk is rotated on the lower limbs, while the feet are firmly placed apart for stability. So, although throwing appears to be a simple action, it involves interrelated movements in most parts of the body.

1924a, b; Gregory, 1929, 1934; Avis, 1962; Tuttle, 1974). These features could also suggest that early hominids, although already bipeds, still made considerable use of trees (Ciochon and Corruccini, 1976).[6]

Hands were in the process of evolving for more effective precision grips and finer manipulative activities; this process was by no means complete. Because the terminal phalanx of the thumb was quite developed, a relatively large thumb flexor muscle was probably already present (Napier, 1962a). The thumb was therefore already capable of powerfully grasping a digging stick, a hand-sized rock for pounding or throwing, or a small flake held between thumb and fingers. The thumb metacarpal from Swartkrans in southern Africa is larger and heavier than in *Homo*, however; in these respects it resembles that bone in chimpanzees (Rightmire, 1972). The structure of the thumb metacarpal suggests considerably less precise movements of the thumb than for humans today. Similarly, one of the wrist bones, the capitate, found in both southern Africa (Sterkfontein) and at Olduvai Gorge, Bed I, in eastern Africa, shows strong affinities with this bone in the African apes and particularly with that of chimpanzees (Lewis, 1972a, 1973). The form of this bone evolved for suspensory locomotion — that is, for hanging and swinging in trees. Its ape-like shape suggests that, unlike humans today, there may have been only limited rotational movement between the thumb and fingers. This means that precision grips must have been less developed in *Australopithecus* than in ourselves (Lewis, 1973). The fingers became shorter and somewhat less curved and the thumb stronger before the wrist bones changed appreciably. Hands were being used differently by the time of *Australopithecus*, but many aspects of form had not yet changed. Australopithecine hands and arms still evinced anatomical resemblance to those of apes. Major changes associated with walking upright occurred before those in hands and arms.

Jaws and teeth are abundant in the hominid fossil record. The hard enamel and dentin in the teeth make them the least edible parts for carnivores and scavengers and the most likely to fossilize. Information on size and wear patterns can be obtained even from single teeth if part of the jaw, skull, or face is also preserved. The reconstruction of associated muscles can suggest how the teeth worked. Teeth alone are insufficient for dietary inferences. But when data on ecological context and comparative information on diet and dentition of primates and human gatherer-hunters liv-

[6] The fossil finger bones from Olduvai Gorge are shorter than in apes but are still strongly curved and have pronounced ridges on them (Napier, 1962a, b), whereas this is not the case on modern human phalanges. In African apes these features are well developed for holding the flexor tendons in place to maintain the powerful flexed position during knuckle walking. This has sometimes been viewed as evidence that the immediate ancestors from which *Australopithecus* evolved were knuckle walkers.

ing in similar environments are combined with dental evidence, a picture of hominid dietary adaptation emerges. The four kinds of australopithecine teeth – incisors, canines, premolars, and molars – together form a pattern (or actually patterns) in size and wear unlike either contemporary apes or humans. Also, it is primarily from the teeth, simply because teeth provide the most extensive fossil documentation, that the contrasts and similarities between different varieties of *Australopithecus* are evident.

First and foremost, the front teeth differ for the australopithecines over time. Here is an evolving complex. It is an important one, and it is related to food, tools, and social communication.

As already mentioned, the basal australopithecines at Laetoli and Afar (Hadar Formation) still have quite large, procumbent incisors and large canines. Although some downward shift in relative size of these front teeth may have occurred from ape ancestor to basal hominid, the pongid affinities are evident. The cheek teeth, also, are still quite small but larger than in common and pygmy chimpanzees and, therefore, probably larger than in the ape ancestor.[7] Overall, then, *A. afarensis* exhibits some, but rather minimal, dental change in a hominid direction.

For all later australopithecines, as for all subsequent hominids, the front teeth – and, most dramatically, the canine teeth – are much reduced. The small size of the canines for both sexes in all but the very earliest basal australopithecines is in contrast to the situation among most living apes and monkeys where canines are large, with males often having even larger ones than females. Canine size tells a complex story (see Figure 9:4). First of all, why are they small? And second, why small in both sexes? Because they are relatively large in most living apes and Old World monkeys (and in many species still larger in males) as well as in most fossil apes compared to hominids, the canine teeth were probably larger in both sexes (and even larger for males) in the ancestral population than in *Australopithecus*. Information on australopithecine canine breadth (one measure of size), as compared to chimpanzees and humans, supports this inference (Wolpoff, 1975). In the australopithecines, both canine "height" (the distance from the base to tip of the canine) and breadth are considerably less than in chimpanzees (LeGros Clark, 1950; Wolpoff, 1971).[8] Interestingly, however, in breadth – which doubtless was slower to change because it was not so directly related to function as was the height – australopithecine

[7]   Whether the cheek teeth of *A. afarensis* were relatively larger than for the ape ancestor depends on how the body sizes of the basal hominid and the ape ancestor compared.
[8]   For the basal hominid, *A. afarensis*, which still has quite large canines (White, 1977), canine height is less than in common chimpanzees (Krogman, 1969) but greater than that of pygmy chimpanzees (Johanson, 1974).

FIGURE 9:4. For common chimpanzees, there is a major contrast in the size of canine teeth between males and females. Women and men do not differ in this way. Human canine teeth are small compared with those of common chimpanzees. Although the basal hominid (*A. afarensis*) still had fairly large canines, subsequent australopithecines exhibit canine reduction.

canines show a bimodal distribution, presumably according to sex (Wolpoff, 1975). In function (as indicated by height and absolute breadth), australopithecine canine teeth were quite similar for males and females. In subsequent hominids, *Homo erectus* and *Homo sapiens,* breadth decreases a bit further and bimodality disappears. Given this trend, the bimodal distribution for canine breadth in the australopithecines strongly suggests that the ancestral population was one in which canines were both functionally and anatomically dimorphic (with differences in both length and breadth), as Darwin (1871) hypothesized long ago.

Several explanations for the reduction of canine teeth for both sexes, and especially for males, have been proposed and, in the context of this model, take on added dimensions.

First, Washburn (1960), as Darwin (1871), suggested that weapons replaced the use of canine teeth for defense and fighting with other animals. Male monkeys and apes use their large canine teeth for fighting when protecting themselves from members of other species; this is especially true for baboons where the males are much larger than the females in body as well as canine size and are the primary protectors of the group. In chimpanzees, canine tooth and body size differences are less marked.[9] Because female chimpanzees do travel alone, have fairly large canines, and do sometimes make use of sticks and upright posture, they are capable of defending themselves against possible predators such as leopards. The argument therefore can be that further reduction of canine teeth means that regular object use (along with bipedal posture) for defense replaced the use of teeth in defense for both female and male australopithecines.

Second, Holloway (1967) hypothesized that changing social and mating patterns led to less intraspecific fighting among males and between males and females. Thus, as female choice increased (correlated with increased maternal investment and with the increased cortical control of sexual behavior consequent to the loss of estrus), the more social (and less aggressive and disruptive) males may well have been more frequently selected as sexual partners. This change in mating patterns would have affected the whole group by increasing sociability among males and between males and females.

Larger canine teeth in male primates combined with dimorphism in body size often correlate with a relatively high degree of intraspecific male-male aggression, as among orangutans and drill baboons (Gartlan, 1970; MacKinnon, 1974). In male and female chimpanzees and in contemporary humans, there is a great deal of overlap in body size and so limited sexual dimorphism in this feature.[10] In addition, for humans there is essentially no sexual dimorphism in canine tooth size. In contrast, male gorillas can be nearly twice the body size of females, with females only 54 to 75 percent the weight and length of males (Schaller, 1963; Napier and Napier, 1967),

---

[9] This trend is emphasized even further among pygmy chimpanzees, in which male and female canine teeth can be distinguished only on the basis of canine breadth, and facial features and cranial capacity show essentially no sexual dimorphism (Cramer, 1974; Almquist, 1974; Johanson, 1974; Zihlman et al., 1978).

[10] Although body size is only a crude measure of features such as strength and aggressiveness, on the average female chimpanzees are some 84 to 92 percent as heavy and long as males, which is very similar to the 83 to 95 percent among humans (Schultz, 1931, 1960, 1969; Lyght et al., 1966; Napier and Napier, 1967; de Benedictis, pers. com.).

and males have considerably larger canines. Difference in degree of sexual dimorphism in body and canine size between chimpanzees and gorillas correlates with their social organizations: Chimpanzee groups are multi-male/multifemale, whereas gorilla groups have one male leader (Eisenberg et al., 1972; Crook, 1972; Leutenegger and Kelly, 1977; Harcourt, 1979). Here degree of sexually dimorphic features fits with extent of male-male social interactions. Similarly, reduction of canines in hominids suggests less male-male aggression and an increase in overall sociability.

Third, the communication system was growing more elaborate (Tanner and Zihlman, 1976b). Actual fighting and gross displays that have anatomical correlates such as large canines are exceedingly rigid means of getting a point across; the information that can thereby be communicated is limited, if impressive. Subtler but more finely discriminating modes of communication were gradually becoming available and were related to the increasing complexity of social relations among a larger number of individuals who did not interact regularly. As communicatory possibilities in the symbolic range began to develop, both sexes could communicate the same types of information and with a similar range of nuances. Therefore, large canines were – at the very least – unnecessary for communication and probably would be a communication liability.

Fourth – finally, and most fundamentally – canine reduction contributes to a more effective grinding mechanism through an elongation of the two side tooth rows.[11] Wolpoff (1978a:124) has demonstrated that there "is a distinct tendency for specimens with larger posterior teeth [i.e., cheek teeth, premolars, and molars] to have both relatively and absolutely smaller canines." This tendency for smaller canines to correlate with larger premolars and molars probably indicates a functional relationship between canines and cheek teeth. The reduction of canine size combined with the enlargement of the molar and premolar teeth thus probably served to improve food processing (Pilbeam, 1972b, 1978a; Wallace, 1975). Canine reduction, with large premolar and molar teeth, therefore meant that australopithecine dentition was well adapted for effective grinding and crushing of a wide range of savanna plant foods.

All four arguments, taken together, can explain reduction of canine teeth in both sexes of early hominids.[12] Objects used by both females and males

[11] In some species of ungulates, such as bovids, the canines have been lost. The loss of canines in such instances probably contributed to a more effective grinding adaptation for dietary needs, with horns replacing the canines in aggressive social interactions (see Geist, 1966a, b).

[12] Other arguments have also been put forward and have been summarized by Washburn and Ciochon (1974). They mention that Kinzey (1971) believes that the canine teeth of the ancestral population were never very large and therefore never reduced. Kinzey's view is

replaced large canine teeth for frightening away potential predators. A more elaborate communication system substituted for considerable intraspecific fighting and displays – in which apes bare their canines – for both sexes. Hands and/or objects were used in the physical fights that did occur. Lessening of intraspecific male-male aggression and female sexual preference of males with smaller canines affected male canine teeth in particular. And selection for a more effective grinding mechanism influenced the species as a whole. Even the canines of the basal hominid (*A. afarensis*) already may have been somewhat reduced from those of the ancestral population, and the reduction is fully evident for all subsequent australopithecines. Further, there is little sexual dimorphism in form and none in function in australopithecine canine teeth subsequent to *A. afarensis*.

Whereas canines simply got smaller, the situation with regard to the cheek teeth (molars and premolars) is more complicated. Initially, for the basal hominids (*A. afarensis*) from approximately 3.77 million or 3.59 million years ago to about 3 million years ago, the cheek teeth were, like those of apes, actually still quite small. But, by the time of the so-called gracile australopithecines (*A. africanus*), which flourished in both eastern and southern Africa (at Omo, Sterkfontein, and Makapansgat) from about 3 million to at least 2 million years ago, and perhaps longer (at Taung, East Turkana, and Olduvai),[13] cheek teeth were notably larger. Then, beginning around 2 million years ago, about the same time the environment in eastern Africa was becoming increasingly arid with greater expanses of grasslands, this trend increased radically. Very robust australopithecines (*A. robustus/boisei*) rapidly became prominent in both eastern and southern Africa, with, if anything, some in eastern Africa even more robust than those in the south. This increasing robusticity meant several things. Cheek teeth became enormous, and the jaw itself increased in size. The muscles moving the jaws became massive, as did their bony attachments at the sides and top of the skull. In fact, a bony crest down the middle of the top of the skull developed. This dental adaptation, with gathering, was initially

contraindicated by fossil evidence discovered subsequent to his 1971 article: The very early hominid fossils at Laetoli and Hadar had noticeably protruding canines. There *has* been relative canine reduction in hominids since that time, initially in length, then later in breadth as well. Washburn and Ciochon also refer to Jolly's (1970a) "seed eating hypothesis" for early hominid canine reduction. But they point out that "recent field studies show that primate diet is much more varied than had previously been thought" and suggest that "the highly diversified diet of the chimpanzee provides a more useful model than [the restricted, seed-eating model of] the gelada [baboon]" (Washburn and Ciochon, 1974:778).
[13] If R. E. F. Leakey's reclassification of some fossils at East Turkana and Olduvai from *H. habilis* to *A. africanus* is correct, *A. africanus* persisted at these sites until after 1.5 Mya (Walker and R. E. F. Leakey, 1978; R. E. F. Leakey et al., 1978). If Taung, southern Africa, is late, *A. africanus* could have persisted there until nearly 1 Mya (but see Chapter 10, footnote 1).

extremely effective. The robust australopithecines very rapidly became commonplace (Figure 9:5). They also were larger than the earlier *A. africanus* (Pilbeam, 1972a). A dental trend, already apparent in *A. africanus*, underwent positive, directional selection in this context of environmental change. Food was probably scarcer after 2 million years ago, and initially these changes in the dentition made it easier to chew large quantities of dry, gritty food gathered on the savanna.

But the environmental shift posed another kind of challenge as well. These were creatures that had been gathering with tools for perhaps 2 million years. Cranial capacities had been slowly increasing. Why not more innovations? I suggest that at least two further inventions occurred about 2 million years ago.

First, a better container was invented. Traveling farther, and staying longer in new places, thus became feasible. It is no accident that the first known hominid fossils outside Africa are dated approximately 1.9 million years ago in Indonesia (Jacob and Curtis, 1971; Jacob, 1972, 1976). With a better container, early gathering hominids could move eastward through the tropics, from Africa to Indonesia. Second, tools to process food – so that large chewing teeth proved to be no longer necessary – were invented. Again, it is no accident that "advanced graciles" (*A.* or *H. habilis*), with larger brains but smaller cheek teeth, also appear in Africa about 2 million to 1.85 million years ago.

Cranial capacity, and by inference intelligence, increased from *A. afarensis* to *A. africanus* to *A. robustus* and, especially, to *A. habilis*. There was a selective advantage for increased cranial capacity over time on a fairly continuous basis, with, as suggested above, an increase in selection pressure starting about 2 million years ago. Significantly, tools made of new materials – stone – also begin to appear in the archeological record about 2 million years ago. This is the archeological evidence for an increase in "cultural" innovation as a means of meeting environmental challenges about this time. Stone tools are found associated with both robust and gracile (especially advanced gracile) fossils. Although some scholars have preferred to think that only *A. habilis* made these tools, such a conclusion is not supported by the evidence.[14]

---

[14] Robust australopithecines have been found near tools at East Turkana (for example, KNM-ER3230 at Area 131, Koobi Fora, and KNM-ER1806 at Area 130, Koobi Fora) and at Olduvai Gorge (OH46 from FLK-NN Middle Bed I, OH5 from FLK Middle Bed I, OH38 from SC Upper Bed II, and OH3 from BK Upper Bed II). At East Turkana, the robust form is associated, in one instance, with the earlier KBS Industry and, in the other, with the Karari Industry. At Olduvai, some robust fossils are associated with the earlier Oldowan Industry and another is associated with the "Developed Oldowan" (M. D. Leakey, 1971, 1978;

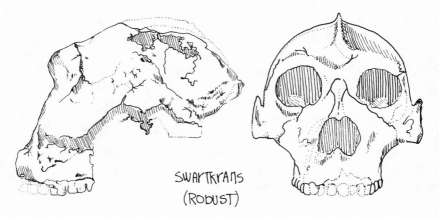

SWARTKRANS
(ROBUST)

Overall, for the australopithecines, the brain is larger than for chimpanzees, and it increases gradually through time. The early hominids already shared in this growth in intelligence that has so characterized human evolution (Figure 9:6).

Increase in absolute brain size implies an increase in number of neurons; but this is not the whole picture (Holloway, 1966). Compared to pongids, considerable reorganization has occurred in the hominid brain (Holloway, 1976a, b, 1978). For instance Holloway (1972a, 1976a), on the basis of extensive comparisons, concludes that the lunate sulcus, the fissure marking off the visual cortex (occipital lobe) from the parietal and temporal cortices, is well back from the pongid position and in a more hominid-like position in an australopithecine endocast from Swartkrans (SK1585). This suggests a relative decrease in at least the surface area of the visual cortex, as well as an increase in the relative volume of the posterior parietal and temporal cortex. The "areas of elaboration" (or "association areas") are found in this part of the hominid brain and have complex, and as yet relatively undefined, capacities (Geschwind, 1965; Lancaster, 1968b; Passingham and Ettlinger, 1974; Granit, 1977).

Brain reorganization enhanced and made more effective the behavioral patterns that formed that basis of the australopithecine adaptation. Reorganization of the cortex, specifically the increased posterior parietal and temporal regions (which suggest more developed areas of elaboration or

R. E. F. Leakey et al., 1978; Isaac and Harris, 1978). Tools have also been found near a robust form at Chesowanja.

Also, at Olduvai are two fossils previously classified as *Homo habilis* but that R. E. F. Leakey et al. (1978) have subsequently suggested are better classified as *A. africanus*. These fossils are also associated with tools: OH24 at DK East in Lower Bed I and OH13 at MNK Skull Site, Lower Middle Bed II (M. D. Leakey, 1971, 1978).

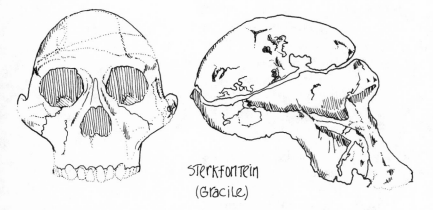

STerkfonTein
(GraciLe)

FIGURE 9:5. Examples of gracile and robust australopithecines. Note the large bony attachments for chewing muscles at the top and sides of the robust skull.

association areas), may well indicate that australopithecine problem-solving abilities, innovativeness, and facility and in communication had increased over that of the ape ancestor (Holloway, 1972b, 1976a). Problem-solving abilities would be useful in finding potential plant foods that were not immediately visible (particularly roots) or always predictably located. Conceptualization, "imagination," memory, and communication became important assets. Experimentation and innovativeness in developing and utilizing tools to obtain plant and animal food and for defense, as well as the foresight and conceptualization involved in finding appropriate materials for tools and in making them, were probably of special significance.

The development of social skills also had a neural base. A capacity for more complex communication was a major aspect of their increasing mental abilities. This communication was both social and about the environment. Communication about finding materials for making tools, for teaching others how to make tools, and for transmitting information about where food sources are located in terms of distance and direction were all involved. With heightened communicatory potential, social organization could become more complex. Breaking up and coming together of groups require remembering numbers of individuals and having the social skills to deal with each of them. Sexual communication probably also assumed increasing significance. Making choices relative to social situations would be an important aspect of their behavior—selecting temporary sexual partners, traveling companions, and friends and choosing where to search for food and water or to camp at night. The reorganized and expanding

australopithecine brain formed the anatomical basis for coordination of increasingly
complex behavioral patterns – more choices
and responses to a greater variety of foods,
locations, group members; enhanced memory and conceptualization; social and environmental communication; hand skills, tool
using, and problem-solving abilities.

My main point . . . is that the endocasts of
the early hominids already display evidence
of reorganization toward a human pattern,
particularly as regards the added development of the temperoparietal regions on the
lateral surface . . . [this] is strongly suggestive that even two or three million years
ago natural selection was operating on eco-
niche adaptation, and that cognitive and
social behavior was surely the main focus.
[Holloway, 1976a:346]

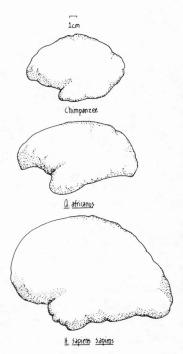

FIGURE 9:6. Brain size in a chimpanzee, an early hominid, and a contemporary human.

Inferences on life processes

Because the brain was still quite small and
the pelvic opening sufficiently large, the birth process was relatively un-
problematic for both mother and infant (Leutenegger, 1972). Births were
perhaps spaced some three to five years apart, an estimate based on comparisons with chimpanzees and human gatherer-hunters (Goodall, 1975a;
Konner, 1976; C. Clark, 1977). The pattern of tooth eruption suggests that
postnatal development was relatively long (Mann, 1968, 1974, 1976),
providing an extended time for offspring to learn where to find food, how
to use tools to obtain it, and where to find materials for making tools. To
learn, the young could observe the mother, siblings, and others closely,
imitate their behavior, and then practice until skillful (Hall, 1963a; Goodall, 1964; Lancaster, 1968a). Equally important would be learning of
social patterns. A young australopithecine would have heterogeneous social relationships, most likely with its mother, siblings, and occasional
additional "kin," with the mother's preferred sex partners, and with "play-
mates" who would be of various ages, because of the fairly small size of
australopithecine social aggregations.

Technical and economic skills plus environmental information would have to be learned by the time an offspring needed to be independent; the economic system would not be so well developed as to sufficiently provide for young indefinitely. Although they would therefore be on their own early, they would of course still have protection from the group and follow along with their mothers and siblings to find food. The capacity to learn complex information and skills early in life would have clear survival value for a young australopithecine. Selection for early intelligence is one basis for expanding brain size and more sophisticated mental capacities.

Because of immaturity at birth and an extended period of development, increased maternal care (both initially and for a longer time) was necessary. Mothers probably carried their infants with them wherever they went. Contact between mothers and their offspring was necessarily intense and of increased duration. Early socialization therefore would be primarily from mothers, and they would form the foci of small genealogically based social groups. Older male and female offspring might also assume a role in caring for and playing with their younger siblings, especially after they were weaned and somewhat independent of the mothers.

Changes in sexual behavior were also probable. The estrous swellings of the female ape genital areas would no longer be selected for, due to the reduced visibility of these body areas as a result of bipedalism. Females and males might become sexual friends who sometimes traveled together, and finding a temporary sex partner could easily occur in the larger groups that camped near water, along river beds and lakes. With the loss of an anatomical signaling device (estrous swellings), females necessarily communicated to males an interest in sex through behavioral and nonverbal cues. These signals could be given at any time and therefore differed significantly from the ape ancestors' hormonally clocked, overt morphological signal. Patterns of sexual interaction among early hominids therefore were consistent with the social structural flexibility—that is, situational changes in size and composition of groups. Shifts in size and composition of groups were made possible by the protection afforded through tool use to australopithecines traveling alone or in very small groups. Social structural flexibility was an effective means of dealing with shifting patterns of food availability on the savanna. Fluid and changeable sexual interaction, depending on what possible partners were available, would be advantageous in this type of socioecological setting.

Females' increasing reliance on voluntary communicatory cues to initiate sexual activities would also intensify female choice of sexual partners, which, in turn, was becoming more conscious as the neural correlates expanded. Greater maternal investment was reflected in more frequent female choice of sex partners.[15] Very early on, hominid females' sexual selection finished off the anatomical symbols of intracommunity aggression – large canine teeth. This is evident in the contrast between the basal hominid *A. afarensis* and all subsequent australopithecines, *A. africanus, A. robustus/boisei,* and *A./H. habilis.* Perhaps early hominid females preferred males who used their mouths to kiss, rather than the ones who bared sharp teeth.

Overall, females apparently were choosing males who were sociable, cooperative, willing to share, and protective. In general, then, sexual intercourse would not be disruptive of either ongoing group interaction or organizational flexibility. Mothers obtained plant food from their own efforts, protein from a variety of sources (insects, plant protein, and some meat from their own efforts, and additional meat from males); had their own tools for protection; and had durable social bonds with sons, daughters, brothers, and sisters who shared the food quest and assisted in protective functions. Thus permanent mates to provide food and protection would be neither necessary nor particularly advantageous. Sexual preference was, however, getting easier to communicate, and it is likely that many australopithecines did have preferred sex partners.

The australopithecines died early. Many had only fairly recently acquired their third molars – which erupt at about 18 years of age – before dying (Mann, 1974). Death from predators may well have been frequent. The process of dying and the fact of death would attract attention. Australopithecines could not yet conceptualize well enough to develop rituals to deal with death, but it was doubtless already posing even more of a problem both socially and emotionally for them than for the ancestral population.[16] The problematic quality of death was related directly to the early hominids' greater capacity (and necessity) for affective interrelationships, which were, in turn, a product of immaturity at birth, longer development in a highly social context, and dependence on socially mediated learning.[17]

Stone tools and animal bones: evidence on food getting?

Except for some probable earlier finds at Hadar, stone tools appear at roughly the same time, approximately 2 million years ago (White and

[15] Maternal investment was high in physical terms (gestation, birth, nursing), in economic terms (gathering, food preparation, sharing), and in social terms (socialization).
[16] See Chapter 5 for examples of how disruption of social bonds due to death influences behavior among chimpanzees. In cases where mothers have died, the viability of even physically independent young can be affected (Teleki, 1973c; Teleki et al., 1976).
[17] Normal primate learning is, in essence, social. Primary reinforcement for all normal primate learning comes from the social context (Hall, 1968). This was further enhanced among hominids.

Harris, 1977). They are found in eastern Africa in the Omo Basin, at Olduvai Gorge, to the east of Lake Turkana, and in the Afar Triangle (M. D. Leakey, 1970, 1971; Merrick et al., 1973; Merrick and Merrick, 1976; Isaac et al., 1976; Isaac, 1976; Isaac and Harris, 1978; Johanson et al., 1980). Stone tools are also found at Swartkrans and the Sterkfontein Extension Site in southern Africa, and probably are somewhat more recent (and the tools slightly more refined) than the earlier eastern African ones.

The early technology in eastern Africa is often called the Oldowan Industry. Although there are some differences from site to site, the general level of technology is similar at all the eastern African sites where stone tools first appear.[18] It was followed first by the "Developed Oldowan" or Early Acheulian, possibly a product of late australopithecines; and later by the Acheulian, often thought to be associated with *Homo erectus* (M. D. Leakey, 1971; Stiles, 1979a).[19]

The earliest stone tools were extremely simple, with minimal working and refinement; yet there was a range of tool forms. A pebble "chopper," for example, is produced by hitting one stone with another, thereby removing a flake. The pebble from which the flake was taken has a sharp edge that can be utilized, and the flake itself may also become a tool. During this period, only a few flakes were struck from a lump of stone to produce a tool. Thus these early tools appear crude. They are without fine retouch or that more elaborate removal of flakes from both sides of a stone pebble, nodule, or angular fragment that later appears in tools called "bifaces." Perhaps crudeness of tools is related to partial lack of ability and skill in the full human sense, both in the hand and in the brain. "The present evidence suggests that the stone implements of early man were as good (or as bad) as the hands that made them" (Napier, 1962b:62).

Stones that might be tools or remains of hominid activity can be recognized most easily when they are found in association with hominid bones, undisturbed and not water rolled; and also when they are foreign objects made from materials naturally occurring some distance from the site where they are found, show evidence of workmanship or use, are clumped together in ways unlikely by natural means, and are plentiful. Archeologists often classify these worked stones on the basis of shape rather than function, mainly because the functions are uncertain; but many references to supposed functions occur as well. The australopithecine stone finds can be grouped into four major categories: "manuports," thought to be intro-

[18] For example, at East Turkana, the "KBS Industry" is the term given the earliest, simplest stone technology – the one similar to the Oldowan – whereas the later, more complex tools are termed the "Karari Industry" (J. Harris and Isaac, 1976; Isaac and Harris, 1978).

[19] Although the African Acheulian Industry is usually assumed to be a product of *Homo erectus,* and the dates are consistent, direct associations are infrequent (Howell, 1978a).

duced into a site by hominids but not shaped by them; "artifacts," covering anything shaped by hominids whether by design or as a by-product; "tools," artifacts judged to show purposive design for use; and "debitage" (Isaac, 1978).

By this definition "stone tools" include the so-called choppers, scrapers, polyhedrons, and discoids, all of which are lumps of stone that have been systematically shaped by removing at least one flake; therefore, they are referred to as core tools (M. D. Leakey, 1971; Isaac, 1978). Flakes, removed from a core in forming a tool, sometimes also show evidence of use. "Spheroids" and "hammerstones" are manuports that were probably carefully selected from around riverbeds and show signs of having been used. Most debitage is composed of broken pieces, as one might expect to result from making and using stone tools.

It is only after the description and classification of stone remains that the fascinating questions actually begin. The most interesting questions all concern what the tools were used for (Figure 9:7). In due time, there will be sufficient systematic experimentation with making duplicate stone tools and testing them in a very wide variety of possible activities, for a real assessment of the most likely uses for each tool. At present, assurance is premature.

There was an initial tendency to assume that stone tools meant hunting. As time has gone on, however, it has become more and more difficult to ascertain how these early stone tools could have been used in hunting. Alternatively, perhaps some of the choppers, for example, may have been used as digging tools. Many are the right size to grasp by hand and have relatively sharp digging edges. Some are pointed at one end, rather like a trowel in shape. Other, flatter stones and choppers were appropriately shaped for use in cutting, pounding, and mashing tough fibrous vegetables. Some of these relatively heavy stone tools may have been used "for breaking open nuts and preparing the otherwise unpalatable parts of plants by the breaking-down of the fibrous portions" (J. D. Clark, 1970:70). Possibly such core tools were used with hammerstones. Small flakes would be useful in scraping off dirt from roots and for dividing and peeling plant food.

In the past it has often been suggested that sharp flakes were used for skinning and cutting up animal flesh (J. D. Clark, 1970; Isaac, 1978; R. E. F. Leakey and Lewin, 1978). Interestingly, however, there is

a suggestion of irregular chipping and damage on the edges [of these flakes] . . . [But the] experimental use of a quartz flake for skinning, disjointing, and cutting the meat from the carcass of a goat has shown that relatively little damage is caused to the edges of the flake when cutting through soft tissues. [M. D. Leakey, 1967: 421–422]

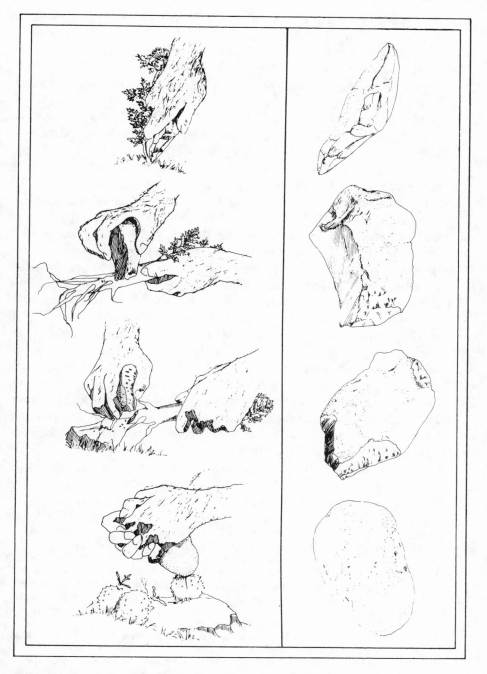

FIGURE 9:7. Oldowan tools: possible uses.

Was, perhaps, this irregular chipping and damage to these flake tools caused by fibrous plants?

Along with the hominids, a wide range of animal species has been found – small mammals, reptiles, shellfish, and fish; medium-sized ungulates such as pigs and numerous antelope, as well as primates such as baboons; many carnivores; and also some large fauna, for example, hippo, giraffe, and elephant (Cooke, 1963, 1978). Most recognizable hominid sites in eastern Africa were near water, which would draw many animals. Because silt accumulates with slight changes in water level, the likelihood of preservation of animals and hominids, should they die there, is much better than in either tropical jungles or open grasslands.

For *Australopithecus,* the evidence for hominid animal-related activity is primarily from the later australopithecine sites of Olduvai Gorge and East Turkana (previously called Lake Rudolf) – both sites that were near water – in Tanzania and Kenya, respectively. At these sites, in many instances where there are hominid fossils there are of course other animal bones as well. In addition, and more significant, there are some locales where artifacts are interspersed with broken animal bones and, sometimes, with hominids.[20] Some of these animal bones were split open and broken in ways that suggested hominid activity to the earlier investigators (M. D. Leakey, 1971; Brain, 1975). Subsequent taphonomic studies – that is, the science of studying animal bone remains – have, however, raised important questions. As Andrew Hill states: "The interpretation of bone fragments as human food debris is common in the archaeological literature, and often with some justification. As yet, however, there are very few criteria by which such assemblages can be distinguished from the food remains of other animals" (1978:96).

Sites with animal remains suggesting human utilization are, for the late australopithecines of the Plio-Pleistocene, very different from the "kill sites" of *Homo erectus* in the Middle Pleistocene.[21] At such later Middle

[20] At East Turkana there is one site complex FxJj20 with artifacts, several types of animal bones, and, at nearby FxJj20 East, a robust mandible, KNM-ER3230. There are also two other sites with animal bones and artifacts but no hominid fossils: FxJj3-HAS, the hippo and artifact site; and FxJj18-IHS, which has a varied bone assemblage and artifacts (Isaac and Harris, 1978). At Olduvai, sites with artifacts, hominids, and fauna include: FLK-NN level 3, FLK North level 5, and FLK "Zinj" (level 22), all in Bed I; and in Bed II, the MNK Skull Site. Two sites at Olduvai also include elephant carcasses and tools (FLK North, level 6, in Bed I and FLK North, Bed II) but no hominid fossils (M. D. Leakey, 1971).
[21] Shipman (1978) has compared eastern African patterns of bovid and primate bone breakage at: first, a pooled sample of all Plio-Pleistocene East Turkana sites that showed no evidence of hominid presence (i.e., no hominid fossils or tools); second, three Plio-Pleistocene Olduvai sites with evidence of hominids (associated tools and/or hominid fossils); and third, a much more recent Middle Pleistocene site, Olorgesailie, dating from only some 700,000 to 400,000

Pleistocene sites, patterns of bone breakage differ (Shipman, 1978). Further, the animal bones are not concentrated at the earlier Plio-Pleistocene sites, and there are fewer tools (Isaac, 1969). The animal species found at sites with stone artifacts on Plio-Pleistocene living floors are in roughly the same proportions as the fauna at sites with no evidence of hominid presence of that period. For the late Australopithecines of the Plio-Pleistocene, specialized intensive utilization of particular animal species had not yet developed. On the contrary, australopithecine meat sources were probably varied and not very extensive, much as for living chimpanzees.

There are three probable explanations for how *Australopithecus* could have obtained meat: (1) catching and killing small animals without tools; (2) coming upon immobilized medium-sized to large dying animals, killing, and butchering them; (3) scavenging medium-sized or large dead animals. Yet, the one less likely explanation – that is, pursuing and killing large animals with tools – has often been assumed. Given small, vulnerable hominids with crude, simple tools, it is most unlikely they were capable of chasing down and killing prey in the size range of hippo and elephant. It would be miraculous if these stone tools, which would have to be thrown, could even scratch the thick hides of such animals, much less do them in.

To summarize what is known about australopithecine tools and what they may have been used for: (1) hominid fossils are known for some 1.5 million years before the appearance of stone tools; (2) data on ape tool use highlight the probable early significance of organic tools; (3) from data on living primates and human gatherer-hunters, there is every reason to assume plants formed a critical part of the diet; (4) comparisons of animal bones support the conclusion that animals were used less intensively by late australopithecines than by *Homo erectus*.

Thus, from what we know of how much organic tools are utilized not

years ago, for which there is clear evidence of hominid presence (Isaac, 1977). Shipman's most interesting finding was the *extent of difference between* all Plio-Pleistocene sites studied, whether or not there was evidence of hominids present (at both East Turkana and Olduvai Gorge) dating from comparatively late australopithecine times *and* the subsequent Middle Pleistocene site (Olorgesailie) dating from mid-*Homo erectus* times. For example, both the East Turkana and Olduvai postcranial animal bones showed fewer breaks than those from Olorgesailie. "The Olorgesailie breakage pattern most clearly attests to hominid activities . . . What can be said with some confidence is that the Olorgesailie primates show very consistent and unusual patterns of breakage that differ widely from those seen in any of the other assemblages examined" (Shipman, 1978:13, 15). Thus, although there were some differences between the animal bones at the nonhominid sites at Turkana and the hominid sites at Olduvai, and although these particular Olduvai sites have been thought to evince hominid usage of animals, the major difference between the breakage patterns of all these Plio-Pleistocene animal bones and those at nearby but Middle Pleistocene Olorgesailie is what is most impressive. If the late australopithecines were utilizing animals, it was not yet in as intensive or effective a manner as among *Homo erectus* in the Middle Pleistocene.

only by chimpanzees but also by human gatherer-hunters, it is highly likely that the earliest hominids – *A. afarensis* and *A. africanus* – primarily utilized organic tools (Goodall, 1970; Teleki, 1974; Goodall and Hamburg, 1975; Tanaka, 1976; McGrew, 1979). Some of the discoids, choppers, or flakes could have been used to prepare wooden tools, such as digging sticks, or branches for defense (J. D. Clark, 1970; Isaac, 1978). "Experiment shows the so-called choppers to be effective for pointing a stick to use for digging out buried plant foods or small burrowing animals as well as for cutting, by means of a sawing action" (J. D. Clark, 1970:70).

Once stone came also to be used systematically for tools, stone tools would then be used with the organic tools. Perhaps pebble "digging tools" (e.g., pointed and sharp-edged choppers) and pebble "pounders" (e.g., some kinds of choppers and possible spheroids together with hammerstones) were used to obtain, open, and crush plant foods. Scrapers, discoids, and flakes could be used to scrape off dirt from plant foods, to divide or peel plant foods, and to make organic tools. Animal bones might also have been used as digging tools.[22] Choppers or discoids also could be used for cracking open bones for marrow, and flakes might be used for skinning and cutting apart animals. Among the organic tools, one was probably particularly important: the digging stick. It, like its stone counterpart, would be widely used for digging up plants but could also be used for protection and for knocking fruits and nuts from trees as the hominids came to climb less frequently. Australopithecines made multipurpose tools. The tools were crude, rapidly fashioned, and sometimes disposed of just as quickly. They were not yet highly specialized and could be used somewhat interchangeably for dealing with plant and animal food or to make other tools. Tools were probably also thrown at predators occasionally. Later, tools will be made for specific activities in order to increase their effectiveness; they will take longer to make, and the materials will be brought from greater distances. This stage had not yet been reached by australopithecine times. Nonetheless, early hominids had already begun to rely on technology to deal with the environment.

---

[22] At various sites at Olduvai there is evidence of bones such as scapulae, which may have been used for digging and shoveling, and bone splinters that could have served as cutting and scraping tools (M. D. Leakey, 1971). A highly polished bovid metacarpal (a limb bone) with longitudinal striations going down to the point was found in Bed I, Olduvai Gorge (M. D. Leakey, 1971). These striations and polishings are similar to the kind of wear resulting from rubbing a hide or digging in the ground (J. D. Clark, 1970). Wear patterns on other stone and bone artifacts might be examined with such possibilities in mind. Some of Mary Leakey's inferences on bone tools at Olduvai Gorge (1971) are quite interesting, even though earlier speculations on bone tools in southern Africa (Dart, 1957) have long been a focus of controversy.

FIGURE 9:8. Worked stone tools could have been used to make digging tools.

Predation and defense

It would not be surprising if danger from predators increased from the chimpanzee-like ancestor to the transitional population and early hominids. They were bipedal and, although this made them better able to frighten predators, it also made them more visible and vulnerable. They were often scattered about the countryside rather than concentrated in large groups, and they had abandoned their arboreal retreat. Bones of many species of carnivores (as well as ungulates) are found at australopithecine sites (Cooke, 1963, 1978; Brain, 1974b, 1978; Vrba, 1974). This at the very least indicates that predators frequented many of the same spots used by *Australopithecus*. At various sites in eastern Africa hominid bones show evidence of having been gnawed or chewed (Behrensmeyer, 1978a). In some instances this may well have been the cause of death. Brain (1970, 1974a, 1978) makes a convincing case that the hominid fossils in the Swartkrans cave in southern Africa were remains of leopard meals (see Figure 9:2). We can surmise that, at other sites as well, some of the australopithecines, plus some of the other animals in association, were killed by predators.

Camping together in fairly large groups (e.g., 15 to 30) at night when many of the large carnivores were seeking prey would provide some protection. The ancestral and transitional populations had doubtless slept in trees, and perhaps early australopithecines still did so. Rapid escape to the trees in an emergency would be less feasible for australopithecines, however, due to the loss of a grasping foot. Yet, camping in clumps of trees around water remained advantageous: ungulates frequent water sources, and their sharp senses of smell and hearing would have been of benefit to the hominids, as to other primates. Throwing sticks, stones, clumps of grass, dirt, and other objects at predators and occasionally scoring a hit would be additional defense, sometimes used at night as well as during the day. Actual fighting with animals as large as themselves—by either males or females—would have been unlikely, however. The australopithecines no longer had large canines and had not yet developed the weaponry to make effective the threat implied in their impressive and frightening displays. In dealing with potential predators, bluff and cunning were more important than force.

Effective defensive behaviors by both sexes and particularly by females not in the company of adult males—a frequent daytime occurrence—were the focus of intensive selection pressure. Females, then, were innovative not only with regard to gathering tools but also for defense. In this way variability in group composition, essential for exploitation of savanna resources, could be maintained. The ecological advantage of flexibility was great; object use for defense by females would be highly adaptive. The australopithecines were able to deal with predators effectively enough to survive and expand, despite reduction of canines and loss of grasping foot. With objects for defense, the loosely structured social pattern present in the ancestral population could persist in the new environment. Flexibility in social organization is as characteristic of the hominid adaptation as tool making or bipedalism.

What were early hominid communities like?

If plant gathering was the basis of the australopithecine adaptation and if mothers were the most regular gatherers, then the basic unit of australopithecine society, as for the transitional population, was probably a mother and one to several offspring. Sometimes this genealogical unit may have been three generational, including an old mother, adult daughter(s) and her infant or juvenile offspring, plus the old mother's adult son(s), and adolescent offspring of both sexes. As generations were short, and life not long, units of more than three generations would be extremely unlikely. These units would not be large; with lengthy nursing a female might bear only four or so children during her childbearing years, and not all would survive. This mother-centered genealogical unit was the most stable group; these individuals might often travel and gather together, with two or three going off to look for meat sporadically. Several of these genealogical units, especially those that were descendants of sisters, may have met frequently and camped with some regularity around well-known water sources.

Adult australopithecine males would have had stronger social bonds with adult females, especially but not exclusively with their mothers and sisters, than is true for living chimpanzees. There was an even longer and more intense association with the mother and with siblings than for the ancestral and transitional populations. Further incorporation of adult males into group life was made possible by increased sociability and decreased disruptiveness of the males (related both to the longer period of maternal care and socialization and to the probable decrease in sexual dimorphism, particularly in canine height). This relatively relaxed incorporation of males into the group was perhaps also reinforced by male contributions to defense and meat acquisition and by male help in bringing raw materials for tool manufacture from some distance to the campsite. Despite this comparative incorporation into group life, males could have gone off from time to time, perhaps for extended periods, alone or with brothers and friends. This would not pose a problem because at any one time adult females were more essential than adult males to group activities.

The social organization that fits the type of economic reconstruction proposed here is one in which groups were flexible in terms of both composition (age and sex) and size. Gathering groups could be quite small and composed of, say, one to three adult females and dependent offspring, or they might be fairly large, combining several mother-centered units. Movements through the extensive range would not be random. The australopithecines possessed a detailed knowledge of their environment; within their range they moved from place to place according to a known sequence of available food sources. Hominids that frequently associated, though separated from time to time, would have had little difficulty finding each other. When food was abundant from fruiting trees around a water hole or near a stream, perhaps 30 or more hominids camped together while the supply lasted. Ecological conditions and food sources strongly influenced how many individuals were together from day to day. The tendency would be: plentiful food, larger groups; scarce food, smaller groups.

Flexible yet organized groups could be maintained if different individuals led in different situations and at different times. In experiments with chimpanzees, for example, leadership with regard to finding food is based less on sex or age and more on personality and situational features (Menzel, 1973a). For early hominids, some division of labor is a distinct possibility. The common assumption that it was primarily or exclusively by sex is, however, an oversimplification. The australopithecines do not evince the degree of sexual dimorphism found in mammalian species in which each sex has a significantly different feeding strategy or other specialized adaptation with clear-cut anatomical correlates. Nor did they already have the reliance on cultural tradition with which to classify activities by sex. There would then be no reason, anatomic or symbolic, for any activity to be confined to one sex. Nonetheless, frequencies of several activities would differ for females with dependent young as compared to old females whose young were grown, females whose offspring had died, juvenile females, and older and younger males. Because mothers gathered for dependent offspring, they spent more time at it and obtained larger quantities. Their gathering techniques and tools might also be more sophisticated. Similarly, it would be females who were not in the last stages of pregnancy or carrying and nursing offspring, plus males – those who happened to be around because of friendships or "kin" relations with the women – that most regularly participated in protective activities during daytime gathering expeditions.

Individuals without small offspring would provide plant food for themselves and occasionally might bring it to their mothers and siblings. Perhaps siblings of both sexes, small groups of male friends, or older mothers with their adolescent offspring went off to search for small animals they could catch by hand or to scavenge for dead animals. These were once assumed to be exclusively male activities. It is now known, however, that some predation is carried out by female chimpanzees and that women are active hunters in some human gathering-hunting societies (Flannery, 1932, 1935; Landes, 1938; Goodall, 1973b; Morris and Goodall, 1977; Griffin, 1978). Among australopithecines, both males and females would have reason to butcher large animals to obtain meat. Perhaps tools were beginning to be sophisticated enough for this to occur among the advanced australopithecines after about 2 million years ago. Males and adolescent females would want to share meat with other group members to obtain social rewards. Mothers would be strongly motivated for butchering, as for gathering, because both activities could provide food to meet their own and their offspring's nutritional requirements. Mothers would have to weigh the advantages of searching for a concentrated and plentiful, but very unpredictable, food source such as a large dead or dying animal versus the far more certain, but less concentrated and more scattered, gathered food sources. On balance, mothers probably more often opted for the comparatively certain plant food but perhaps encouraged their juvenile daughters and sons as well as their brothers and adolescent sisters to search for meat sources.

Patterns of sharing likely differed for plant and animal food. Plant food, as the basic staple, was probably shared primarily between a mother and her most dependent offspring and secondarily with her juvenile offspring, who foraged for itself but whose diet was occasionally supplemented by food from its mother. Others foraged for themselves. Meat—even from a fairly small animal—probably would have been relatively widely shared in a genealogical unit and among friends, as it is among chimpanzees. Butchered meat, which meant an abundance of food for a short time, was probably shared with all australopithecines in the area. Plant food was the daily staple and meat the occasional delicacy.

Effective communication would be important for social relations and "economic" activities among both individuals seen regularly and those seen irregularly or infrequently. A variety of activities were performed by different individuals. Some coordination might be feasible with increasing communicatory range. Given their small brains, however, language per se was very unlikely—and evidently unnecessary, for they survived and continued to evolve. Menzel's experiments on chimpanzees have shown that even specific information can be communicated nonverbally (1973a). The australopithecines were more intelligent. By this time a relatively complex nonverbal system of communication—more complex than among chimpanzees with their surprising communicatory capacities—was in use.

Chimpanzees have been estimated to have ranges of as little as 7 to 20 square kilometers in a tropical forest to about 190 square kilometers in a savanna woodlands area, and in one very arid region a group of chimpanzees probably has a range as large as 700 to 750 square kilometers (Kano, 1972; Sugiyama, 1973a; Itani, 1979). It is therefore not unreasonable to postulate that hominids (who were both more intelligent and bipedal) had at least as extensive ranges. They thus covered an impressively large area by foot. As ranges grew larger, knowledge of the environment also expanded. Information about group members, food and water sources, raw materials, predators, and other animal species in this large area would all be essential. Alternating wet and dry periods meant that vegetation, and therefore food sources, changed according to the annual cycle. Specific foods were likely available for only limited periods (such as are termites for Gombe chimpanzees). As the hominids increased their geographic range, their capacity to conceptualize and communicate the "where," "when," and relative abundance of a variety of potential food sources was also developing.

Summary: the generic adaptation

Australopithecus is precisely the sort of early hominid one would expect, given (1) a chimpanzee-like ancestral population and (2) the sort of transition to regular utilization of the mosaic savanna hypothesized in Chapter 7. Early hominid anatomy, compared with the ancestral population, was modified for new behaviors: changes in the pelvis, legs, and feet for bipedal locomotion; developing hand skills for tool use; large grinding molars and premolars with reduced canines for effective chewing of savanna plant foods; minimal sexual dimorphism because of selection for a common behavioral adaptation for both females and males; brain expansion and reorganization for their developing memory, conceptualization, problem solving, innovativeness, and more sophisticated communication, as well as for increased hand skills; and the expansion of the brain and reduced sexual dimorphism, in turn, interrelated with the social and technological aspects of the new adaptation.

All of the foregoing are related to gathering plant food on the savanna as the primary adaptation. Females were innovators in gathering. Because of nutritional requirements of pregnancy and nursing and overt demands from hungry children, women had more motivation for technological inventiveness, for creativity in dealing with the environment, for learning about plants, and for developing tools to increase productivity and save time. Males continued to forage for plants without tools as did the ape ancestors and probably also borrowed some of the gathering technology. Selection was for increasingly efficient, time-saving, energy-saving ways of getting food: "Necessity is the mother of invention." Vegetation from the savanna and the woodlands that border streams and lakes was the primary food resource; but meat eating also was increasing somewhat. Inventions, especially of digging and cutting tools, were associated with gathering and sharing. A technology of butchering perhaps had also begun to develop toward the end of *Australopithecus*'s tenure, but there was not yet a technology of hunting. Bipedalism, combined with increasing use of hands and tools, was fundamental to the new way of life.

The ability to communicate social and environmental information was enhanced and formed the basis for hominid communities. Social organization was flexible and perhaps relatively complex; groups could vary in size because sufficient protection was provided by object use, rather than by anatomical specializations such as large canines. The social organization was one of dispersion and aggregation occurring according to situation. With larger aggregations not having a regular or stable membership, everyday communication might become more elaborate in order to deal with a fairly large number of individuals that are not all equally well known or seen in any regular sequence.

A steady food supply was obtained through a flexible social organization, effective communication, anatomical structures appropriate to the new adaptation, and the use of tools. Gathering many kinds of plants and a few types of insects with tools, killing some small game by hand, and, later on, perhaps occasionally butchering large immobile animals together provided a regular omnivorous diet. Objects were used successfully for protection in the environment in which the food was found. Tools were made and used for obtaining and, subsequently, for preparing the food itself. This highly successful adaptation worked for a very long time; it lasted for some 2 million years.

TEN

Early hominid lifeways: the critical role of an interpretive framework

THE preservation of evidence at an archaeological site older than a few millennia is seldom ideal, while the quality and comprehensiveness of research projects are rarely appropriate for an optimal exploitation of all the potential information available even at an average site . . . Similarly, hominid sites mainly yield fragmentary bones that are difficult to reconstruct as a single individual, let alone as representative of a prehistoric group. As a result, genetic variability is poorly understood and much of the taxonomic discussion generated is correspondingly controversial, if not querulous and trivial.

Karl W. Butzer, 1977

TODAY in eastern Africa early hominid fossil discoveries are occurring with bewildering frequency. The evidence is far from complete, difficult to interpret, but enormously richer than in only the early part of this century when the first hominid "ape-man" was unearthed at Taung limeworks in southern Africa and named *Australopithecus africanus* by Dart (1925). The diversity of the fossils—in relative robusticity and shape of jaws, teeth and skull, and in cranial capacity—has engendered a great deal of speculation. Attempts to explain such differences have ranged from the postulation of one polytypic or sexually dimorphic species to the recognition of two, three, or four species of *Australopithecus* (generally considered to be the first hominid genus), and also to the suggestion that more than one genus—both *Australopithecus* and *Homo*, our own genus—may have been present.

Myriad early hominid fossil fragments have been unearthed in eastern and southern Africa. Each year is likely to bring significant new discoveries. This discussion of sites and dates attempts to sort out the existing mass of published information in terms of a time line and the geographic distribution of finds; to present, in a very general way, the nature of the hominid fossil evidence available at each site; and to discuss how these remains have been or might be classified. My preliminary objective here, as I set the stage for hypothesizing about patterning and variability among early

225

hominids, is to delineate morphological variations and change within a time frame. What I shall attempt to demonstrate is that, with an interpretive framework based on the gathering hypothesis, the variation among early hominids becomes explicable.

The fossils to be considered here are a diverse group that fall roughly between *Australopithecus afarensis,* the earliest known basal hominids found at Laetoli and Afar (Hadar Formation), and *Homo erectus,* early members of our own genus. I consider all of the hominids of this general grade to be members of one genus, *Australopithecus.* Save for two jaw fragments from Java and a few teeth from China, all these fossils were found in eastern or southern Africa. They date from *A. afarensis,* starting about 3.77 million to 3.59 million years ago or earlier to approximately 1.5 million years ago when *Homo erectus* appears, with some members perhaps still extant for up to a few hundred thousand years past that date.

After *A. afarensis,* the subsequent australopithecine fossils are from: first, Omo in eastern Africa and the southern African sites, which together cover an extensive time span and therefore provide important information on fossil sequences; second, the roughly contemporaneous sites of Olduvai and East Turkana (Lake Rudolf) in eastern Africa with their particularly rich, and quite similar, remains; and finally, the more recent sites of Chesowanja and Peninj.

In general, the pattern is as follows. The earliest established hominids at Laetoli and Hadar, dating from less than 4 million years ago to about 3 million years ago, are distinctly hominid because of their bipedalism yet retain many features reminiscent of the ape ancestor. These very early hominids exhibited considerable variability – so much so that various fossils were initially compared to two different species of later *Australopithecus* (a gracile and a robust variety) as well as to *Homo,* our own genus (Johanson and Taieb, 1976). The initial tendency to find many species among the earliest known hominids at Laetoli and Hadar subsequently settled down into a well-considered assessment of all these remains as representing one very early, variable, and still quite "primitive" hominid species, *A. afarensis* (Johanson, White, Coppens, 1978; Johanson and White, 1979; Johanson and Edey, 1981).

So much for the situation from somewhat after 4 million years ago to somewhat after 3 million years ago. For the period of about 3 million to 2 million years ago the available fossils are those from Omo in eastern Africa and from the Sterkfontein Type Site and Makapansgat in southern Africa. These fossils have all been considered gracile and termed *A. africanus* (Howell and Coppens, 1976; Tobias, 1978). There is, in fact, considerable variability among them, particularly in the size of the molars and premolars. The earliest hominid remains at Omo (about 3 Mya) have the smallest molars and premolars. In this respect they exhibit continuity with the basal hominid, *A. afarensis*.[1] Subsequent gracile finds between 3 million and 2 million years ago, both at Omo and in southern Africa, show various degrees of enlargement of the molars and premolars.

After 2 million years ago, the fossil record becomes quite prolific, particularly at Omo, Olduvai Gorge, and East Turkana in eastern Africa but also in southern Africa. At Swartkrans and Kromdraai in southern Africa and at Omo, Olduvai, and East Turkana in eastern Africa, a robust form (variously called *A. robustus, A. boisei,* or *Zinjanthropus*) appears. Although it is much more extreme, it nonetheless exhibits clear continuity with prior gracile forms. Gracile forms continue; some have quite large cranial capacities (the "advanced graciles," *A.* or *H. habilis*). By 1.5 million years ago there are still robust and advanced gracile australopithecines in evidence. But the first known *Homo erectus* has already appeared at East Turkana in eastern Africa. *Homo erectus* is also found somewhat later at Olduvai and, from 1.2 million to 1 million years ago, at Omo. Similarly, in the relatively recent, although undated, Sterkfontein Extension Site in southern Africa, there are remains of *Homo erectus* (or at least of an advanced gracile) as well as of Early Acheulian stone tools. The Acheulian tool tradition is usually thought to be associated with *Homo erectus*.

The overall pattern therefore is: first, early, rather ape-like "graciles," the basal hominid (*A. afarensis*); later, more robust graciles (*A. africanus*); then, advanced super graciles (*A./H. habilis*), on the one hand, and advanced super robusts (*A. robustus/boisei*) on the other hand. Presumably, the advanced graciles evolve into *Homo erectus* (which later evolves into *Homo sapiens*), whereas the robust line eventually disappears.

The subsequent description of sites and dates presents the data on which the above pattern is based. It is followed by a discussion of how the gathering hypothesis can shed light on the adaptive meaning of this sequence of variation among these early African hominids.

Sites and dates: an approach to sorting out patterns of variation

The geological formations and fossils at Omo, Ethiopia, in eastern Africa provide exceptional evidence: Here is a continuous record of hominid evolution covering a period of over 2 million years, from

[1] The earliest finds at Omo were initially classified as *A. africanus* (Howell and Coppens, 1976) but may well be *A. afarensis* (Howell, pers. com.).

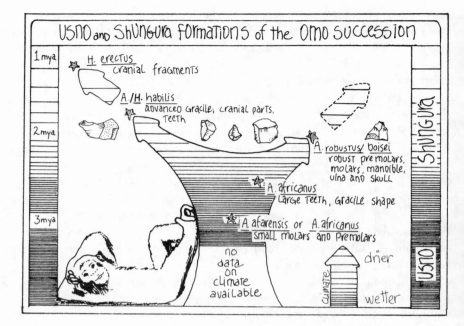

FIGURE 10:1. Omo—the early hominid sequence. At Omo the fossil sequence is particularly instructive. First comes the early basal hominid, *A. afarensis*, or a very gracile australopithecine, *A. africanus*. For the next three quarters of a million years are remains of the "gracile" *A. africanus*, some of which are actually fairly robust. Still later come the more robust australopithecines (*A. robustus/boisei*), the advanced graciles (*A./H. habilis*), and stone tools. Tools were found at several locales but not associated with the fossils. And, finally, *Homo erectus* appears.

about 3 million to 1 million years ago—with strata and dates worked out! The observable sequence of hominid forms is particularly interesting (Howell and Coppens, 1976; Howell, 1976, 1978a). Figure 10:1 portrays this sequence, presenting a possible picture of early hominid variation at Omo plotted against a time line, and Figure 10:2 presents a chart summarizing the fossil and archeological remains.

No hominid remains have been found at Omo in the very early Mursi Formation, dating from about 4.2 million years ago (Boaz,1977a). An early hominid did, however, live in the Omo river basin roughly 3 million years ago (Howell and Coppens, 1976). This early hominid is known from just 21 teeth discovered in the Usno Formation. These teeth, mostly molars and premolars, are similar to those of gracile *Australopithecus africanus* from the Sterkfontein Type Site and Makapansgat in southern Africa but are considerably smaller. Although initially classified as an ordinary gracile australopithecine, *A. africanus* (Howell and Coppens, 1976), it is probable that these early hominids at Omo were part of a population continuous in space and time with the basal hominid, *A. afarensis*, found at Laetoli and Hadar (Howell, pers. com.). These Omo molars and premolars from about 3 million years ago—like *A. afarensis* and probably like the previous ape ancestor—are smaller than those of subsequent gracile australopithecines.

Not far from the early Usno Formation (with its deposits from about 3 Mya), is the more recent Shungura Formation. Its layers, several of which contain hominid remains, span from roughly 2.9 million to 0.9 million years ago (Brown and Shuey, 1976). The period from about 3 million to 2 million years ago at Omo is especially interesting because this is the only site yet known for eastern Africa that has fossils during this time span. At this time, the Omo environment still contained closed and/or open woodland, along with grasslands (Carr, 1976), and was therefore probably quite diverse. Significantly, in the Shungura Formation during this period, roughly 2.9 million to 1.9 million years ago (in Members B, C, D, lower E, most levels of F, and G), there are plentiful remains of *A. africanus*. And in the earlier period, 2.9 million to 2.4 million years ago, only *A. africanus* is found. For these specimens, the dental morphology resembles that of the southern African gracile australopithecines at the Sterkfontein Type Site. The tooth morphology is also similar to that of the earliest fossils at Omo—the 21 molars, premolars, and an incisor from the Usno Formation—but the later molars and premolars are larger, with some even entering the robust size range. Between 3 million and 2 million years ago at Omo, the gracile population was becoming less gracile.

In sum, then, at Omo, there are gracile hominid teeth and a jaw that appear early (about 3 Mya to 2.5 Mya). These finds may represent the early gracile hominid, *A. africanus*, evolving from the basal hominid, *A. afarensis*. Remains of early gracile hominids, classified as *A. africanus*, persist at Omo to 1.8 million years ago.

Slightly before the end of the tenure of *A. africanus* at Omo, about 2 million years ago, a similar but more gracile and more "advanced" hominid appears. It is comparable to a form at Olduvai Gorge (OH7) that has been called *Homo habilis* but that I currently prefer to consider an advanced gracile australopithecine, *A. habilis* (Campbell, 1978). Slightly before that, however, perhaps about 2.1 million years ago or somewhat earlier, a robust australopithecine, *A. robustus* (also called *A. boisei*) appears and is present until at least 1.4 million to 1.2 million years ago at East Turkana and Olduvai, respectively (M. D. Leakey, 1978; R. E. F. Leakey et al., 1978; Walker and R. E. F. Leakey, 1978). It seems reasonable to conclude that some 2.1 million to 1.85 million years ago at Omo both an

Site/date (Mya)		Remains
SHUNGURA FORMATION		
Member L (±1.05–< 0.9)		1 incisor, 1 molar
Member K (±1.35–1.05)	Top	Part of cranium
	Lower	Molar
Member H (1.8–1.65)		Premolar; foot bone
Member G (±2.0–1.8); hominid sediments		Molars, premolars, mandibles, partial crania, part ulna, femoral fragments
Member F (±2.1–2.0)	Upper	2 premolars, 1 mo
	Basal	27 teeth, mandible tools
Member E (±2.25–2.1)	Upper	Tools; partial mandible, premolars, molars, complete ulna (forearm)
	Middle	Molars, premolars, partial juvenile cranium
	Lower	Teeth, mandible frag
	Uncertain	Upper molar, premo
Member D (±2.4–2.25)		10 teeth: 9 molars, incisor; humerus
Member C (±2.65–2.4)		30 teeth (incisors, molars, premolars mandible without tooth crowns, pal. frag., skull parieta frag., hand bone
Member B (±2.95–2.65)		1 premolar, 8 mola
USNO FORMATION About 3.5±0.7–2.97±0.3		21 teeth: 1 incisor, 20 molars, premola

Current classification	Comments
Undetermined	Molar rather like OH13 (*A./H. habilis*)
Homo erectus	Part of top and side of cranium like *Homo erectus* in intracranial morphology, thick cranial vault
Undetermined	Very worn
A./ H. habilis	Tooth almost duplicate of OH13 (*A./H. habilis*)
A. robustus/boisei, A. africanus, and *A./H. habilis*	Many teeth; some robust; many not robust, resemble *A. afr.* and/or *A./H. habilis;* one of crania suggests "early *Homo*" (i.e., advanced gracile *A./H. habilis*)
A. africanus	Tooth size, morphology like *A. africanus*
A. robustus/boisei, A. africanus, and *A./H. habilis*	Some molars, premolars like robust; canine, premolars, molars like *A. africanus;* mandible like advanced gracile (ER1802) at E. Turkana. Crude *established* stone tools (small, introduced quartz); tools localized at several sites; not associated with fossils
⇨ Chopper, flake *A. robustus/boisei* and undetermined	Evidence of *possible* early stone tools, not associated with fossils. Mandible, ulna: morphology and size like robust (ulna longer than for *Homo*); fragmentary teeth undiagnostic
A. robustus/boisei and undetermined	Dental morphology and size like robust; brain 420 cm^3, est. adult size 440 cm^3; some aspects like *A. africanus,* some (esp. skull rear) appear distinctive
A. africanus	Dental morphology and size like *A. africanus*
A. africanus	Dental morphology and size like *A. africanus*
Probably *A. africanus*	3 molars and an incisor like *A. africanus,* 4 too worn to classify; some especially large molars, with morphology like *A. africanus;* one unusual; humerus not small, resembles *A. africanus*
A. africanus	Tooth morphology and size like gracile *A. afr.;* but some within robust size range (*size increase from Usno Formation*); V-shaped mandible, like Sterkfontein gracile *A. afr.;* skull frag. has some indication of crest (as in robusts); hand bone is rare specimen, similar to OH7 (*A./H. habilis*)
A. africanus ⇨	Tooth morphology like prior Usno formation and S. African graciles from Sterkfontein and Makapansgat; size varies, some within range of robust (1 molar, like prior Usno; 3 like Sterkfontein and Makapansgat; another within size range of robust but shape like Sterkfontein)
A. afarensis or *A. africanus*	Unusually small, but shape similar to Sterkfontein and Makapansgat (*A. africanus*); small tooth size, premolar morphology most like *A. afarensis.*

FIGURE 10:2. Early hominid remains in northeastern Africa from approximately 3 Mya to 1 Mya from the Omo Basin, southeastern Ethiopia: Usno and Shungura formations.

advanced robust form and an advanced gracile form evolved from the earlier gracile australopithecines. These, in turn, doubtless evolved from the basal hominid, *A. afarensis.*

Around the time that the two varieties of advanced australopithecines appear at Omo, pollen analysis shows a greater proportion of grasses and fewer trees, indicating a drying trend by 2 million years ago; faunal evidence supports this inference (Carr, 1976; Bonnefille, 1976a; Jaeger and Wesselman, 1976). Some forests were still present, probably close to rivers (Dechamps, 1976; Boaz, 1977a). In addition, also approximately then or slightly earlier, crude stone tools appear in the fossil record at several sites in or about Members E or F of the Shungura Formation, about 2.25 to 2 million years ago (Howell, 1976, 1978b; Merrick and Merrick, 1976; Guilmet, 1977). They are not immediately associated with the fossils. These artifacts are primarily small quartz fragments, flakes, and cores; at one site there is also indication of a possible bone industry but not at the other site. Chavaillon asks: "What could be the use of these very small fragments? It cannot be said that they were for butchering animals or cutting up meat. But there is nothing to gainsay the argument that they could have been used to cut up roots, rhizomes and branches" (1976:572). Given the drying trend about 2 million years ago, it is indeed very plausible that such tools might be used on the less succulent savanna plant foods, which were perhaps now coming to comprise a higher proportion of the edible vegetation. With the gracile form still present at 1.9 million years ago and the robust form already on the scene by 2.1 million years ago (and joined soon thereafter by the advanced gracile), one must ask whether all of them made and used these tools and, if so, whether they used them in identical ways. By 1.1 million years ago *Homo erectus* is present at Omo (Howell and Coppens, 1976; Howell, 1978a, b).

Southern African fossil hominids were discovered first and therefore are considered the type specimens of the gracile and robust forms, even though more recent discoveries in eastern Africa are from stratified sites, are dated, and go back further in time. The southern African fossils may cover a time span roughly contemporaneous with Omo, that is, about 3 million to 1 million years ago, or perhaps a somewhat shorter period of about 3 million to 1.5 million years ago. The primary method used to date early hominid sites in southern Africa consists of comparisons of the associated faunal assemblages with the fauna of radiometrically dated eastern African sites.

Remains of a gracile hominid, termed *Australopithecus africanus*, at Makapansgat and the Sterkfontein Type Site, are the oldest finds in southern Africa and, based on faunal and paleomagnetic comparisons, probably date from about 3 million to more than 2 million years ago (Vrba, 1974, 1975; Brown and Shuey, 1976; Brock et al., 1977; White and Harris, 1977; Partridge, 1973). It is noteworthy that the earliest known hominids in southern Africa, as in eastern Africa, were relatively gracile compared to some of the later forms in both areas. Nonetheless, for their body weight, even these relatively gracile fossils had massive jaws and teeth compared with humans today. Their cheek teeth were also more massive than both the earliest finds at Omo (those 21 teeth in the Usno Formation) and the earlier basal hominids at Laetoli and Hadar, *A. afarensis* (Howell and Coppens, 1976; Johanson and White, 1979).

Quite an impressive array of skeletal parts has been unearthed at these two early sites: skulls, jaws, teeth, part of an upper limb and scapula fragments, part of the vertebral column and pelvis, pieces of an upper and of a distal femur. From such remains it is clear that these early gracile hominids walked on two legs, were small in body and brain, had teeth and jaws adapted to grinding, and died quite young. Despite their clear physical adaptation for upright walking, their arms were still relatively long compared with humans today (Pilbeam, 1972a). This was also the case for fossils from this period at Omo and earlier at Hadar (Johanson and Taieb, 1976; Howell, 1978a). A fossil shoulder bone, part of a scapula from the Sterkfontein Type Site, also retains strong similarities to those of apes (Vrba, 1979). The physical changes that made bipedalism feasible had already occurred, but these early hominids retained anatomical characteristics of the upper arm and shoulder usually associated with hanging and climbing in trees. The environment in southern Africa, like that at Omo during this early period, evidently was still quite varied, with wooded, bush, and open areas; it was not yet nearly so arid as it is today (Howell, 1978a). Walking was crucial for daytime gathering, but trees probably still provided both some food and a critical place for safe sleeping.

The somewhat more recent early hominid sites in southern Africa – Taung, Swartkrans, Kromdraai, and the Sterkfontein Extension Site – may date from around 2.5 million to 1.5 million years ago and conceivably may be younger. The Taung child, the first australopithecine discovered a half century ago, appears to be fairly gracile.[2] Significantly, maturity was

---

[2] Some geological evidence has suggested that the Taung fossil might be the most recent of the southern African australopithecines (Partridge, 1973; Butzer, 1974b), but this is by no means confirmed (Boaz, 1977a).

Partridge (1973) has put forward a method for estimating approximate dates for cave openings for Makapansgat and Sterkfontein, for Swartkrans (but not Kromdraai), and for Taung. He concludes that the caves at Makapansgat and Sterkfontein opened earlier than
Continued on page 236

Sites in southern Africa	Relative Dates	Remains found
STERKFONTEIN Member 5, middle breccia, extension site	Younger than Sterkfontein Type Site; perhaps 1.5 Mya	Maxilla; teeth, mandible; cranium with dentition; stone tools
KROMDRAAI	Younger than Swartkrans (Member 1/A), Sterkfontein (lower breccia), and Makapansgat	Skull parts; teeth; humerus; talus; 5–6 individuals; stone tool(s)
SWARTKRANS Member 2/B, outer cave	Considerably younger than Makapansgat and Sterkfontein; much younger than Member 1/A, Swartkrans	Mandibles; piece of maxilla; part of cranium; teeth; radius; tools
Member 1/A, base of inner cave	Younger than Makapansgat and Sterkfontein Type Site; probably less than 2 Mya	Remains of over 70 individuals: parts of skulls; endocast; jaw; many teeth; fragments of pelvis; femora; hand bones; distal humerus; tools
TAUNG	Uncertain	Child's skull and lower jaw
MAKAPANSGAT	Older than Swartkrans or Kromdraai; approx. 3–2.5 Mya or less	Remains of several individuals: crania; mandibles; teeth; some postcranial remains
STERKFONTEIN Member 4, beds B & C, lower breccia, type site (Sts)	Approx. 3–2.8 Mya or less; older than Sterkfontein extension site	About 40 individuals: skulls; pelves; vertebrae; jaws; teeth; capitate; scapular, humeral parts; femora

Current taxonomic classification	Comments
Possibly *Homo erectus* and/or "*Homo*"	Teeth small compared to main assemblage (*A. africanus*) at Sterkfontein Type Site; tools: Early African Acheulian or "Developed Oldowan"
➡ *A. robustus* and/or *A. indeterminate* (prev. "*Paranthropus robustus*" and "*Homo*"?)	In some respects, more robust than *A. africanus* at Sterkfontein Type Site; less robust than most Swartkrans robusts; one specimen's first molar as small as smallest first molar from Sterkfontein; hominids possible leopard prey; tool(s)
Uncertain, perhaps *A./H. habilis* or *H. erectus* (prev. "*Telanthropus capensis*")	Compared to other Swartkrans remains, teeth smaller and resemble *H. erectus*; cranial crests and ridges, jaws and face less robust than Member 1/A remains; tools, perhaps early Acheulian or "Developed Oldowan"
A. robustus (or *A. crassidens*) and "*Homo*"	Many robust australopithecines, and possible "*Homo*"; brain approx. 530cm^3; molars and body larger than for *A. africanus*; many australopithecines probably immature at death; all younger than 40; probable leopard predation; simple tools resemble those from Olduvai Bed II ("Developed Oldowan")
A. africanus, but rather robust	Gracile size and shape for skull, jaw, teeth; cranial capacity (est. for adult) approx. 440cm^3; teeth large compared to *H. sapiens*
A. africanus, possibly some *A. robustus*	Relatively gracile; some specimens rather robust; cranial capacity approx. 435cm^3; possibly rocks and bone used as tools
➡ *A. africanus*, possibly some *A. robustus*	Relatively gracile; no tools; mean cranial capacity 443cm^3; differential molar wear; possible lair of saber-toothed felid

FIGURE 10:3. Southern Africa: early hominid fossil remains from about 3 Mya to roughly 1.5 Mya. The earliest southern African finds are relatively gracile australopithecines (*A. africanus*). Subsequent hominid fossils tend to be either more robust or advanced gracile forms, the latter probably evolving into *Homo erectus*.

delayed for the Taung child – a hominid feature (Mann, 1968, 1975; Howell, 1978a). There was more time for learning than among the ape ancestors. At Swartkrans are many remains of a form with much more robust chewing teeth, jaw, and skull; it was probably also larger than the earlier gracile forms (see Figure 10:3). Another find at Swartkrans is quite gracile: Its teeth resemble those of *Homo erectus* (Read, 1975), and it is from a portion of the cave that was filled subsequently. The remains from Kromdraai are more robust than the earlier gracile remains at Sterkfontein but less robust than the majority of remains at Swartkrans. At the Sterkfontein Extension Site are finds that may be *Homo* or *Homo erectus*. The stone tools found there are more "advanced" than the earliest stone tools found in eastern Africa. These Sterkfontein Extension Site tools have been classified as Early Acheulian (Stiles, 1979a). This is of interest because the Acheulian tool tradition is often thought to be associated with *Homo erectus* (J. D. Clark, 1975).

Overall, there is considerable variability, with some southern African remains (especially those at Kromdraai) difficult to classify. When plotted along a time line, however, patterns do emerge. Figure 10:3 summarizes the evidence. The oldest australopithecines at Makapansgat and Sterkfontein are relatively gracile, as are the early remains at Omo. Later, probably after 2 million years ago but prior to 1 million years ago, robust forms (*A. robustus* or, previously, *A. crassidens*) appear at Swartkrans with contrasting skull shape and teeth. At Kromdraai fossils are also rather robust but seem more intermediate in nature. The gracile line may persist (if Taung is fairly late), and what might be a more evolved gracile or *Homo erectus* appears later at Swartkrans and at the Sterkfontein Extension Site. The similarities to the sequence at Omo in eastern Africa are striking.

Continued from page 233
the caves at Swartkrans. In terms of the relative order of Makapansgat and Sterkfontein (gracile hominids: early) as compared to Swartkrans (robust hominids: later), Partridge's conclusions concur with those based on the faunal evidence. However, Partridge also concludes that the cave at Taung opened most recently, which is not consistent with the faunal evidence (Boaz, 1977b; Cooke, 1978). Bishop strongly questions the viability of the assumptions about river movements and erosion rates underlying the cave-opening date estimations in general. And, specifically, with regard to Taung, he states: "The most likely explanation for the young 'date' at Taung is that the locality is on a different river system from the Transvaal sites [i.e., Makapansgat, Sterkfontein, Swartkrans, and Kromdraai]. The river flows over a contrasting substrate and through a series of different morphological settings to an Atlantic rather than an Indian Ocean base-level" (1978:263). Taung, unlike the other four cave sites in the Transvaal, is in Cape Province.

Faunal sequences provide relatively reliable indications of chronological order. However, attempting to assign actual dates based on correlations with dated fauna in other environments (for example, eastern Africa as contrasted to southern Africa) is quite risky (Bishop, 1978).

Olduvai Gorge is probably the most famous of the eastern African early hominid sites. It is also a site for which extremely thorough and careful geological, archeological, and fossil analyses are now complete (see Figures 10:4 and 10:5).[3] Both robust australopithecines and advanced graciles have been found at Bed I.[4] Significantly, this is about the same time they appear at Omo. Also, *A. africanus* may persist at Olduvai, in both Bed I and subsequent Bed II times, that is, until about 1.5 million years ago. These possible gracile australopithecines were originally classified as advanced graciles.[5] More pertinent than whether these fossils are *A. africanus* or *A. habilis* is the difficulty there has been in differentiating them. Some "advanced gracile" and "early gracile" fossils closely resemble each other—just as do some "robusts" and "graciles."[6] This is doubtless because both the advanced graciles and the robusts evolved from the earlier graciles, which in turn evolved from the basal hominid stock, *A. afarensis*.

The hominids recovered from the living sites of Olduvai Beds I and II lived fairly near a shallow lake (M. D. Leakey, 1978; Hay, 1976a, b). The lake was largely surrounded by forested highlands, with savanna extending from the lake margins to the wooded uplands. The lake flooded the surrounding flat terrain from time to time, and there were marshy areas near

[3] There is, however, beginning to be some reevaluation of how hominids were classified at Olduvai, particularly with regard to gracile australopithecines and advanced graciles (R. E. F. Leakey et al., 1978). Mary Leakey also states that "the terminology used in describing Plio-Pleistocene hominids may be ripe for revision" (1978:5).

[4] The combination of K/Ar dating and geomagnetic polarity measurements gives the upper part of Bed I "one of the firmest dates of any hominid-bearing lower Pleistocene stratigraphic unit. Potassium-argon dates clearly indicate an age on the order of 1.7–1.8 Mya for the fossiliferous deposits" (Hay, 1976b:212–213). Using evidence from magnetic stratigraphy, stratal thickness, and development of paleosols, Hay, a geologist, estimates that the hominid and tool-bearing part of Bed I spans only 50,000 to 100,000 years (1976b).

[5] R. E. F. Leakey and associates (1978), by comparison with forms they have reclassified from *A./H. habilis* (advanced gracile) to *A. africanus* (gracile) at East Turkana, suggest that OH24, in Lower Bed I, and OH13, of Middle Bed II, are ordinary gracile australopithecines (*A. africanus*) rather than advanced graciles (*A.* or *H. habilis*) as originally thought (M. D. Leakey, 1971). OH24 is composed of a crushed cranium with some teeth, and OH13 is a juvenile's broken skull with jaws and teeth (M. D. Leakey, 1971, 1978).

[6] There is considerable overlap between some of the premolar and molar sizes (upper and lower M_3, lower P_4, for example) for southern African graciles (Taung, Makapansgat, Sterkfontein Type Site) and robusts (Kromdraai, Swartkrans), according to measurements reported by Johanson and White (1979). And the Kromdraai (robust) material is intermediate in some respects between that at Sterkfontein (gracile) and Swartkrans (robust): molars are smaller than Swartkrans and as small at Sterkfontein, but body size is greater than Sterkfontein (Pilbeam, 1972a). The Kromdraai specimens are less robust than many eastern African robusts (Howell, 1978a). Thus, although fossils at Kromdraai are indeed "robust," are they so robust that they are no longer "gracile"?

Bed	Site/Remains	Current classification
BED II (1.7–1.15 Mya) Upper	LLK: Cranium (OH9)	*Homo erectus/Homo leakeyi*

	TKUF,TKLF: tools
	SC: molar and incisors (OH38),
	  ulna (OH36); tools
	BK: molar (OH3) and canine;
	  tools
		Homo erectus and possibly *A.
		  robustus/boisei*
		A. robustus/boisei

Middle	FCWF: molar (OH19); tools
	EF-HR: tools
	MNK **skull site**: juvenile skull
	  and jaws (OH13)
	  Juvenile skull fragments,
	    teeth
	  Tools
	Molars, partial mandible
	Molar
		"Homo"?
		
		A. africanus or *A./H. habilis*
		
		Undetermined, *"Homo"?*
		
		A./H. habilis
		"Homo"?

Lower	FLK North: elephant bones
	  with tools; possible
	  "butchery site"
	Femoral fragment
	Molar; tools
	
	Teeth and cranial fragments
	Crushed skull, teeth; tools
		No hominid fossils
		
		A. robustus/boisei
		A./H. habilis?
		
		Possibly *A. robustus/boisei, A. indet.*
		Possibly *A./H. habilis* or *A. africanus*

BED I
(1.9–1.7 Mya)
Upper
	HWK: **molar**
	FLK North: elephant bones
	  with tools; possible
	  "butchery site"
	FLK North: 3 antelope
	  skulls, 1 near hominid toe
	  bone (OH10) and "debris"
		A./H. habilis? "Homo"?
		No hominid fossils
		
		A./H. habilis? "Homo"?

Middle	FLK: skull, jaw, teeth (OH5);
	  teeth, skull fragments, leg
	  bones; tools
	FLK NN: skull fragments,
	  mandible, teeth, hand
	  bones (all OH7); tools
	Foot (OH8), shoulder, rib,
	  hand, arm bones
	Teeth
	
	Skull fragments
		A. robustus/boisei(OH5), *A./H.
		  habilis?*
		
		A./H. habilis, "Homo," or
		  A. africanus
		
		Possibly *A./H. habilis* and unclas-
		  sified
		Possibly *A. robustus/boisei* and
		  A./H. habilis
		Unclassified

Lower	MK: mandible and teeth
	  (OH4)
	DK East: crushed cranium
	  and teeth (OH24); tools
		A. africanus, "Homo," or
		  A./H. habilis (OH24)
		A./H. habilis (OH4) or undeter-
		  mined

Comments

Acheulian tools (many hand axes) about 91 m from OH9; animal bones, some
broken, possibly to remove marrow
Indeterminate tools: "Developed Oldowan" or Early Acheulian
Inferred "Developed Oldowan"

"Giant" hominid tooth; "Developed Oldowan"

Indeterminate tools: "Developed Oldowan" or Early Acheulian
Early Acheulian
OH13 resembles KNM-ER1813 at E. Turkana, which has a small cranial capacity
and has been reclassified from *H. habilis* to *A. africanus* by R. E. Leakey

Probable Oldowan tools
No tools
No tools

Many probable Oldowan tools; possible "butchered"
elephant (*Deinotherium*) car-
cass partly crushed in excavation
No tools
"Developed Oldowan" or Early
    Acheulian tools

Probable Oldowan tools

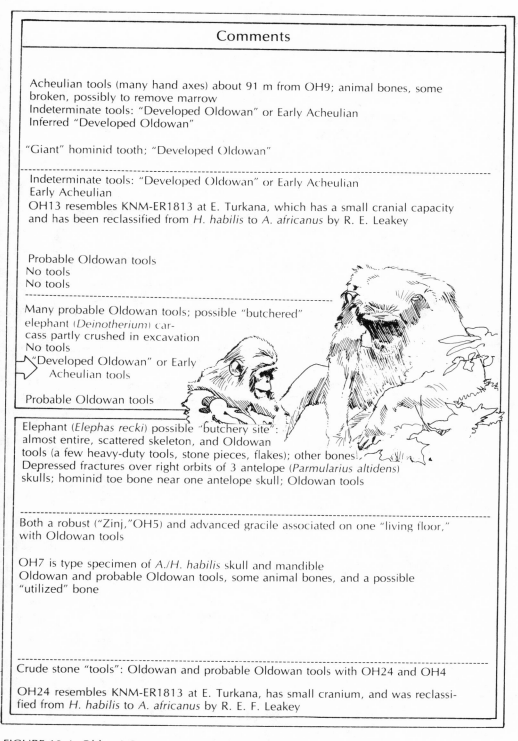

Elephant (*Elephas recki*) possible "butchery site":
almost entire, scattered skeleton, and Oldowan
tools (a few heavy-duty tools, stone pieces, flakes); other bones
Depressed fractures over right orbits of 3 antelope (*Parmularius altidens*)
skulls; hominid toe bone near one antelope skull; Oldowan tools

----

Both a robust ("Zinj,"OH5) and advanced gracile associated on one "living floor,"
with Oldowan tools

OH7 is type specimen of *A./H. habilis* skull and mandible
Oldowan and probable Oldowan tools, some animal bones, and a possible
"utilized" bone

Crude stone "tools": Oldowan and probable Oldowan tools with OH24 and OH4

OH24 resembles KNM-ER1813 at E. Turkana, has small cranium, and was reclassified from *H. habilis* to *A. africanus* by R. E. F. Leakey

FIGURE 10:4. Olduvai Gorge: summary of some of the fossil and archeological
remains for Beds I and II, approximately 1.9 to 1.15 Mya.

the lake (Hay, 1976b). Two possible butchery sites have been located at Olduvai: the first in Upper Bed I (FLK North), the second in Lower Bed II (also FLK North), thus probably roughly 1.8 million to slightly less than 1.7 million years ago. Both seemed to be swampy areas and, in each instance, it was a type of elephant (*Elephas recki* and *Deinotherium*) that was associated with Oldowan tools (M. D. Leakey, 1971; Potts, 1978). These two sites, and a similarly dated one at East Turkana, are the earliest known possible butchery sites. They occur nearly 2 million years after fully bipedal hominids lived at nearby Laetoli some 3.77 million to 3.59 million years ago.[7]

The possible Upper Bed I "butchery site" at Olduvai is particularly interesting because it differs so strikingly from later Middle or Upper Pleistocene butchery sites (Clark and Haynes, 1970; Potts, 1978).[8] This Upper Bed I locale is presumed to be a butchery site because tools were found near the elephant bones.[9] However, at this Upper Bed I "butchery site" — unlike the much later, well-verified butchery site at Mwanganda's village in Malawi, Africa (Clark and Haynes, 1970) — the Olduvai elephant skeleton is remarkably complete and the bones surprisingly intact (Potts, 1978).[10] This indicates, I suggest, that butchery was not yet a well-developed skill even as recently as Upper Bed I times, some 1.8 million or 1.7 million years ago. At this time, meat eating probably was still largely confined to chimpanzee-style predation (without tools) on small animals, a possible beginning of occasional efforts to kill medium-sized animals (such as antelopes) with tools, and rare attempts to cut off some pieces of meat from large animals (like elephants) that got stuck in swampy areas and were either then killed or died of natural causes. The fact that the Olduvai Bed I elephant carcass is largely intact, despite the association of stone tools, seems to indicate that butchery skills had not yet advanced to the point where large pieces could be removed and carried away.

[7] Also from about this time, in Upper Bed I at Olduvai, three "antelope" skulls with depressed fractures over the right eye orbits have been recovered. The fractures have been suggested as indicative of lethal blows by hominids (M. D. Leakey, 1978). Although the three fractured antelope skulls are intriguing, the lack of reports of associated hominid tools or fossils for two of them must leave their status in doubt. For the third (Upper Bed I, FLK North, level 5), "occupation debris" and a hominid toe bone (OH10) are found in the same level as the antelope skull (M. D. Leakey, 1971), providing somewhat suggestive proximity. There seems to be no indication or evidence of antelope butchery, however.

[8] Unfortunately, the bones at the Bed II "butchery site" were crushed during excavation, and information is not as complete for this site as for the "butchery site" in Bed I.

[9] At the other Olduvai possible butchery site, there were also elephant bones and tools.

[10] Whereas the possible butchery site at Olduvai in Beds I and II are from the Late Pliocene to early Pleistocene, the established butchery site at Mwanganda's village is considerably later. It dates from the Middle Pleistocene or early Upper Pleistocene (Clark and Haynes, 1970).

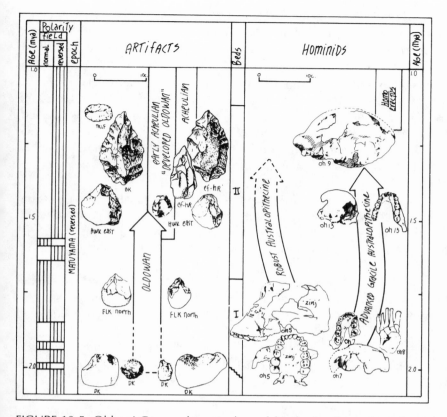

FIGURE 10:5. Olduvai Gorge—dates, tools, and fossils. Fossil remains reflect hominid evolution, from australopithecines (both robust and advanced gracile plus possible gracile) to further advanced gracile fossils (and possible gracile ones), then to *Homo erectus* (OH9), an early member of our own genus. Tools change over time, from very simple ones in Lower Bed I to quite complex ones in Upper Bed II. The time covered here has been measured by several techniques and extends over roughly three quarters of a million years—from less than 2 Mya to somewhat over 1 Mya.

Crude pebble tools from what is usually called the Oldowan Industry have been recovered from Bed I (Figure 10:5). In this bed, pebble tools were found associated with remains of robust australopithecines, advanced graciles, and possible graciles at several different sites. Tools were also found near these types of hominids at more recent sites in Bed II (M. D. Leakey, 1971, 1978; R. E. F. Leakey et al., 1978; Howell, 1978a). In Bed II, although probable Oldowan and/or Developed Oldowan tools persist (M. D. Leakey, 1971, 1978), the Early Acheulian and/or Acheulian Industry appears (M. D. Leakey, 1971; Stiles, 1979b). Stiles (1979b) has argued that for four living floors in Middle and Upper Bed II (dated about 1.5 Mya or after), sets of artifacts called Developed Oldowan and Acheulian are really not distinct tool traditions but simply show differences in the extent of flaking and biface making because of differences in how easy or difficult it is to detach flakes from the type of rock used. In other words, the quartz used for the Developed Oldowan tools was less conducive to flake detachment than the lava used for the Acheulian. Thus, at approximately one time level, there really is not evidence for two distinct tool traditions.

Over time, however, a growing sophistication in tool making occurs. The tools in Bed I are mostly "choppers." In Bed II, the Developed Oldowan, or Early Acheulian, does not yet include bifacial "handaxes," but there are choppers, spheroids, and small tools. From the middle of Bed II on, this Developed Oldowan or Early Acheulian includes small bifacial tools. The Acheulian Industry appears in Upper Bed II and is made up largely of bifacial tools (tools with flakes chipped off on both sides). Another contrast between the earlier Bed I and the subsequent Bed II is in terms of animal bones exhibiting indications of utilization (possibly as bone tools): There are only 5 in Bed I but at least 105 in Bed II (M. D. Leakey,. 1971).

In Bed I, there may well be remains of both graciles (*A. africanus*) and advanced graciles (*A.* or *H. habilis*) resembling those at East Turkana (Tobias, 1976; R. E. F. Leakey et al., 1978). There are also robust forms (formerly called *"Zinjanthropus"*) resembling those at East Turkana (*"A. boisei"*) and Swartkrans (*A. robustus*) (Walker and R. E. F. Leakey, 1978). In Bed II, *Homo erectus* appears (M. D. Leakey, 1971). A likely interpretation is that *Homo erectus,* in Bed II, has further evolved from the advanced graciles. The remaining robust, gracile, and advanced gracile specimens in Bed II could be considered archaic forms, evolutionary remnants from an earlier stage. At Olduvai, then, there appear to be both graciles and advanced graciles as well as robust forms in Bed I. They persist on into Bed II, with *Homo erectus* appearing in Bed II at least by about 1.2 million years ago (Hay, 1976a; Howell, 1978a).

From East Turkana, Kenya, comes the well-known KNM-ER1470 skull. It has a comparatively large cranial capacity of about 770 to 775 cubic centimeters (R. E. F. Leakey et al., 1978). This is bigger than the southern African averages for early gracile *Australopithecus* (422 cm^3), for the southern African and Olduvai average for robust forms (530 cm^3), or for the advanced gracile (*A. habilis*) at Olduvai (633 to 684 cm^3), although it is still smaller than *Homo erectus* (R. E. F. Leakey, 1973b). Dating is, of course, critical to understanding where KNM-ER1470 and the many other interesting fossil hominids at East Turkana fit into the evolutionary sequence (see Figures 10:6 and 10:7). Radiometric dates at East Turkana have been under dispute, but the issue now appears resolved.

Numerous hominid remains have been found at East Turkana at several locales, in particular Ileret and Koobi Fora. The now famous large-brained early hominid KNM-ER1470 was recovered from an inland part of the Koobi Fora Formation, area 131, stratigraphically below the KBS Tuff and above the Tulu Bor Tuff, perhaps roughly midway through these approximately 60-meter-thick deposits (R. E. F. Leakey, 1973b).

The KBS Tuff has had a fascinating history of dating controversy.[11] Preliminary dating attempts on the KBS Tuff by the regular potassium-argon (K/Ar) technique resulted in a scatter of dates (Fitch and Miller, 1970). Determinations by the $^{40}Ar/^{39}Ar$ step heating technique were made in an attempt to resolve the uncertainty (Behrensmeyer, 1978b). The dates obtained were: KBS Tuff complex, 2.54 million years ago and 2.61 ± 0.26 million years ago; and for the lower Tulu Bor Tuff, 3.18 ± 0.09 million years ago (Fitch and Miller, 1970; Fitch et al., 1974; Fitch and Miller, 1976). If these dates had been correct it would have meant that a large-brained hominid (KNM-ER1470) lived about the same time as small-brained, gracile *Australopithecus* and long before either the robust or the advanced gracile lineages! However, these early dates obtained by the $^{40}Ar/^{39}Ar$ step heating technique were not consistent with faunal correlations.

The relative age of the hominid fossils at East Turkana can be ascertained by comparisons of fossil faunal sequences. For example, a comparison of fossil suid ("pig") sequences for sites that also bear early hominid remains not only helps to place these early hominid sites relative to each other (J. M. Harris, 1977; White and Harris, 1977) but also, on the whole, correlates very well with available radiometric dates (see Figure 10:7). The consistency of this picture, therefore, helped to resolve the dating controversy at East Turkana. John M. Harris (1977:670) concluded that "from available vertebrate evidence . . . the Tulu Bor Tuff [at Koobi Fora] is not, in terms of conventional radiometric dates, as old as 3.18 m.y." He goes on to point out that "the suid faunas from the upper part of the Lower Member of the Koobi Fora Formation [just below the KBS Tuff] are evolutionarily equivalent to those from Omo Shungura Member G and Olduvai Bed I." The upper part of Bed I at Olduvai is firmly dated at 1.8 million to 1.7 million years ago (Hay, 1976b).

[11] There is both a KBS Tuff, which is continuous over a rather wide area and discussed above and in Figures 10:6 and 10:7, and a KBS site, as is shown on Figure 10:9.

Formation	Ileret Region			
	Marker tuff date	Remains found	Current classification	Comments
Guomde Formation		1 cranium, 1 femur	None	No information
	Chari avg. 1.3 Mya			
Upper Member Koobi Fora Formation		Several fossils: crania, jaws, postcranials	Several unclassified; 1 A. robustus/boisei femur; 1 A. africanus (or A./H. habilis) mandible; H. erectus skull (ER3883)	Interesting diversity, including an early Homo erectus
	middle/ Lower 1.57–1.48 Mya	Tools, some fossils	Most unclassified; 1 A. robustus/boisei	Concentrated tools, probably Karari industry, very near several hominids (1 robust)
		Many fossils: crania, jaw, postcranials	Many unclassified; some A. robustus/boisei (incl. ER406), and a gracile (ER732)	Early A robustus at Ileret, E. Turkana but later than at Olduvai, Omo, or southern Africa; gracile ER732 originally classified as female A. boisei by R. E. F. Leakey
Lower Member Koobi Fora Formation	KBS equivalent 1.8 Mya.	Juvenile cranial fragments and teeth	A./H. habilis	A. habilis also appears about this time elsewhere at E. Turkana and Olduvai, and slightly later at Omo

Marker tuff date	Remains found	Current classification	Comments
Karari avg. 1.3 Mya			
	Postcranials	Unclassified	No information
⇨	ER3230: lower jaw and teeth; tools	A. robustus/boisei; Karari Industry	Many Karari tools and some animal bones at site near A. robustus mandible site
Okote 1.57 – 1.48 Mya			
	Many fossils, including skull ER3733; ER1813 skull and upper jaw; ER1805 cranium and jaws; ER1806 jaw fragments; tools	H. erectus (ER3733); A. africanus or A./H. habilis (ER1813); unclassified (ER1805) A. robustus/boisei (ER1806); KBS (early Oldowan) Industry	Remarkably complete, very early H. erectus skull: 850cm³ (ER3733); ER1813, perhaps A. africanus, small cranial capacity (505–510 cm³) but A. habilis-like jaw and teeth. Many unclassified fossils: ER1805 has small molars but robust-like crests for jaw muscle attachments; cranial capacity 582cm³. Tools, probably KBS, near ER1805 and robust mandible (ER1806)
KBS 1.8 Mya			
⇨	Many cranial, dental, postcranial remains, incl. ER1470, 1482, 1469; tools; possible hippo "butchery" site	Many unclassified; several classified as A./H. habilis or "Homo" (incl. ER1470 and ER1482); another probably A. robustus/boisei (ER1469)	ER1470 is earliest known large-brained form, est. at 770–775cm³ cranial capacity; KBS Industry tools ("Early Oldowan"), not with hominid fossils; possible "butchery" site: hippo, KBS tools, no hominid fossils
Tulu Bor.	Hominid tooth fragments	None	No evidence of stone tools or "butchery"

Above table titled: **Koobi Fora Region**

FIGURE 10:6. East Turkana, Kenya: hominid remains at two regions, Ileret and Koobi Fora. Marker tuffs provide an estimate of fossil dates.

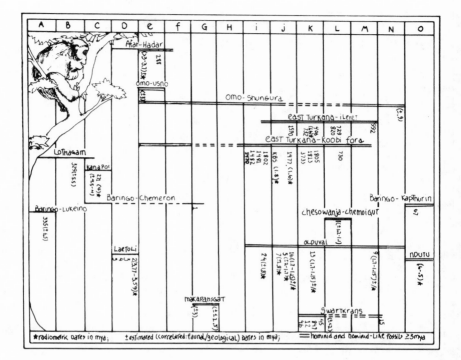

FIGURE 10:7. Comparison of fossil animals at various hominid sites can show the relative ages of these sites. Here, hominid fossils and sites are compared according to fossil "pig" (suid) sequences. Dates have been added where available. The date of 1.8 Mya for the KBS tuff at East Turkana correlates with fauna and dates at other sites.

Further, pumice from the KBS Tuff was tested with conventional K/Ar dating techniques but with innovations in laboratory processes for more effective separating out of the datable pumice prior to testing (Curtis et al., 1975). Samples of pumice from the KBS Tuff from Area 131 (where the KNM-ER1470 skull was recovered) gave an age of 1.82 ± 0.04 million years ago and, from other areas, 1.6 million years ago. These dates are consistent with the faunal evidence (J. M. Harris, 1977; White and Harris, 1977).

More recently, several tuffs in the Koobi Fora Formation at East Turkana – including the controversial KBS Tuff – have been found to correlate with tuffs in the nearby Shungura Formation at Omo. The KBS Tuff at East Turkana and Tuff H2 at Omo correlate in terms of composition, paleomagnetism, fauna, and a date of 1.8 million years ago (Cerling et al., 1979). Two even more recent K/Ar studies (Drake et al., 1980; McDougall et al., 1980) have reported mean dates of 1.8 ± 0.1 million years ago and 1.89 ± 0.01 million years ago, respectively. With a date of about 1.8 million years ago for the KBS Tuff, KNM-ER1470 is no longer such an enigma: it becomes roughly similar in age to advanced graciles at Omo and Olduvai, Bed I.

Robust australopithecines also were present in deposits underlying the KBS Tuff—thus slightly earlier than 1.8 million years ago—as indicated, for example, by the left half mandible, KNM-ER1469 (R. E. F. Leakey, 1973a). Further, a partial V-shaped mandible, KNM-ER1482, of uncertain affinities, was found below the KBS Tuff (R. E. F. Leakey, 1973a). KNM-ER1482 is not a very robust mandible,[12] nor does it appear to be an advanced gracile or gracile form (R. E. F. Leakey and Wood, 1974). Is it a somewhat robust descendant of the more archaic, relatively gracile basal australopithecine, *A. afarensis?*[13]

Somewhat later in time, above the KBS Tuff, a small-brained gracile is represented by a cranium (KNM-ER1813). Despite being considerably more recent, and with teeth similar to those of advanced graciles, the cranium still resembles the early gracile *A. africanus* found at Sterkfontein in southern Africa. It has a moderate cranial capacity of about 505 to 510 cubic centimeters (Holloway, pers. com. to R. E. F. Leakey et al., 1978). Another skull (KNM-ER1805)—which faunal correlations place about the same time as Olduvai, Lower Middle Bed II, namely, less than 1.7 million years ago—is quite enigmatic. "Its relatively large cranium bears sagittal and nuchal crests but has small teeth; this combination is in contrast to all the specimens previously recovered from East Rudolf" (R. E. F. Leakey, 1974:655).

Variability among these hominids at East Turkana about 2 million to 1.6 million years ago (somewhat above and somewhat below the KBS Tuff and KBS Tuff equivalent) is really very striking. There are relatively gracile, robust, and advanced large-brained gracile fossils (Figure 10:8). This is also roughly the same period that two or more forms of early hominid can be identified at Omo, at Olduvai Gorge, and at sites in southern Africa. The variety at East Turkana does, however, appear to surpass that at other sites that sample the populations about this time.

The fact that the variability at East Turkana appears to cluster in age around the KBS Tuff becomes especially interesting when considered in light of other events occurring then. An important shift in climate is detect-

[12] It could be classified as a comparatively small female robust, however (Howell, pers. com.).
[13] Some of the basal *A. afarensis*'s jaws may have been roughly V-shaped. For a comparison of Laetoli jaw LH4 to both *Ramapithecus* and a pygmy chimpanzee, see Figures 3:8 and 8:7.

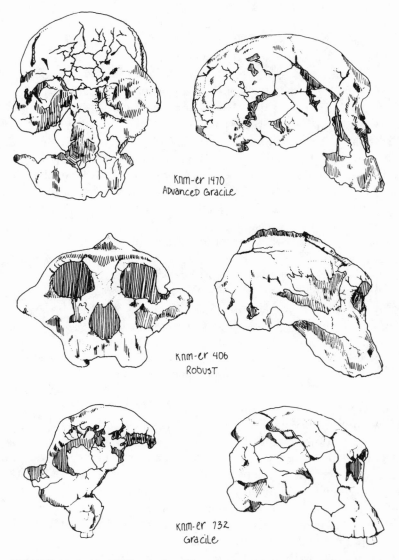

Knm-er 1470
ADvanceD Gracile

Knm-er 406
RobusT

Knm-er 732
Gracile

FIGURE 10:8. Variability in fossil hominids at Ileret and Koobi Fora, East Tur-kana, Kenya about 2 Mya to 1.6 Mya. Note that the robust form (KNM-ER406) has bony crests for muscle attachments for heavy jaws with large grinding teeth. KNM-ER1470 already exhibits cranial enlargement for a bigger brain.

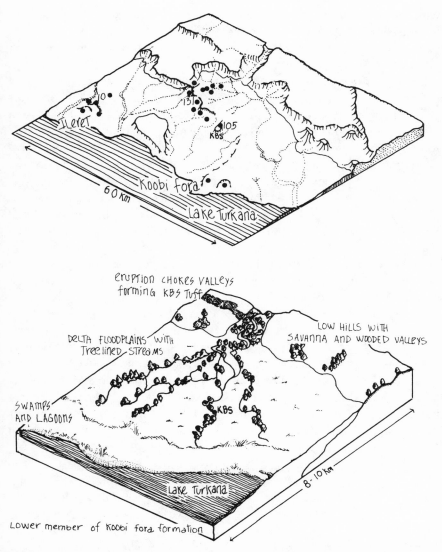

FIGURE 10:9. East Turkana: *above,* fossil sites today are shown; *below,* the richer environment in which the fossil hominids lived is pictured.

able through changing percentages of carbonates in the soil; the KBS Tuff marks this change. About that time, most likely 2 million to 1.8 million years ago, there was a drastic decrease in rainfall (Cerling et al., 1977). East Turkana, like Omo, was entering a drier period. Lake Turkana receded, and "rivers and streams coming from the northeast established winding distributory channels across the newly emergent flats" (Isaac et al., 1976:534). A volcano also erupted about then; its effluvia spread down through the stream channels. This is what is now known as the KBS Tuff (Figure 10:9).

Even extensive hominid variability and climatic change do not exhaust the list of significant occurrences at East Turkana some 1.8 million years ago. Early stone tools were discovered associated with the KBS Tuff in Area 105 by Behrensmeyer in 1969; this site has now been excavated thoroughly, and several other tool-bearing sites discovered since then have been examined (Isaac et al., 1976). Most of these were located on the shores of tree-bordered streams (Isaac et al., 1976). These stream-edge sites doubtless had more vegetation than the increasingly dry surroundings (Figure 10:9). At several sites tools alone are found, with little or no animal bone (Isaac and Harris, 1978). The circumstantial evidence suggests that many of these tools were used for obtaining and/or preparing the plant food, which was more abundant near water than elsewhere.

In one site dating from somewhat before 1.8 million years ago, a concentration of tools was found associated with hippo bones; the hippo probably lay in a hollow or pool within a silted-up channel (Isaac et al., 1976; Isaac and Harris, 1978). In this instance, small, sharp flakes predominated (Isaac et al., 1976). These early East Turkana hominids may have been beginning to utilize meat from large animals when feasible—here from a hippo that had perhaps floundered in the sand and mud of the stream bed. Whether this animal was killed and then butchered or whether hominids scavenged an animal that had already died is unclear. This occurs at approximately the same time as the indications of butchery at Olduvai but possibly slightly earlier.

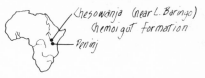

At Chesowanja to the east of Lake Baringo, and at Peninj some 320 kilometers farther south, are finds that sample a late robust australopithecine population or populations. The Peninj mandible has extremely small canine teeth and progressively larger cheek teeth; it was an isolated find, without other parts of cranium or skeleton, and was not in association with artifacts (Tobias, 1965). The Chesowanja cranial fragment (KNM-CH1) shows features that are quite different from earlier robust specimens. It may date from less than 1.5 million years ago; its cranial capacity may be larger than other known robust specimens; and the teeth, though large, are surprisingly unworn. It came from the gray tuffaceous grit within the Chemoigut Formation (Carney et al., 1971). Fragments of two molar teeth (KNM-CH302), also of a robust australopithecine, were found 3 meters higher in the same formation (Bishop et al., 1975). Many artifacts have also been found at Chesowanja; they come from at least eight levels, spanning some 50 meters of sediments, all within about 1 kilometer of each other. There are four groups of artifacts, from oldest to youngest. The earliest, Group A, is an assemblage of cores, chopping tools, and flakes (without "bifaces" or "cleavers") and is confined to the Chemoigut Formation – the formation in which the robust cranial fragments and molar teeth were found.[14]

The robust hominid population sampled by the remains at Chesowanja lived along the shores of a slightly salty lake, fed by fresh-water streams. Animal bones found in the vicinity include remains adapted to both a bush grassland environment (elephants, giraffes, rhinos, antelopes, equids, and suids) and river and lake mammals and reptiles such as hippos, crocodiles, and turtles (J. W. K. Harris and Bishop, 1976).[15]

Although the date for the Chesowanja partial cranium is not entirely clear, it does seem certain that this is a relatively late robust australopithecine. Clear robust finds at Omo are dated about 2.1 million years ago, so that even if the Chesowanja finds were as old as 1.5 million years ago the robust line could have had some half a million more years of evolution behind it by then.

With fragments of two late robust australopithecines unearthed in the Chemoigut Formation and many artifacts also found in this formation (Bishop et al., 1975), the evidence points to the conclusion that robust australopithecines, at least by this time, were using stone tools regularly. Carney and colleagues note that "the absence of marked wear on any tooth is most striking" (1971:514). The Chesowanja late robust population appears to be one that still had large grinding molars and premolars, that regularly used stone tools, and whose teeth showed little wear. These robust gatherers might already be using tools not only to gather but also to clean, chop, cut, crush, and otherwise prepare plant food prior to eating it. Probably this robust population had not used tools to prepare plant foods for very long; this would account for the fact that their molars were not yet reduced in size, but do not show extensive wear.

A controversy over reconstruction of skull shape and size – and therefore

[14] Much later tools are also found, the earliest of which are the Group B Acheulian artifacts dating from about 0.5 Mya (Bishop et al., 1975).
[15] These fauna suggest an age over 1.34 Mya (Bishop et al., 1975). The sediments show reversed paleomagnetic polarity, which most likely places them within the Matuyama Reversed Epoch (0.7 Mya to 2.4 Mya). A date of 1.2 Mya was obtained on the Chepchuk trachyte (originally thought to be older than the fossils), but unfortunately the relationship of this trachyte to the fossil-bearing sediments is not yet established (Carney et al., 1971; Bishop, 1972; Howell, 1972; Bishop et al., 1975).

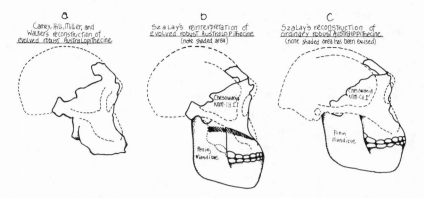

FIGURE 10:10. The Chesowanja robust specimen and Peninj mandible—an ordinary or an evolved robust australopithecine?

over probable cranial capacity—has enlivened the anatomical descriptions of the Chesowanja fossil fragments (Carney et al., 1971; Szalay, 1971; Walker, 1972).[16] Three large pieces were recovered: part of the upper jaw, most of one side of the face, and part of the other side. Most of the upper skull (over the brain) is in fact missing. Reconstruction of its size and shape must therefore be based on the curvature of the preserved bones of the forehead. The face is set under the cranium in a manner that seems more "progressive" or "modern" than in earlier robust specimens at other sites. The Chesowanja cranial vault rises relatively steeply. Cranial capacity was probably larger than 530 cubic centimeters, the average for robust specimens (Carney et al., 1971).

Szalay, in contrast to the above authors, thinks that the specimen was "subjected to, and altered by, great pressures after burial" (1971:229). He therefore excised a segment from the side of the face and redrew his reconstruction of face and skull to look like other robust australopithecines (Figure 10:10). Walker, one of the original authors of the first article, strongly protests this pictorial removal of a wedge of bone by Szalay. Walker acknowledges a slight "faulting" of the bone under pressure but states that "none of these 'faults' has a throw of more than one mm." He goes on to point out that the frontal fragment

cannot be placed where Szalay would like it, for two reasons. First, when freshly cleaned with an air abrasive machine . . . the two pieces matched

[16] In their initial description of the remains, Carney et al. state, "The specimen . . . consists of most of the right facial skeleton . . . parts of the left facial skeleton, part of the right frontal bone and the right basal part of the calvaria . . . The right maxillary teeth from canine to third molar are well preserved. Distortion is slight" (1971:513).

in fracture shape and fine detail at the position I showed in the photograph; and second, the bone thicknesses are identical at the position I
showed whereas the bone on the main fragment is no less than three
times as thick as the bone of the posterior wall of the frontal sinus if
Szalay's placement is attempted.   [Walker, 1972:108]

Walker seems to have effectively countered Szalay's proposal and to have
adequately defended the initial reconstruction of the Chesowanja find as a
fairly "progressive" and probably relatively large-brained robust australopithecine. This interpretation fits with the probable late date, the tools, and
the minimal tooth wear.

Summary of fossil sequences

There is a long sequence of dated sites in eastern Africa. From about 6
million to 4 million years ago, remains are scarce. Interestingly, however,
possible ancestral remains appear in the Lukeino Formation at Baringo,
and what could be transitional remains have been found at Lothagam.
Other possible transitional or very early hominid fossils have been found at
Kanapoi and Baringo. At 3.77 million to 3.59 million years ago at Laetoli
and over 3 million to 3.7 million years ago at Hadar are remains from
creatures that are bipedal and clearly hominid, but that still retain distinctive ape-like features. Only after 3 million years ago are hominid remains
found in southern Africa; and hominid fossils do not appear outside Africa,
in Indonesia, until less than 2 million years ago. At present, therefore, the
fossil evidence supports the interpretation that the transition to *Australopithecus* occurred in eastern Africa and was completed prior to 3.75 million years ago.

  All of the earliest hominid fossils are found in or near the eastern African
rift system. This rift valley complex is interesting from an ecological standpoint: The terrain was and is irregular, forming numerous small basins,
many of which included stream-fed lakes bordered by trees (Shackleton,
1978). Streams from forested volcanic highlands flowed into these basins
or geological pockets bringing water, which in turn fostered the growth of
rich patches of vegetation. Overall, this area is one of savanna grasslands.
But the nature of the terrain promoted diversity of habitats and an exceptionally varied flora and fauna, remains of which have been found at Omo
and Hadar, for example, about the time of *A. afarensis* and *A. africanus*
(Howell, 1978a). Somewhat earlier, one can imagine a population of apes-
becoming-hominids living in the gallery forests along rivers and around
lakes in one or more of the basins of the eastern rift valley system in Africa
some 5 million to 4 million years ago. They were beginning to utilize

grasslands in addition to woodlands, beginning to gather plant food with tools and continuing to collect some small fauna, walking upright, and adapting in jaws and teeth for chewing and grinding the savanna plant foods. There is no need to postulate other transitions; a successful population expands. After 3 million years ago, early hominid finds occur in both eastern and southern Africa.

Where stratified fossil sequences are known, "gracile" fossils precede robust ones.[17] The extremely robust hominids do not appear on the scene until around 2 million years ago, followed shortly thereafter by an "advanced" gracile. Both the advanced gracile and robust forms probably evolved from earlier gracile australopithecines. It is usually assumed that the late, comparatively large-brained eastern African advanced gracile evolved into *Homo erectus*, possibly as early as 1.5 million years ago but certainly by at least 1.1 million years ago, with the robust form perhaps persisting as late as about 1.4 million to 1.2 million years ago (Howell, 1978a; Walker and R. E. F. Leakey, 1978; M. D. Leakey, 1978; R. E. F. Leakey et al., 1978).[18]

Evolutionary processes: the gathering hypothesis and the question of speciation among early hominids

Variability is extensive among early hominids. Early on, from the ape ancestry, to *A. afarensis* and *A. africanus* (Laetoli, Hadar, Makapansgat, and the Sterkfontein Type Site), jaw shapes ranged from U-shaped to roughly V-shaped to mildly parabolic during a period of some million years (Le Gros Clark, 1950; Day, 1965; Oakley et al., 1977; White, 1977; Johanson and White, 1979).[19] Also at Omo in the Usno and early Shungura formations (3 Mya to about 2.4 Mya), molar and premolar tooth size varied, with some teeth still very small and others already within the size

[17] The earliest "gracile" forms (*A. afarensis*) are actually gracile primarily in the sense of simply having small premolars and molars – the smallness presumably descendant from the ape ancestors, though already larger than living African apes and therefore probably also larger than the ape ancestor. They therefore already show a significant hominid increase in this feature. Also, they are simply generally small gracile creatures. Their large canine teeth, diastema (space between teeth for the opposite canine), and protruding jaws, however, are hardly like those of the subsequent "gracile" *A. africanus*, robust *A. robustus/boisei*, or advanced gracile *A./H. habilis*. The three later australopithecine varieties all have human-like jaws, whereas the jaws of the basal hominid *A. afarensis* still display these ape-like features (see Figure 8:10).

[18] If Taung is as late as Partridge (1973) and Butzer (1974b) have suggested, a small-brained gracile form may have also persisted there until about 1 Mya or even longer. (But see footnote 2, this chapter.)

[19] See Figures 3:8, 8:7, 8:9, and 8:10 for drawings of jaws from Laetoli (LH4) and **Hadar** (AL288, AL200), which exemplify both a U-shaped jaw and roughly V-shaped ones.

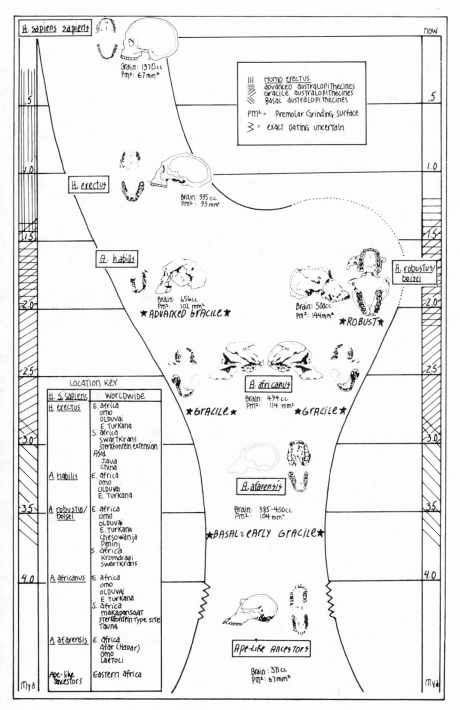

FIGURE 10:11. Summary of human evolutionary patterns, after emergence from ape-like ancestors, with dates and locations.

range of later robust australopithecines. That such variation should have existed is not at all surprising. The population at this especially early period was in a state of flux: The new adaptation tied to bipedalism and use of the hands in gathering – with resultant freeing of these our ancestors from their prior heavy dependence on the forest – was just being established. Their jaws, teeth, and jaw musculature were just becoming adapted to the diet that was made possible by savanna gathering.

Probably, at any one time level between about 3.75 million and 2 million years ago, this variable population living in eastern Africa was one species. In other words, I think it more likely than not that sexual interaction and reproduction occurred among the very early bipedal gatherers who inhabited the same ranges – regardless of their varying jaw shapes or somewhat differing tooth sizes. Through time, however, it is useful to delineate species. Thus, the early, basal hominids at Laetoli, Hadar, and Omo are termed *A. afarensis,* and their immediate descendants at Omo, as well as at the Sterkfontein Type Site and Makapansgat in southern Africa, are known as *A. africanus.* This serves to signify that the basal hominids are earlier, and more ape-like, than their "gracile" hominid descendants.

Intrapopulation variability in shape of jaw, size of teeth, related skull features, and other characteristics is to be expected for the very early basal hominids at Laetoli and Hadar (*A. afarensis*). Nor is the variability in the subsequent gracile *A. africanus* surprising – though the apparent direction of change for at least some of the fossils (getting more and more robust through time) – is significant.[20] *A. africanus* is a highly probable ancestor of both the advanced gracile *A. habilis* and the robust *A. robustus/boisei.*

But what about the much more patterned variability starting approximately 2 million years ago? Both dental proportions and at least some cranial capacities are strikingly different (Pilbeam, 1978b). The environment at Omo shows a distinct drying trend about 2 million years ago (Bonnefille, 1976a; Carr, 1976; Cooke, 1976; Gentry, 1976). Slightly later, at Olduvai, conditions appear to have been variable, with shifts from drier to wetter to drier again (Howell, 1978a).[21] Stone tools begin to occur

---

[20] The relatively early gracile (*A. africanus*), dating from approximately 3 Mya to about 2 Mya or somewhat after, can usually be differentiated from its direct descendant *A. habilis* (an advanced gracile dating from approximately 2 Mya to 1.5 Mya), although this has proved somewhat complicated at East Turkana and Olduvai. Thus *A. africanus* and *A. habilis* can be considered different chronospecies. However, exactly where the line between them is drawn is necessarily arbitrary.

[21] Near Lake Turkana at Ileret somewhat later, about 1.5 Mya, conditions allowed more woodlands and a wetter and/or cooler climate than at present (Bonnefille, 1976b; Howell, 1978a). Nonetheless, faunal evidence from nearby Koobi Fora, also east of Lake Turkana, indicates grasslands with little bush just above the KBS Tuff or about 1.8 Mya (Cooke,

in the archeological record about this time (Howell, 1976; Merrick and Merrick, 1976; Guilmet, 1977). The gracile hominid, *A. africanus,* can – at least according to some – still be found (R. E. F. Leakey et al., 1978; Walker and R. E. F. Leakey, 1978). And what can be interpreted as two lines of "advanced" australopithecines appear: a robust line, *A. robustus,*[22] and an advanced gracile form called *Australopithecus habilis* or *Homo habilis.* Robust teeth, jaws, muscles, and shape of bony attachments on the skull differ considerably from those of both the graciles and the advanced graciles. That at least two patterns – robust and gracile/advanced gracile – existed about 2 million years ago seems clear. Nonetheless, rather "intermediate" fossils also exist.

Were the advanced robust and advanced gracile (plus the remaining gracile) hominids who lived somewhat less than 2 million years ago part of one interbreeding polytypic species, or did they represent two species that were reproductively isolated?[23] I think the former is marginally more likely. They overlapped in time, lived in the same areas, and had the same ape-like basal hominid and then gracile hominid ancestors. They shared many, many anatomical and behavioral features. Both used tools and utilized the mosaic savanna. What would keep them totally apart sexually?

Today there are cultural distinctions that strongly support racial, linguistic, ethnic, religious, class, and national distinctions plus traditions that militate against intermarriage between racial, economic, and cultural groups. Nevertheless, sexual contact – sometimes socially legitimized, sometimes not – between individuals from different groups occurs continuously. The human species today is highly gregarious in a sexual sense. The ancestral population, as reconstructed in Chapters 4, 5, and 6, was also sexually gregarious. There is no compelling reason for assuming the australopithecines were not sexually sociable as well. Before cultural meaning systems and language developed, there would be even less to keep these early "pre-people" who shared so many behavioral characteristics and lived at the same time and in the same areas from intermingling sexually now and then.

1976). And about 2 Mya to 1.8 Mya, just below the KBS Tuff, there was an impressive decrease in rainfall (Cerling et al., 1977). Some variation in climate between 2 Mya and 1.5 Mya seems indicated at Turkana as well as at Olduvai.

[22] It has been variously termed *Zinjanthropus/Australopithecus boisei* in eastern Africa, and *Paranthropus crassidens* at Swartkrans in southern Africa.

[23] Wolpoff, for example, has pointed out that differences in cheek and anterior teeth dimensions between different "lines" of australopithecines are not as great as for differences between species of apes. One possibility is that "the continuity in variation between these [early hominid] examples could be interpreted to show that gene flow occurred between them" (Wolpoff, 1978b:479).

There is at least one anomalous fossil from this time period – the unusual KNM-ER1805 skull found at East Turkana, which has sagittal and nuchal crests like a robust australopithecine but small cheek teeth like a gracile form (R. E. F. Leakey, 1974).[24] This fossil might be interpreted as the offspring (obviously viable even though unusual) of a robust and a gracile or advanced gracile – the crests from its robust forebear, the small teeth from its gracile parent. Similarly, modern human skulls and their muscle joints show similarities with both gracile *A. africanus* and robust *A. robustus* fossils. As Du Brul has stated: "It is clear that joint surfaces and relations in modern man retain certain features of *both* australopithecine forms" (1977:315). Thus, rather than assume there were contemporaneous robust and gracile/advanced gracile species of *Australopithecus* with full reproductive isolation, I prefer to hypothesize subspecific differences with reduced but still some sexual contact.

Homo erectus and *Homo sapiens* do, nonetheless, resemble the advanced gracile more than they resemble the superrobust form (Tobias and Von Koenigswald, 1964; Walker and R. E. F. Leakey, 1978). There was no future for ultrarobust characteristics.

At first, however, selection appears to have favored robust features. Remains until about 3 million years ago are gracile in terms of the cheek teeth (Howell and Coppens, 1976; White, 1977; Johanson and White, 1979). After that, larger cheek teeth begin to appear in the fossil record, and for some australopithecines they got larger and larger through time (Johanson and White, 1979). By 2 million years ago, a distinct robust cluster of features had evolved: larger premolars and molars and smaller canines, large jaws, large bony protuberances above each side of the jaw for muscle attachments, and, most striking, a bony crest along the midline of the top of the skull from front to back – also for muscle attachments (Boaz, 1977a; Du Brul, 1977). These superrobust features further enhanced the already highly effective australopithecine grinding mechanism. The robust australopithecine was superbly formed for crushing and grinding tough, gritty savanna plant foods (Wallace, 1975). At this time rainfall was decreasing in at least some places, and woodlands were diminishing in extent, although there continued to be gallery forests bordering streams and lakes (Bonnefille, 1976a; Carr, 1976; Boaz, 1977a). As a consequence hominids would be further increasing their use of savanna foods. Such a shift in dental equipment, therefore, made excellent anatomical and ecological sense: The larger molars and heavier chewing muscles would aid in processing this higher proportion of tough, dry plant foods.

[24] This fossil is from the Koobi Fora region, more recent than the KBS Tuff but older than the Okote Tuff and therefore dating roughly 1.8 Mya to 1.5 Mya.

Australopithecus was already using organic tools to obtain food, however. Some individuals and small groups doubtless began to experiment with using tools to process food as well – to scrape it clean, to break or pry it open, and to crush or grind particularly tough items, thereby saving their teeth (Krantz, 1973). For some, tools came to substitute for teeth to prepare and process these tough foods (Wallace, 1975). Selection pressure for an anatomical adaptation to savanna plant use was therefore reduced for groups that used tools in food preparation. Thus, used as dental substitutes in altered environmental circumstances (that put increased pressure on teeth) could enable some individuals to live beyond the period when dental wear and attrition might pose a serious survival problem (Krantz, 1973). In order for brain size to increase within a population, infants must be born ever more immature and rely on their mothers for an increasing period for food and instruction. However, if gracile australopithecine mothers began to face "dental death" at an earlier age when the climate became more arid and the environment more thoroughly savanna, about 2 million years ago, the extended mothering necessary for survival of more intelligent, bigger-brained offspring would not be feasible without an added innovation. It would be those mothers who invented and used stone tools as dental substitutes, thereby extending their own survival, who could be available for extended care of infants born increasingly immature with bigger brains. For these reasons, selection acted on expansion of cranial capacity and dental reduction simultaneously in one group of australopithecines. Tools for processing, as well as obtaining, food became central to the hominid adaptation. More advanced, complex social traditions of tool making and use eventually became established throughout an extensive population. Selection for a somewhat larger brain and reduced dental apparatus – that is, selection for intelligence rather than teeth – was underway. The result was the advanced gracile, *A. habilis*.

In other words, there was a robust anatomical and behavioral "experiment" within the genus that, although initially very effective, had little future. I think that advanced graciles and superrobusts represent two different sorts of attempts to utilize the mosaic savanna more effectively than either the very early "gracile" but still ape-like basal hominids or the somewhat later gracile (but already rather robust) australopithecines. Both advanced gracile and superrobust patterns apparently developed as the climate became drier and use of savanna plants increased. At Omo, where a long fossil sequence exists, the robust anatomical adaptation to the savanna became established somewhat earlier than the advanced gracile adaptation, based on partial substitution of tools for teeth. As a result of the effectiveness of the robust anatomical adaptation to savanna living (larger molars and premolars, bigger muscles, more effective grinding/chewing apparatus), a larger body could be supported. Robust individuals may have been bigger and heavier because their teeth could process more food.

Reasons for the variability among early hominids have been obscure. In the context of the gathering hypothesis, however, a straightforward explanation emerges: It is likely that the differences between the robust australopithecines and the advanced graciles in face, skull, and teeth relate to differential use of tools in preparing plant food. Perhaps the advanced graciles pounded and chopped tough plant food with tools and thereby minimized the amount of chewing needed to break down the material. They also may have scraped off sand and dirt with tools, again minimizing dental wear. This attention to tool use for plant food processing may have been associated with beginning to make and use more effective containers on a regular basis. With containers they could carry food back to a camping spot for food processing, that is, for scraping, chopping, cutting, or pounding with the new tools. Members of the robust population, although they also used tools to obtain food, may have consumed more food on the spot and, at least initially, used tools less in food preparation. The robust line therefore needed a heavier masticatory apparatus. More extensive on-the-spot eating of savanna plant food, combined with minimal use of tools for food preparation in a changing environment, could account for the larger molars and heavier faces and skulls in the robust specimens without invoking arguments concerning the presence or absence of tools per se, tool using versus tool making, or vegetarian versus omnivorous diet. The importance of an interpretive framework is, therefore, evident not only in reconstructing the transition to *Australopithecus* but also in explicating the notable variability among these early hominids.

Robust australopithecines represent a thoroughgoing anatomical adaptation to the savanna (Wallace, 1975). Initially they would have been considerably better adapted to the savanna environment than the earlier graciles from which they evolved. Massive jaw musculature was useful for chewing tough savanna plant foods; therefore, selection would have favored even more extreme development. As might be expected from this line of reasoning, relatively large molars and premolars for all forms are found between 2.5 million and 2 million years ago. This was after the adaptation to the savanna was established but prior to widespread use of stone tools for processing plant food before eating. After 2 million years ago to about 1.5 million years ago a bimodal distribution of molar and premolar tooth size existed (Pilbeam and Zwell, 1972). By this time robust molars and premolars had become even larger for part of the hominid population, with the eastern African robusts having the most pronounced features. In contrast, starting around 2 million years ago, individuals begin to appear with grinding teeth that are distinctly smaller. Tools for food preparation were, by then, probably used extensively by this advanced gracile population. This marked an intensification of a tool-using adaptation to savanna living. Learning had become critical to the adaptation.

We can, but need not, assume that gracile and robust australopithecines forever parted company at this point, with the robust line dying out, leaving no descendants. It seems somewhat more likely that the robust population eventually also learned to expand their tool use to include food preparation. This could explain the absence of marked wear on the teeth of the late robust fossil at Chesowanja. Such learning would result in a relaxation of selection pressure for large molars and for the muscular and bony features of the skull related to such molars, and enhanced selection for increased intelligence for more effective innovation and learning, particularly with regard to tool making and use. If further fossil data on late robusts were to confirm that teeth began to show less wear (and, especially, if they also became smaller) in the robust as well as in the gracile line, this would support the latter interpretation.

The two populations, once very close to full speciation, could have merged again. If so, genes from both variants might be part of our human heritage.[25] Systematic comparative studies could assist in checking out this possibility. Whichever occurred – a merging of advanced gracile and robust gene pools leading into *Homo erectus,* or *Homo erectus* evolving exclusively from the *A. habilis* population – it was the adaptive direction that was significant. Greater reliance on tools, and on other learned behavior, for a broader assortment of purposes was what was critical at this point in human evolution.

A tool using tradition of some sophistication already existed among late australopithecines. Such a technology presumes mental envisioning of effective tools to be made and used; it must also involve socially mediated learning about tool making and use. Similarly, social traditions related to finding food and camping spots, sharing, and the care and "socialization" of young likely existed. Such social traditions were necessarily prior to the development of culture as we know it. What might such antecedents to culture have been like? First and foremost, australopithecine social interac-

[25] Again, with regard to the late robust Chesowanja specimen, Carney et al. state that "Some features resemble those of *A. robustus* and *A. boisei,* some *A. africanus* and some show trends that have been taken before as typical developments towards *Homo.* The tantalizing suggestive evidence of enlarged cranial capacity, the tucking of the face under the braincase, either reduction or refinement of the masticatory apparatus . . . are all pointers to development in the lineage of trends towards *Homo* that are, perhaps, demonstrable in other hominid lines" (1971:514).

tions, particularly the communicatory aspects, provided the matrix for the development of human culture. The increased intelligence and heightened affect of young australopithecines, as compared to the ancestral population, were interrelated with the growing importance of socially mediated learning after birth. Learning took place in an affectively rich and socially intimate context.

Culture has been described, in a broadly functional sense, as an "extra-somatic, extragenetic, outside-the-skin [set of] control mechanisms . . . for ordering . . . behavior" (Geertz, 1966, as reprinted 1973:44). In this very general sense, culture was beginning to exist in australopithecine times. It was in the form of a developing social tradition of patterns of interaction, knowledge about the environment, and conceptualizations underlying tool making and using and embodied, as it were, in the tools themselves and in the communication (the teaching and learning) of those "traditions." Our language fails us here, for everything was at its beginning and interrelated. Yet the late australopithecines almost certainly were, to some extent and in an incipient fashion, dependent on extragenetic "control mechanisms" such as these to guide their day-to-day behavior.[26] It seems relatively certain that this reliance was a prime factor both in selection for evolution into *Homo erectus* and in the later development of human culture.

[26] In a narrower, more qualitative sense (what culture *is* rather than what it does for us), a culture—any culture—can be defined as "an ordered system of meanings and symbols . . . in terms of which individuals define their world, express their feelings and make their judgments" (Geertz, 1959, as reprinted 1973:144—145; 1966, as reprinted 1973:68). Clearly, for the australopithecines, culture—in this specific and more essentialist sense—was rudimentary indeed. The fact that culture as we know it is always in the form of a specific culture is significant and will be discussed in the Conclusion, Chapter 11.

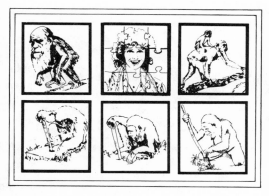

ELEVEN

Conclusion: becoming human

THE modification and transportation of objects probably emerged in con-
junction with subsistence activities. Whereas sticks need not be modified
for use as clubs, twigs must usually be modified for use as probes.

Geza Teleki, 1974

THE search for origins is an insistent and particularly human quest. In times
past—and in many parts of the world yet today—it has found expression in
origin myths. More recently in the West, with the development of a "scientific" view of the world, understanding and explanation of human origins
have been sought from that vast jigsaw puzzle called evolution. We all
want to know who our ancestors were, how we came to be, and, in a very
real sense, what sort of creatures we have become. The origins, development, and very nature of our humanness is at the same time one of the
most intriguing and most enigmatic of evolutionary riddles.

In this reconstruction of early human lifeways my objective has been to
construct a sequential model that builds in, as fundamental to the model
itself, the probable ranges of behavior and the social and cultural contributions of both sexes. I have tried, on the one hand, to be as rigorous as
possible—to integrate several types of disparate information into a model
that is reasonably consistent and that makes some predictions feasible—
and, on the other hand, to be broadly humanistic and to consider a wide
range of human potentialities, not only those reflected in the manners and
mores of the industrial West. Methodologically, cross-cultural research,
particularly of peoples who still live by gathering and hunting today, combined with the comparative study of primate social behavior are essential
to the reconstruction of early human social life. Only by in-depth research
of cultures very different from our own can one hope to minimize a Western bias in the reconstruction of the lifeways of our ape and early human
ancestors.

263

What kind of ancestor?

Recent studies have demonstrated that the African apes are far more closely related to humans than once imagined. Anatomically, common and pygmy chimpanzees provide an excellent model of what the generalized ancestral ape population may have been like. The other African ape, the gorilla, which is also closely related to us, provides a much less useful model because gorilla anatomy and adaptation are far more specialized. For example, there is a great deal more size difference between males and females in gorillas than occurs in chimpanzees or humans. Although chimpanzees provide an excellent anatomical model for what the generalized ancestral apes might have looked like, this is not the  primary reason they are such a superb model for the ancestral population. It is the study of chimpanzee behavior that has proved particularly instructive. Of special interest are: chimpanzee intelligence, communication, and sociability; the flexibility and variability, with structure, apparent in chimpanzee groups; the  durability of mother–child and sibling relationships; bipedal and manipulatory capacities; the surprising extent of object modification and tool use; the heavy reliance on plant food combined with insect collecting and some predation; a chimpanzee's immaturity at birth, the extended period of contact with its mother and the significance of this extended contact for learning both relational and technical skills; extensive food sharing by mothers; and the important roles that social tradition and environmental context play in patterns of social interaction, diet, and the use of tools. All these features make *Pan* unusually interesting in the attempt to postulate the capacities and behaviors that could have provided a base for the hominid divergence from an ape ancestor.

When we look at humans living today, there is one fact that especially stands out. Humans have many cultures with social and economic systems ranging from small communities of gatherer-hunters or horticulturalists to ancient, agriculturally based states and the recent industrial nations. All humans today are members of just one biological species, *Homo sapiens sapiens*. Culturally, however, we are a most various species. Language, clothing styles, rituals, art forms, values, beliefs, kinship arrangements, community size and organization, the personal characteristics considered masculine or feminine, the role of the aged, and many other features vary from society to society (Figure 11:1). Furthermore, our ecological adapta-

FIGURE 11:1. Human cultural diversity: *Top left,* Orchid Island near Taiwan. A Yami wears his forged coin helmet, a prized symbol of wealth. *Bottom left,* Madison Avenue, New York. Stars of the rock group "Kiss." *Middle,* Zululand, southern Africa. A woman diviner with vials of herbs around her neck. *Upper right,* Malaysia. In trance, a man fulfills his religious vows during the ceremony of Thaipusam. *Bottom right,* Thailand. The Lakon, danced for centuries in northern Thailand, is here performed in a Bangkok restaurant.

tions differ enormously from one society to the next (Figure 11:2). Humans are unique in having such an enormous adaptive range. Biologically speaking, we are able to utilize many extremely different ecological niches, from the Sahara to the Arctic, as well as to create and destroy niches (Figure 11:4).

FIGURE 11:2. In human horticulture and agriculture, technologies differ. *Above,* Zulu women hoeing in southern Africa. *Middle,* Chinese men plowing with a wooden plow drawn by a water buffalo. *Below,* Canadian farmer reaps barley with a motor-driven harvester.

Our species' exceptional reliance on culture is what makes this extraordinary adaptive range possible. It is this human uniqueness—the fundamental role of culture in our species' adaptation—that must be understood if we are to reconstruct the behavioral capacities of the ancestral population. Chimpanzee intelligence, tool use, sociability, flexible social organization, effective nonverbal communication, minimal sexual dimorphism, the importance of mother—offspring ties, nurturing, and the social context of learning for the young indicate what sorts of behavioral bases may have existed for evolution of the human capacity for culture, just as dietary omnivorousness and locomotor patterns that include occasional bipedalism help us understand how our earliest bipedal, savanna-living ancestors could have physically evolved from early apes.

The nature of the transition

We know that a transition from an ancestral pongid population to an early hominid one occurred. This book has tried to explore how and why it happened. I think a key innovation was central to the hominid divergence. There are a number of excellent reasons for the hypothesis that gathering plants (and small animals such as insects) by mothers for sharing with their offspring was that key innovation (Linton [Slocum], 1971; Zihlman and Tanner, 1974, 1979; Tanner, 1975; Tanner and Zihlman, 1976a; Zihlman, 1978a, b, d). That early technologi-

cal innovations should largely focus on plant food is only logical given the preeminence of plants in the diets both of nonhuman primates and among non-Western, tropical gathering-hunting peoples today (Gould, 1978). The PPb and complex Pb proteins in human saliva—thought to be involved in protecting the teeth of primates that are primarily plant eaters from plant-carbohydrate and/or texture-induced dental caries — are, in fact, still those of plant-eating primates (Azen et al., 1978). Indeed, a heavy reliance on plant carbohydrate persists for tropical, non-Western peoples regardless of whether they obtain

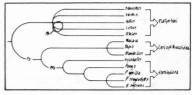

their food through gathering and hunting, horticulture, or agriculture (Gaulin and Konner, 1977).

The innovation that produced more food would be most likely to occur initially among those on whom there was the most nutritional stress.[1]

These are women. It is women who bear babies and nurse infants. Above and beyond such physical nutritional stress on females, it was also early women who had the most responsibility for the survival of the next generation. Mothers' sharing of food with offspring — well documented for both chimpanzees and humans — meant that the gathering innovation made the utmost sense. By gathering with tools, early mothers could obtain enough food for themselves and to share with their young, even on the savanna.

It is, therefore, highly probable that it was women with offspring who developed the new gathering technology and that this was the innovation critical to the ape—human divergence. It is further reasonable to suppose that the technological innovations associated with gathering had a powerful impact on subsequent biological evolution. Mothers who were the best gatherers — that is, who were most intelligent, who used tools most effectively, who walked and carried most efficiently, and who shared gathered food — had children who were the most likely to survive. Among these surviving children, those best able to learn and improve on their mothers' techniques and those who, like their mothers, were willing to share in turn had the children who were most likely to live long enough to reproduce.

Natural selection — the fitness of the individual (e.g., surviving long enough to reproduce) and, especially, the survival and fitness of the progeny — is of course a prime feature in human evolution. The intelligence to

[1] Chimpanzee females, for example, use tools more frequently and for longer periods for insect collecting than males (McGrew, 1977, 1979; Nishida, 1973).

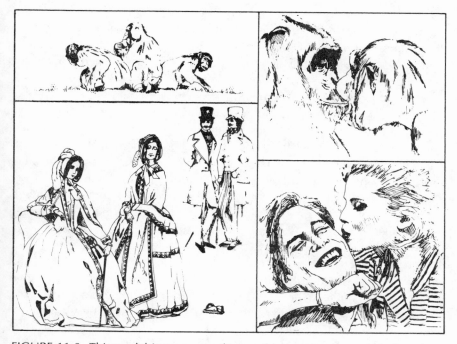

FIGURE 11:3. This model incorporates the possible impact of sexual choice of males by females in the evolutionary process of "becoming human."

gather (i.e., to learn, improve upon, and teach this crucial innovation) and the sociability to share with offspring doubtless were enhanced by natural selection just as were anatomical changes related to bipedalism and skilled use of the hands. These changes enhanced the survival of the mothers themselves and of their children.

In addition, sexual selection may have contributed to similar ends (Figure 11:3). In many species, the number of ova released, fetuses carried, live births, and children who survive are all infinitesimally small compared to sperm produced and available. In addition, among mammals (and especially primates where single births are the rule), the physical and other input of the female into her progeny is enormous; it far exceeds that of the male. For both these reasons, the female and her ova are the "limiting resources." Most sperm will not fertilize ova. If some males have a better chance than others of having their sperm fertilize an ovum, then we say sexual selection is occurring.

Sexual selection has two components: (1) the direct selection by the female of the male(s) with whom she chooses to copulate and (2) competition among the males for opportunity to copulate. Darwin discussed both aspects in *The Descent of Man and Selection in Relation to Sex* (1871). Strangely, however, since Darwin almost all attention has been directed to the second component; the former—the sexual choice of males by females—has been largely ignored. The present model incorporates the possible impact of this first aspect during the hominid divergence.

After gathering became common, the mother's contribution to the life chances of her offspring increased dramatically as compared to that of the pongid ancestor. At the time of the initial divergence, when the earliest hominids still resembled the ape-like ancestor in many features, it is extremely unlikely that social fatherhood had yet been invented. In other words, the increase in maternal contribution through gathering was not counterbalanced at that time by any like increase in paternal "investment." This provided a genetic and social context for an increase in female sexual selectivity. Let us suppose for a moment that female choice was, in fact, heightened during the divergence. If females chose males who—like themselves—were intelligent and sociable, adept with their hands, and comparatively effective bipeds, then natural and sexual selection could reinforce each other (Tanner, 1975; Tanner and Zihlman, 1976a). With gathering, the maternal contribution to a surviving offspring was intensified. A corresponding intensification of sexual selection, combined with the increased natural selection consequent to gathering, makes probable a rapid transition from ancestral ape to early hominid.

This fits very well with the appearance of a few hominid-like fossils in eastern Africa some 6 million to 4 million years ago, followed by the sudden appearance of fairly plentiful early hominid remains (*Australopithecus*) there after about 3.5 million years ago. This fossil record is also consistent with the evidence from molecular 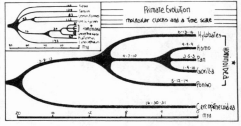 evolution for a particularly close relationship between apes and humans, and for a comparatively recent pongid—hominid divergence.

The evolutionary result is ourselves—creatures in which bipedalism, hand—eye coordination with effective manipulatory ability, tool making and use, intelligence, the ability to symbol, a multifaceted communication system, extended infant dependence on the mother, and extensive reliance on learning are characteristic of both sexes. This provides some evidence that natural and sexual selection did indeed work to the same ends. For sexual selection to have reinforced natural selection, females must have chosen males fairly similar to themselves. The alternative picture of sexual selection, where male competition for females is stressed, is one in which the males that differ greatly from females biologically—whether in size, strength, or special attention-getting features such as peacocks' tails—engage in the most sexual activity and have a better chance to pass on their genes. This is the case, for example, when some males prevent other males from mating through establishment of physical dominance and/or territorial exclusion. Such sexual patterns accompanied by extreme sexual dimorphism do occur in some animals. An example is the stellar sea lion, where the male weighs about three times as much as the female and males who come to shore first establish territories to exclude other males (Gentry, 1970; Le Boeuf, 1974). Presumably bigger males have a better chance of establishing and defending territories than small males. Thus the bigger males are there, available for the females when they come to shore, and the smaller males are not. Therefore, larger males can contribute more to the gene pool than smaller males: There is sexual selection for large males. No like selection pressure exists for large females. Apparently, over time, the stellar sea lion males came to differ more and more from the females.

This is not what happened in human evolution. As among chimpanzees, there is only a minimal average size difference between human males and females, and there is extensive overlap. Further, sexual dimorphism may even have decreased during and since the divergence. If the males of the ancestral ape population, like most apes today, had longer and larger canines than the females, then during the transition to humanity male canines must have decreased in size more than those of females, because there is little difference between female and male canines in humans.[2]

Therefore, there may have been stronger selection for a reduced canine in males than in females during the transition from ape to human. If females were choosing to copulate with the sociable males—ones who did not bare large canine "fighting teeth" at them—then sexual selection supported reduction of male canines. This could reinforce the concurrent natural selection for reduced canines (for a more effective chewing appara-

[2] Similarly, if the very early hominids from Afar (Hadar Formation) are more sexually dimorphic than subsequent australopithecines and *Homo,* as appears to be the case, then selection for decreasing sexual dimorphism also continued during early human evolution.

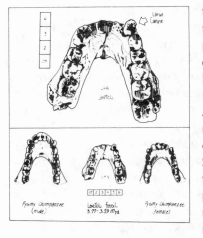

Pygmy Chimpanzee (male)   LaeTolil fossil 3.77-3.59 mya   Pygmy Chimpanzee (female)

tus) that was acting on both sexes. From the fossil record, canine reduction appears to have occurred very rapidly indeed. The earliest type specimen of a hominid jaw (LH4), found in the Laetolil Formation at Laetoli, Tanzania, in eastern Africa, is dated about 3.77 million to 3.59 million years ago. It still has a pronounced canine (M. D. Leakey et al., 1976). Similarly, one of the oldest jaws, AL200, from the Hadar Formation at Afar, Ethiopia, dating from over 3 million to 3.7 million years ago, also still has a prominent canine (Johanson and Taieb, 1976; Johanson et al., 1976; Taieb et al., 1976). Later hominids—both *Australopithecus* and *Homo*—do not, however.

The likelihood that sexual and natural selection could reinforce each other is also great with regard to features such as effective manipulatory hands, bipedalism, sociability, and intelligence. Males who used their mobile hands to groom and otherwise engage in tactile contact with fe-

Bipedalism

males would be likely sex partners. The readily visible erect penis of a bipedal male provided a visual attraction. Males who were effective bipeds could better deal with the savanna themselves, and also better keep up with the wide-ranging, bipedal, gathering females; these males

Sociability

therefore were available for copulation. And an intelligent male had a

Intelligence and communication

better chance of getting a busy, intelligent female to pay attention to him. Therefore, in all the

Hands and Tools

key features of the hominid adaptation—bipedalism, hand manipulative ability, sociability, and intelligence—both natural and sexual selection could have been significant. The transition from pongid to hominid could have occurred relatively rapidly under such circumstances.

The evolution of an ape-like being into one that can be recognized as having "human" qualities therefore probably entailed, from the initial stages onward, evolution toward a similar adaptation for the entire population. In contrast to some mammalian species in which each sex possesses highly distinctive behaviors correlated with marked anatomical differences, the early hominids were developing what was essentially one adaptation for males and females. This is not to suggest that all group members did the same things; quite the contrary, the essence of the adaptation was one of flexibility and variability; behaviors were not rigidly programmed genetically or confined to one sex. During hominid evolution, similarities between the sexes increased in both physical features and in range of social and technological potentialities. Between males and females today, physical dimorphism is relatively minor. As compared with many other mammals and, in all probability, with the ape ancestor and the very earliest hominids themselves, there was a reduction of anatomical and behavioral differences between the sexes—with a resulting enhancement of social organizational flexibility and increase in the potential for male, as well as female, sociability.

From the earliest hominid, *A. afarensis,* to *Homo* there was notable expansion of the brain. This physical evolution occurred in the context of

increased social organizational flexibility, which in turn enhanced communicatory possibilities, thereby providing a sound basis for complex learning and the development of mental capacities—particularly in the context of the rich, affective interaction experienced by

the young. These features are at the root of the development of the exceptional intelligence exhibited by our species. Intelligence is the ability to deal effectively with variability and changeability in both social situations and environmental contexts and to develop nonsomatic guidelines for conceiving of and implementing behaviors that work; it is this ability that forms the biological base for the development and elaboration of culture. The early hominid capacity to learn social, technical, and environmental patterns—a capacity that laid the foundation for what subsequently would become cultural learning in its full sense—was developing in a luxuriant social matrix. A growing capacity for learning how to communicate many meanings facilitated both the expression of individual emotions and the dissemination of information learned by individuals; both came to be shared at the group level.

Early hominid "experiments": the lifeway that worked

Among the early hominids the new two-legged, upright method of getting about – bipedalism – freed the arms and hands from locomotor functions and thereby opened up many possibilities for their use in other ways. Free hands, combined with hand–eye motor coordination and developing mental abilities, laid the foundation for the elaboration of technology as a further significant dimension in the hominid adaptation.

Initially, among the early gracile australopithecines, tools were used  primarily for obtaining food by gathering and for defense from predators. Tools for defense made it possible to maintain social flexibility – for groups to merge or split and even for individuals to sometimes travel alone or in the company of only one or two other individuals – even on the more exposed savanna and without a grasping toe for quick escape into trees. In terms of natural selection, tools for defense meant that intelligent moth-ers could defend their offspring effectively.

Tools for gathering meant mothers could collect  more food for offspring who, then, could be supported longer before becoming independent. The children therefore had a longer period to learn social and technological traditions.

Because savanna plant foods were tough and gritty, there was a premium on an effective chewing mechanism to process this food. Therefore, the cheek teeth or molars, that is, the chewing teeth, became progressively larger. In one australopithecine line, this strengthening of the chewing apparatus bestowed such an advantage that the molars and associated musculature became very large indeed. In another line, however, the chewing teeth, although they too became somewhat larger over time, never approached the size of the robust variety. It is hypothesized that, in this less robust line, the use of tools was extended from gathering to also include tool use in processing and preparing plant food prior to eating. Tools came to substitute for some of the functions of teeth.

This line therefore became even more reliant on tools. The hominid innovation (substitution of ideas or equipment that can be invented and made for "built-in" behavior patterns and anatomical "equipment" that one must be born with) was thus pushed even further along. From these advanced gracile hominids presumably our own genus *Homo* evolved.

Reliance on tools and social tradition are part of our genus's earliest heritage. The social transmission of gathering skills and technology was a critical aspect of the transition from ape-ancestor to early hominid. This increasing importance of social and technological tradition — "incipient culture," if you will — proceeded together with biological evolution from the very beginning of the hominid divergence.

The capacity for culture, the magnification of technology, extended infant dependence on and interaction with the mother, and the elaboration of social and referential communication developed together in human evolution. The learning of multiple modes of communication, of patterns for social behavior, and of ways to make and use tools took place from infancy onward in the tactile intimacy of the mother–child relationship. Also, the young grew, observed, and learned in a broader social context that included older sisters and brothers, sexual and other friends of the mother, and her traveling companions.

Initially, interior visualization and simple conceptualization were related to social interaction and nascent tool use. These are abilities that the ancestral ape population already possessed if it was as intelligent as chimpanzees are today. Such abilities formed the nexus of elaboration for the hominid line. From this simple base, the capacity for symbolization and conceptual thought evolved. The biological capacity for symbolization formed the foundation for the development of many human lifeways — the distinct linguistic, social, technological, and artistic traditions characteristic of different social groups. The ability to symbol, that is, the capacity for conceptual thought, made possible the development of the variety of human cultures found throughout the world. Doubtless it was the developing human capacity to build new cultures suitable to new environments that made possible the extraordinary spread of *Homo sapiens sapiens* over the globe (Figure 11:4).

Cultures, as we know them today, are the accumulated and systematized resultants of the ability to symbol. The symbolic "products" — whether tools, language, kinship organization, art — are the outcome of historical processes; and it is these that we commonly label "culture." Equally important is the fact that the direction taken by the hominid line was one that led inexorably to human reliance on culture. Our species, *Homo sapiens sapiens*, is at the end of a long line of hominids for whom natural and

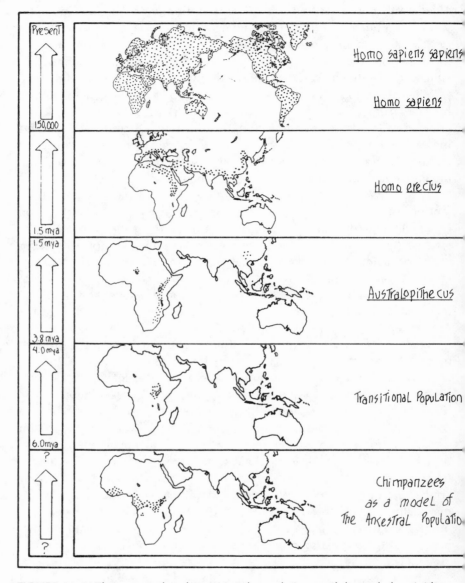

FIGURE 11:4. The ancestral and transitional populations and the early hominids (*Australopithecus*) had comparatively limited ranges. An effective container and greater intelligence may have assisted the expansion eastward of Homo erectus through the tropics to Indonesia and north to China and Europe. Culture itself is the primary adaptation of our even more widespread species, *Homo sapiens sapiens*.

sexual selection enhanced social flexibility, social and technological traditions, and a rich and complex communication system. We have evolved with both the potential and the necessity for culture (Geertz, 1973).

Culture is part of our biological heritage; the capacity for it evolved along with other characteristically human qualities. *Cultures can be changed by human choice.* More often, cultures change almost unbeknownst to the society concerned because of ad hoc cultural borrowings from other societies, inventions that have greater impact than anticipated and that generate subsidiary changes, and because of many economic and political factors. Such changes occur with astounding rapidity in comparison with genetic change. Nonetheless, cultural values and behavioral guidelines are deeply embedded in each society's traditions, and cultural change is very hard to plan, initiate, facilitate, or control. Our species relies on its many cultures. Indeed, in a sense culture *is* the human adaptation. For *Homo sapiens sapiens* culture is elemental and necessary: people cannot function apart from a specific culture for it is only through one's own culture that an individual knows what can be done and how to do it. This simple fact is what often leads to an enormous tenacity of belief in the face of a changing world. Ironically, it was the development of culture that made elaboration or dichotomization possible in any direction; a lopsided society such as ours that either ignores or infantilizes half the species—women—can exist. Whether or not it can survive is another matter. For the challenges of a world society suddenly able to destroy itself, full, mature, and equal participation by both sexes in problem solving and culture building would seem necessary.

Bibliography

ACKNOWLEDGMENTS

Geertz, Clifford
   1973   *The Interpretation of Cultures: Selected Essays.* New York: Basic
           Books.
Geertz, Hildred
   1961   *The Javanese Family: A Study of Kinship and Socialization.* New
           York: Free Press of Glencoe.
Tanner, Nancy M.
   1974   Matrifocality in Indonesia and Africa and among Black Americans. In
           Woman, Culture, and Society, Michelle Rosaldo and Louise Lamphere
           (eds.), pp. 129–156. Stanford: Stanford University Press.
Tanner, Nancy M., and Adrienne L. Zihlman
   1976a   Women in Evolution. 1. Innovation and Selection in Human Origins.
           Signs: Journal of Women in Culture and Society 1:585–608.
   1976b   The Evolution of Human Communication: What Can Primates Tell
           Us? In *Origins and Evolution of Language and Speech,* Stevan R. Har-
           nad, Horst D. Steklis, and Jane Lancaster, (eds.), pp. 467–480, An-
           nals of the New York Academy of Sciences, vol. 280. New York:
           New York Academy of Sciences.
Zihlman, Adrienne L.
   1974   Review of *Sexual Selection and the Descent of Man, 1871–1971,*
           Bernard Campbell (ed.),. *American Anthropologist* 76:475–478.
   1978a   Motherhood in Transition: From Ape to Human. In *Family Formation
           and First Child,* W. Miller and L. Newman (eds.), pp. 35–50. Chapel
           Hill: Carolina Population Center Publications.
   1978b   Women and Evolution. 2. Subsistence and Social Organization
           among Early Hominids. *Signs: Journal of Women in Culture and Soci-
           ety* 4:4–20.
Zihlman, Adrienne L., and Nancy M. Tanner
   1979   Gathering and the Hominid Adaptation. In *Female Hierarchies,* Lionel
           Tiger and Heather M. Fowler (eds.), pp. 163–194. Chicago: Beres-
           ford Book Service.

CHAPTER 1. DARWIN AND THE DESCENT OF "MAN"

Alland, Alexander, Jr.
   1974   Why Not Spencer? *Journal of Anthropological Research* 30:271–280.

Bock, Kenneth E.
1955   Darwin and Social Theory. *Philosophy of Science* 22:123–133.
Campbell, Bernard, ed.
1972a   *Sexual Selection and the Descent of Man, 1871–1971*. Chicago: Aldine.
Darwin, Charles
1859   *The Origin of Species by Means of Natural Selection; or, The Preservation of Favored Races in the Struggle for Life*. London: John Murray. (Reprinted, 1936.)
1869   *The Origin of Species by Means of Natural Selection; or, The Preservation of Favored Races in the Struggle for Life*. 5th ed. London: John Murray.
1871   *The Descent of Man and Selection in Relation to Sex*. London: John Murray. (Reprinted 1936. New York: Modern Library.)
Freeman, Derek
1974   The Evolutionary Theories of Charles Darwin and Herbert Spencer. *Current Anthropology* 15:211–237.
Gould, Stephen Jay
1974   Darwin's Dilemma. *Natural History* 83:16, 20–21.
Hofstadter, Richard
1959   *Social Darwinism in American Thought*. Rev. ed. New York: Braziller.
Huxley, Thomas Henry
1888   The Struggle for Existence in Human Society. *Nineteenth Century* 23:161–180. (Reprinted 1896, in *Evolution and Ethics and Other Essays*, pp. 195–236. New York: Appleton.)
1894   Prolegomena. Introduction to *Evolution and Ethics*. New York: Appleton. (Reprinted 1896, in *Evolution and Ethics and Other Essays*, pp. 1–45. New York: Appleton.)
Levi-Strauss, Claude
1949   *Les structures élémentaires de la parenté*. Paris: Presses Universitaires de France. (Reprinted in English in 1967 as *The Elementary Structures of Kinship*. Boston: Beacon Press.)
Lorenz, Konrad
1966   *On Aggression*. New York: Harcourt, Brace and World.
Montagu, Ashley
1976   *The Nature of Human Aggression*. New York: Oxford University Press.
Morgan, Lewis Henry
1877   *Ancient Society; or, Researches in the Lines of Human Progress from Savagery through Barbarism to Civilization*. Chicago: Kerr. (Reprinted 1963. Cleveland: World.)
Morris, Desmond
1967   *The Naked Ape: A Zoologist's Study of the Human Animal*. New York: McGraw-Hill.
Sahlins, Marshall
1977   *The Use and Abuse of Biology*. Ann Arbor: University of Michigan Press.

Spencer, Herbert
    1852a The Development Hypothesis. *Leader,* March 20. (Reprinted 1904, in *Essays, Scientific, Political, and Speculative,* pp. 1–7. New York: Appleton.)
    1852b A Theory of Population, Deduced from the General Law of Animal Fertility. *Westminster Review,* April, pp. 468–501.
    1857 Progress: Its Law and Cause. *Westminster Review,* April. (Reprinted 1904, in *Essays, Scientific, Political, and Speculative,* pp. 8–62. New York: Appleton.)
    1864 *First Principles.* New York: Appleton.
    1866 *The Principles of Biology.* New York: Appleton.
Stocking, George W., Jr.
    1968 *Race, Culture, and Evolution: Essays in the History of Anthropology.* New York: Free Press.
Tiger, Lionel
    1969 *Men in Groups.* New York: Random House.
Tiger, Lionel, and Robin Fox
    1971 *The Imperial Animal.* New York: Holt, Rinehart and Winston.
Trivers, Robert L.
    1972 Parental Investment and Sexual Selection. In *Sexual Selection and the Descent of Man 1871–1971,* Bernard Campbell (ed.), pp. 136–179. Chicago: Aldine.
Tylor, Edward B.
    1871 *Primitive Culture.* 2 vols. London: John Murray.
Wallace, Alfred Russel
    1855 On the Law Which Has Regulated the Introduction of New Species. *Annals and Magazine of Natural History* 16:184–196.
    1858 On the Tendency of Varieties to Depart Indefinitely from the Original Type. *Journal of the Proceedings of the Linnean Society, Zoology* 3:53–62. (Reprinted 1958, in *Evolution by Natural Selection,* by Charles Darwin and Alfred Russel Wallace, pp. 268–279. Cambridge: Cambridge University Press.)
Wilson, Edward O.
    1975 *Sociobiology: The New Synthesis.* Cambridge: Harvard University Press, Belknap Press.
Zihlman, Adrienne L.
    1974 Review of *Sexual Selection and the Descent of Man 1871–1971,* Bernard Campbell (ed.), *American Anthropologist* 76:475–478.

CHAPTER 2. MODELS IN EVOLUTION

Aldrich-Blake, F. P. G.
    1970 Problems of Social Structure in Forest Monkeys. In *Social Behaviour in Birds and Mammals,* John H. Crook (ed.), pp. 79–101. New York: Academic Press.
Ardrey, Robert
    1976 *The Hunting Hypothesis.* New York: Atheneum.

Bartholomew, George A., Jr., and Joseph B. Birdsell
   1953   Ecology and the Protohominids. *American Anthropologist* 55:481–
          598. (Reprinted 1962, in *Culture and the Evolution of Man*, Ashley
          Montagu (ed.), pp. 20–37. New York: Oxford University Press.)
Curtin, Richard, and Phyllis Dolhinow
   1978   Primate Social Behavior in a Changing World. *American Scientist*
          66:468–475.
Dart, Raymond A.
   1949   The Predatory Implemental Technique of *Australopithecus. American
          Journal of Physical Anthropology* 7:1–38.
Darwin, Charles
   1869   *The Origin of Species by Means of Natural Selection; or, The Preser-
          vation of Favored Races in the Struggle for Life.* 5th ed. London: John
          Murray.
Dawkins, Richard
   1976   *The Selfish Gene.* London: Oxford University Press.
de Beer, Gavin
   1958   Foreword to *Evolution by Natural Selection,* by Charles Darwin and
          Alfred Russel Wallace. Cambridge: Cambridge University Press.
DeVore, Irven, and K. R. L. Hall
   1965   Baboon Ecology. In *Primate Behavior: Field Studies of Monkeys and
          Apes,* I. DeVore (ed.), pp. 20–52. New York: Holt, Rinehart and
          Winston.
DeVore, Irven, and Sherwood L. Washburn
   1963   Baboon Ecology and Human Evolution. In *African Ecology and Hu-
          man Evolution,* F. C. Howell and F. Bourlière (eds.), pp. 335–367.
          Chicago: Aldine.
Dolhinow, Phyllis Jay
   1972   The North Indian Langur. In *Primate Patterns,* P. Dolhinow (ed.), pp.
          181–238. New York: Holt, Rinehart and Winston.
Engels, Frederick
   1891   *The Origin of Family, Private Property, and the State.* 4th ed. Pub-
          lished in the journal *Die neue Zeit 2,* no. 41, and in the book *Der
          Ursprung der Familie, des Privateigenthums und des Staats,* Stuttgart.
          (Reprinted 1968, in *Karl Marx and Frederick Engels: Selected Works,*
          pp. 455–593. New York: International Publishers.)
   1895– The Part Played by Labour in the Transition from Ape to Man. *Die
   1896   neue Zeit 2,* no. 44. (Reprinted 1968, in *Karl Marx and Frederick
          Engels: Selected Works,* pp. 359–368. New York: International
          Publishers.)
Etkin, William
   1954   Social Behavior and the Evolution of Man's Mental Faculties. *Ameri-
          can Naturalist* 88:129–142. (Reprinted 1962, in *Culture and the Evo-
          lution of Man,* Ashley Montagu (ed.), pp. 131–145. New York: Ox-
          ford University Press.)
Gartlan, J. S.
   1973   Influences of Phylogeny and Ecology on Variations in the Group Or-
          ganization of Primates. In *Precultural Primate Behavior: Symposia of*

the *Fourth International Congress of Primatology,* vol. 1, E. W. Menzel (ed.), pp. 80–101. Basel: Karger.

1975   Adaptive Aspects of Social Structure in *Erythrocebus patas.* In *Proceedings from the Symposia of the 5th Congress of the International Primatological Society, 1974,* S. Kondo, M. Kawai, A. Ehara, and S. Kawamura (eds.), pp. 161–171. Tokyo: Japan Science Press.

Geertz, Clifford

1973   Religion as a Cultural System. In *The Interpretation of Cultures,* pp. 87–125. New York: Basic Books.

Goodall, Jane, and David A. Hamburg

1975   Chimpanzee Behavior as a Model for the Behavior of Early Man. In *New Psychiatric Frontiers,* D. A. Hamburg and H. K. H. Brodie (eds.), pp. 14–43. New York: Basic Books.

Hall, K. R. L.

1965a   Behaviour and Ecology of the Wild Patas Monkey, *Erythrocebus patas,* in Uganda. *Journal of Zoology 148:*15–87.

Hall, K. R. L., and Irven DeVore

1965   Baboon Social Behavior. In *Primate Behavior: Field Studies of Monkeys and Apes,* I. DeVore (ed.), pp. 53–110. New York: Holt, Rinehart and Winston.

Haraway, Donna

1978   Animal Sociology and a Natural Economy of the Body Politic. 2. The Past Is the Contested Zone: Human Nature and Theories of Production and Reproduction in Primate Behavior Studies. *Signs: Journal of Women in Culture and Society 4:*37–60.

Hodgson, Harry E., and Joseph S. Larson

1973   Some Sexual Differences in Behaviour within a Colony of Marked Beavers (*Castor canadensis*). *Animal Behavior 21:*147–152.

Huxley, Thomas Henry

1893   *Evolution and Ethics. The Romanes Lectures.* (Reprinted 1896, in *Evolution and Ethics and Other Essays,* pp. 46–86. New York: Appleton.)

1894   Prolegomena. Introduction to *Evolution and Ethics.* New York: Appleton. (Reprinted 1896, in *Evolution and Ethics and Other Essays,* pp. 1–45. New York: Appleton.)

Hyman, Stanley Edgar

1962   *The Tangled Bank: Darwin, Marx, Frazer, and Freud as Imaginative Writers.* New York: Atheneum.

Kummer, Hans

1968   *Social Organization of Hamadryas Baboons: A Field Study.* Basel: Karger.

1971   *Primate Societies: Group Techniques of Ecological Adaptation.* Chicago: Aldine.

Lee, Richard B., and Irven DeVore, eds.

1968   *Man the Hunter.* Chicago: Aldine.

McKim, Donald, Jr., and Thomas C. Hutchinson

1975   Phylogenetic Implications of Comparative Primate Growth Rates. *American Journal of Physical Anthropology 42:*495–500.

Morgan, Lewis Henry
    1877   *Ancient Society; or, Researches in the Lines of Human Progress from Savagery through Barbarism to Civilization.* Chicago: Kerr. (Reprinted 1963. Cleveland: World.)

Morris, Desmond
    1967   *The Naked Ape: A Zoologist's Study of the Human Animal.* New York: McGraw-Hill.

Napier, John
    1976   Review of *The Hunting Hypothesis,* by Robert Ardrey. *New Scientist* 71:242.

Pilbeam, David
    1978a Rearranging Our Family Tree. *Human Nature* 1:38–45.

Pilbeam, David; Grant E. Meyer; Catherine Badgley; M. D. Rose; M. H. K. Pickford; A. K. Behrensmeyer; and S. M. Ibrahim Shah.
    1977   New Hominoid Primates from the Siwaliks of Pakistan and Their Bearing on Hominoid Evolution. *Nature* 270:689–695.

Read, Carveth
    1920   *The Origin of Man and of His Superstitions.* Cambridge: Cambridge University Press.

Rowell, Thelma E.
    1966   Forest Living Baboons in Uganda. *Journal of Zoology* 149:344–364.
    1969   Long-Term Changes in a Population of Ugandan Baboons. *Folia Primatologica* 11:241–254.
    1972   *The Social Behaviour of Monkeys.* Baltimore: Penguin Books.
    1974   The Concept of Social Dominance. *Behavioral Biology* 11:131–154.

Schaller, George B.
    1972   *The Serengeti Lion: A Study of Predator-Prey Relations.* Chicago: University of Chicago Press.

Spencer, Herbert
    1866   *The Principles of Biology.* New York: Appleton.

Struhsaker, Thomas T.
    1969   Correlates of Ecology and Social Organization among African Cercopithecines. *Folia Primatologica* 11:80–118.

Struhsaker, Thomas T., and J. Stephen Gartlan
    1970   Observations on the Behavior and Ecology of the Patas Monkey (*Erythrocebus patas*) in the Waza Reserve, Cameroon. *Journal of Zoology* 161:49–63.

Tennyson, Alfred Lord
    1850   *In Memoriam.* London: Edward Moxon.

Tiger, Lionel
    1969   *Men in Groups.* New York: Random House.

Tiger, Lionel, and Robin Fox
    1971   *The Imperial Animal.* New York: Holt, Rinehart and Winston.

Washburn, Sherwood L.
    1978   What We Can't Learn about People from Apes. *Human Nature* 1:70–75.

284   *On becoming human*

Washburn, Sherwood L., and Irven DeVore
    1961a Social Behavior of Baboons and Early Man. In *Social Life of Early
        Man,* S. L. Washburn (ed.), pp. 91–105. Chicago: Aldine. (Reprinted
        in *Yearbook of Physical Anthropology 9:91–105.*)
    1961b The Social Life of Baboons. *Scientific American 204:62–71.*
Washburn, Sherwood L., and C. S. Lancaster
    1968 The Evolution of Hunting. In *Perspectives on Human Evolution,* vol.
        1, S. L. Washburn and Phyllis C. Jay (eds.), pp. 213–229. New York:
        Holt, Rinehart and Winston.
Yoshiba, Kenji
    1968 Local and Intertroop Variability in Ecology and Social Behavior of Com-
        mon Indian Langurs. In *Primates: Studies in Adaptation and Variability,*
        P. Jay (ed.), pp. 217–242. New York: Holt, Rinehart and Winston.
Zuckerman, Solly
    1932 *The Social Life of Monkeys and Apes.* New York: Harcourt, Brace.
    1933 Functional Affinities of Man, Monkeys, and Apes. New York: Har-
        court, Brace.

CHAPTER 3. AFRICAN APES AND HUMAN EVOLUTION

Almquist, Alan J., and John E. Cronin
    1977 *Origin of Man: Problems in the Interpretation of New Evidence.* Rev.
        ed. AAAS Study Guides on Contemporary Problems. A part of the
        NSF Chautauqua-type short courses for college teachers program.
Andrews, Peter
    1971 *Ramapithecus wickeri* Mandible from Fort Ternan, Kenya. *Nature
        231:192–194.*
    1974 New Species of *Dryopithecus* from Kenya. *Nature 249:188–190.*
Andrews, Peter; W. R. Hamilton; and P. J. Whybrow
    1978 Dryopithecines from the Miocene of Saudi Arabia. *Nature 274:249–
        251.*
Andrews, Peter, and Judith A. H. Van Couvering
    1975 Palaeoenvironments in the East African Miocene. In *Approaches in
        Primate Paleobiology,* F. Szalay (ed.), pp. 62–103. Basel: Karger.
Ankel, Friderun
    1965 Der Canalis sacralis als Indikator für die Länge der Caudalregion der
        Primaten [The sacral canal as an indicator of the length of the caudal
        region in primates]. *Folia Primatologica 3:263–276.*
Avis, Virginia
    1962 Brachiation: The Crucial Issue for Man's Ancestry. *Yearbook of Physi-
        cal Anthropology 10:99–128.*
Ayala, Francisco J., ed.
    1976 *Molecular Evolution.* Sunderland, Mass.: Sinauer Associates.
Badrian, Alison, and Noel Badrian
    1977 Pygmy Chimpanzees. *Oryx 13:463–468.*
Barry, J. M., and E. M. Barry
    1973 *Molecular Biology: An Introduction to Chemical Genetics.* Englewood
        Cliffs, N.J.: Prentice-Hall.

Bender, M. A., and E. H. Y. Chu
  1963 The Chromosomes of Primates. In *Evolutionary and Genetic Biology of Primates,* vol. 1, John Buettner-Janusch (ed.), pp. 261–310. New York: Academic Press.
Berggren, W. A.
  1972a Cenozoic Time Scale: Some Implications for Regional Geology and Palaeobiogeography. *Lethaia* 5:195–215.
Bilsborough, A.
  1971 Evolutionary Change in the Hominoid Maxilla. *Man* 6:473–485.
Bingham, Harold C.
  1932 *Gorillas in a Native Habitat.* Washington, D.C.: Carnegie Institution.
Bruce, Elizabeth J., and Francisco J. Ayala
  1978 Humans and Apes Are Genetically Very Similar. *Nature* 276:264–265.
Butzer, Karl W.
  1978 Geo-ecological Perspectives on Early Hominid Evolution. In *Early Hominids of Africa,* Clifford J. Jolly (ed.), pp. 191–217. London: Duckworth.
Campbell, B. G., and R. L. Bernor
  1976 The Origin of the Hominidae: Africa or Asia? *Journal of Human Evolution* 5:441–454.
Carlson, Steven S.; Allan C. Wilson; and Richard D. Maxson
  1978 Do Albumin Clocks Run on Time? 2. *Science* 200:1183–1185.
Coolidge, Harold J., Jr.
  1933 *Pan paniscus:* Pygmy Chimpanzee from South of the Congo River. *American Journal of Physical Anthropology* 18:1–60.
Corruccini, Robert S.; Russell L. Ciochon; and Henry M. McHenry
  1976 The Postcranium of Miocene Hominoids: Were Dryopithecines Merely "Dental Apes"? *Primates* 17:205–223.
Cramer, Douglas L., and Adrienne L. Zihlman
  1978 Sexual Dimorphism in Pygmy Chimpanzees (*Pan paniscus*). In *Recent Advances in Primatology,* vol. 3, D. J. Chivers and K. A. Joysey (eds.), pp. 487–490. New York: Academic Press.
Cronin, John E.
  1975 Molecular Systematics of the Order Primates. Dissertation, University of California, Berkeley.
  1977a Anthropoid Evolution: The Molecular Evidence. *Kroeber Anthropological Society Papers,* no. 50:75–84.
  1977b Pygmy Chimpanzee (*Pan paniscus*) Systematics. Paper presented at the 46th Annual Meeting, American Association of Physical Anthropologists, Seattle.
Darwin, Charles
  1859 *The Origin of Species by Means of Natural Selection; or, The Preservation of Favored Races in the Struggle for Life.* London: John Murray.
  1871 *The Descent of Man and Selection in Relation to Sex.* London: John Murray.
DeJong, W. W. W.
  1971 Structure of the β-chain of Chimpanzee Haemoglobin Az. *Nature New Biology* 234:176–177.

Delson, Eric
    1975a Paleoecology and Zoogeography of the Old World Monkeys. In *Primate Functional Morphology and Evolution,* Russell H. Tuttle (ed.), pp. 37–64. The Hague: Mouton.
    1975b Evolutionary History of the *Cercopithecidae.* In *Approaches to Primate Paleobiology,* F. S. Szalay (ed.), pp. 167–217. Basel: Karger.
Doolittle, R. F., and G. A. Mross
    1970 Identity of Chimpanzee and Human Fibrinopeptides. *Nature* 225:643–644.
Doolittle, R. F.; G. L. Wooding; Y. Lin; and M. Riley
    1971 Hominoid Evolution as Judged by Fibrinopeptide Structures. *Journal of Molecular Evolution* 1:74–83.
Eckhardt, Robert B.
    1977 Hominid Origins: The Lothagam Problem. *Current Anthropology* 18:356.
Fitch, Walter M.
    1977 The Phyletic Interpretation of Macromolecular Sequence Information: Sample Cases. In *Major Patterns in Vertebrate Evolution,* Max K. Hecht, Peter C. Goody, and Bessie M. Hecht (eds.), pp. 211–248. New York: Plenum Press.
Frayer, David W.
    1976 A Reappraisal of *Rampithecus [sic]. Yearbook of Physical Anthropology, 1974, 18:*19–30.
Gantt, David G.; David Pilbeam; and Gregory P. Steward
    1977 Hominoid Enamel Prism Patterns. *Science 198:*1155–1157.
Goodall, Jane van Lawick
    1968b A Preliminary Report on Expressive Movements and Communication in the Gombe Stream Chimpanzees. In *Primates: Studies in Adaptation and Variability,* Phyllis C. Jay (ed.), pp. 313–374. New York: Holt, Rinehart and Winston.
    1976 Continuities between Chimpanzee and Human Behavior. In *Human Origins: Louis Leakey and the East African Evidence,* Glynn Ll. Isaac and Elizabeth R. McCown (eds.), pp. 81–95. Menlo Park: Benjamin.
Goodall, Jane, and David A. Hamburg
    1975 Chimpanzee Behavior as a Model for the Behavior of Early Man. In *New Psychiatric Frontiers,* D. A. Hamburg and H.´K. H. Brodie (eds.), pp. 14–43. New York: Basic Books.
Goodman, Morris
    1976 Toward a Genealogical Description of the Primates. In *Molecular Anthropology,* M. Goodman, R. E. Tashian, and J. H. Tashian (eds.), pp. 321–352. New York: Plenum Press.
Goodman, Morris, and Gabriel W. Lasker
    1975 Molecular Evidence as to Man's Place in Nature. In *Primate Functional Morphology and Evolution,* R. H. Tuttle (ed.), pp. 71–101. The Hague: Mouton.
Goodman, Morris; Richard E. Tashian; and Jeanne H. Tashian, eds.
    1976 *Molecular Anthropology: Genes and Proteins in the Evolutionary Ascent of the Primates.* New York: Plenum Press.

Greenfield, L. O.
 1978 On the Dental Arcade Reconstructions of *Ramapithecus. Journal of Human Evolution* 7:345–359.
Haq, Bilal U.; W. A. Berggren; and John A. Van Couvering
 1977 Corrected Age of the Pliocene/Pleistocene Boundary. *Nature* 269:483–488.
Hill, W. C. Osman
 1969 The Nomenclature, Taxonomy, and Distribution of Chimpanzees. In *The Chimpanzee,* vol. 1, G. H. Bourne (ed.), pp. 22–46. Basel: Karger.
 1972 *Evolutionary Biology of the Primates.* New York: Academic Press.
Hsiung, G. D.; F. L. Black; and J. R. Henderson
 1964 Susceptibility of Primates to Viruses in Relation to Taxonomic Classification. In *Evolutionary and Genetic Biology of Primates,* vol. 2, John Buettner-Janusch (ed.), pp. 1–24. New York: Academic Press.
Huxley, Thomas Henry
 1863 *Evidence as to Man's Place in Nature.* London: Williams and Norgate. (Reprinted 1959 as *Man's Place in Nature.* Ann Arbor: University of Michigan Press.)
Jacob, Teuku
 1972 The Absolute Date of the Djetis Beds at Modjokerto. *Antiquity* 46:36.
 1976 Man in Indonesia: Past, Present, and Future. In *Modern Quaternary Research in Southeast Asia,* vol. 2, Gert-Jan Bartstra and Willem Arnold Casparie (eds.), pp. 39–48. Rotterdam: Balkema.
Jacob, Teuku, and Garniss H. Curtis
 1971 Preliminary Potassium-Argon Dating of Early Man in Java. *Contributions of the University Archaeological Research Facility* 12:50.
Kano, Takayoshi
 1979 A Pilot Study of the Ecology of Pygmy Chimpanzees (*Pan paniscus*). In *The Great Apes.* Perspectives on Human Evolution, vol. 5, D. Hamburg and E. McCown (eds.), pp. 123–185. Menlo Park: Benjamin/Cummings.
 1980 Social Behavior of Wild Pygmy Chimpanzees (*Pan paniscus*) of Wamba: A Preliminary Report. *Journal of Human Evolution* 9(4):243–260.
Kennedy, G. E.
 1978 Hominoid Habitat Shifts in the Miocene. *Nature* 271:11–12.
King, Mary-Claire, and A. C. Wilson
 1975 Evolution at Two Levels in Humans and Chimpanzees. *Science* 188:107–116.
Klinger, Harold P.; John L. Hamerton; David Mutton; and Ernst M. Lang
 1963 The Chromosomes of the Hominoidea. In *Classification and Human Evolution,* Sherwood L. Washburn (ed.), pp. 235–242. Chicago: Aldine.
Köhler, Wolfgang
 1927 *The Mentality of Apes.* 2d ed. New York: Harcourt, Brace.
Kohne, David E.
 1970 Evolution of Higher-Organism DNA. *Quarterly Review of Biophysics* 3:327–375.

288   *On becoming human*

Kohne, David E.; J. A. Chiscon; and B. H. Hoyer
    1972   Evolution of Primate DNA Sequences. *Journal of Human Evolution*
            1:627–644.
Kohts, Nadezhda Nikolaevna
    1935   Infant Ape and Human Child: Instincts, Emotions, Play, Habits. *Sci-*
            entific Memoirs of the Museum Darwinianum in Moscow 3:1–596.
            [Name also spelled Kots.]
Korey, Kenneth A.
    1979   Species Number, Sample Size, and the Estimation of Divergence Times
            from Molecular Evidence. Paper presented at the 48th Annual Meeting,
            American Association of Physical Anthropologists, San Francisco.
Lark, David
    1953   Darwin's Finches. *Scientific American 188*:66–72.
Lewis, O. J.
    1972a   Osteological Features Characterizing the Wrists of Monkeys and
            Apes, with a Reconsideration of this Region in *Dryopithecus* (Procon-
            sul) *africanus*. *American Journal of Physical Anthropology 36*:45–58.
    1972b   The Evolution of the Hallucial Tarsometatarsal Joint in the *Anthropoi-*
            dea. *American Journal of Physical Anthropology 37*:13–34.
Lewontin, R. C.
    1974   *The Genetic Basis of Evolutionary Change.* New York: Columbia Uni-
            versity Press.
Lillegraven, Jason A.
    1974   Biogeographical Considerations of the Marsupial-Placental Dichot-
            omy. In *Annual Review of Ecology and Systematics,* R. F. Johnston,
            P. W. Frank, and C. D. Michener (eds.), pp. 263–283. Palo Alto:
            Annual Reviews.
MacKinnon, John
    1976   Mountain Gorillas and Bonobos. *Oryx 13*:372–382.
McClure, H. M., and N. B. Guilloud
    1971   Comparative Pathology of the Chimpanzee. In *The Chimpanzee,* vol.
            4, *Behavior, Growth, and Pathology of Chimpanzees,* G. H. Bourne
            (ed.), pp. 104–272. Basel: Karger.
McHenry, Henry M.
    1975   Fossils and the Mosaic Nature of Human Evolution. *Science*
            190:425–431.
Miller, Dorothy A.
    1977   Evolution of Primate Chromosomes. *Science 198*:1116–1124.
Moore, G. W.; M. Goodman; C. Callahan; R. Holmquist; and M. Herbert
    1976   Estimation of Superimposed Mutations in the Divergent Evolution of
            Protein Sequences: Stochastic vs. Augmented Maximum Parsimony
            Method-Cytochrome c Phylogeny. *Journal of Molecular Biology*
            10:15–37.
Morbeck, Mary Ellen
    1972   A Re-examination of the Forelimb of the Miocene *Hominoidea.* Dis-
            sertation, University of California, Berkeley.
    1975a   The *Dryopithecus africanus* Forelimb. *Journal of Human Evolution*
            4:39–46.

1979 Hominoidea Postcranial Remains from Rudabanya, Hungary. Paper presented at the 48th Annual Meeting, American Association of Physical Anthropologists, San Francisco.

Napier, John
1963 Brachiation and Brachiators. *Symposia of the Zoological Society of London* 10:183–195.

Nei, Masatoshi
1975 Molecular Population Genetics and Evolution. New York: American Elsevier.

Ninkovich, D., and L. H. Burckle
1978 Absolute Age of the Base of the Hominid-Bearing Beds in Eastern Java. *Nature* 275:306–307.

Nishida, Toshisada
1972b Preliminary Information on the Pygmy Chimpanzees *(Pan paniscus)* of the Congo Basin. *Primates* 13:415–425.

Nissen, Henry W.
1931 *A Field Study of the Chimpanzee: Observations of Chimpanzee Behavior and Environment in Western French Guinea.* Comparative Psychology Monographs, no. 8. Baltimore: Johns Hopkins University Press.

Oxnard, C. E.
1963 Locomotor Adaptation in the Primate Forelimb. *Symposia of the Zoological Society of London* 10:165–182.

Patterson, Francine
1978a The Gestures of a Gorilla: Sign Language Acquisition in Another Pongid Species. *Brain and Language* 5:72–97.
1978b Conversations with a Gorilla. *National Geographic* 154:438–465.

Pilbeam, David R.
1966 Notes on *Ramapithecus,* the Earliest Known Hominid, and *Dryopithecus. American Journal of Physical Anthropology* 25:1–5.
1969 *Tertiary Pongidae of East Africa: Evolutionary Relationships and Taxonomy.* Peabody Museum of Natural History, Bulletin no. 31.
1978a Rearranging Our Family Tree. *Human Nature* 1:38–45.

Pilbeam, David; John Barry; Grant E. Meyer; S. M. Ibrahim Shah; M. H. K. Pickford; W. W. Bishop; Herbert Thomas; and Louis L. Jacobs
1977 Geology and Palaeontology of Neogene Strata of Pakistan. *Nature* 270:684–689.

Pilbeam, David; Grant E. Meyer; Catherine Badgley; M. D. Rose; M. H. K. Pickford; A. K. Behrensmeyer; and S. M. Ibrahim Shah
1977 New Hominoid Primates from the Siwaliks of Pakistan and Their Bearing on Hominoid Evolution. *Nature* 270:689–695.

Poirier, Frank E.
1977 *Fossil Evidence: The Human Evolutionary Journey.* 2d ed. Saint Louis: Mosby.

Preuschoft, H.
1973 Body Posture and Locomotion in Some East African Miocene *Dryopithecinae.* In *Human Evolution,* M. H. Day (ed.), pp. 13–46. London: Taylor and Francis.

Radinsky, Leonard
    1978   Do Albumin Clocks Run on Time? *Science 200*:1182–1183.
Romero-Herrera, A. E.; H. Lehmann; K. A. Joysey; and A. E. Friday
    1973   Molecular Evolution of Myoglobin and the Fossil Record: A Phyloge-
            netic Synthesis. *Nature 246*:389–395.
Rumbaugh, Duane M.
    1970   Learning Skills of Anthropoids. In *Primate Behavior: Developments in
            Field and Laboratory Research*, vol. 1, L. A. Rosenblum (ed.), pp. 1–
            70. New York: Academic Press.
Sabater Pí, Jorge
    1974   An Elementary Industry of the Chimpanzees in the Okorobikó Moun-
            tains, Rio Muni (Republic of Equatorial Guinea), West Africa. *Pri-
            mates 15*:351–364.
Sarich, Vincent M.
    1968   The Origin of the Hominids: An Immunological Approach. In *Per-
            spectives on Human Evolution*, vol. 1, S. L. Washburn and Phyllis C.
            Jay (eds.), pp. 94–121. New York: Holt, Rinehart and Winston.
    1973   Just How Old Is the Hominid Line? *Yearbook of Physical Anthropol-
            ogy 17*:98–112.
Sarich, Vincent M., and John E. Cronin
    1976   Molecular Systematics of the Primates. In *Molecular Anthropology:
            Genes and Proteins in the Evolutionary Ascent of the Primates*, Morris
            Goodman, Richard E. Tashian, and Jeanne H. Tashian (eds.), pp.
            141–170. New York: Plenum Press.
    1977   Generation Length and Rates of Hominoid Molecular Evolution. *Na-
            ture 269*:354.
Sarich, Vincent M., and Allan C. Wilson
    1967   Immunological Time Scale for Hominid Evolution. *Science
            158*:1200–1203.
Savage, E. Sue, and Roger Bakeman
    1978   Sexual Dimorphism and Behavior in *Pan paniscus*. In *Recent Ad-
            vances in Primatology*, vol. 1, D. J. Chivers and J. Herbert (eds.), pp.
            613–616. New York: Academic Press.
Savage, E. Sue, E. O. Smith; and J. Songo Bululu
    1976   *Pan paniscus*: Sexual Morphology and Behaviour. Paper presented at
            the 6th Congress of the International Primatological Society, Cam-
            bridge.
Savage-Rumbaugh, E. Sue, and Beverly J. Wilkerson
    1978   Socio-sexual Behavior in *Pan paniscus* and *Pan troglodytes*: A Com-
            parative Study. *Journal of Human Evolution 7*:327–344.
Savage-Rumbaugh, E. Sue; Beverly J. Wilkerson; and Roger Bakeman
    1977   Spontaneous Gestural Communication among Conspecifics in the
            Pygmy Chimpanzee *(Pan paniscus)*. In *Progress in Ape Research*,
            G. H. Bourne (ed.), pp. 97–116. New York: Academic Press.
Simons, Elwyn L.
    1972   *Primate Evolution: An Introducion to Man's Place in Nature*. New
            York: Macmillan.
    1976   The Fossil Record of Primate Phylogeny. In *Molecular Anthropology:*

Genes and Proteins in the Evolutionary Ascent of the Primates, Morris Goodman, Richard E. Tashian, and Jeanne H. Tashian (eds.), pp. 35–62. New York: Plenum Press.

1977   *Ramapithecus. Scientific American 236:*28–35.

1978   Diversity among the Early Hominids: A Vertebrate Palaeontologist's Viewpoint. In *Early Hominids of Africa,* Clifford J. Jolly (ed.), pp. 543–566. London: Duckworth.

Simons, Elwyn L., and David R. Pilbeam

1965   Preliminary Revision of the Dryopithecinae (Pongidae, Anthropoidea). *Folia Primatologica 3:*81–152.

Swindler, Daris S.

1976   *Dentition of Living Primates.* New York: Academic Press.

Szalay, F. S.

1975   Haplorhine Phylogeny and the Status of the Anthropoidea. In *Primate Functional Morphology and Evolution,* Russell H. Tuttle (ed.), pp. 3–22. The Hague: Mouton.

Tanner, Nancy M., and Adrienne L. Zihlman

1976a   Women in Evolution. 1. Innovation and Selection in Human Origins. *Signs: Journal of Women in Culture and Society 1:*585–608.

1976b   The Evolution of Human Communication: What Can Primates Tell Us? In *Origins and Evolution of Language and Speech,* Stevan R. Harnad, Horst D. Steklis, and Jane Lancaster (eds.), pp. 467–480. Annals of the New York Academy of Sciences, vol. 280. New York: New York Academy of Sciences.

Tauxe, Lisa

1979   A New Date for *Ramapithecus. Nature 282:*399–401.

Uzzell, Thomas, and David Pilbeam

1971   Phyletic Divergence Dates of Hominoid Primates: A Comparison of Fossil and Molecular Data. *Evolution 25:*615–635.

Van Couvering, Judith A. H.

1975   Forest Habitat of Early Miocene Hominoids. Paper presented at the 44th Annual Meeting, American Association of Physical Anthropologists, Denver.

Van Couvering, Judith A. H., and John A. Van Couvering

1976   Early Miocene Mammal Fossils from East Africa: Aspects of Geology, Faunistics, and Paleoecology. In *Human Origins: Louis Leakey and the East African Evidence,* Glynn Ll. Isaac and Elizabeth R. McCown (eds.), pp. 155–207. Menlo Park: Benjamin.

Vrba, Elisabeth S., and Fred E. Grine

1978   Australopithecine Enamel Prism Patterns. *Science 202:*890–892.

Wade, Nicholas

1978   New Vaccine May Bring Man and Chimpanzee into Tragic Conflict. *Science 200:*1027–1030.

Walker, Alan

1976   Splitting Times among Hominoids Deduced from the Fossil Record. In *Molecular Anthropology: Genes and Proteins in the Evolutionary Ascent of the Primates,* Morris Goodman, Richard E. Tashian, and Jeanne H. Tashian (eds.), pp. 63–77. New York: Plenum Press.

Washburn, Sherwood L.
    1950   The Analysis of Primate Evolution with Particular Reference to the
            Origin of Man. *Cold Spring Harbor Symposia on Quantitative Biology*
            15:67–78.
    1963   Behavior and Human Evolution. In *Classification and Human Evolu-
            tion,* pp. 190–203. Chicago: Aldine.
Washburn, Sherwood L., and Ruth Moore
    1974   *Ape into Man. A Study of Human Evolution.* Boston: Little, Brown.
Wilson, Allan C.; Steven S. Carlson; and Thomas J. White
    1977   Biochemical Evolution. In *Annual Review of Biochemistry* 46:573–
            639.
Wilson, Allan C., and Vincent M. Sarich
    1969   A Molecular Time Scale for Human Evolution. *Proceedings of the Na-
            tional Academy of Sciences* 63:1088–1093.
Yerkes, Robert M., and Ada W. Yerkes
    1929   *The Great Apes: A Study of Anthropoid Life.* New Haven: Yale Uni-
            versity Press.
Yunis, Jorge J.; Jeffrey R. Sawyer; and Kelly Dunham
    1980   The Striking Resemblance of High-Resolution G-Banded Chromo-
            somes of Man and Chimpanzee. *Nature 208:*1145–1148.
Zihlman, Adrienne L.
    1977   Implications of Pygmy Chimpanzee Morphology for Interpretations of
            Early Hominids. Paper presented at the 46th Annual Meeting, Ameri-
            can Association of Physical Anthropologists, Seattle.
    1979   Pygmy Chimpanzee Morphology and the Interpretation of Early
            Hominids. *South African Journal of Science 5:*165–168.
Zihlman, Adrienne L., and Douglas L. Cramer
    1978   Skeletal Differences between Pygmy *(Pan paniscus)* and Common
            Chimpanzees *(Pan troglodytes). Folia Primatologica* 29:86–94.
Zihlman, Adrienne L.; John E. Cronin; Douglas Cramer; and Vincent M. Sarich
    1978   Pygmy Chimpanzee as a Possible Prototype for the Common Ancestor
            of Humans, Chimpanzees, and Gorillas. *Nature 275:*744–746.
Zihlman, Adrienne L., and Nancy M. Tanner
    1979   Gathering and the Hominid Adaptation. In *Female Hierarchies,* Lionel
            Tiger and Heather M. Fowler (eds.). Chicago: Beresford Book Service.
Zuckerkandl, Emile, and Linus Pauling
    1962   Molecular Disease, Evolution, and Genic Heterogeneity. In *Horizons
            in Biochemistry,* Michael Kasha and Bernard Pullman (eds.), pp.
            189–225. New York: Academic Press.

CHAPTER 4. CHIMPANZEES AS A MODEL OF THE ANCESTRAL POPULATION:
LOCOMOTION, TOOLS, AND DIET

Albrecht, Helmut, and Sinclair C. Dunnett
    1971   *Chimpanzees in Western Africa.* Studies in Ethology. Munich: Piper.
Altmann, Stuart A., and Jeanne Altmann
    1970   *Baboon Ecology: African Field Research.* Bibliotheca Primatologica,
            no. 12. Basel: Karger.

Bauer, Harold R.
   1977   Chimp Bipedal Locomotion in the Gombe National Park. *Primates*
          18:913–921.
DeVore, Irven, and K. R. L. Hall
   1965   Baboon Ecology. In *Primate Behavior: Field Studies of Monkeys and*
          Apes, I. DeVore (ed.), pp. 20–52. New York: Holt, Rinehart and
          Winston.
DeVore, Irven, and Sherwood L. Washburn
   1963   Baboon Ecology and Human Evolution. In *African Ecology and Hu-*
          man Evolution, F. Clark Howell and F. Bourlière (eds.), pp. 335–367.
          Chicago: Aldine.
Goodall, Jane van Lawick
   1963   Feeding Behaviour of Wild Chimpanzees: A Preliminary Report. *Sym-*
          posia of the Zoological Society of London, no. 10:39–48.
   1965   Chimpanzees of the Gombe Stream Reserve. In *Primate Behavior:*
          Field Studies of Monkeys and Apes, I. DeVore (ed.), pp. 425–473.
          New York: Holt, Rinehart and Winston.
   1968a The Behaviour of Free-living Chimpanzees in the Gombe Stream Re-
          serve. *Animal Behaviour Monographs 1*:161–311.
   1970   Tool-Using in Primates and Other Vertebrates. In *Advances in the*
          Study of Behavior, vol. 3, Daniel S. Lehrman, Robert A. Hinde,
          and Evelyn Shaw (eds.), pp. 195–249. New York: Academic
          Press.
   1973b Cultural Elements in a Chimpanzee Community. In *Precultural Pri-*
          mate Behavior, Symposia of the Fourth International Congress of
          Primatology, vol. 1, E. W. Menzel, Jr. (ed.), pp. 144–185. Basel:
          Karger.
Gregory, William K.
   1949   The Bearing of Australopithecinae upon the Problem of Man's Place
          in Nature. *American Journal of Physical Anthropology 7*:485–512.
Hall, K. R. L.
   1963b Tool-Using Performances as Indicators of Behavioral Adaptability.
          Current Anthropology 4:479–487.
Harding, Robert S. O., and Shirley C. Strum
   1976   The Predatory Baboons of Kekopey. *Natural History 85*:46–53.
Hayes, Cathy
   1951   *The Ape in Our House.* New York: Harper and Brothers.
Hladik, C. M.
   1973   Alimentation et activité d'un groupe de chimpanzés réintroduits en
          Forêt Gabonais. *Terre et la vie 27*:343–413.
Jay, Phyllis C.
   1968   Primate Field Studies and Human Evolution. In *Primates: Studies in*
          Adaptation and Variability, Phyllis C. Jay (ed.), pp. 487–503. New
          York: Holt, Rinehart and Winston.
Jones, Clyde, and Jorge Sabater Pí
   1971   *Comparative Ecology of* Gorilla gorilla *(Savage and Wyman) and* Pan
          troglodytes *(Blumenbach) in Rio Muni, West Africa.* Bibliotheca Pri-
          matologica, no. 13. Basel: Karger.

294   *On becoming human*

Kawabe, Munemi
    1966   One Observed Case of Hunting Behavior among Wild Chimpanzees
            Living in the Savanna Woodland of Western Tanzania. *Primates*
            7:393–396.
King, Mary-Claire, and A. C. Wilson
    1975   Evolution at Two Levels in Humans and Chimpanzees. *Science*
            188:107–116.
Köhler, Wolfgang
    1927   *The Mentality of Apes.* 2d ed. New York: Harcourt, Brace.
Kortlandt, Adriaan
    1965   How Do Chimpanzees Use Weapons When Fighting Leopards? *Year-
            book of the American Philosophical Society,* pp. 327–332.
    1967   Experimentation with Chimpanzees in the Wild. In *Neue Ergebnisse
            der Primatologie* [Progress in primatology], First Congress of the Inter-
            national Primatological Society, Frankfurt, D. Starck, R. Schneider,
            and H. J. Kuhn (eds.), pp. 208–224. Stuttgart: Gustav Fischer.
Kortlandt, Adriaan, and M. Kooij
    1963   Protohominid Behaviour in Primates (Preliminary Communication). In
            The Primates, Symposia of the Zoological Society of London, no. 10,
            John Napier and N. A. Barnicot (eds.), pp. 61–88. London: Zoologi-
            cal Society.
Kruuk, H.
    1972   *The Spotted Hyena.* Chicago: University of Chicago Press.
Lancaster, Jane B.
    1968a   On the Evolution of Tool-Using Behavior. *American Anthropologist*
            70:56–66.
McGrew, William C.
    1974   Tool Use by Wild Chimpanzees in Feeding upon Driver Ants. *Journal
            of Human Evolution* 3:501–508.
    1977   Socialization and Object Manipulation of Wild Chimpanzees. In *Pri-
            mate Bio-Social Development: Biological, Social, and Ecological De-
            terminants,* Suzanne Chevalier-Skolnikoff and Frank E. Poirier (eds.),
            pp. 261–288. New York: Garland.
    1979   Evolutionary Implications of Sex Differences in Chimpanzee Predation
            and Tool Use. In *The Great Apes,* Perspectives on Human Evolution,
            vol. 5, D. A. Hamburg and E. R. McCown (eds.), pp. 441–463.
            Menlo Park: Benjamin/Cummings.
McGrew, William C., and Caroline E. G. Tutin
    1973   Chimpanzee Tool Use in Dental Grooming. *Nature* 241:477–478.
McGrew, William C.; Caroline E. G. Tutin; and P. J. Baldwin
    1979   Chimpanzees, Tools, and Termites: Cross-Cultural Comparisons of
            Senegal, Tanzania, and Rio Muni. *Man* 14:185–214.
Menzel, Emil W., Jr.
    1973b   Further Observations on the Use of Ladders in a Group of Young
            Chimpanzees. *Folia Primatologica* 19:450–457.
    1973c   Chimpanzee Spatial Memory Organization. *Science* 182:943–945.
    1974   A Group of Young Chimpanzees in a One-Acre Field. In *Behavior of
            Nonhuman Primates: Modern Research Trends,* vol. 5, A. M. Schrier
            and F. Stollnitz (eds.), pp. 83–153. New York: Academic Press.

Morris, Kathryn, and Jane Goodall
    1977   Competition for Meat between Chimpanzees and Baboons of the
            Gombe National Park. *Folia Primatologica* 28:109–121.
Morton, Dudley J.
    1935   *The Human Foot: Its Evolution, Physiology, and Functional Disorders.*
            New York: Columbia University Press. (Reprinted 1964. New York:
            Hafner.)
Nishida, Toshisada
    1968   The Social Group of Wild Chimpanzees in the Mahali Mountains.
            Primates 9:167–224.
    1972a   A Note on the Ecology of the Red-Colobus Monkeys (*Colobus badius
            tephroscelos*) Living in the Mahali Mountains. *Primates* 13:57–64.
    1973   The Ant Gathering Behavior by the Use of Tools among Wild Chim-
            panzees of the Mahali Mountains. *Journal of Human Evolution*
            2:357–370.
Nissen, Henry W.
    1931   *A Field Study of the Chimpanzee: Observations of Chimpanzee Behav-
            ior and Environment in Western French Guinea.* Comparative Psychol-
            ogy Monographs, no. 8. Baltimore: Johns Hopkins University Press.
Oakley, Kenneth P.
    1961   On Man's Use of Fire, with Comments on Tool-Making and Hunting.
            In *Social Life of Early Man*, Sherwood L. Washburn (ed.), pp. 176–
            192. Chicago: Aldine.
Rahm, U.
    1971   L'emploi d'outils par les chimpanzés de l'ouest de la Côte-d'Ivoire.
            Terre et la vie 25:506–509.
Reynolds, Vernon
    1967   *The Apes: The Gorilla, Chimpanzee, Orangutan, and Gibbon–Their
            History and Their World.* New York: Dutton.
Reynolds, Vernon, and Frances Reynolds
    1965   Chimpanzees of the Budongo Forest. In *Primate Behavior: Field
            Studies of Monkeys and Apes*, Irven DeVore (ed.), pp. 425–473.
            New York: Holt, Rinehart and Winston.
Riss, David C., and Curt D. Busse
    1977   Fifty-Day Observation of a Free-ranging Adult Male Chimpanzee. *Fo-
            lia Primatologica* 28:283–297.
Rowell, Thelma E.
    1966   Forest Living Baboons in Uganda. *Journal of Zoology* 149:344–364.
Schaller, George B.
    1963   *The Mountain Gorilla: Ecology and Behavior.* Chicago: University of
            Chicago Press.
    1972   *The Serengeti Lion: A Study of Predator-Prey Relations.* Chicago: Uni-
            versity of Chicago Press.
Struhsaker, T. T., and P. Hunkeler
    1971   Evidence of Tool-Using by Chimpanzees in the Ivory Coast. *Folia Pri-
            matologica* 15:212–219.
Strum, Shirley C.
    1975   Primate Predation: Interim Report on the Development of a Tradition
            in a Troop of Olive Baboons. *Science* 187:755–757.

Sugiyama, Yukimaru

　1969　Social Behavior of Chimpanzees in the Budongo Forest, Uganda. *Primates* 10:197–225.

　1972　Social Characteristics and Socialization of Wild Chimpanzees. In *Primate Socialization,* Frank E. Poirier (ed.), pp. 145–258. New York: Random House.

Suzuki, Akira

　1966　On the Insect-Eating Habits among Wild Chimpanzees Living in the Savanna Woodland of Western Tanzania. *Primates* 7:481–487.

　1969　An Ecological Study of Chimpanzees in a Savanna Woodland. *Primates* 10:103–148.

Tanner, Nancy M., and Adrienne L. Zihlman

　1976a　Women in Evolution. 1. Innovation and Selection in Human Origins. *Signs: Journal of Women in Culture and Society* 1:585–608.

Teleki, Geza

　1973a　The Omnivorous Chimpanzee. *Scientific American* 228:32–42.

　1973b　*The Predatory Behavior of Wild Chimpanzees.* Lewisburg, Pa.: Bucknell University Press.

　1975　Primate Subsistence Patterns: Collector-Predators and Gatherer-Hunters. *Journal of Human Evolution* 4:125–184.

In press　Environmental Parameters of Chimpanzee Behavior and Society in Gombe National Park, Tanzania: A Field Study of Adaptive Strategies.

Tuttle, Russell H.

　1967　Knuckle-Walking and the Evolution of Hominoid Hands. *American Journal of Physical Anthropology* 26:171–206.

　1969　Knuckle-Walking and the Problem of Human Origins. *Science* 166:953–961.

Washburn, Sherwood L.

　1968b　The Study of Human Evolution. Condon Lectures. Eugene: Oregon State System of Higher Education.

Wrangham, Richard W.

　1974　Artificial Feeding of Chimpanzees and Baboons in Their Natural Habitat. *Animal Behaviour* 22:83–93.

CHAPTER 5. CHIMPANZEES AS A MODEL OF THE ANCESTRAL POPULATION: SOCIAL ORGANIZATION AND INTERACTION

Albrecht, Helmut, and Sinclair C. Dunnett

　1971　*Chimpanzees in Western Africa.* Studies in Ethology. Munich: Piper.

Boaz, Noel T.

　1979　Early Hominid Population Densities: New Estimates. *Science* 206:592–595.

Bygott, J. David

　1979　Agonistic Behaviour, Dominance, and Social Structure in Wild Chimpanzees of the Gombe National Park. In *The Great Apes,* Perspectives on Human Evolution, vol. 5, D. A. Hamburg and E. R. McCown (eds.), pp. 405–427. Menlo Park: Benjamin/Cummings.

Chavaillon, J.
  1976 Evidence for the Technical Practices of Early Pleistocene Hominids. In *Earliest Man and Environments in the Lake Rudolf Basin.* Yves Coppens, F. Clark Howell, Glynn Ll. Isaac, and Richard E. F. Leakey (eds.), pp. 565–573. Chicago: University of Chicago Press.
Clark, Cathleen B.
  1977 A Preliminary Report on Weaning among Chimpanzees of the Gombe National Park, Tanzania. In *Primate Bio-Social Development,* Suzanne Chevalier-Skolnikoff and Frank E. Poirier (eds.), p. 235–260. New York: Garland.
Curtin, Richard, and Phyllis Dolhinow
  1978 Primate Social Behavior in a Changing World. *American Scientist* 66:468–475.
Garn, Stanley M.; Rose S. Kerewsky; and Daris S. Swindler
  1966 Canine "Field" in Sexual Dimorphism of Tooth Size. *Nature* 212:1501–1502.
Goodall, Jane van Lawick
  1965 Chimpanzees of the Gombe Stream Reserve. In *Primate Behavior: Field Studies of Monkeys and Apes,* I. DeVore (ed.), pp. 425–473. New York: Holt, Rinehart and Winston.
  1967a Mother-Offspring Relationships in Free-Ranging Chimpanzees. In *Primate Ethology,* Desmond Morris (ed.), pp. 287–347. Chicago: Aldine.
  1968a The Behaviour of Free-living Chimpanzees in the Gombe Stream Reserve. *Animal Behaviour Monographs* 1:161–311.
  1968b A Preliminary Report on Expressive Movements and Communication in the Gombe Stream Chimpanzees. In *Primates: Studies in Adaptation and Variability,* Phyllis C. Jay (ed.), pp. 313–374. New York: Holt, Rinehart and Winston.
  1969 Some Aspects of Reproductive Behaviour in a Group of Wild Chimpanzees, *Pan troglodytes schweinfurthi,* at the Gombe Stream Chimpanzee Reserve, Tanzania, East Africa. *Journal of Reproduction and Fertility, Supplement* 6:353–355.
  1970 Tool-Using in Primates and Other Vertebrates. In *Advances in the Study of Behavior,* vol. 3, D. S. Lehrman, R. A. Hinde, and E. Shaw (eds.), pp. 195–249. New York: Academic Press.
  1971 *In the Shadow of Man.* Boston: Houghton Mifflin.
  1973a The Behavior of Chimpanzees in Their Natural Habitat. *American Journal of Psychiatry* 130:1–12.
  1973b Cultural Elements in a Chimpanzee Community. In *Precultural Primate Behavior,* Symposia of the Fourth International Congress of Primatology, vol. 1, E. W. Menzel, Jr. (ed.), pp. 144–185. Basel: Karger.
  1975a The Behavior of the Chimpanzee. In *Hominisation and Behavior,* G. Kurth and I. Eibl-Eibesfeldt (eds.), pp. 74–136. Stuttgart: Gustav Fischer.
  1975b The Chimpanzee. In *The Quest for Man,* Vanne Goodall (ed.), pp. 131–170. New York: Praeger.

1977   Infant Killing and Cannibalism in Free-Living Chimpanzees. *Folia Primatologica* 28:259–282.

1979   Life and Death at Gombe. *National Geographic* 155:593–621.

Goodall, J.; A. Bandora; E. Bergmann; C. Busse; H. Matama; E. Mpongo; A. Pierce; and D. Riss

1979   Intercommunity Interactions in the Chimpanzee Population of the Gombe National Park. In *The Great Apes,* Perspectives on Human Evolution, vol. 5, D. A. Hamburg and E. R. McCown (eds.), pp. 13–53. Menlo Park: Benjamin/Cummings.

Hafez, E. S. E.

1971   Reproductive Cycles. In *Comparative Reproduction of Nonhuman Primates,* E. S. E. Hafez (ed.), pp. 160–204. Springfield, Ill.: Charles C Thomas.

Hladik, C. M.

1973   Alimentation et activité d'un groupe de chimpanzés réintroduits en Forêt gabonais. *Terre et la vie* 27:343–413.

Howell, F. Clark

1976   An Overview of the Pliocene and Earlier Pleistocene of the Lower Omo Basin, Southern Ethiopia. In *Human Origins: Louis Leakey and the East African Evidence,* Glynn Ll. Isaac and Elizabeth R. McCown (eds.), pp. 227–268. Menlo Park: Benjamin.

Isaac, Glynn Ll.

1978   The Archaeological Evidence for the Activities of Early African Hominids. In *Early Hominids of Africa,* Clifford J. Jolly (ed.), pp. 219–254. London: Duckworth.

Itani, Junichiro

1979   Distribution and Adaptation of Chimpanzees in an Arid Area. In *The Great Apes,* Perspectives on Human Evolution, vol. 5, D. A. Hamburg and E. R. McCown (eds.), pp. 55–71. Menlo Park: Benjamin/Cummings.

Itani, Junichiro, and Akira Suzuki

1967   The Social Unit of Chimpanzees. *Primates* 8:355–381.

Izawa, Kosei

1970   Unit Groups of Chimpanzees and Their Nomadism in the Savanna Woodland. *Primates* 11:1–46.

Johanson, Donald C.; Yves Coppens; and Maurice Taieb

1976   Pliocene Hominid Remains from Hadar, Central Afar, Ethiopia. Ms. from Les plus anciens hominidés, UISPP, 9th Congress.

Johanson, Donald C., and Maurice Taieb

1976   Plio-Pleistocene Hominid Discoveries in Hadar, Ethiopia. *Nature* 260:293–297.

Johanson, Donald, and Maitland Edey

1981   *Lucy: The Beginnings of Humankind.* New York: Simon and Schuster.

Jones, Clyde, and Jorge Sabater Pí

1971   *Comparative Ecology of* Gorilla gorilla (*Savage and Wyman*) *and* Pan troglodytes (*Blumenbech*) *in Rio Muni, West Africa.* Bibliotheca Primatologica, no. 13. Basel: Karger.

Kano, Takayoshi

1972   Distribution and Adaptation of the Chimpanzee on the Eastern Shore of Lake Tanganyika. *Kyoto University African Studies* 7:37–129.

Kawanaka, Kenji, and Toshisada Nishida
   1975   Recent Advances in the Study of Inter-Unit-Group Relationships and
          Social Structure of Wild Chimpanzees of the Mahali Mountains. *Pro-
          ceedings from the Symposia of the 5th Congress of the International
          Primatological Society*, S. Kondo, M. Kawai, A. Ehara, and S. Kaw-
          amura (eds.), pp. 173–186. Tokyo: Japan Science Press.

Kortlandt, Adriaan
   1967   Experimentation with Chimpanzees in the Wild. In *Neue Ergebnisse
          der Primatologie* [Progress in primatology], First Congress of the Inter-
          national Primatological Society, Frankfurt, D. Starck, R. Schneider,
          and H. J. Kuhn (eds.), pp. 208–224. Stuttgart: Gustav Fischer.

Lee, Richard Borshay
   1979   *The !Kung San: Men, Women, and Work in a Foraging Society.* Cam-
          bridge: Cambridge University Press.

Lemmon, William Burton, and Melvin Lloyd Allen
   1978   Continual Sexual Receptivity in the Female Chimpanzee (*Pan troglo-
          dytes*). *Folia Primatologica* 30:80–88.

Lyght, Charles E.; Chester S. Keefer; Francis D. W. Lukens; Dickinson W. Rich-
          ards; W. Henry Sebrell; and John M. Trapnell, eds.
   1966   *The Merck Manual of Diagnosis and Therapy.* 11th ed. Rahway, N.J.
          and West Point, Pa.: Merck Sharp and Dohme Research Laboratories.

Mason, W. A.
   1970   Chimpanzee Social Behavior. In *The Chimpanzee*, vol. 2, *Physiology,
          Behavior, Serology, and Diseases of Chimpanzees*, G. H. Bourne
          (ed.), pp. 265–288. Baltimore: University Park Press.

McGinnis, Patrick R.
   1979   Sexual Behavior in Free-Living Chimpanzees: Consort Relationships.
          In *The Great Apes*, Perspectives on Human Evolution, vol. 5,
          D. Hamburg and E. R. McCown (eds.), pp. 429–439. Menlo Park:
          Benjamin/Cummings.

McGrew, William C.
   1975   Patterns of Plant Food Sharing by Wild Chimpanzees. In *Contempo-
          rary Primatology*, Proceedings of the Fifth International Congress of
          Primatology, S. Kondo, M. Kawai, and A. Ehara (eds.), pp. 304–309.
          Basel: Karger.
   1977   Socialization and Object Manipulation of Wild Chimpanzees. In *Pri-
          mate Bio-Social Development: Biological, Social, and Ecological De-
          terminants*, Suzanne Chevalier-Skolnikoff and Frank E. Poirier (eds.),
          pp. 261–288. New York: Garland.

Menzel, Emil W., Jr.
   1973a Leadership and Communication in Young Chimpanzees. In *Precul-
          tural Primate Behavior*, Symposia of the Fourth International Congress
          of Primatology, E. W. Menzel, Jr. (ed.), pp. 192–225. Basel: Karger.
   1974   A Group of Young Chimpanzees in a One-Acre Field. In *Behavior of
          Nonhuman Primates: Modern Research Trends*, vol. 5, A. M. Schrier
          and F. Stollnitz (eds.), pp. 83–153. New York: Academic Press.
   1975   Natural Language of Young Chimpanzees. *New Scientist* 65:127–
          130.

Merrick, H. V., and J. P. S. Merrick
   1976   Archeological Occurrences of Earlier Pleistocene Age, from the Shun-
          gura Formation. In *Earliest Man and Environments in the Lake Rudolf
          Basin,* Yves Coppens, F. Clark Howell, Glynn Ll. Isaac, and Richard E.
          F. Leakey (eds.), pp. 574–585. Chicago: University of Chicago Press.
Napier, J. R., and P. H. Napier
   1967   *A Handbook of Living Primates.* New York: Academic Press, 1970 ed.
Nishida, Toshisada
   1968   The Social Group of Wild Chimpanzees in the Mahali Mountains.
          Primates 9:167–224.
   1970   Social Behavior and Relationship among Wild Chimpanzees of the
          Mahali Mountains. *Primates* 11:47–87.
   1979   The Social Structure of Chimpanzees of the Mahale Mountains. In
          The Great Apes, Perspectives on Human Evolution, vol. 5, D. A.
          Hamburg and E. R. McCown (eds.), pp. 73–121. Menlo Park: Benja-
          min/Cummings.
Nishida, Toshisada, and Kenji Kawanaka
   1972   Inter-Unit-Group Relationships among Wild Chimpanzees of the Ma-
          hali Mountains. *Kyoto University African Studies* 7:131–169.
Pusey, Anne
   1979   Intercommunity Transfer of Chimpanzees in Gombe National Park. In
          The Great Apes, Perspectives on Human Evolution, vol. 5, D. A.
          Hamburg and E. R. McCown (eds.), pp. 465–479. Menlo Park: Ben-
          jamin/Cummings.
Reynolds, Vernon, and Frances Reynolds
   1965   Chimpanzees of the Budongo Forest. In *Primate Behavior: Field
          Studies of Monkeys and Apes,* Irven DeVore (ed.), pp. 425–473.
          New York: Holt, Rinehart and Winston.
Reynolds, V., and G. Luscombe
   1969   Chimpanzee Rank Order and the Function of Displays. In *Behavior,*
          Proceedings of the 2nd International Congress of Primatology, vol. 1,
          C. R. Carpenter (ed.), pp. 81–86. Basel: Karger.
Riss, David C., and Curt D. Busse
   1977   Fifty-Day Observation of a Free-ranging Adult Male Chimpanzee. *Fo-
          lia Primatologica* 28:283–297.
Riss, David, and Jane Goodall
   1976   Sleeping Behavior and Associations in a Group of Captive Chimpan-
          zees. *Folia Primatologica* 25:1–11.
Schultz, Adolph H.
   1931   Man as a Primate. *Scientific Monthly* 33:385–412.
   1960   Einige Beobachtungen und Malze am Skelett von *Oreopithecus;* im
          Vergleich mit Anderen catarrhinen Primaten. *Z. Morph. Anthrop.*
          50:136–149.
Silk, Joan B.
   1978   Patterns of Food Sharing among Mother and Infant Chimpanzees at
          Gombe National Park, Tanzania. *Folia Primatologica* 29:129–141.
Sugiyama, Yukimaru
   1968   Social Organization of Chimpanzees in the Budongo Forest, Uganda.
          Primates 9:225–258.

1969 Social Behavior of Chimpanzees in the Budongo Forest, Uganda. *Primates 10*:197–225.

1972 Social Characteristics and Socialization of Wild Chimpanzees. In *Primate Socialization*, Frank E. Poirier (ed.), pp. 145–258. New York: Random House.

1973a The Social Structure of Wild Chimpanzees. In *Comparative Ecology and Behavior of Primates*, R. P. Michael and J. H. Crook (eds.), pp. 376–410. New York: Academic Press.

1973b Social Organization of Wild Chimpanzees. In *Behavioral Regulators of Behavior in Primates*, C. R. Carpenter (ed.), pp. 68–80. Lewisburg, Pa.: Bucknell University Press.

Sugiyama, Yukimaru, and Jeremy Koman
1979 Social Structure and Dynamics of Wild Chimpanzees of Boussou, Guinea. *Primates 20*:323–339.

Suzuki, Akira
1969 An Ecological Study of Chimpanzees in a Savanna Woodland. *Primates 10*:103–148.

Teleki, Geza
1973a The Omnivorous Chimpanzee. *Scientific American 228*:32–42.

1973b *The Predatory Behavior of Wild Chimpanzees.* Lewisburg, Pa.: Bucknell University Press.

1973c Group Response to the Accidental Death of a Chimpanzee in Gombe National Park, Tanzania. *Folia Primatologica 20*:81–94.

In press Environmental Parameters of Chimpanzee Behavior and Society in Gombe National Park, Tanzania: A Field Study of Adaptive Strategies.

Teleki, Geza; E. E. Hunt, Jr.; and J. H. Pfifferling
1976 Demographic Observations (1963–1973) on the Chimpanzees of Gombe National Park, Tanzania. *Journal of Human Evolution 5*:559–598.

Trivers, Robert L.
1972 Parental Investment and Sexual Selection. In *Sexual Selection and the Descent of Man, 1871–1971*, B. Campbell (ed.), pp. 136–179. Chicago: Aldine.

Tutin, Caroline E. G.
1975 Exceptions to Promiscuity in a Feral Chimpanzee Community. In *Contemporary Primatology*, Proceedings of the Fifth International Congress of Primatology, S. Kondo, M. Kawai and A. Ehara (eds.), pp. 445–449. Basel: Karger.

Wrangham, Richard W.
1974 Artificial Feeding of Chimpanzees and Baboons in Their Natural Habitat. *Animal Behaviour 22*:83–93.

CHAPTER 6. CHIMPANZEES AS A MODEL OF THE ANCESTRAL POPULATION: MENTAL CAPACITIES, COMMUNICATION, AND SOCIATION – BASES FOR THE EVOLUTION OF THE CAPACITY FOR CULTURE

Birdwhistell, Ray L.
1970 *Kinesics and Context: Essays on Body Motion Communication.* Philadelphia: University of Pennsylvania Press.

Boas, Franz
1911 Introduction to *Handbook of American Indian Languages,* F. Boas
(ed.), pp. 59–73. Washington, D.C.: Smithsonian Institution. (Reprinted 1964 as "Linguistics and Ethnology" and as "On Grammatical Categories" in *Language in Culture and Society: A Reader in Linguistics and Anthropology,* Dell Hymes, ed., pp. 15–26, 121–123.
New York: Harper and Row.)
Chapple, Eliot D.
1970 *Culture and Biological Man: Explorations in Behavioral Anthropology.*
New York: Holt, Rinehart and Winston.
Chevalier-Skolnikoff, Suzanne
1973 Facial Expression of Emotion in Nonhuman Primates. In *Darwin and
Facial Expression: A Century of Research in Review,* Paul Ekman
(ed.), pp. 11–89. New York: Academic Press.
Cowey, Alan, and Lawrence Weiskrantz
1975 Demonstration of Cross-Modal Matching in Rhesus Monkeys, *Macaca
mulatta. Neuropsychologia 13:*117–120.
Darwin, Charles
1871 *The Descent of Man and Selection in Relation to Sex.* London: John
Murray.
1872 *The Expression of the Emotions in Man and Animals.* London: John
Murray.
Davenport, Richard K.
1976 Cross-Modal Perception in Apes. In *Origins and Evolution of
Language and Speech.* Stevan R. Harnad, Horst D. Steklis, and
Jane Lancaster (eds.), pp. 143–149, Annals of the New York
Academy of Sciences, vol. 280. New York: New York Academy of
Sciences.
Davenport, Richard K., and Charles M. Rogers
1970 Intermodal Equivalence of Stimuli in Apes. *Science 168:*279–280.
Davenport, Richard K.; Charles M. Rogers; and I. Steele Russell
1973 Cross Modal Perception in Apes. *Neuropsychologia 11:*21–28.
1975 Cross-Modal Perception in Apes: Altered Visual Cues and Delay.
*Neuropsychologia 13:*229–235.
Fouts, Roger S.
1975 Communication with Chimpanzees. In *Hominisation and Behavior,*
G. Kurth and I. Eibl-Eibesfeldt (eds.), pp. 137–158. Stuttgart: Gustav
Fischer.
1977 Ameslan in *Pan.* In *Progress in Ape Research,* Geoffrey H. Bourne
(ed.), pp. 117–123. New York: Academic Press.
Fouts, Roger S., and Joseph B. Couch
1976 Cultural Evolution of Learned Language in Chimpanzees. In *Commu-
nicative Behavior and Evolution,* Martin E. Hahn and Edward C. Sim-
mel (eds.), pp. 141–161. New York: Academic Press.
Fouts, Roger S., and Randall L. Rigby
1977 Man–Chimpanzee Communication. In *How Animals Communicate,*
Thomas A. Sebeok (ed.), pp. 1034–1054. Bloomington: Indian University Press.

Galaburda, Albert M.; Marjorie LeMay; Thomas L. Kemper; and Norman Gesch-
      wind
   1978   Right—Left Asymmetries in the Brain. *Science 199*:852—856.
Gallup, Gordon G., Jr.
   1970   Chimpanzees: Self-Recognition. *Science 167*:86—87.
Gardner, Beatrice T., and R. Allen Gardner
   1971   Two-Way Communication with an Infant Chimpanzee. In *Behavior of
      Nonhuman Primates: Modern Research Trends,* vol. 4, A. M. Schrier
      and F. Stollnitz (eds.), pp. 117—184. New York: Academic Press.
   1975b Evidence for Sentence Constituents in the Early Utterances of Child
      and Chimpanzee. *Journal of Experimental Psychology: General
      104*:244—267.
Gardner, R. Allen, and Beatrice T. Gardner
   1969   Teaching Sign Language to a Chimpanzee. *Science 165*:664—672.
   1972   Communication with a Young Chimpanzee: Washoe's Vocabulary. In
      Modeles animaux de comportement humain, Colloques Internatio-
      naux du Centre National de la Recherche Scientifique, no. 198,
      Rémy Chauvin (ed.), pp. 241—264. Paris: Editions du Centre National
      de la Recherche Scientifique.
   1975a Early Signs of Language in Child and Chimpanzee. *Science 187*:752—
      753.
Geertz, Clifford
   1962   The Growth of Culture and the Evolution of Mind. In *Theories of the
      Mind,* J. Scher (ed.), pp. 713—740. New York: Macmillan. (Reprinted
      1973, in *The Interpretation of Cultures: Selected Essays by Clifford
      Geertz,* pp. 55—83. New York: Basic Books.)
   1966   The Impact of the Concept of Culture on the Concept of Man. In
      New Views of the Nature of Man, J. Platt (ed.), pp. 93—118. Chicago:
      University of Chicago Press. (Reprinted 1973, in *The Interpretation of
      Cultures: Selected Essays by Clifford Geertz,* pp. 33—54. New York:
      Basic Books.)
Geschwind, Norman
   1965   Disconnexion Syndromes in Animals and Man. *Brain 88*:237—294.
   1970a Intermodal Equivalence of Stimuli in Apes. *Science 168*:1249.
   1970b The Organization of Language and the Brain. *Science 170*:940—944.
Geschwind, Norman, and Walter Levitsky
   1968   Human Brain: Left—Right Asymmetries in Temporal Speech Region.
      Science 161:186—187.
Gill, Timothy V.
   1977a Conversations with Lana. In *Langauge Learning by a Chimpanzee:
      The Lana Project,* Duane M. Rumbaugh (ed.), pp. 225—246. New
      York: Academic Press.
   1977b Talking to Lana: The Question of Conversation. In *Progress in Ape
      Research,* Geoffrey H. Bourne (ed.), pp. 125—132. New York: Aca-
      demic Press.
Goffman, Erving
   1963   *Behavior in Public Places: Notes on the Social Organization of
      Gatherings.* New York: Free Press.

1969   Expression Games: An Analysis of Doubts at Play. In *Strategic Interaction*, Erving Goffman and Dell Hymes (eds.), pp. 3–81. Philadelphia: University of Pennsylvania Press.

Goodall, Jane van Lawick
1968b   A Preliminary Report on Expressive Movements and Communication in the Gombe Stream Chimpanzees. In *Primates: Studies in Adaptation and Variability*, Phyllis C. Jay (ed.), pp. 313–374. New York: Holt, Rinehart and Winston.
1970   Tool-Using in Primates and Other Vertebrates. In *Advances in the Study of Behavior*, vol. 3, Daniel S. Lehrman, Robert A. Hinde, and Evelyn Shaw (eds.), pp. 195–249. New York: Academic Press.
1971   *In the Shadow of Man*. Boston: Houghton Mifflin.
1976   Continuities between Chimpanzees and Human Behavior. In *Human Origins: Louis Leakey and the East African Evidence*, Glynn Ll. Isaac and Elizabeth R. McCown (eds.), pp. 81–95. Menlo Park: Benjamin.

Goodall, Jane, and David A. Hamburg
1975   Chimpanzee Behavior as a Model for the Behavior of Early Man. In *New Psychiatric Frontiers*, D. A. Hamburg and H. K. H. Brodie (eds.), pp. 14–43. New York: Basic Books.

Goodenough, Ward H.
1971   *Culture, Language, and Society*. Addison-Wesley Module in Anthropology, no. 7, Reading, Mass: Addison-Wesley.

Gumperz, John J., and Dell Hymes, eds.
1972   *Directions in Sociolinguistics: The Ethnography of Communication*. New York: Holt, Rinehart and Winston.

Hall, Edward T.
1959   *The Silent Language*. New York: Doubleday.

Hayes, Cathy
1951   *The Ape in Our House*. New York: Harper and Brothers.

Hayes, Keith J., and Catherine H. Nissen
1971   Higher Mental Functions of a Home-Raised Chimpanzee. In *Behavior of Non-Human Primates: Modern Research Trends*, vol. 4, A. M. Schrier and F. Stollnitz (eds.), pp. 59–115. New York: Academic Press.

Hewes, Gordon W.
1973a   Primate Communication and the Gestural Origin of Language. *Current Anthropology 14*:5–12.
1973b   Pongid Capacity for Language Acquisition. In *Precultural Primate Behavior*, Symposia of the Fourth International Congress of Primatology, vol. 1, E. W. Menzel, Jr. (ed.), pp. 124–143. Basel: Karger.

Itani, Junichiro
1979   Distribution and Adaptation of Chimpanzees in an Arid Area. In *The Great Apes*, Perspectives on Human Evolution, vol. 5, D. A. Hamburg and E. R. McCown (eds.), pp. 55–71. Menlo Park: Benjamin/Cummings.

Jarvis, M. J., and G. Ettlinger
1978   Cross-Modal Performance in Monkeys and Apes: Is There a Substantial Difference? In *Recent Advances in Primatology*, vol. 1, D. J.

Chivers and J. Herbert (eds.), pp. 953–956. New York: Academic Press.

Kano, Takayoshi
    1972   Distribution and Adaptation of the Chimpanzee on the Eastern Shore of Lake Tanganyika. *Kyoto University African Studies* 7:37–129.

Kochman, Thomas, ed.
    1972   *Rappin' and Stylin' Out: Communication in Urban Black America.* Urbana: University of Illinois Press.

Lancaster, Jane B.
    1968b Primate Communication Systems and the Emergence of Human Language. In *Primates: Studies in Adaptation and Variability,* Phyllis C. Jay (ed.), pp. 439–457. New York: Holt, Rinehart and Winston.

LeMay, Marjorie
    1976   Morphological Cerebral Asymmetries of Modern Man, Fossil Man, and Nonhuman Primate. In *Origins and Evolution of Language and Speech,* Stevan R. Harnad, Horst D. Steklis, and Jane Lancaster (eds.), pp. 349–366, Annals of the New York Academy of Sciences, vol. 280. New York: New York Academy of Sciences.

LeMay, Marjorie, and Norman Geschwind
    1975   Hemispheric Differences in the Brains of Great Apes. *Brain, Behavior, and Evolution* 11:48–52.

Marler, Peter
    1977   Primate Vocalization: Affective or Symbolic? In *Progress in Ape Research,* G. H. Bourne (ed.), pp. 85–96. New York: Academic Press.

Marler, Peter, and Richard Tenaza
    1977   Signaling Behavior of Apes with Special Reference to Vocalization. In *How Animals Communicate,* Thomas A. Sebeok (ed.), pp. 965–1033. Bloomington: Indiana University Press.

McGrew, William C.
    1979   Evolutionary Implications of Sex Differences in Chimpanzee Predation and Tool Use. In *The Great Apes,* Perspectives on Human Evolution, vol. 5, D. A. Hamburg and E. R. McCown (eds.), pp. 441–463. Menlo Park: Benjamin/Cummings.

Menzel, Emil W., Jr.
    1969   Chimpanzee Utilization of Space and Responsiveness to Objects: Age Differences and Comparisons with Macaques. In *Behavior,* Proceedings of the Second International Congress of Primatology, vol. 1, C. R. Carpenter (ed.), pp. 72–80. Basel: Karger.
    1971a Communication about the Environment in a Group of Young Chimpanzees. *Folia Primatologica* 15:220–232.
    1973c Chimpanzee Spatial Memory Organization. *Science* 182:943–945.
    1974   A Group of Young Chimpanzees in a One-Acre Field. In *Behavior of Nonhuman Primates: Modern Research Trends,* vol. 5, A. M. Schrier and F. Stollnitz (eds.), pp. 83–153. New York: Academic Press.
    1975   Natural Language of Young Chimpanzees. *New Scientist* 65:127–130.
    1978   Implications of Chimpanzee Language-Training Experiments for Primate Field Research – and Vice Versa. In *Recent Advances in Prima-*

tology vol. 1, D. J. Chivers and J. Herbert (eds.), pp. 884–895. New York: Academic Press.

Menzel, Emil W., Jr.; R. K. Davenport; and C. M. Rogers
1972 Protocultural Aspects of Chimpanzees' Responsiveness to Novel Objects. *Folia Primatologica* 17:161–170.

Menzel, Emil W., Jr., and Stewart Halperin
1975 Purposive Behavior as a Basis for Objective Communication between Chimpanzees. *Science* 189:652–654.

Menzel, Emil W., Jr.; David Premack; and Guy Woodruff
1978 Map Reading by Chimpanzees. *Folia Primatologica* 29:241–249.

Nishida, Toshisada
1970 Social Behavior and Relationship among Wild Chimpanzees of the Mahali Mountains. *Primates* 11: 47–87.
1973 The Ant Gathering Behavior by the Use of Tools among Wild Chimpanzees of the Mahali Mountains. *Journal of Human Evolution* 2:357–370.

Passingham, R. E.
1973 Anatomical Differences between the Neocortex of Man and Other Primates. *Brain, Behavior, and Evolution* 7:337–359

Patterson, Francine G.
1978a The Gestures of a Gorilla: Sign Language Acquisition in Another Pongid Species. *Brain and Language* 5:72–97.
1978b Conversations with a Gorilla. *National Geographic* 154:438–465.

Premack, Ann James, and David Premack
1972 Teaching Language to an Ape. *Scientific American* 227:92–99.

Premack, David
1970 A Functional Analysis of Language. *Journal of the Experimental Analysis of Behavior* 14:107–125.
1971a Language in Chimpanzee? *Science* 172:808–822.
1971b On the Assessment of Language Competence in the Chimpanzee. In *Behavior of Nonhuman Primates: Modern Research Trends*, A. M. Schrier and F. Stollnitz (eds.), pp. 185–228. New York: Academic Press.
1976a *Intelligence in Ape and Man*. Hillsdale, N. J.: Lawrence Erlbaum.
1976b Language and Intelligence in Ape and Man. *American Scientist* 64:674–683.
1978 Comparison of Language-Related Factors in Ape and Man. In *Recent Advances in Primatatology*, vol. 1, D. J. Chivers and J. Herbert (eds.), pp. 867–881. New York: Academic Press.

Pride, J. B., and Janet Holmes, eds.
1972 *Sociolinguistics. Selected Readings*. Baltimore: Penguin Books.

Reynolds, Vernon, and Frances Reynolds.
1965 Chimpanzees of the Budongo Forest. In *Primate Behavior: Field Studies of Monkeys and Apes*, Irven DeVore (ed.), pp. 425–473. New York: Holt, Rinehart and Winston.

Rumbaugh, Duane M.
1970 Learning Skills of Anthropoids. In *Primate Behavior: Developments in Field and Laboratory Research*, vol. 1, L. A. Rosenblum (ed.), pp. 1–70. New York: Academic Press.

1977b The Emergence and State of Ape Language Research. In *Progress in Ape Research,* Geoffrey H. Bourne (ed.), pp. 75–83. New York: Academic Press.

1977c Language Behavior of Apes. In *Behavioral Primatology: Advances in Research and Theory,* vol. 1, Allan M. Schrier (ed.), pp. 105–138. Hillsdale, N.J.: Lawrence Erlbaum.

1978 Ape Language Projects: A Perspective. In *Recent Advances in Primatology,* vol. 1, D. J. Chivers and J. Herbert (eds.), pp. 855–859. New York: Academic Press.

Rumbaugh, Duane M., ed.

1977a *Language Learning by a Chimpanzee: The Lana Project.* New York: Academic Press.

Rumbaugh, Duane M., and Timothy V. Gill

1977 Lana's Acquisition of Language Skills. In *Language Learning by a Chimpanzee: The Lana Project.* Duane M. Rumbaugh (ed.), pp. 165–192. New York: Academic Press.

Rumbaugh, Duane. M.; E. C. von Glasersfeld; T. V. Gill; H. Warner; P. Pisani; J. V. Brown; and C. L. Bell

1973 A Computer-Controlled Language Training System for Investigating the Language Skills of Young Apes. *Behavioral Research Methods and Instrumentation* 5:385–392.

Sapir, Edward

1931 Conceptual Categories in Primitive Languages. *Science* 74:578. (Reprinted 1964, in *Language in Culture and Society: A Reader in Linguistics and Anthropology,* Dell Hymes (ed.), p. 128. New York: Harper and Row.)

Savage, E. Sue, and Roger Bakeman

1978 Sexual Dimorphism and Behavior in *Pan paniscus.* In *Recent Advances in Primatology,* vol. 1, D. J. Chivers and J. Herbert (eds.), pp. 613–616. New York: Academic Press.

Savage-Rumbaugh, E. Sue, and Duane M. Rumbaugh

1978 Symbolization, Language, and Chimpanzees: A Theoretical Reevaluation Based on Initial Language Acquisition Processes in Four Young *Pan troglodytes. Brain and Language* 6:265–300.

Savage-Rumbaugh, E. Sue; Beverly J. Wilkerson; and Roger Bakeman

1977 Spontaneous Gestural Communication among Conspecifics in the Pygmy Chimpanzee *(Pan paniscus).* In *Progress in Ape Research,* G. H. Bourne (ed.), pp. 97–116. New York: Academic Press.

Tanner, Nancy M., and Adrienne L. Zihlman

1976b The Evolution of Human Communication: What Can Primates Tell Us? In *Origins and Evolution of Language and Speech,* Stevan R. Harnad, Horst D. Steklis, and Jane Lancaster (eds.), pp. 467–480, Annals of the New York Academy of Sciences, vol. 280. New York: New York Academy of Sciences.

Warren, J. M., and A. J. Noneman

1976 The Search for Cerebral Dominance in Monkeys. In *Origins and Evolution of Language and Speech,* Stevan R. Harnad, Horst D. Steklis, and Jane Lancaster (eds.), pp. 732–744, Annals of the New York

    Academy of Sciences, vol. 280. New York: New York Academy of
    Sciences.
Washburn, Sherwood L.
    1973   The Promise of Primatology. *American Journal of Physical Anthropol-
            ogy 38*:177–182.
Washburn, Sherwood L., and Shirley C. Strum
    1972   Concluding Comments. In *Perspectives on Human Evolution,* vol. 2,
            S. L. Washburn and P. Dolhinow (eds.), pp. 469–491. New York:
            Holt, Rinehart and Winston.
Whorf, Benjamin Lee
    1956   A Linguistic Consideration of Thinking in Primitive Communities. In
            *Language, Thought, and Reality: Selected Writings of Benjamin Lee
            Whorf,* John B. Carroll (ed.), pp. 65–86. New York: Wiley. (Re-
            printed 1964, in *Language in Culture and Society: A Reader in Lin-
            guistics and Anthropology,* Dell Hymes (ed.), pp. 129–141. New
            York: Harper and Row.)
Yeni-Komshian, Grace H., and Dennis A. Benson
    1976   Anatomical Study of Cerebral Asymmetry in the Temporal Lobe of
            Humans, Chimpanzees, and Rhesus Monkeys. *Science 192*:387–389.
Zihlman, Adrienne L.
    1967   Human Locomotion: A Reappraisal of the Functional and Anatomical
            Evidence. Dissertation, University of California, Berkeley.

CHAPTER 7. THE TRANSITION TO *AUSTRALOPITHECUS:* NATURAL AND
SEXUAL SELECTION IN HUMAN ORIGINS

Albrecht, Helmut, and Sinclair C. Dunnett
    1971   *Chimpanzees in Western Africa.* Studies in Ethology. Munich: Piper.
Andrews, Peter, and Judith A. H. Van Couvering
    1975   Palaeoenvironments in the East African Miocene. In *Approaches to
            Primate Paleobiology,* F. Szalay (ed.), pp. 62–103. Basel: Karger.
Baker, B. H.; L. A. J. Williams; J. A. Miller; and F. J. Fitch
    1971   Sequence and Geochronology of the Kenya Rift Volcanics. *Tectono-
            physics 11*:191–215.
Baker, B. H., and J. Wohlenberg
    1971   Structure and Evolution of the Kenya Rift Valley. *Nature 229*:538–542.
Boaz, Noel T.
    1979   Early Hominid Population Densities: New Estimates. *Science
            206*:592–595.
Bond, Geoffrey
    1963   Pleistocene Environment in Southern Africa. In *African Ecology and
            Human Evolution,* F. C. Howell and F. Bourlière (eds.), pp. 308–
            334. Chicago: Aldine.
Bonnefille, Raymonde
    1976a   Palynological Evidence for an Important Change in the Vegetation of
            the Omo Basin between 2.5 and 2 Million Years Ago. In *Earliest Man
            and Environments in the Lake Rudolf Basin,* Yves Coppens, F. Clark
            Howell, Glynn Ll. Isaac, and Richard E. F. Leakey (eds.), pp. 421–
            431. Chicago: University of Chicago Press.

Bourlière, François
1963 Observations on the Ecology of Some Large African Mammals. In *African Ecology and Human Evolution*, F. C. Howell and F. Bourlière (eds.), pp. 43–54. Chicago: Aldine.
Bourlière, François, and Malcolm Hadley
1970 The Ecology of Tropical Savannas. In *Annual Review of Ecology and Systematics*, R. F. Johnston, P. W. Frank, and C. D. Michener (eds.), pp. 125–152. Palo Alto: Annual Reviews.
Butzer, Karl W.
1971 *Environment and Archaeology: An Ecological Approach to Prehistory.* Chicago: Aldine-Atherton.
1978 Geo-ecological Perspectives on Early Hominid Evolution. In *Early Hominids of Africa*, C. J. Jolly (ed.), pp. 191–217. London: Duckworth.
Campbell, Bernard
1972c Man for All Seasons. In *Sexual Selection and the Descent of Man 1871–1971*, Bernard Campbell (ed.), pp. 40–58. Chicago: Aldine.
Carpenter, C. R.
1940 A Field Study in Siam of the Behavior and Social Relations of the Gibbon, *Hylobates lar. Comparative Psychology Monographs* 16:112–141.
Chalmers, N. R., and T. E. Rowell
1971 Behaviour and Female Reproductive Cycles in a Captive Group of Mangabeys. *Folia Primatologica* 14:1–14.
Darwin, Charles
1871 *The Descent of Man and Selection in Relation to Sex.* London: John Murray. (Reprinted 1936. New York: Modern Library.)
DeVore, Irven
1963 A Comparison of the Ecology and Behavior of Monkeys and Apes. In *Classification and Human Evolution*, S. L. Washburn (ed.), pp. 301–319. Chicago: Aldine.
Dobzhansky, Theodosius
1958 Evolution at Work. *Science 127*:1091–1098.
1970 *Genetics of the Evolutionary Process.* New York: Columbia University Press.
Draper, Patricia
1976 Social and Economic Constraints on Child Life among the !Kung. In *Kalahari Hunter-Gatherers: Studies of the !Kung San and Their Neighbors*, R. B. Lee and I. DeVore (eds.), pp. 199–217. Cambridge: Harvard University Press.
Ehrman, Lee
1972 Genetics and Sexual Selection. In *Sexual Selection and the Descent of Man 1871–1971*, Bernard Campbell (ed.), pp. 105–135. Chicago: Aldine.
Ellefson, John O.
1968 Territorial Behavior in the Common White-handed Gibbon, *Hylobates lar Linn.* In *Primates: Studies in Adaptation and Variability*, P. C. Jay (ed.), pp. 180–199. New York: Holt, Rinehart and Winston.

Frisch, Rose E.
    1978   Population, Food Intake, and Fertility. *Science 199*:22–30.
Goodall, Jane van Lawick
    1965   Chimpanzees of the Gombe Stream Reserve. In *Primate Behavior: Field Studies of Monkeys and Apes,* I. DeVore (ed.), pp. 425–473. New York: Holt, Rinehart and Winston.
    1968a   The Behaviour of Free-living Chimpanzees in the Gombe Stream Reserve. *Animal Behaviour Monographs 1*:165–311.
    1970   Tool-Using in Primates and Other Vertebrates. In *Advances in the Study of Behavior,* vol. 3, D. S. Lehrman, R. A. Hinde, and E. Shaw (eds.), pp. 195–249. New York: Academic Press.
    1972   A Preliminary Report on Expressive Movements and Communication in the Gombe Stream Chimpanzees. In *Primate Patterns,* Phyllis Dolhinow (ed.), pp. 25–84. New York: Holt, Rinehart and Winston.
    1973b   Cultural Elements in a Chimpanzee Community. In *Precultural Primate Behavior,* Symposia of the Fourth International Congress of Primatology, vol. 1, E. W. Menzel, Jr. (ed.), pp. 144–184. Basel: Karger.
    1975a   The Behavior of the Chimpanzee. In *Hominisation and Behavior,* G. Kurth and I. Eibl-Eibesfeldt (eds.), pp. 74–136. Stuttgart: Gustav Fischer.
    1979   Life and Death at Gombe. *National Geographic 155(5)*:592–620.
Gwynne, M. D., and R. H. V. Bell
    1968   Selection of Vegetation Components by Grazing Ungulates in the Serengeti National Park. *Nature 220*:390–393.
Hafez, E. S. E.
    1971   Reproductive Cycles. In *Comparative Reproduction of Nonhuman Primates,* E. S. E. Hafez (ed.), pp. 160–204. Springfield, Ill.: Charles C. Thomas.
Hall, K. R. L.
    1965a   Behaviour and Ecology of the Wild Patas Monkey, *Erythrocebus patas,* in Uganda. *Journal of Zoology 148*:15–87.
    1965b   Social Organization of the Old World Monkeys and Apes. *Symposia of the Zoological Society of London 14*:265–289.
Hall, K. R. L., and Irven DeVore
    1965   Baboon Social Behavior. In *Primate Behavior: Field Studies of Monkeys and Apes,* I. DeVore (ed.), pp. 53–110. New York: Holt, Rinehart and Winston.
Hamilton, William D.
    1963   The Evolution of Altruistic Behavior. *American Naturalist 97*:354–356.
    1964   The Genetical Evolution of Social Behavior. 1 and 2. *Journal of Theoretical Biology 7*:1–52.
    1971   Selection of Selfish and Altruistic Behavior in Some Extreme Models. In *Man and Beast,* J. F. Eisenberg and W. S. Dillon (eds.), pp. 59–91. Washington, D. C.: Smithsonian Institution Press.
Holloway, Ralph L.
    1976a   Paleoneurological Evidence for Language Origins. In *Origins and Evolution of Language and Speech,* Stevan R. Harnad, Horst D. Steklis, and

Jane Lancaster (eds.), pp. 330–348, Annals of the New York Academy of Sciences, vol. 280. New York: New York Academy of Sciences.

Itani, Junichiro

1965 On the Acquisition and Propagation of a New Food Habit in a Troop of Japanese Monkeys at Takasakiyama. In *Japanese Monkeys: A Collection of Translations,* S. Altmann (ed.), pp. 52–65. Published by the editor.

1979 Distribution and Adaptation of Chimpanzees in an Arid Area. In *The Great Apes, Perspectives on Human Evolution,* vol. 5, D. A. Hamburg and E. R. McCown (eds.), pp. 55–71. Menlo Park: Benjamin/Cummings.

Jochim, Michael A.

1976 *Hunter-Gatherer Subsistence and Settlement: A Predictive Model.* New York: Academic Press.

King, B. C., and G. R. Chapman

1972 Volcanism of the Kenya Rift Valley. *Philosophical Transactions of the Royal Society of London,* Ser. A, 271:185–208.

Köhler, Wolfgang

1927 *The Mentality of Apes.* 2d ed. New York: Harcourt, Brace.

Kummer, Hans

1968 *Social Organization of Hamadryas Baboons: A Field Study.* Basel: Karger.

Kummer, Hans; W. Goetz; and W. Angst

1970 Cross-Species Modification of Social Behavior in Baboons. In *Old World Monkeys: Evolution, Systematics, and Behavior,* J. R. Napier and P. H. Napier (eds.), pp. 351–363. New York: Academic Press.

Lee, Richard Borshay

1965 Subsistence Ecology of !Kung Bushmen. Dissertation, University of California, Berkeley.

1968 What Hunters Do for a Living, or, How to Make Out on Scarce Resources. In *Man the Hunter,* R. B. Lee and I. DeVore (eds.), pp. 30–48. Chicago: Aldine.

1969 !Kung Bushmen Subsistence: An Input-Output Analysis. In *Environment and Cultural Behavior: Ecological Studies in Cultural Anthropology,* A. P. Vayda (ed.), pp. 47–79. New York: National History Press.

1972 The !Kung Bushmen of Botswana. In *Hunters and Gatherers Today,* M. G. Bicchieri, (ed.), pp. 326–368. New York: Holt, Rinehart and Winston.

1976 !Kung Spatial Organization: An Ecological and Historical Perspective. In *Kalahari Hunter-Gatherers: Studies of the !Kung San and Their Neighbors,* Richard B. Lee and Irven DeVore (eds.), pp. 74–97. Cambridge: Harvard University Press.

1979 *The !Kung San: Men, Women, and Work in a Foraging Society.* Cambridge: Cambridge University Press.

Lemmon, William Burton, and Melvin Lloyd Allen

1978 Continual Sexual Receptivity in the Female Chimpanzee *(Pan troglodytes). Folia Primatologica* 30:80–88.

Leutenegger, Walter
    1978   Scaling of Sexual Dimorphism in Body Size and Breeding Systems in Primates. *Nature 272*:610–611.
Loy, James D.
    1971   Estrous Behavior of Free-Ranging Rhesus Monkeys *(Macaca mulatta). Primates 12*:1–31.
Marshall, Lorna
    1976   *The !Kung of Nyae Nyae.* Cambridge: Harvard University Press.
Mayr, E.
    1970   *Populations, Species, and Evolution: An Abridgment of Animal Species and Evolution.* Cambridge: Harvard University Press, Belknap Press.
McGinnis, Patrick R.
    1979   Sexual Behavior in Free-Living Chimpanzees: Consort Relationships. In *The Great Apes,* Perspectives on Human Evolution, vol. 5, D. A. Hamburg and E. R. McCown (eds.), pp. 429–439. Menlo Park: Benjamin/Cummings.
Menzel, Emil W., Jr.
    1971a Communication about the Environment in a Group of Young Chimpanzees. *Folia Primatologica 15*:220–232.
    1979   Communication of Object Locations in a Group of Young Chimpanzees. In *The Great Apes,* Perspectives on Human Evolution, vol. 5, D. A. Hamburg and E. R. McCown (eds.), pp. 357–371. Menlo Park: Benjamin/Cummings.
Menzel, Emil W., Jr.; R. K. Davenport; and C. M. Rogers
    1972   Protocultural Aspects of Chimpanzees' Responsiveness to Novel Objects. *Folia Primatologica 17*:161–170.
Menzel, Emil W., Jr., and Stewart Halperin
    1975   Purposive Behavior as a Basis for Objective Communication between Chimpanzees. *Science 189*:652–654.
Nagel, U.
    1973   A Comparison of Anubis Baboons, Hamadryas Baboons, and Their Hybrids at a Species Border in Ethiopia. *Folia Primatologica 19*:104–165.
Riss, David C., and Curt D. Busse
    1977   Fifty-Day Observation of a Free-ranging Adult Male Chimpanzee. *Folia Primatologica 28*:283–297.
Riss, David, and Jane Goodall
    1976   Sleeping Behavior and Associations in a Group of Captive Chimpanzees. *Folia Primatologica 25*:1–11.
Sarich, Vincent M., and John E. Cronin
    1977   Generation Length and Rates of Hominoid Molecular Evolution. *Nature 269*:354.
Savage-Rumbaugh, E. Sue, and Beverly J. Wilkerson
    1978   Socio-sexual Behavior in *Pan paniscus* and *Pan troglodytes:* A Comparative Study. *Journal of Human Evolution 7*:327–344.
Schaller, George B.
    1972   *The Serengeti Lion: A Study of Predator-Prey Relations.* Chicago: University of Chicago Press.
Silberbauer, George B.
    1972   The G/wi Bushmen. In *Hunters and Gatherers Today,* M. G. Bicchieri

(ed.), pp. 271–325. New York: Holt, Rinehart and Winston.

Simpson, George Gaylord
1953   *The Major Features of Evolution.* New York: Columbia University Press.
1972   The Evolutionary Concept of Man. In *Sexual Selection and the Descent of Man, 1871–1971,* Bernard Campbell (ed.), pp. 17–39. Chicago: Aldine.

Struhsaker, Thomas T.
1967   Ecology of Vervet Monkeys *(Cercopithecus aethiops)* in the Masai-Amboseli Game Reserve, Kenya. *Ecology 48*:891–904.

Struhsaker, Thomas T., and J. Stephen Gartlan
1970   Observations on the Behavior and Ecology of the Patas Monkey *(Erythrocebus patas)* in the Waza Reserve, Cameroon. *Journal of Zoology 161*:49–63.

Suzuki, Akira
1966   On the Insect-eating Habits among Wild Chimpanzees Living in the Savanna Woodland of Western Tanzania. *Primates 7*:481–487.
1969   An Ecological Study of Chimpanzees in a Savanna Woodland. *Primates 10*:103–148.

Tanaka, Jiro
1976   Subsistence Ecology of Central Kalahari San. In *Kalahari Hunter-Gatherers: Studies of the !Kung San and Their Neighbors,* Richard B. Lee and Irven DeVore (eds.), pp. 98–119. Cambridge: Harvard University Press.

Tanner, Nancy
1974   Matrifocality in Indonesia and Africa and among Black Americans. In *Woman, Culture, and Society,* M. Z. Rosaldo and L. Lamphere (eds.), pp. 129–156. Stanford: Stanford University Press.

Tanner, Nancy M., and Adrienne L. Zihlman
1976a   Women in Evolution. 1. Innovation and Selection in Human Origins. *Signs: Journal of Women in Culture and Society 1*:585–608.
1976b   The Evolution of Communication: What Can Primates Tell Us? In *Origins and Evolution of Language and Speech,* Stevan R. Harnad, Horst D. Steklis, and Jane Lancaster (eds.), pp. 467–480, Annals of the New York Academy of Sciences, vol. 280. New York: New York Academy of Sciences.

Teleki, Geza
1975   Primate Subsistence Patterns: Collector-Predators and Gatherer-Hunters. *Journal of Human Evolution 4*:125–184.

Trivers, Robert L.
1971   The Evolution of Reciprocal Altruism. *Quarterly Review of Biology 46*:35–57.
1972   Parental Investment and Sexual Selection. In *Sexual Selection and the Descent of Man, 1871–1971,* B. Campbell (ed.), pp. 136–179. Chicago: Aldine.

Tutin, Caroline E. G.
1975   Exceptions to Promiscuity in a Feral Chimpanzee Community. In *Contemporary Primatology,* Proceedings of the Fifth International Congress of Primatology, S. Kondo, M. Kawai, and A. Ehara (eds.), pp. 445–449. Basel: Karger.

314   *On becoming human*

Washburn, Sherwood L., and Irven DeVore
    1961b The Social Life of Baboons. *Scientific American* 204:62–71.
Williams, B. J.
    1977   Investigations of a Little-Known Way of Life. (Review of *Kalahari Hunter-Gatherers*, Richard B. Lee and Irven DeVore (eds.), Cambridge: Harvard University Press, 1976.) *Science* 196:761–763.
Wilson, Edward O.
    1975   *Sociobiology: The New Synthesis*. Cambridge: Harvard University Press, Belknap Press.
Yellen, John, and Henry Harpending
    1972   Hunter-Gatherer Populations and Archaeological Inference. *World Archaeology* 4:244–253.
Zihlman, Adrienne L.
    1967   Human Locomotion: A Reappraisal of the Functional and Anatomical Evidence. Dissertation, University of California, Berkeley.
    1978c Interpretations of Early Hominid Locomotion. In *Early Hominids of Africa*. Clifford J. Jolly (ed.), pp. 361–377. London: Duckworth.
Zihlman, Adrienne L., and Nancy M. Tanner
    1979   Gathering and the Hominid Adaptation. In *Female Hierarchies*, Lionel Tiger and Heather M. Fowler (eds.). Chicago: Beresford Book Service.

CHAPTER 8. EVIDENCE ON THE TRANSITION: WHAT CAN THE EARLIEST HOMINID FOSSILS REVEAL ABOUT THE ANCESTRAL POPULATION AND THE TRANSITION?

Aronson, J. L.; T. J. Schmitt; R. C. Walter; M. Taieb; J. J. Tiercelin; D. J. Johanson; C. W. Naeser; A. E. M. Nairn
    1977   New Geochronologic and Palaeomagnetic Data for the Hominid-Bearing Hadar Formation of Ethiopia. *Nature* 267:323–327.
Azen, Edwin A.; Walter Leutenegger; and Erwin H. Peters
    1978   Evolutionary and Dietary Aspects of Salivary Basic (Pb) and Post Pb (PPb) Proteins in Anthropoid Primates. *Nature* 273:775–778.
Behrensmeyer, A. K.
    1976   Lothagam Hill, Kanapoi, and Ekora: A General Summary of Stratigraphy and Faunas. In *Earliest Man and Environments in the Lake Rudolf Basin*, Yves Coppens, F. Clark Howell, Glynn Ll. Isaac, and Richard E. F. Leakey (eds.), pp. 163–170. Chicago: University of Chicago Press.
Butzer, Karl W.
    1978   Geo-ecological Perspectives on Early Hominid Evolution. In *Early Hominids of Africa*, C. J. Jolly (ed.), pp. 191–217. London: Duckworth.
Cooke, H. B. S.
    1978a Faunal Evidence for the Biotic Setting of Early African Hominids. In *Early Hominids of Africa*, C. J. Jolly (ed.), pp. 267–281. London: Duckworth.
    1978b Pliocene-Pleistocence Suidae from Hadar, Ethiopia. *Kirtlandia* 29. Cleveland Museum of Natural History.
Eckhardt, Robert B.
    1977   Hominid Origins: The Lothagam Problem. *Current Anthroplogy* 18:356.

Howell, F. Clark
    1978a Hominidae. In *Evolution of African Mammals,* Vincent J. Maglio and
        H. B. S. Cooke (eds.), pp. 154–248. Cambridge: Harvard University
        Press.
Itani, Junichiro
    1979 Distribution and Adaptation of Chimpanzees in an Arid Area. In *The
        Great Apes,* Perspectives on Human Evolution, vol. 5, D. A. Hamburg
        and E. R. McCown (eds.), pp. 55–71. Menlo Park: Benjamin/Cummings.
Johanson, Donald C.
    1974 Some Metric Aspects of the Permanent and Deciduous Dentition of
        the Pygmy Chimpanzee *(Pan paniscus). American Journal of Physical
        Anthropology 41*:39–48.
    1976 Ethiopia Yields First "Family" of Early Man. *National Geographic
        150*: 791–811.
Johanson, Donald C.; Yves Coppens; and Maurice Taieb
    1976 Pliocene Hominid Remains from Hadar, Central Afar, Ethiopia. Ms.
        from Les plus anciens hominidés, UISPP, 9th Congress.
Johanson, Donald C., and Maurice Taieb
    1976 Plio-Pleistocene Hominid Discoveries in Hadar, Ethiopia. *Nature
        260*:293–297.
Johanson, Donald C.; Maurice Taieb; B. T. Gray; and Yves Coppens
    1978 Geological Framework of the Pliocene Hadar Formation (Afar, Ethio-
        pia) with Notes on Paleontology, Including Hominids. In *Geological
        Background to Fossil Man,* Walter W. Bishop (ed.), pp. 549–564.
        Edinburgh: Scottish Academic Press.
Johanson, Donald C., and Tim D. White
    1979 A Systematic Assessment of Early African Hominids. *Science
        203*:321–330.
Johanson, Donald C.; Tim D. White; and Yves Coppens
    1978 A New Species of the Genus *Australopithecus* (Primates: Hominidae)
        from the Pliocene of Eastern Africa. *Kirtlandia 28.* Cleveland Museum
        of Natural History.
Johanson, Donald C; Maurice Taieb; Yves Coppens; Hélène Roche
    1980 New Discoveries of Pliocene Hominids and Artifacts in Hadar: Inter-
        national Afar Research Expedition to Ethiopia (Fourth and Fifth Field
        Seasons, 1975–1977). *Journal of Human Evolution 9(8)*:583–585.
Johanson, Donald C, and Maitland Edey
    1981 *Lucy: The Beginnings of Humankind.* New York. New York: Simon
        and Schuster.
Kimbel, W. H.
    1979 Characteristics of Fossil Hominid Cranial Remains, Hadar, Ethiopia.
        Paper presented at the 48th Annual Meeting, American Association of
        Physical Anthropologists, San Francisco.
Kortlandt, Adriaan
    1978 The Ecosystem in Which the Incipient Hominines Could Have Evolved.
        In *Recent Advances in Primatology,* vol. 3, *Evolution,* D. J. Chivers and
        K. A. Joysey (eds.), pp. 503–506. New York: Academic Press.
Leakey, Mary D.
    1979 Footprints in the Ashes of Time. *National Geographic 155*:446–457.

Leakey, M. D., and R. L. Hay
    1979   Pliocene Footprints in the Laetolil Beds at Laetoli, Northern Tanzania. *Nature 278*:317–323.
Leakey, M. D.; R. L. Hay; G. H. Curtis; R. E. Drake; M. K. Jackes; T. D. White
    1976   Fossil Hominids from the Laetolil Beds. *Nature 262*:460–466.
Le Gros Clark, W. E.
    1950   Hominid Characters of the Australopithecine Dentition. *Journal of the Royal Anthropological Institute 80*:37–54.
Mahler, Paul Emil
    1973   Metric Variation in the Pongid Dentition. Dissertation, University of Michigan.
Martyn, John, and Philip V. Tobias
    1967   Pleistocene Deposits and New Fossil Localities in Kenya. *Nature 215*:476–480.
McHenry, Henry M., and Robert S. Corruccini
    1980   Late Tertiary Hominids and Human Origins. *Nature 285*:397–398.
Patterson, Bryan; Anna K. Behrensmeyer; and William D. Sills
    1970   Geology and Fauna of a New Pliocene Locality in Northwestern Kenya. *Nature 226*:918–921.
Patterson, Bryan, and W. W. Howells
    1967   Hominid Humeral Fragment from Early Pleistocene of Northwestern Kenya. *Science 156*:64–66.
Pickford, Martin
    1975   Late Miocene Sediments and Fossils from the Northern Kenya Rift Valley. *Nature 256*:279–284.
Robinson, J. T.
    1953   *Meganthropus*, Australopithecines, and Hominids. *American Journal of Physical Anthropology 11*:1–37.
Ryan, Alan S.
    1979   Scanning Electron Miscroscopy of Tooth Wear on Anterior Teeth of *Australopithecus afarensis*. Paper presented at the 48th Annual Meeting, American Association of Physical Anthropologists, San Francisco.
Taieb, M.; D. C. Johanson; Y. Coppens; and J. L. Aronson
    1976   Geological and Palaeontological Background of Hadar Hominid Site, Afar, Ethiopia. *Nature 260*:289–293.
Tanner, Nancy M.
    1975   Selection and Hominid Origins: The Role of Females in Speciation. Paper presented at the Behavioral Genetics Association Meetings (Spring), Dallas.
Tanner, Nancy M., and Adrienne L. Zihlman
    1976a Women in Evolution. 1. Innovation and Selection in Human Origins. *Signs: Journal of Women in Culture and Society 1*:585–608.
Van Couvering, Judith A. H.
    1975   Forest Habitat of Early Miocene Hominoids. Paper presented at the 44th Annual Meeting, American Association of Physical Anthropologists, Denver.
White, Tim. D.
    1977   New Fossil Hominids from Laetolil, Tanzania. *American Journal of Physical Anthropology 46*:197–229.

1980 Evolutionary Implications of Pliocene Hominid Footprints. *Nature* 208:175–176.

White, T. D., and J. M. Harris
1977 Suid Evolution and Correlation of African Hominid Localities. *Science* 198:13–21.

Wolpoff, Milford
1971 *Metric Trends in Hominid Dental Evolution.* Case Western Reserve University Studies in Anthropology, no.2. Cleveland: Press of Case Western Reserve University.

Zihlman, Adrienne L., and Nancy M. Tanner
1974 Becoming Human: Putting Women in Evolution. Paper presented at the Annual Meetings of the American Anthropological Association, Mexico City.

CHAPTER 9. GATHERING AND THE AUSTRALOPITHECINE WAY OF LIFE

Almquist, A. J.
1974 Sexual Difference in the Anterior Dentition in African Primates. *American Journal of Physical Anthropology* 40:359–367.

Avis, Virginia
1962 Brachiation: The Crucial Issue for Man's Ancestry. *Yearbook of Physical Anthropology* 10:99–128.

Behrensmeyer, A. K.
1978a The Habitat of Plio-Pleistocene Hominids in East Africa: Taphonomic and Micro-Stratigraphic Evidence. In *Early Hominids of Africa,* Clifford J. Jolly (ed.), pp. 165–190. London: Duckworth.

Brain, C. K.
1970 New Finds at the Swartkrans Australopithecine Site. *Nature* 225:1112–1119.
1974a A Hominid Skull's Revealing Holes. *Natural History* 553:44–45.
1974b Some Aspects of the South African Australopithecine Sites and Their Bone Accumulations. Conference on the African Hominidae of the Plio-Pleistocene: Evidence, Problems, and Strategies. Sponsored by Wenner-Gren Foundation for Anthropological Research, New York.
1975 An Interpretation of the Bone Assemblage from the Kromdraai Australopithecine Site, South Africa. In *Paleoanthropology: Morphology and Paleoecology,* Russell H. Tuttle (ed), pp. 225–244. The Hague: Mouton.
1978 Some Aspects of the South African Australopithecine Sites and Their Bone Accumulations. In *Early Hominids of Africa,* Clifford J. Jolly (ed.), pp. 131–161. London: Duckworth.

Campbell, Bernard G.
1972b Conceptual Progress in Physical Anthropology: Fossil Man. *Annual Reviews of Anthropology* 1:27–54.
1973 A New Taxonomy of Fossil Man. *Yearbook of Physical Anthropology* 17:194–201.
1978 Some Problems in Hominid Classification and Nomenclature. In *Early Hominids of Africa,* Clifford J. Jolly (ed.), pp. 567–581. London: Duckworth.

Ciochon, Russell L., and Robert S. Corruccini
　1976　Shoulder Joint of Sterkfontein *Australopithecus*. *South African Journal of Science* 72:80–82.
Clark, Cathleen B.
　1977　A Preliminary Report on Weaning among Chimpanzees of the Gombe National Park, Tanzania. In *Primate Bio-Social Development,* Suzanne Chevalier-Skolnikoff and Frank E. Poirier (eds.), pp. 235–260. New York: Garland.
Clark, J. Desmond
　1970　*The Prehistory of Africa.* New York: Praeger.
Cooke, H.B.S.
　1963　Pleistocene Mammal Faunas of Africa, with Particular Reference to Southern Africa. In *African Ecology and Human Evolution,* F. Clark Howell and François Bourlière (eds.), pp. 65–116. Chicago: Aldine.
　1978　Faunal Evidence for the Biotic Setting of Early African Hominids. In *Early Hominids of Africa,* Clifford J. Jolly (ed.), pp. 267–281. London: Duckworth.
Cramer, Douglas L.
　1974　Cranio-Facial Form in Two African Pongidae, with Special Reference to the Pygmy Chimpanzee, *Pan paniscus.* Dissertation, University of Chicago.
Crook, John Hurrell
　1972　Sexual Selection, Dimorphism, and Social Organization in the Primates. In *Sexual Selection and the Descent of Man, 1871–1971,* Bernard Campbell (ed.), pp. 231–281. Chicago: Aldine.
Dart, Raymond A.
　1957　*The Osteodontokeratic Culture of* Australopithecus prometheus. Transvaal Museum Memoir No. 10. Pretoria: Transvaal Museum.
Darwin, Charles
　1871　*The Descent of Man and Selection in Relation to Sex.* London: John Murray.
Du Brul, E. Lloyd
　1977　Early Hominid Feeding Mechanisms. *American Journal of Physical Anthropology* 47:305–320.
Eisenberg, J. F.; N. A. Muckenhirn; and R. Rudran
　1972　The Relation between Ecology and Social Structure in Primates. *Science* 176:863–874.
Flannery, Regina
　1932　The Position of Woman among the Mescalero Apache. *Primitive Man* 10:26–32.
　1935　The Position of Woman among the Eastern Cree. *Primitive Man* 12:81–86.
Gartlan, John S.
　1970　Preliminary Notes on the Ecology and Behavior of the Drill, *Mandrillus leucophaeus* Ritgen, 1824. In *Old World Monkeys: Evolution, Systematics, and Behavior,* J. R. Napier and P. H. Napier (eds.), pp. 445–480. New York: Academic Press.
Geist, Valerius
　1966a　The Evolution of Horn-like Organs. *Behavior* 27:175–214.

1966b The Evolutionary Significance of Mountain Sheep Horns. *Evolution* 20:558–566.

Geschwind, Norman
1965 Disconnexion Syndromes in Animals and Man. *Brain* 88:237–294.

Goodall, Jane van Lawick
1964 Tool-Using and Aimed Throwing in a Community of Free-Living Chimpanzees. *Nature* 201:1264–1266.
1970 Tool-Using in Primates and Other Vertebrates. In *Advances in the Study of Behavior,* vol. 3, D. S. Lehrman, R. A. Hinde, and E. Shaw (eds.), pp. 195–249. New York: Academic Press.
1973b Cultural Elements in a Chimpanzee Community. In *Precultural Primate Behavior,* Symposia of the Fourth International Congress of Primatology, vol. 1, E. W. Menzel, Jr. (ed.), pp. 144–185. Basel: Karger.
1975a The Behavior of the Chimpanzee. In *Hominisation and Behavior,* G. Kurth and I. Eibl-Eibesfeldt (eds.), pp. 74–136. Stuttgart: Gustav Fischer.

Goodall, Jane, and David A. Hamburg
1975 Chimpanzee Behavior as a Model for the Behavior of Early Man. In *New Psychiatric Frontiers,* D. A. Hamburg and H. K. H. Brodie (eds), pp. 14–43. New York: Basic Books.

Gould, Richard A.
1969 *Yiwara: Foragers of the Australian Desert.* New York: Scribners.

Granit, Ragnar
1977 *The Purposive Brain.* Cambridge: MIT Press.

Gregory, William K.
1929 Were the Ancestors of Man Primitive Brachiators? *Proceedings of the American Philosophical Society* 67:129–150.
1934 *Man's Place among the Anthropoids.* Oxford: Clarendon Press.

Griffin, P. Bion
1978 Agta Negrito Women Hunter-Gatherers. Paper presented at the 47th Annual Meeting of the American Anthropological Association, University of Toronto.

Hall, K. R. L.
1963a Observational Learning in Monkeys and Apes. *British Journal of Psychology* 54:201–226.
1968 Social Learning in Monkeys. In *Primates: Studies in Adaptation and Variation,* Phyllis C. Jay (ed.), pp. 383–397. New York: Holt, Rinehart and Winston.

Harcourt, A. H.
1979 The Social Relations and Group Structure of Wild Mountain Gorillas. In *The Great Apes,* Perspectives on Human Evolution, vol. 5, D. A. Hamburg and E. R. McCown (eds.), pp. 187–192. Menlo Park: Benjamin/Cummings.

Harris, John W. K., and Glynn Ll. Isaac
1976 The Karari Industry: Early Pleistocene Archaeological Evidence from the Terrain East of Lake Turkana, Kenya. *Nature* 262:102–107.

Harris, Marvin
1972 You Are What They Ate. *Natural History* 81:24–25.

Hill, Andrew
    1978   Taphonomical Background to Fossil Man: Problems in Palaeoecology.
            In *Geological Background to Fossil Man,* Walter W. Bishop (ed.), pp.
            87–101. Edinburgh: Scottish Academic Press.
Holloway, Ralph L.
    1966   Cranial Capacity, Neural Reorganization, and Hominid Evolution: A
            Search for More Suitable Parameters. *American Anthropologist*
            68:103–121.
    1967   Tools and Teeth: Some Speculations Regarding Canine Reduction.
            American Anthropologist 69:63–67.
    1972a   New Australopithecine Endocast, SK1585, from Swartkrans, South Af-
            rica. *American Journal of Physical Anthropology* 37:173–186.
    1972b   Australopithecine Endocasts, Brain Evolution in the Hominoidea, and
            a Model of Hominid Evolution. In *The Functional and Evolutionary
            Biology of Primates,* Russell H. Tuttle (ed.), pp. 185–203. Chicago:
            Aldine.
    1976a   Paleoneurological Evidence for Language Origins. In *Origins and Evo-
            lution of Language and Speech,* S. R. Harnad, H. D. Steklis, and J.
            Lancaster (eds.), pp. 330–348, Annals of the New York Academy of
            Sciences, vol. 280. New York: New York Academy of Sciences.
    1976b   Some Problems of Hominid Brain Endocast Reconstruction, Allome-
            try, and Neural Reorganization. Ms. from Les plus anciens
            hominidés, UISPP, 9th Congress.
    1978   Problems of Brain Endocast Interpretation and African Hominid Evolu-
            tion. In *Early Hominids of Africa,* Clifford J. Jolly (ed.), pp. 379–401.
            London: Duckworth.
Howell, F. Clark
    1978a   Hominidae. In *Evolution of African Mammals,* Vincent J. Maglio and
            H. B. S. Cooke (eds.), pp. 154–248. Cambridge: Harvard University
            Press.
Isaac, Glynn Ll.
    1969   Studies of Early Culture in East Africa. *World Archaeology* 1:1–28.
    1976   Traces of Early Hominid Activities from the Lower Member of the
            Koobi Fora Formation, Kenya. Ms. from Les plus anciennes industries
            en Afrique, UISPP, 9th Congress.
    1977   *Olorgesailie: Archeological Studies of a Middle Pleistocene Lake
            Basin in Kenya.* Assisted by Barbara Isaac. Chicago: University of
            Chicago Press.
    1978   The Archaeological Evidence for the Activities of Early African Homi-
            nids. In *Early Hominids of Africa,* Clifford J. Jolly (ed.), pp. 219–254.
            London: Duckworth.
Isaac, Glynn Ll., and John W. K. Harris
    1978   Archaeology. In *Koobi Fora Research Project,* vol. 1, *The Fossil
            Hominids and an Introduction to Their Context: 1968–1974,* Meave
            G. Leakey and Richard E. F. Leakey (eds.), pp. 64–85. Oxford: Cla-
            rendon Press.
Isaac, Glynn Ll.; J. W. K. Harris; and D. Crader
    1976   Archeological Evidence from the Koobi Fora Formation. In *Earliest
            Man and Environments in the Lake Rudolf Basin,* Yves Coppens,

F. Clark Howell, Glynn Ll. Isaac, and Richard E. F. Leakey (eds.), pp. 533–551. Chicago: University of Chicago Press.

Itani, Junichiro
    1979   Distribution and Adaptation of Chimpanzees in an Arid Area. In *The Great Apes*, Perspectives on Human Evolution, vol. 5, D. A. Hamburg and E. R. McCown (eds.), pp. 55–71. Menlo Park: Benjamin/Cummings.

Jacob, Teuku
    1972   The Absolute Date of the Djetis Beds at Modjokerto. *Antiquity* 46:36.
    1976   Man in Indonesia: Past, Present, and Future. In *Modern Quaternary Research in Southeast Asia*, vol. 2, Gert-Jan Bartstra and Willem Arnold Casparie (eds.), pp. 39–48. Rotterdam: Balkema.

Jacob, Teuku, and Garniss H. Curtis
    1971   Preliminary Potassium-Argon Dating of Early Man in Java. *Contributions of the University of California Archaeological Research Facility* 12:50.

Johanson, Donald C.
    1974   Some Metric Aspects of the Permanent and Deciduous Dentition of the Pygmy Chimpanzee *(Pan paniscus)*. *American Journal of Physical Anthropology* 41:39–48.

Johanson, Donald C.; Maurice Taieb; B. T. Gray; and Yves Coppens
    1978   Geological Framework of the Pliocene Hadar Formation (Afar, Ethiopia) with Notes on Paleontology, Including Hominids. In *Geological Background to Fossil Man*, Walter W. Bishop (ed.), pp. 549–564. Edinburgh: Scottish Academic Press.

Johanson, Donald C., and Tim D. White
    1979   A Systematic Assessment of Early African Hominids. *Science* 203:321–330.

Jolly, Clifford J.
    1970a The Seed-Eaters: A New Model of Hominid Differentiation Based on a Baboon Analogy. *Man* 5:5–25.

Kano, Takayoshi
    1972   Distribution and Adaptation of the Chimpanzee on the Eastern Shore of Lake Tanganyika. *Kyoto University African Studies* 7:37–129.

Keith, Arthur
    1923   Man's Posture: Its Evolution and Disorders. *British Medical Journal* 1:451–454.

Kinzey, Warren G.
    1971   Evolution of the Human Canine Tooth. *American Anthropologist* 73:680–694.

Konner, Melvin J.
    1976   Maternal Care, Infant Behavior and Development among the !Kung. In *Kalahari Hunter-Gatherers: Studies of the !Kung San and Their Neighbors*, Richard B. Lee and Irven DeVore (eds.), pp. 218–245. Cambridge: Harvard University Press.

Krogman, W. M.
    1969   Growth Changes in Skull, Face, Jaws, and Teeth of the Chimpanzee. In *The Chimpanzee*, vol. 1, *Anatomy, Behavior, and Diseases of Chimpanzees*, G. H. Bourne (ed.), pp. 104–164. Basel: Karger.

Kuhn, Thomas S.
   1962   *The Structure of Scientific Revolutions.* Chicago: University of Chicago Press.
Lancaster, Jane B.
   1968a On the Evolution of Tool-Using Behavior. *American Anthropologist* 70:56–66.
   1968b Primate Communication Systems and the Emergence of Human Language. In *Primates: Studies in Adaptation and Variability,* Phyllis C. Jay (ed.), pp. 439–457. New York: Holt, Rinehart and Winston.
Landes, Ruth
   1938   *The Ojibwa Woman.* New York: Columbia University Press.
Leakey, Mary D.
   1967   Preliminary Survey of the Cultural Material from Beds I and II, Olduvai Gorge, Tanzania. In *Background to Evolution in Africa,* W. W. Bishop and J. D. Clark (eds.), pp. 417–446. Chicago: University of Chicago Press.
   1970   Early Artifacts from the Koobi Fora Area. *Nature* 226:228–230.
   1971   *Olduvai Gorge,* vol. 3, *Excavations in Beds I and II, 1960–1963.* Cambridge: Cambridge University Press.
   1978   Olduvai Fossil Hominids: Their Stratigraphic Positions and Associations. In *Early Hominids of Africa,* Clifford J. Jolly (ed.), pp. 3–16. London: Duckworth.
   1979   Footprints in the Ashes of Time. *National Geographic* 155:446–457.
Leakey, M. D., and R. L. Hay
   1979   Pliocene Footprints in the Laetolil Beds at Laetoli, Northern Tanzania. *Nature* 278:317–323.
Leakey, Richard E. F.; Meave G. Leakey; and Anna K. Behrensmeyer
   1978   The Hominid Catalogue. In *Koobi Fora Research Project,* vol. 1, *The Fossil Hominids and an Introduction to Their Context, 1968–1974.* Meave G. Leakey and Richard E. F. Leakey (eds.), pp. 86–182. Oxford: Clarendon Press.
Leakey, Richard E. F., and Roger Lewin
   1978   *People of the Lake.* Garden City: Anchor Press.
Lee, Richard Borshay
   1968   What Hunters Do for a Living, or, How to Make Out on Scarce Resources. In *Man the Hunter,* R. B. Lee and I. DeVore, (eds.), pp. 30–48. Chicago: Aldine.
   1979   *The !Kung San: Men, Women, and Work in a Foraging Society.* Cambridge: Cambridge University Press.
Lee, Richard Borshay, and Irven DeVore, eds.
   1968   *Man the Hunter.* Chicago: Aldine.
   1976   *Kalahari Hunter-Gatherers: Studies of the !Kung San and Their Neighbors.* Cambridge: Harvard University Press.
Le Gros Clark, W. E.
   1950   Hominid Characters of the Australopithecine Dentition. *Journal of the Royal Anthropological Institute* 80:37–54.
Leutenegger, Walter
   1972   Newborn Size and Pelvic Dimensions of *Australopithecus. Nature* 240:568–569.

Leutenegger, Walter, and James T. Kelly
    1977   Relationship of Sexual Dimorphism in Canine Size and Body Size to Social, Behavioral, and Ecological Correlates in Anthropoid Primates. *Primates 18*:117–136.

Lewis, O. J.
    1972a Osteological Features Characterizing the Wrists of Monkeys and Apes, with a Reconsideration of This Region in *Dryopithecus* (Proconsul) *africanus. American Journal of Physical Anthropology 36*:45–58.
    1973   The Hominid Os Capitatum, with Special Reference to the Fossil Bones from Sterkfontein and Olduvai Gorge. *Journal of Human Evolution 2*:1–11.

Linton, Sally
    1971   Woman the Gatherer: Male Bias in Anthropology. In *Women in Cross-Cultural Perspective: A Preliminary Sourcebook,* Sue-Ellen Jacobs (ed.), pp. 9–21. Urbana: University of Illinois Press. (Reprinted 1975, under the name of Sally Slocum, in *Toward an Anthropology of Women,* Rayna R. Reiter (ed.), pp. 36–50. New York: Monthly Review Press.)

Lovejoy, C. Owen
    1978   A Biomechanical Review of the Locomotor Diversity of Early Hominids. In *Early Hominids of Africa,* Clifford J. Jolly (ed.), pp. 403–429. London: Duckworth.
    1979   A Reconstruction of the Pelvis of AL-288 (Hadar Formation, Ethiopia). Paper presented at the 48th Annual Meeting, American Association of Physical Anthropologists, San Francisco.

Lyght, Charles E.; Chester S. Keefer; Francis D. W. Lukens; Dickinson W. Richards; W. Henry Sebrell; and John M. Trapnell, eds.
    1966   *The Merck Manual of Diagnosis and Therapy.* 11th ed. Rahway, N.J., and West Point, Pa.: Merck Sharp and Dohme Research Laboratories.

MacKinnon, John
    1974   The Behavior and Ecology of Wild Orang-utans. (*Pongo pygmaeus*). *Animal Behavior 22*:3–74.

Mann, Alan E.
    1968   The Paleodemography of *Australopithecus.* Dissertation, University of California, Berkeley.
    1974   Australopithecine Demographic Patterns. Ms. from the African Hominidae of the Plio-Pleistocene: Evidence, Problems, and Strategies, Wenner-Gren Foundation for Anthropological Research.
    1976   Australopithecine Demography. Ms. from Les plus anciens hominidés, UISPP, 9th Congress.

McGrew, William C.
    1979   Evolutionary Implications of Sex Differences in Chimpanzee Predation and Tool Use. In *The Great Apes,* Perspectives on Human Evolution, vol. 5, D. A. Hamburg and E. R. McCown (eds.), pp. 441–463. Menlo Park: Benjamin/Cummings.

McHenry, Henry M., and L. Alis Temerin
    1979   The Evolution of Hominid Bipedalism: Evidence from the Fossil Record. *Yearbook of Physical Anthropology 22.*

Menzel, Emil W., Jr.

1973a Leadership and Communication in Young Chimpanzees. In *Precultural Primate Behavior,* Symposia of the Fourth International Congress of Primatology, E. W. Menzel, Jr. (ed.), pp. 192–225. Basel: Karger.

Merrick, H. V.; J. de Heinzelin; P. Haesaerts; and F. C. Howell

1973 Archaeological Occurrences of Early Pleistocene Age from the Shungura Formation, Lower Omo Valley, Ethiopia. *Nature 242*:572–575.

Merrick, H. V., and J. P. S. Merrick

1976 Archeological Occurrences of Earlier Pleistocene Age, from the Shungura Formation. In *Earliest Man and Environments in the Lake Rudolf Basin,* Yves Coppens, F. Clark Howell, Glynn Ll. Isaac, and Richard E. F. Leakey (eds.), pp. 574–585. Chicago: University of Chicago Press.

Morris, Kathryn, and Jane Goodall

1977 Competition for Meat between Chimpanzees and Baboons of the Gombe National Park. *Folia Primatologica 28*:109–121.

Morton, Dudley J.

1924a Evolution of the Human Foot. 2. *American Journal of Physical Anthropology 7*:1–52.

1924b Evolution of the Longitudinal Arch of the Human Foot. *Journal of Bone and Joint Surgery 6*:56–90.

Napier, J. R.

1962a Fossil Hand Bones from Olduvai Gorge. *Nature 196*:409–411.

1962b The Evolution of the Hand. *Scientific American 207*:56–62.

Napier, J. R., and P. H. Napier

1967 *A Handbook of Living Primates.* New York: Academic Press.

Passingham, R. E., and G. Ettlinger

1974 A Comparison of Cortical Functions in Man and the Other Primates. In *International Review of Neurobiology,* vol. 16, pp. 233–299, Carl C. Pfeiffer and John R. Smythies (eds.). New York: Academic Press.

Pilbeam, David

1972a *The Ascent of Man: An Introduction to Human Evolution.* New York: Macmillan.

1972b Evolutionary Changes in Hominoid Dentition through Geological Time. In *Calibration of Hominoid Evolution,* W. W. Bishop and J. A. Miller (eds.), pp. 369–380. Edinburgh: Scottish Academic Press.

1978a Rearranging Our Family Tree. *Human Nature 1*:38–45.

Rightmire, G. P.

1972 Multivariate Analysis of an Early Hominid Metacarpal from Swartkrans. *Science 176*:159–161.

Schaller, George B.

1963 *The Moutain Gorilla.* Chicago: University of Chicago Press.

Schultz, Adolph H.

1931 Man as a Primate. *Scientific Monthly 33*:385–412.

1960 Einige Beobachtungen und Malze am Skelett von *Oreopithecus;* im Vergleich mit Anderen Catarrhinen Primaten. *Z. Morph. Anthrop. 50*:136–149.

1969 *The Life of Primates.* New York: Universe Books.

Shipman, Pat
1978   Patterns of Bone Breakage and Early Hominid Behavior. Paper presented at the 47th Annual Meeting, American Association of Physical Anthropologists, University of Toronto.
Stiles, Daniel
1979a Recent Archaeological Findings at the Sterkfontein Site. *Nature* 277:381–382.
Sugiyama, Yukimaru
1973a The Social Structure of Wild Chimpanzees. In *Comparative Ecology and Behavior of Primates*, R. P. Michael and J. H. Crook (eds.), pp. 376–410. New York: Academic Press.
Tanaka, Jiro
1976   Subsistence Ecology of Central Kalahari San. In *Kalahari Hunter-Gatherers: Studies of the !Kung San and Their Neighbors*, Richard B. Lee and Irven DeVore (eds.), pp. 98–119. Cambridge: Harvard University Press.
Tanner, Nancy M., and Adrienne L. Zihlman
1976a Women in Evolution. 1. Innovation and Selection in Human Origins. *Signs: Journal of Women in Culture and Society* 1:585–608.
1976b The Evolution of Human Communication: What Can Primates Tell Us? In *Origins and Evolution of Language and Speech*, Stevan R. Harnad, Horst D. Steklis, and Jane Lancaster (eds.), pp. 467–480, New York Academy of Sciences, vol. 280. New York: New York Academy of Sciences.
Teleki, Geza
1973c Group Response to the Accidental Death of a Chimpanzee in Gombe National Park, Tanzania. *Folia Primatologica* 20:81–94.
1974   Chimpanzee Subsistence Technology: Materials and Skills. *Journal of Human Evolution* 3:575–594.
1975   Primate Subsistence Patterns: Collector-Predators and Gatherer-Hunters. *Journal of Human Evolution* 4:125–184.
Teleki, Geza; E. E. Hunt, Jr.; and J. H. Pfifferling
1976   Demographic Observations (1963–1973) on the Chimpanzees of Gombe National Park, Tanzania. *Journal of Human Evolution* 5:559–598.
Tuttle, Russell
1974   Darwin's Apes, Dental Apes, and the Descent of Man: Normal Science in Evolutionary Anthropology. *Current Anthropology* 15:389–398.
Vrba, E. S.
1974   Chronological and Ecological Implications of the Fossil Bovidae at the Sterkfontein Australopithecine Site. *Nature* 250:19–23.
Walker, Alan, and Richard E. F. Leakey
1978   The Hominids of East Turkana. *Scientific American* 239:54–66.
Wallace, John A.
1975   Dietary Adaptations of *Australopithecus* and Early *Homo*. In *Paleoanthropology: Morphology and Paleoecology*, Russell H. Tuttle (ed.), pp. 203–223. The Hague: Mouton.

Washburn, Sherwood L.
   1960   Tools and Human Evolution. *Scientific American 203*:62–75. (Re-
          printed 1974 in *Biological Anthropology: Readings from "Scientific
          American,"* pp. 47–60. San Francisco: Freeman.)
   1968   One Hundred Years of Biological Anthropology. In *One Hundred
          Years of Anthropology,* J. O. Brew (ed.), pp. 97–115. Cambridge:
          Harvard University Press.
Washburn, Sherwood L., and R. L. Ciochon
   1974   Canine Teeth: Notes on Controversies in the Study of Human Evolu-
          tion. *American Anthropologist 76*:765–784.
White, Tim D.
   1977   New Fossil Hominids from Laetolil, Tanzania. *American Journal of
          Physical Anthropology 46*:197–229.
White, T. D., and J. M. Harris
   1977   Suid Evolution and Correlation of African Hominid Localities. *Science
          198*:13–21.
Wolpoff, Milford
   1971   *Metric Trends in Hominid Dental Evolution.* Case Western Reserve
          University Studies in Anthropology, no. 2. Cleveland: Press of Case
          Western Reserve University.
   1975   Sexual Dimorphism in the Australopithecines. In *Paleoanthropology:
          Morphology and Paleoecology,* Russell H. Tuttle (ed.), pp. 245–284.
          The Hague: Mouton.
   1978a Some Aspects of Canine Size in the Australopithecines. *Journal of Hu-
          man Evolution 7*:115–126.
   1978b Analogies and Interpretation in Palaeoanthropology. In *Early Hominids
          of Africa,* Clifford J. Jolly (ed.), pp. 461–504. London: Duckworth.
Zihlman, Adrienne L.
   1978c Interpretations of Early Hominid Locomotion. In *Early Hominids of
          Africa,* Clifford J. Jolly (ed.), pp. 361–377. London: Duckworth.
Zihlman, Adrienne, and Lynda Brunker
   1979   Hominid Bipedalism: Then and Now. *Yearbook of Physical Anthro-
          pology 22.*
Zihlman, Adrienne L.; John E. Cronin; Douglas L. Cramer; and Vincent M. Sarich
   1978   Pygmy Chimpanzee as a Possible Prototype for the Common Ancestor
          of Humans, Chimpanzees and Gorillas. *Nature 275*:744–746.
Zihlman, Adrienne L., and Nancy M. Tanner
   1979   Gathering and the Hominid Adaptation. In *Female Hierarchies,* Lionel
          Tiger and Heather M. Fowler (eds.), Chicago: Beresford Book Service.

CHAPTER 10. EARLY HOMINID LIFEWAYS: THE CRITICAL ROLE OF AN
INTERPRETIVE FRAMEWORK

Behrensmeyer, A. K.
   1978b Correlation of Plio-Pleistocene Sequences in the Northern Lake Tur-
          kana Basin: A Summary of Evidence and Issues. In *Geological Back-
          ground to Fossil Man,* Walter W. Bishop (ed.), pp. 421–440. Edin-
          burgh: Scottish Academic Press.

Bishop, W. W.
    1972   Stratigrapahic Succession 'Versus' Calibration in East Africa. In *Calibration of Hominoid Evolution*, W. W. Bishop and J. A. Miller (eds.), pp. 219–246. Edinburgh: Scottish Academic Press.
    1978   Geochronological Framework for African Plio-Pleistocene Hominidae: As Cerberus Sees It. In *Early Hominids of Africa*, Clifford J. Jolly (ed.), pp. 255–265. London: Duckworth.
Bishop, W. W.; M. Pickford; and A. Hill
    1975   New Evidence Regarding the Quaternary Geology, Archaeology, and Hominids of Chesowanja, Kenya. *Nature 258*:204–208.
Boaz, Noel T.
    1977a   Paleoecology of Plio-Pleistocene Hominidae in the Lower Omo Basin, Ethiopia. Dissertation, University of California, Berkeley.
    1977b   Paleoecology of Early Hominidae in Africa. Kroeber Anthropological Society Papers, no. 50:37–62.
Bonnefille, Raymonde
    1976a   Palynological Evidence for an Important Change in the Vegetation of the Omo Basin between 2.5 and 2 Million Years Ago. In *Earliest Man and Environments in the Lake Rudolf Basin*, Yves Coppens, F. Clark Howell, Glynn Ll. Isaac, and Richard E. F. Leakey (eds.), pp. 421–431. Chicago: University of Chicago Press.
    1976b   Implications of Pollen Assemblage from the Koobi Fora Formation, East Rudolf, Kenya. *Nature 264:* 403–407.
Brock, A.; P. L. McFadden; and T. C. Partridge
    1977   Preliminary Paleomagnetic Results from Makapansgat and Swartkrans. *Nature 266*:249–250.
Brown, F. H., and R. T. Shuey
    1976   Magnetostratigraphy of the Shungura and Usno Formations, Lower Omo Valley, Ethiopia. In *Earliest Man and Environments in the Lake Rudolf Basin*, Yves Coppens, F. Clark Howell, Glynn Ll. Isaac, and Richard E. F. Leakey (eds.), pp. 64–78. Chicago: University of Chicago Press.
Butzer, Karl W.
    1974b   Paleoecology of South African Australopithecines: Taung Revisited. *Current Anthropology 15*:367–382.
    1977   Geo-Archaeology in Practice. *Reviews in Anthropology 4*:125–131.
Campbell, Bernard G.
    1978   Some Problems in Hominid Classification and Nomenclature. In *Early Hominids of Africa*, Clifford J. Jolly (ed.), pp. 567–581. London: Duckworth.
Carney, J.; A. Hill; J. A. Miller; and A. Walker
    1971   Late Australopithecine from Baringo District, Kenya. *Nature 230*:509–514.
Carr, C. J.
    1976   Plant Ecological Variation and Pattern in the Lower Omo Basin. In *Earliest Man and Environments in the Lake Rudolf Basin*, Yves Coppens, F. Clark Howell, Glynn Ll. Isaac, and Richard E. F. Leakey (eds.), pp. 432–467. Chicago: University of Chicago Press.

Cerling, T. E.; F. H. Brown; B. W. Cerling; G. H. Curtis; and R. E. Drake
    1979   Preliminary Correlations between the Koobi Fora and Shungura For-
            mations, East Africa. *Nature* 279:118–121.
Cerling, T. E.; R. L. Hay; and J. R. O'Neil
    1977   Isotopic Evidence for Dramatic Climatic Changes in East Africa during
            the Pleistocene. *Nature* 267:137–138.
Chavaillon, J.
    1976   Evidence for the Technical Practices of Early Pleistocene Hominids. In
            Earliest Man and Environments in the Lake Rudolf Basin, Yves Cop-
            pens, F. Clark Howell, Glynn Ll. Isaac, and Richard E. F. Leakey
            (eds.), pp. 565–573. Chicago: University of Chicago Press.
Clark, J. Desmond
    1975   A Comparison of the Late Acheulian Industries of Africa and the
            Middle East. In *After the Australopithecines,* Karl W. Butzer and
            Glynn Ll. Isaac (eds.), pp. 605–659. The Hague: Mouton.
Clark, J. Desmond, and C. Vance Haynes, Jr.
    1970   An Elephant Butchery Site at Mwanganda's Village, Karonga, Malawi,
            and Its Relevance for Palaeolithic Archaeology. *World Archaeology*
            1:390–411.
Cooke, H. B. S.
    1976   Suidae from Plio-Pleistocene Strata of the Rudolf Basin. In *Earliest
            Man and Environments in the Lake Rudolf Basin,* Yves Coppens, F.
            Clark Howell, Glynn Ll. Isaac, and Richard E. F. Leakey (eds.), pp.
            251–263. Chicago: University of Chicago Press.
    1978   Faunal Evidence for the Biotic Setting of Early African Hominids. In
            Early Hominids of Africa, Clifford J. Jolly (ed.), pp. 267–281. Lon-
            don: Duckworth.
Curtis, G. H.; R. E. Drake; T. E. Cerling; B. W. Cerling; and J. H. Hampel
    1975   Age of KBS Tuff in Koobi Fora Formation, East Rudolf, Kenya. *Nature*
            258:395–398.
Dart, Raymond A.
    1925   *Australopithecus africanus:* The Man-Ape of South Africa. *Nature*
            115:195–199.
Day, Michael H.
    1965   *Guide to Fossil Man: A Handbook of Human Palaeontology.* London:
            Cassell.
Dechamps, R.
    1976   Résultats préliminaires de l'étude des bois fossiles de la Basse Vallée
            de l'Omo. Annals, Mus. Roy. Afrique Cent., Tervuren.
Drake, R. E.; G. H. Curtis; T. E. Cerling; B. W. Cerling; and J. Hampel
    1980   KBS Dating and Geochronology of Tuffaceous Sediments in the Koobi
            Fora and Shungura Formations, East Africa. *Nature* 283:368–372.
Du Brul, E. Lloyd
    1977   Early Hominid Feeding Mechanisms. *American Journal of Physical
            Anthropology* 47:305–320.
Fitch, Frank J.; Jan C. Findlater; Ronald T. Watkins; and J. A. Miller
    1974   Dating of the Rock Succession Containing Fossil Hominids at East
            Rudolf, Kenya. *Nature* 251:213–215.

Fitch, Frank J., and J. A. Miller
1970   Radioisotopic Age Determinations of Lake Rudolf Artefact Site. *Nature* 226:226–228.
1976   Conventional Potassium-Argon and Argon-40/Argon-39 Dating of Volcanic Rocks from East Rudolf. In *Earliest Man and Environments in the Lake Rudolf Basin,* Yves Coppens, F. Clark Howell, Glynn Ll. Isaac, and Richard E. F. Leakey (eds.), pp. 123–147. Chicago: University of Chicago Press.

Geertz, Clifford
1959   Ritual and Social Change: A Javanese Example. *American Anthropologist* 61:991–1012. (Reprinted 1973, in *The Interpretation of Cultures: Selected Essays by Clifford Geertz,* pp. 142–169. New York: Basic Books.)
1966   The Impact of the Concept of Culture on the Concept of Man. In *New Views of the Nature of Man,* J. Platt (ed.), pp. 93–118. Chicago: University of Chicago Press. (Reprinted 1973, in *The Interpretation of Cultures: Selected Essays by Clifford Geertz,* pp. 33–54. New York: Basic Books.)

Gentry, A. W.
1976   Bovidae from the East Rudolf Succession. In *Earliest Man and Environments in the Lake Rudolf Basin,* Yves Coppens, F. Clark Howell, Glynn Ll. Isaac, and Richard E. F. Leakey (eds.), pp. 275–292. Chicago: University of Chicago Press.

Guilmet, George M.
1977   The Evolution of Tool-Using and Tool-Making Behaviour. *Man* 12:33–47.

Harris, John M.
1977   Palaeomagnetic Stratigraphy of the Koobi Fora Formation, East of Lake Turkana (Lake Rudolf), Kenya. *Nature* 268:699–670.

Harris, J. W. K., and W. W. Bishop
1976   Sites and Assemblages from the Early Pleistocene Beds of Karari and Chesowanja. Ms. from Les plus anciennes industries en Afrique, UISPP, 9th Congress.

Hay, Richard L.
1976a   *Geology of the Olduvai Gorge: A Study of Sedimentation in a Semiarid Basin.* Berkeley: University of California Press.
1976b   Environmental Setting of Hominid Activities in Bed I, Olduvai Gorge. In *Human Origins: Louis Leakey and the East African Evidence,* Glynn Ll. Isaac and Elizabeth R. McCown (eds.), pp. 209–226. Menlo Park: Benjamin.

Howell, F. Clark
1972   Pliocene/Pleistocene Hominidae in Eastern Africa, Absolute and Relative Ages. In *Calibration of Hominoid Evolution,* W. W. Bishop and J. A. Miller (eds.), pp. 331–368. Edinburgh: Scottish Academic Press.
1976   An Overview of the Pliocene and Earlier Pleistocene of the Lower Omo Basin, Southern Ethiopia. In *Human Origins: Louis Leakey and the East African Evidence,* Glynn Ll. Isaac and Elizabeth R. McCown (eds.), pp. 227–268. Menlo Park: Benjamin.
1978a   Hominidae. In *Evolution of African Mammals,* Vincent J. Maglio and

H. B. S. Cooke (eds.), pp. 154–248. Cambridge: Harvard University Press.

1978b Overview of the Pliocene and Earlier Pleistocene of the Lower Omo Basin, Southern Ethiopia. In *Early Hominids of Africa*, Clifford J. Jolly (ed.), pp. 85–130. London: Duckworth.

Howell, F. Clark, and Yves Coppens
1976 An Overview of Hominidae from the Omo Succession, Ethiopia. In *Earliest Man and Environments in the Lake Rudolf Basin*, Yves Coppens, F. Clark Howell, Glynn Ll. Isaac, and Richard E. F. Leakey (eds.), pp. 522–532. Chicago: University of Chicago Press.

Isaac, Glynn Ll., and John W. K. Harris
1978 Archaeology. In *Koobi Fora Research Project*, vol. 1, *The Fossil Hominids and an Introduction to Their Context: 1968–1974*, Meave G. Leakey and Richard E. F. Leakey (eds.), pp. 64–85. Oxford: Clarendon Press.

Isaac, Glynn Ll.; J. W. K. Harris; and D. Crader
1976 Archeological Evidence from the Koobi Fora Formation. In *Earliest Man and Environments in the Lake Rudolf Basin*, Yves Coppens, F. Clark Howell, Glynn Ll. Isaac, and Richard E. F. Leakey (eds.), pp. 533–551. Chicago: University of Chicago Press.

Jaeger, J.-J., and H. B. Wesselman
1976 Fossil Remains of Micromammals from the Omo Group Deposits. In *Earliest Man and Environments in the Lake Rudolf Basin*, Yves Coppens, F. Clark Howell, Glynn Ll. Isaac, and Richard E. F. Leakey (eds.), pp. 351–360. Chicago: University of Chicago Press.

Johanson, Donald C., and Maitland Edey
1981 *Lucy: The Beginnings of Humankind.* New York: Simon and Schuster.

Johanson, Donald C., and Maurice Taieb
1976 Plio-Pleistocene Hominid Discoveries in Hadar, Ethiopia. *Nature* 260:293–297.

Johanson, Donald C., and Tim D. White
1979 A Systematic Assessment of Early African Hominids. *Science* 203:321–330.

Johanson, Donald C.; Tim D. White; and Yves Coppens
1978 A New Species of the Genus *Australopithecus* (Primates: Hominidae) from the Pliocene of Eastern Africa. *Kirtlandia 28:1–14.*

Krantz, Grover S.
1973 Romer's Rule and the Origin of Stone Tools. *Man* 8:631–633.

Leakey, Mary D.
1971 *Olduvai Gorge*, vol. 3, *Excavations in Beds I and II, 1960–1963.* Cambridge: Cambridge University Press.

1978 Olduvai Fossil Hominids: Their Stratigraphic Positions and Associations. In *Early Hominids of Africa*, Clifford J. Jolly (ed.), pp. 3–16. London: Duckworth.

Leakey, Richard E. F.
1973a Further Evidence of Lower Pleistocene Hominids from East Rudolf, North Kenya, 1972. *Nature* 242:170–173.

1973b Evidence for an Advanced Plio-Pleistocene Hominid from East Rudolf, Kenya. *Nature 242:447–450.*

1974   Further Evidence of Lower Pleistocene Hominids from East Rudolf, North Kenya, 1973. *Nature 248*:653–656.

Leakey, Richard E. F.; Meave G. Leakey; and Anna K. Behrensmeyer

1978   The Hominid Catalogue. In *Koobi Fora Research Project*, vol. 1, *The Fossil Hominids and an Introduction to Their Context, 1968–1974,* Meave G. Leakey and Richard E. F. Leakey (eds.), pp. 86–182. Oxford: Clarendon Press.

Leakey, Richard E. F., and B. A. Wood

1974   A Hominid Mandible from East Rudolf, Kenya. *American Journal of Physical Anthropology 41*:245–249.

Le Gros Clark, W. E.

1950   Hominid Characters of the Australopithecine Dentition. *Journal of the Royal Anthropological Institute 80*:37–54.

Mann, Alan E.

1968   The Paleodemography of *Australopithecus*. Dissertation, University of California, Berkeley.

1975   Some Paleodemographic Aspects of the South African Australopithecines. *University of Pennsylvania Publications in Anthropology 1*:1–171.

McDougall, Ian; Robyn Maier; P. Sutherland-Hawkes; and A. J. W. Gleadow

1980   K-Ar Age Estimate for the KBS Tuff, East Turkana, Kenya. *Nature 284*:230–234.

Merrick, H. V., and J. P. S. Merrick

1976   Archeological Occurrences of Earlier Pleistocene Age, from the Shungura Formation. In *Earliest Man and Environments in the Lake Rudolf Basin*, Yves Coppens, F. Clark Howell, Glynn Ll. Isaac, and Richard E. F. Leakey (eds.), pp. 574–585. Chicago: University of Chicago Press.

Oakley, Kenneth P.; Bernard G. Campbell; and Theya I. Molleson, eds.

1977   *Catalogue of Fossil Hominids,* part 1, *Africa* 2d ed. London: Trustees of the British Museum.

Partridge, T. C.

1973   Geomorphological Dating of Cave Openings at Makapansgat, Sterkfontein, Swartkrans, and Taung. *Nature 246*:75–79.

1979   Re-appraisal of Lithostratigraphy of Makapansgat Limeworks Hominid Site. *Nature 279*:484–488.

Pilbeam, David R.

1972a *The Ascent of Man: An Introduction to Human Evolution.* New York: Macmillan.

1978b Recognizing Specific Diversity in Heterogeneous Fossil Samples. In *Early Hominids of Africa*, Clifford J. Jolly (ed.), pp. 505–516. London: Duckworth.

Pilbeam, David R., and Michael Zwell

1972   The Single Species Hypothesis, Sexual Dimorphism, and Variability in Early Hominids. *Yearbook of Physical Anthropology 16*:69–79.

Potts, Richard

1978   Site Statistics: A Search for Hominid Activity Patterns at Olduvai Gorge. Paper presented at the 47th Annual Meeting, American Association of Physical Anthropologists, Toronto.

Read, Dwight W.
    1975   Hominid Teeth and Their Relationship to Hominid Phylogeny. *American Journal of Physical Anthropology 42*:105–125.
Shackleton, Robert M.
    1978   Structural Development of the East African Rift System. In *Geological Background to Fossil Man,* Walter W. Bishop (ed.), pp. 19–28. Edinburgh: Scottish Academic Press.
Stiles, Daniel
    1979a   Recent Archaeological Findings at the Sterkfontein Site. *Nature 277*:381–382.
    1979b   Early Acheulian and Developed Oldowan. *Current Anthropology 20*:126–129.
Szalay, Frederick S.
    1971   Biological Level of Organization of the Chesowanja Robust Australopithecine. *Nature 234*:229–230.
Tobias, Phillip V.
    1965   The Early *Australopithecus* and *Homo* from Tanzania. *Anthropologie 3*:43–48.
    1976   African Hominids: Dating and Phylogeny. In *Human Origins: Louis Leakey and the East African Evidence,* Glynn Ll. Isaac and Elizabeth R. McCown (eds.), pp. 377–422. Menlo Park: Benjamin.
    1978   The South African Australopithecines in Time and Hominid Phylogeny with Special Reference to the Dating and Affinities of the Taung Skull. In *Early Hominids of Africa,* Clifford J. Jolly (ed.), pp. 45–84. London: Duckworth.
Tobias, Phillip V., and G. H. R. von Koenigswald
    1964   A Comparison between the Olduvai Hominines and Those of Java and Some Implications for Hominid Phylogeny. *Nature 204*:515–518.
Vrba, E. S.
    1974   Chronological and Ecological Implications of the Fossil Bovidae at the Sterkfontein Australopithecine Site. *Nature 250*:19–23.
    1975   Some Evidence of Chronology and Palaeoecology of Sterkfontein, Swartkrans, and Kromdraai from the Fossil Bovidae. *Nature 254*:301–304.
    1979   A New Study of the Scapula of *Australopithecus africanus* from Sterkfontein. *American Journal of Physical Anthropology 51*:117–130.
Walker, Alan
    1972   Chesowanja Australopithecine. *Nature 238*:108–109.
Walker, Alan, and Richard E. F. Leakey
    1978   The Hominids of East Turkana. *Scientific American 239*:54–66.
Wallace, John A.
    1975   Dietary Adaptations of *Australopithecus* and Early *Homo*. In *Paleoanthropology: Morphology and Paleoecology,* Russell H. Tuttle (ed.), pp. 203–223. The Hague: Mouton.
White, Tim D.
    1977   New Fossil Hominids from Laetolil, Tanzania. *American Journal of Physical Anthropology 46*:197–229.

White, Tim D., and J. M. Harris
    1977   Suid Evolution and Correlation of African Hominid Localities. *Science*
            198:13–21.
Wolpoff, M. H.
    1978b   Analogies and Interpretation in Palaeoanthropology. In *Early Hominids*
            of Africa, Clifford J. Jolly (ed.), pp. 461–504. London: Duckworth.

CHAPTER 11. CONCLUSION: BECOMING HUMAN

Azen, Edwin A.; Walter Leutenegger; and Erwin H. Peters
    1978   Evolutionary and Dietary Aspects of Salivary Basic (Pb) and Post Pb
            (PPb) Proteins in Anthropoid Primates. *Nature 273*:775–778.
Darwin, Charles
    1871   *The Descent of Man and Selection in Relation to Sex.* London: John
            Murray.
Gaulin, Steven J. C., and Melvin Konner
    1977   On the Natural Diet of Primates, Including Humans. In *Nutrition and*
            the Brain, vol. 1, R. J. Wurtman and J. J. Wurtman (eds.), pp. 1–87.
            New York: Raven Press.
Geertz, Clifford
    1973   *The Interpretation of Cultures: Selected Essays.* New York: Basic
            Books.
Gentry, Roger
    1970   Social Behavior of the Stellar Sea Lion. Dissertation, University of
            California, Santa Cruz.
Gould, Richard A.
    1978   Review of *Kalahari Hunter-Gatherers: Studies of the !Kung San and*
            Their Neighbors, Richard B. Lee and Irven DeVore (eds.), *American*
            Journal of Physical Anthropology 48:262–266.
Johanson, Donald C; Yves Coppens; and Maurice Taieb
    1976   Pliocene Hominid Remains from Hadar, Central Afar, Ethiopia. Ms.
            from Les plus anciens hominidés, UISPP, 9th Congress.
Johanson, Donald C., and Maurice Taieb
    1976   Plio-Pleistocene Hominid Discoveries in Hadar, Ethiopia. *Nature*
            260:293–297.
Leakey, M. D.; R. L. Hay; G. H. Curtis; R. E. Drake; M. K. Jackes; and T. D.
            White
    1976   Fossil Hominids from the Laetolil Beds. *Nature 262*:460–466.
Le Boeuf, Burney J.
    1974   Male-Male Competition and Reproductive Success in Elephant Seals.
            American Zoologist 14:163–176.
Linton, Sally
    1971   Woman the Gatherer: Male Bias in Anthropology. In *Women in*
            Cross-Cultural Perspective: A Preliminary Sourcebook, Sue-Ellen Jac-
            obs (ed.), pp. 9–21. Urbana: University of Illinois Press. (Reprinted
            1975, under the name of Sally Slocum, in *Toward an Anthropology*
            of Women, Rayna R. Reiter (ed.), pp. 36–50. New York: Monthly
            Review Press.)

McGrew, William C.
　　1977　Socialization and Object Manipulation of Wild Chimpanzees. In *Primate Bio-Social Development: Biological, Social, and Ecological Determinants*, Suzanne Chevalier-Skolnikoff and Frank E. Poirier (eds.), pp. 261–288. New York: Garland.
　　1979　Evolutionary Implication of Sex Differences in Chimpanzee Predation and Tool Use. In *The Great Apes*, Perspectives on Human Evolution, vol. 5, D. A. Hamburg and E. R. McCown (eds.), pp. 441–463. Menlo Park: Benjamin/Cummings.

Nishida, Toshisada
　　1973　The Ant Gathering Behavior by the Use of Tools among Wild Chimpanzees of the Mahali Mountains. *Journal of Human Evolution* 2:357–370.

Taieb, M.; D. C. Johanson; Y. Coppens; and J. L. Aronson
　　1976　Geological and Palaeontological Background of Hadar Hominid Site, Afar, Ethiopia. *Nature* 260:289–293.

Tanner, Nancy M.
　　1975　Selection and Hominid Origins: The Role of Females in Speciation. Paper presented at the Behavioral Genetics Association Meetings (Spring), Dallas.

Tanner, Nancy M., and Adrienne L. Zihlman
　　1976a　Women in Evolution. 1. Innovation and Selection in Human Origins. *Signs: Journal of Women in Culture and Society* 1:585–608.

Teleki, Geza
　　1974　Chimpanzee Subsistence Technology: Materials and Skills. *Journal of Human Evolution* 3:575–594.

Zihlman, Adrienne L.
　　1978a　Motherhood in Transition: From Ape to Human. In *Family Formation and First Child*, W. Miller and L. Newman (eds.), pp. 35–50. Chapel Hill: Carolina Population Center Publications.
　　1978b　Women and Evolution. 2. Subsistence and Social Organization among Early Hominids. *Signs: Journal of Women in Culture and Society* 4:4–20.
　　1978d　The Importance of the Invention of Gathering by Females as an Innovation in Human Evolution. Paper presented at the Distinguished Lecture Series, Foundation for Research into the Origin of Man, New York.

Zihlman, Adrienne L., and Nancy M. Tanner
　　1974　Becoming Human: Putting Women in Evolution. Paper presented at the Annual Meetings of the American Anthropological Society, Mexico City.
　　1979　Gathering and the Hominid Adaptation. In *Female Hierarchies*, Lionel Tiger and Heather M. Fowler (eds.), pp. 163–194. Chicago: Beresford Book Service.

Acknowledgments and bibliography for illustrations

The illustrations, maps, and charts in this book present the work of myself and the artist Dee Anne Hooker, our interpretations of data, photographs, and illustrations, with the research assistance of Tina de Benedictis, Mary Hilger, and John Olmsted. I wish to acknowledge the many important sources of inspiration and information that went into these figures. Illustrations, maps, and charts are listed separately, with illustrations listed first, maps second, and charts and diagrams last.

ILLUSTRATIONS

Title page

Goodall, Jane van Lawick. 1967b. *My Friends the Wild Chimpanzees.* Washington: National Geographic Society.

Opening, Chapter 1

Gruber, Howard E. 1974. *Darwin on Man: A Psychological Study of Scientific Creativity.* New York: Dutton.

Figure 1:1

Heiser, Charles B., Jr. 1973. *Seed to Civilization: The Story of Man's Food.* San Francisco: Freeman.
White, Peter T. 1967. Hopes and Fears in Booming Thailand. *National Geographic 132:76–125.*
Williams, A. W. 1973. Dietary Patterns in Three Mexican Villages. In *Man and His Foods: Studies in the Ethnobotany of Nutrition – Contemporary, Primitive, and Pre-Historic Non-European Diets,* C. Earle Smith, Jr. (ed.), pp. 51–73. University: University of Alabama Press.

Figure 1:2

Squire, Geoffrey. 1974. *Dress and Society, 1560–1970.* New York: Viking Press.

Figure 1:3

Howell, Nancy. 1976. The Population of the Dobe Area !Kung. In *Kalahari Hunter-Gatherers: Studies of the !Kung San and Their Neighbors,* Richard B. Lee and Irven DeVore (eds.), pp. 137–151. Cambridge: Harvard University Press.

Figure 1:4

Truswell, A. Stewart, and John D. L. Hansen. 1976. Medical Research among the !Kung. In *Kalahari Hunter-Gatherers: Studies of the !Kung San and Their Neighbors*, Richard B. Lee and Irven DeVore (eds.), pp. 166–194. Cambridge: Harvard University Press.

Figure 2:1

Scott, Laurence K., and David Baze. 1977. *My Childbirth Coloring Book*. Chicago: Academy Press.

Figure 2:2

Napier, John. 1976. *Monkeys without Tails*. London: British Broadcasting Corporation.

Figure 2:3

Oakley, Kenneth P. 1951. A Definition of Man. In *Culture and the Evolution of Man*, M. F. Ashley Montagu (ed.), pp. 3–12. New York: Oxford University Press. Reprint, 1962.

Figure 2:4

Lee, Richard B., and Irven DeVore, eds. 1976. *Kalahari Hunter-Gatherers: Studies of the !Kung San and Their Neighbors*. Cambridge: Harvard University Press.
Lee, Richard B. 1979. *The !Kung San: Men, Women, and Work in a Foraging Society*. Cambridge: Cambridge University Press.
Marshall, Lorna. 1976. *The !Kung of Nyae Nyae*. Cambridge: Harvard University Press.
Richards, Audrey I. 1939. *Land, Labour and Diet in Northern Rhodesia: An Economic Study of the Bemba Tribe*. London: Oxford University Press.

Opening, Chapter 3

Leakey, Louis S. B. 1969. *The Wild Realm: Animals of East Africa*. Washington, D.C.: National Geographic Society.

Figure 3:1

Eimerl, Sarel; Irven DeVore; and the Editors of Time-Life Books. 1965. *The Primates*. New York: Time-Life Books. Reprint, 1968.
Goodall, Jane van Lawick. 1968. The Behaviour of Free-living Chimpanzees in the Gombe Stream Reserve. *Animal Behaviour Monographs* 1:161–311.
Penfield, Wilder. 1968. Engrams in the Human Brain: Mechanisms of Memory. *Proceedings of the Royal Society of Medicine* 61(8):831–840.
Schultz, Adolph H. 1926. Fetal Growth of Man and Other Primates. *Quarterly Review of Biology* 1:465–521.
   1931. Man as a Primate. *Scientific Monthly* 33:385–412.
   1956. Postembryonic Age Changes. *Primatologia: Handbook of Primatology* 1:887–964.
   1969. The Skeleton of the Chimpanzee. In *The Chimpanzee*, vol. 1, *Anatomy*,

Behavior and Diseases of Chimpanzees, G. H. Bourne (ed.), pp. 50–103. Basel: Karger.

Washburn, Sherwood L. 1968. *The Study of Human Evolution.* Condon Lectures. Eugene: Oregon State System of Higher Education.

Washburn, S. L., and Ruth Moore. 1974. *Ape into Man: A Study of Human Evolution.* Boston: Little, Brown.

Weiner, J. S. 1971. *The Natural History of Man.* New York: Universe Books.

Figure 3:2

McGrew, W. C. 1977. Socialization and Object Manipulation of Wild Chimpanzees. In *Primate Bio-Social Development: Biological, Social, and Ecological Determinants,* Suzanne Chevalier-Skolnikoff and Frank E. Poirier (eds.), pp. 261–288. New York: Garland.

Figure 3:3

Goodall, Jane van Lawick. 1971. *In the Shadow of Man.* Boston: Houghton Mifflin.

   1975a. The Behavior of the Chimpanzee. In *Hominisation and Behavior,* G. Kurth and I. Eibl-Eibesfeldt (eds.), pp. 74–136. Stuttgart: Gustav Fischer.

Figure 3:4

Sarich, Vincent M., and John E. Cronin. 1976. Molecular Systematics of the Primates. In *Molecular Anthropology: Genes and Proteins in the Evolutionary Ascent of the Primates,* Morris Goodman, Richard E. Tashian, and Jeanne H. Tashian (eds.), pp. 141–170. New York: Plenum Press.

Figure 3:6

Eimerl, Sarel; Irven DeVore; and the Editors of Time-Life Books. 1965. *The Primates.* New York: Time-Life Books. Reprint, 1968.

Goodall, Jane van Lawick. 1968. The Behaviour of Free-living Chimpanzees in the Gombe Stream Reserve. *Animal Behaviour Monographs* 1:161–311.

Washburn, S. L., and Ruth Moore. 1974. *Ape into Man: A Study of Human Evolution.* Boston: Little, Brown.

Figure 3:7

Leakey, Louis S. B. 1969. *The Wild Realm: Animals of East Africa.* Washington, D.C.: National Geographic Society.

Van Couvering, Judith A. H. and John A. 1976. Early Miocene Mammal Fossils from East Africa: Aspects of Geology, Faunistics and Palio-ecology. In *Human Origins: Louis Leakey and the East African Evidence,* G. Ll. Isaac, and E. R. McCown (eds), pp. 155–207. Menlo Park: Benjamin.

Figure 3:8

Leakey, M. D.; R. L. Hay; G. H. Curtis; R. E. Drake; M. K. Jackes; and T. D. White. 1976. Fossil Hominids from the Laetolil Beds. *Nature* 262:460–466.

Pilbeam, David; Grant E. Meyer; Catherine Badgley; M. D. Rose; M. H. L. Pickford; A. K. Behrensmeyer; and S. M. Ibrahim Shah. 1977. New Hominoid Primates from the Siwaliks of Pakistan and Their Bearing on Hominoid Evolution. *Nature* 270:689–695.

Tauxe, Lisa. 1979. A New Date for *Ramapithecus*. *Nature 282*:399–401.
White, Tim D. 1977. New Fossil Hominids from Laetolil, Tanzania. *American Journal of Physical Anthropology 46*:197–229.

Figure 3:10

Goodall, Jane van Lawick. 1967. *My Friends the Wild Chimpanzees*. Washington, D.C.: National Geographic Society.
Hill, W. C. Osman. 1969. The Nomenclature, Taxonomy, and Distribution of Chimpanzees. In *The Chimpanzee*, vol. 1, *Anatomy, Behavior, and Diseases of Chimpanzees*, G. H. Bourne (ed.), pp. 22–49. Basel: Karger.
Jolly, Alison. 1972. *The Evolution of Primate Behavior*. New York: Macmillan.

Opening, Chapter 4

Goodall, Jane van Lawick. 1967. *My Friends the Wild Chimpanzees*. Washington, D.C.: National Geographic Society.

Figure 4:2

Albrecht, Helmut, and Sinclair C. Dunnett. 1971. *Chimpanzees in Western Africa*. Studies in Ethology. Munich: Piper.
Goodall, Jane van Lawick. 1968. The Behaviour of Free-living Chimpanzees in the Gombe Stream Reserve. *Animal Behaviour Monographs 1*:161–311.
        1971. *In the Shadow of Man*. Boston: Houghton Mifflin.

Figure 4:3

Goodall, Jane van Lawick. 1967. *My Friends the Wild Chimpanzees*. Washington, D.C.: National Geographic Society.

Figure 4:4

Albrecht, Helmut, and Sinclair C. Dunnett. 1971. *Chimpanzees in Western Africa*. Studies in Ethology. Munich: Piper.

Figure 4:5

Biegert, J., and R. Maurer. 1972. Rumpfskelettlänge, Allometrien und Körperproportionen bei catarrhinen Primaten. *Folia Primatologica 17*:142–156.
Coleman, H. 1971. Comparison of the Pelvic Growth Patterns of Chimpanzee and Man. In *Proceedings of the Third International Congress of Primatology, Zurich 1970*, vol. 1, *Taxonomy, Anatomy, Reproduction*, J. Biegert and W. Leutenegger (eds.), pp. 176–182. Basel: Karger.
Eimerl, Sarel; Irven DeVore; and the Editors of Time-Life Books. 1965. *The Primates*. New York: Time-Life Books. Reprint, 1968.
Fick, Rudolf Armin. 1911. *Handbuch der Anatomie und Mechanik der Gelenke unter Berucksichtigungter bewegenden Muskeln*, vol. 3, *T1. Spezielle Gelunk und Muselmechanik*. Jena: Fischer.
Kummer, B. 1962. Gait and Posture under Normal Conditions, with Special Reference to the Lower Limbs. In *Clinical Orthopaedics*, vol. 25, Anthony F. De Palma (ed.), with the assistance of the Associate Editors, Board of Advi-

sory Editors, and Board of Corresponding Editors, pp. 32–41. Philadelphia: Lippincott.

Schultz, Adolph H. 1950. The Specializations of Man and His Place among the Catarrhine Primates. *Cold Spring Harbor Symposia on Quantitative Biology 15* (Origin and Evolution of Man):37–53.

1957. Past and Present Views of Man's Specializations. *Irish Journal of Medical Science*, no. 380, 6th ser.:341–356.

1969. The Skeleton of the Chimpanzee. In *The Chimpanzee*, vol. 1, *Anatomy, Behavior and Diseases of Chimpanzees*, G. H. Bourne (ed.), pp. 50–103. Basel: Karger.

Zihlman, Adrienne L. 1967. Human Locomotion: A Reappraisal of the Functional and Anatomical Evidence. Dissertation, University of California, Berkeley.

Figure 4:6

Goodall, Jane. 1965. Chimpanzees of the Gombe Stream Reserve. In *Primate Behavior: Field Studies of Monkeys and Apes*, Irven DeVore (ed.), pp. 425–473. New York: Holt, Rinehart and Winston.

Goodall, Jane van Lawick. 1967. *My Friends the Wild Chimpanzees*. Washington, D.C.: National Geographic Society.

1971. *In the Shadow of Man*. Boston: Houghton Mifflin.

Figure 4:7

Albrecht, Helmut, and Sinclair C. Dunnett. 1971. *Chimpanzees in Western Africa*. Studies in Ethology. Munich: Piper.

Goodall, Jane van Lawick. 1971. *In the Shadow of Man*. Boston: Houghton Mifflin.

Figure 4:8

Goodall, Jane van Lawick. 1967. *My Friends the Wild Chimpanzees*. Washington, D.C.: National Geographic Society.

1971. *In the Shadow of Man*. Boston: Houghton Mifflin.

Opening, Chapter 5

Goodall, Jane van Lawick. 1967. *My Friends the Wild Chimpanzees*. Washington, D.C.: National Geographic Society.

Figure 5:1

Goodall, Jane van Lawick. 1975a. The Behavior of the Chimpanzee. In *Hominisation and Behavior*, G. Kurth and I. Eibl-Eibesfeldt (eds.), pp. 74–136. Stuttgart: Gustav Fischer.

Figure 5:2

Goodall, Jane van Lawick. 1975a. The Behavior of the Chimpanzee. In *Hominisation and Behavior*, G. Kurth and I. Eibl-Eibesfeldt (eds.), pp. 74–136. Stuttgart: Gustav Fischer.

Figure 5:3

Goodall, Jane van Lawick. 1968. A Preliminary Report on Expressive Movements and Communication in the Gombe Stream Chimpanzees. In *Primates: Studies in Adaptation and Variability,* Phyllis C. Jay (ed.), pp. 313–374. New York: Holt, Rinehart and Winston.

Figure 5:4

Goodall, Jane van Lawick. 1967. *My Friends the Wild Chimpanzees.* Washington, D.C.: National Geographic Society.

Figure 5:5

Edey, Maitland A., and the Editors of Time-Life Books. 1972. *The Missing Link.* New York: Time-Life Books.

Figure 5:6

Albrecht, Helmut, and Sinclair C. Dunnett. 1971. *Chimpanzees in Western Africa.* Studies in Ethology. Munich: Piper.

Figure 5:7

Goodall, Jane van Lawick. 1975a. The Behavior of the Chimpanzee. In *Hominisation and Behavior,* G. Kurth and I. Eibl-Eibesfeldt (eds.), pp. 74–136. Stuttgart: Gustav Fischer.

Figure 5:8

Goodall, Jane van Lawick. 1975a. The Behavior of the Chimpanzee. In *Hominisation and Behavior,* G. Kurth and I. Eibl-Eibesfeldt (eds.), pp. 74–136. Stuttgart: Gustav Fischer.

Figure 5:9

Goodall, Jane van Lawick. 1971. *In the Shadow of Man.* Boston: Houghton Mifflin.

Figure 5:10

Goodall, Jane van Lawick. 1967. *My Friends the Wild Chimpanzees.* Washington, D.C.: National Geographic Society.

Figure 5:11

Goodall, Jane van Lawick. 1967. *My Friends the Wild Chimpanzees.* Washington, D.C.: National Geographic Society.

Figure 5:12

Mann, William M. 1938. Monkey Folk. *National Geographic* 73:615–655.

Opening, Chapter 6

Goodall, Jane van Lawick. 1967. *My Friends the Wild Chimpanzees.* Washington, D.C.: National Geographic Society.

Figure 6:1

Albrecht, Helmut, and Sinclair C. Dunnett. 1971. *Chimpanzees in Western Africa.* Studies in Ethology. Munich: Piper.
Goodall, Jane van Lawick. 1967. *My Friends the Wild Chimpanzees.* Washington, D.C.: National Geographic Society.

1968. The Behaviour of Free-living Chimpanzees in the Gombe Stream Reserve. *Animal Behaviour Monographs* 1:161–311.

Figure 6:2

Goodall, Jane van Lawick. 1971. *In the Shadow of Man.* Boston: Houghton Mifflin.

Figure 6:3

Fouts, R. S. 1975. Communication with Chimpanzees. In *Hominisation and Behavior,* G. Kurth and I. Eibl-Eibesfeldt (eds.), pp. 137–158. Stuttgart: Gustav Fischer.
Linden, Eugene. 1976. *Apes, Men, and Language.* New York: Penguin Books.

Figure 6:4

Rumbaugh, Duane M., ed. 1977. Frontispiece. *Language Learning by a Chimpanzee: The Lana Project.* New York: Academic Press.
Warner, Harold, and Charles L. Bell. 1977. The System: Design and Operation. In *Language Learning by a Chimpanzee: The Lana Project,* Duane M. Rumbaugh (ed.), pp. 143–155. New York: Academic Press.

Figure 6:5

Savage-Rumbaugh, E. Sue; Beverly J. Wilkerson; and Roger Bakeman. 1977. Spontaneous Gestural Communication among Conspecifics in the Pygmy Chimpanzee. In *Progress in Ape Research,* G. H. Bourne (ed.), pp. 97–116. New York: Academic Press.

Figure 7:2

Sabater Pí, Jorge. 1974. An Elementary Industry of the Chimpanzees in the Okorobikó Mountains, Rio Muni (Republic of Equatorial Guinea), West Africa. *Primates* 15:351–364.

Figure 7:3

Lee, Richard B., and Irven DeVore. 1976. *Kalahari Hunter-Gatherers: Studies of the !Kung San and Their Neighbors.* Cambridge: Harvard University Press.

Figure 7:4

Goodall, Jane van Lawick. 1968. The Behaviour of Free-living Chimpanzees in the Gombe Stream Reserve. *Animal Behaviour Monographs* 1:161–311.

Figure 7:5

Draper, Patricia. 1976. Social and Economic Constraints on Child Life among the !Kung. In *Kalahari Hunter-Gatherers: Studies of the !Kung San and Their Neighbors,* Richard B. Lee and Irven DeVore (eds.), pp. 199–217. Cambridge: Harvard University Press.

Figure 7:6

Goodall, Jane van Lawick. 1967. *My Friends the Wild Chimpanzees.* Washington, D.C.: National Geographic Society.

Figure 7:7

Kortlandt, Adriaan. 1967. Experimentation with Chimpanzees in the Wild. In *Neue Ergebnisse der Primatologie* [Progress in primatology], First Congress of the International Primatological Society, Frankfurt. D. Starck, R. Schneider, and H. J. Kuhn (eds.), pp. 208–244. Stuttgart: Gustav Fischer.

Reynolds, Vernon. 1967. *The Apes: The Gorilla, Chimpanzee, Orangutan, and Gibbon – Their History and Their World.* London: Cassell.

Figure 7:8

Goodall, Jane van Lawick. 1971. *In the Shadow of Man.* Boston: Houghton Mifflin.

Figure 7:9

Jolly, Alison. 1972. *The Evolution of Primate Behavior.* New York: Macmillan.

Figure 8:6

Goodall, Jane. 1965. Chimpanzees of the Gombe Stream Reserve. In *Primate Behavior: Field Studies of Monkeys and Apes,* Irven DeVore (ed.), pp. 425–473. New York: Holt, Rinehart and Winston.

Figure 8:7

Fenart, R., and R. Deblock. 1973. Pan paniscus *et* Pan troglodytes *Craniométrie: étude Comparative et Ontogénique Selon les Méthodes Classiques et Vestibulaire,* vol. 1. Tervuren, Belgium: Musée Royal de l'Afrique Centrale, Annales, ser. in-8^0, *Sciences Zoologiques,* no. 204:1–473.

Leakey, M. D.; R. L. Hay; G. H. Curtis; R. E. Drake; M. K. Jackes; and T. D. White. 1976. Fossil Hominids from the Laetolil Beds. *Nature* 262:460–466.

White, Tim D. 1977. New Fossil Hominids from Laetolil, Tanzania. *American Journal of Physical Anthropology* 46:197–229.

Figure 8:9

Johanson, Donald C. 1976. Ethiopia Yields First "Family" of Early Man. *National Geographic 150:791–811.*

Taieb, Maurice; D. Carl Johanson; and Yves Coppens. 1975. Expédition Internationale de l'Afar, Ethiopie (3e Campagne 1974); Découverte d'Hominidés Plio-Pléistocènes à Hadar. Académie des Sciences, Paris: *Comptes Rendus Hebdomadaires des Séances* 281, ser. D:1297–1300.

Figure 8:10

Johanson, D. C., and M. Taieb. 1976. Plio-Pleistocène Hominid Discoveries in Hadar, Ethiopia. *Nature* 260:293–297.

Kinzey, W. G. 1970. Basic Rectangle of the Mandible. *Nature 228:289–290.*

Tobias, P. V. 1967. *Olduvai Gorge,* L. S. B. Leakey (ed.), vol. 2, *The Cranium and Maxillary Dentition of Australopithecus (Zinjanthropus) boisei.* Cambridge: Cambridge University Press.

Figure 8:11

Azen, Edwin A.; Walter Leutenegger; and Erwin H. Peters. 1978. Evolutionary and Dietary Aspects of Salivary Basic (Pb) and Post Pb (PPb) Proteins in Anthropoid Primates. *Nature* 273:775–778.

Figure 8:12

Palmer, Eve, and Norah Pitman. 1972. *Trees of Southern Africa: Covering All Known Indigenous Species in the Republic of South Africa, South-West Africa, Botswana, Lesotho, and Swaziland,* vol. 2. Cape Town: Balkema.

Figure 9:3

Howell, F. Clark, and the Editors of Time-Life Books. 1965. *Early Man.* New York: Time-Life Books. Reprint, 1970.

Figure 9:4

Goodall, Jane van Lawick. 1968. The Behaviour of Free-living Chimpanzees in the Gombe Stream Reserve. *Animal Behaviour Monographs* 1:161–311.
Schultz, Adolph H. 1940. Growth and Development of the Chimpanzee. *Contributions to Embryology,* no. 170 (Carnegie Institution of Washington Publication no. 518):1–64.

Figure 9:5

Day, Michael H. 1965. *Guide to Fossil Man: A Handbook of Human Palaeontology.* London: Cassell.
Koenigswald, G. H. R. von. 1962. *The Evolution of Man.* Ann Arbor: University of Michigan Press. Reprint, 1976.
Pilbeam, David. 1972a. *The Ascent of Man: An Introduction to Human Evolution.* New York: Macmillan.

Figure 9:6

Penfield, Wilder. 1968. Engrams in the Human Brain: Mechanisms of Memory. *Proceedings of the Royal Society of Medicine* 61:831–840.
Schepers, G. W. H. 1946. *The South African Fossil Ape-Men, the Australopithecinae. 2. The Endocranial Casts of the South African Ape-Men.* Transvaal Museum Memoir no. 2:155–272.
Swindler, Daris R., and Chas. D. Wood. 1973. *An Atlas of Baboon, Chimpanzee and Man.* Seattle and London: University of Washington Press.
Weiner, J. S. 1971. *The Natural History of Man.* New York: Universe Books.

Figure 9:7

Coon, Nelson. 1974. *The Dictionary of Useful Plants.* Emmaus, Pa.: Rodale Press.
Leakey, M. D. 1971. *Olduvai Gorge,* vol. 3, *Excavations in Beds I and II, 1960–1963.* Cambridge: Cambridge University Press.
Story, R. 1958. Some Plants Used by the Bushmen in Obtaining Food and Water. Botanical Survey Memoir no. 30. Union of South Africa: Dept. of Agriculture, Division of Botany.

Figure 9:8

Harrison, S. G.; G. B. Masefield; and Michael Wallis. 1969. *The Oxford Book of Food Plants*. London: Oxford University Press.
Leakey, M. D. 1971. *Olduvai Gorge*, vol. 3, *Excavations in Beds I and II, 1960–1963*. Cambridge: Cambridge University Press.

Figure 10:8

Day, M. H.; R. E. F. Leakey; A. C. Walker; and B. A. Wood. 1975. New Hominids from East Rudolf, Kenya, 1. *American Journal of Physical Anthropology* 42:461–475.
Leakey, R. E. F. 1971. Further Evidence of Lower Pleistocene Hominids from East Rudolf, North Kenya. *Nature 231*:241–245.
Leakey, R. E. F.; J. M. Mungai; A. C. Walker. 1971. New Australopithecines from East Rudolf, Kenya. *American Journal of Physical Anthropology 35*:175–186.

Figure 10:10

Carney, J.; A. Hill; J. A. Miller; and A. Walker. 1971. Late Australopithecine from Baringo District, Kenya. *Nature 230*:509–514.
Szalay, Frederick S. 1971. Biological Level of Organization of the Chesowanja Robust Australopithecine. *Nature 234*:229–230.

Figure 11:1

Chang, Shuhua. 1977. The Gentle Yamis of Orchid Island. *National Geographic 151*:98–109.
Ellis, William S. 1977. Malaysia: Youthful Nation with Growing Pains. *National Geographic 151*:635–667.
Judge, Joseph. 1971. The Zulus: Black Nation in a Land of Apartheid. *National Geographic 140*:738–775.
Robinson, Richard. 1979. The Ace Frehley Solo Interview. *Hit Parader*, no. 175 (February):34–36.
White, Peter T. 1967. Hopes and Fears in Booming Thailand. *National Geographic 132*:76–125.

Figure 11:2

Jordan, Robert Paul. 1976. Pioneers Head North from Edmonton, Gateway to Canada's "Now" Frontier. *National Geographic 150*:480–511.
Judge, Joseph. 1971. The Zulus: Black Nation in a Land of Apartheid. *National Geographic 140*:738–775.
Topping, Audrey. 1971. Return to Changing China. *National Geographic 140*:800–833.

Figure 11:3

1978. Advertisement for Chanel. *Vogue 168* (November).

Figure 11:4

Day, M. H.; M. D. Leakey; C. Magori, 1980. A New Hominid Fossil Skull (L. H. 18) from the Ngaloba Beds, Laetoli, Northern Tanzania. *Nature 284*:55–56.

MAPS

Figures 3:9, 4:1, 7:1, 8:3, 8:4, 9:1, 11:4

Adinegro, Adam Bachtiar; W. F. Heinemeyer; J. E. Romein; and Sutopo. 1952. *Atlas Semesta Dunia*. Djakarta, Indonesia: Badan Penerbit Djambatan N. V.

Aubreville, A.; P. Duvigneaud; A. C. Hoyle; R. W. J. Keay; F. A. Mondonça; and R. E. G. Pichi-Sermolli. 1958. Vegetation Map of Africa South of the Tropic of Cancer. Published on behalf of the Association pour l'Etude Taxonomique de la Flore d'Afrique Tropicale, with the assistance of UNESCO. London: Cooke, Hammond and Kell.

Baker, B. H.; P. A. Mohr; and L. A. J. Williams. 1972. Geology of the Eastern Rift System of Africa. Geological Society of America, Special Paper 136.

Clark, J. Desmond. 1967. *Atlas of African Prehistory*. Wenner-Gren Foundation. Chicago: University of Chicago Press.

Cooke, H. B. S. 1978. Africa: The Physical Setting. In *Evolution of African Mammals*, Vincent J. Maglio and H. B. S. Cooke (eds.). Cambridge: Harvard University Press.

Cooke, H. B. S., and V. J. Maglio. 1972. Plio-Pleistocene Stratigraphy in East Africa in Relation to Proboscidean and Suid Evolution. In *Calibration of Hominoid Evolution*, W. W. Bishop and J. A. Miller (eds.), pp. 303–329. Edinburgh: Scottish Academic Press.

Editors of Time-Life Books. 1973. *The First Men*. New York: Time-Life Books.

Hill, Osman W. C. 1969. The Nomenclature, Taxonomy, and Distribution of Chimpanzees. In *The Chimpanzee*, vol. 1, *Anatomy, Behavior and Diseases of Chimpanzees*, G. H. Bourne (ed.), pp. 22–46. Basel: Karger.

Howells, W. W. 1973. *Evolution of the Genus Homo*. Reading, Mass.: Addison Wesley.

Isaac, Glynn Ll.; and Elizabeth R. McCown. 1976. *Human Origins: Louis Leakey and the East African Evidence*. Menlo Park: Benjamin.

Johanson, Donald C. 1976. Ethiopia Yields "First Family" of Early Man. *National Geographic 150*:791–811.

Kano, Takayoshi. 1972. Distribution and Adaptation of the Chimpanzee on the Eastern Shore of Lake Tanganyika. *Kyoto University African Studies 7*:37–129.

Leakey, M. D., and R. L. Hay. 1979. Pliocene Footprints in the Laetolil Beds at Laetoli, Northern Tanzania. *Nature 278*:317–323.

Leakey, M. D.; R. L. Hay; G. H. Curtis; R. E. Drake; M. K. Jackes; and T. D. White. 1976. Fossil Hominids from the Laetolil Beds. *Nature 262*:460–466.

Merrick, H. V.; J. De Heinzelin; P. Haesarts; and F. C. Howell. 1973. Archaeological Occurrences of Early Pleistocene Age from the Shungura Formation, Lower Omo Valley, Ethiopia. *Nature 242*:572–575.

Merrick, H. V., and J. P. S. Merrick. 1976. Archeological Occurrences of Earlier Pleistocene Age from the Shungura Formation. In *Earliest Man and Environments in the Lake Rudolf Basin: Stratigraphy, Paleoecology, and Evolution*, Yves Coppens, F. Clark Howell, Glynn Ll. Isaac, and Richard E. F. Leakey (eds.), pp. 574–584. Chicago: University of Chicago Press.

Oakley, Kenneth P.; Bernard G. Campbell; and Theya I. Molleson, eds. 1977. *Catalogue of Fossil Hominids*, part 1, *Africa*. 2d ed. London: Trustees of the British Museum.

Palmer, Eve, and Norah Pitman. 1972. *Trees of Southern Africa: Covering All Known Indigenous Species in the Republic of South Africa, South-West Africa, Botswana, Lesotho, and Swaziland,* vol. 2. Cape Town: Balkema.
Schultz, Adolph H. 1969. *The Life of Primates.* New York: Universe Books and London: Weidingfeld and Nicolson.
U.S. Central Intelligence Agency. 1977. *Maps of World's Nations,* vol. 2, *Africa.* Washington, D.C.: U.S. Government Printing Office.

Figure 10:9

Isaac, Glynn Ll., J. W. K. Harris, and D. Crader. 1976. Archeological Evidence from the Koobi Fora Formation. In *Earliest Man and Environments in the Lake Rudolf Basin: Stratigraphy, Paleoecology, and Evolution,* Yves Coppens, F. Clark Howell, Glynn Ll. Isaac, and Richard E. F. Leakey (eds.), pp. 533–551. Chicago: University of Chicago Press.
Leakey, Richard, and Glynn Isaac. 1976. East Rudolf: An Introduction to the Abundance of New Evidence. In *Human Origins: Louis Leakey and the East African Evidence,* Glynn Ll. Isaac and Elizabeth R. McCown (eds.), pp. 307–332. Menlo Park: Benjamin.

CHARTS AND DIAGRAMS

Figure 3:5

Andrews, Peter, and Ibrahim Tekkaya. 1976. *Ramapithecus* in Kenya and Turkey. Ms. from Les plus anciens hominidés, UISPP, 9th Congress.
Andrews, Peter, and H. Tobien. 1977. New Miocene Locality in Turkey with Evidence on the Origin of *Ramapithecus* and *Sivapithecus. Nature* 268:699–701.
Behrensmeyer, A. K. 1976. Lothagam Hill, Kanapoi, and Ekora: A General Summary of Stratigraphy and Faunas. In *Earliest Man and Environments in the Lake Rudolf Basin,* Yves Coppens, F. Clark Howell, Glynn Ll. Isaac, and Richard E. F. Leakey (eds.), pp. 163–170. Chicago: University of Chicago Press.
Berggren, W. A., and J. A. Van Couvering. 1974. The Late Neogene: Biostratigraphy, Geochronology, and Paleoclimatology of the Last 15 Million Years in Marine and Continental Sequences. *Palaeogeography, Palaeoclimatology, Palaeoecology* 16:1–216.
Boaz, Noel T. 1977. Paleoecology of Early Hominidae in Africa. Kroeber Anthropological Society Papers, no. 50:37–62.
Brace, C. L.; P. E. Mahler; R. B. Rosen. 1972. Tooth Measurements and the Rejection of the Taxon *Homo habilis. Yearbook of Physical Anthropology* 16:50–68.
Brain, C. K. 1974b. Some Aspects of the South African Australopithecine Sites and Their Bone Accumulations. Conference on the African Hominidae of the Plio-Pleistocene: Evidence, Problems, and Strategies. Sponsored by Wenner-Gren Foundation for Anthropological Research, New York.
  1978. Some Aspects of the South African Australopithecine Sites and Their Bone Accumulations. In *Early Hominids of Africa,* Clifford J. Jolly (ed.), pp. 131–161. London: Duckworth.
Brock, A.; P. L. McFadden; and T. C. Partridge. 1977. Preliminary Palaeomagnetic Results from Makapansgat and Swartkrans. *Nature* 266:249–250.

Brown, F. H., and R. T. Shuey. 1976. Magnetostratigraphy of the Shungura and Usno Formations, Lower Omo Valley, Ethiopia. In *Earliest Man and Environments in the Lake Rudolf Basin*, Yves Coppens, F. Clark Howell, Glynn Ll. Isaac, and Richard E. F. Leakey (eds.), pp. 64–78. Chicago: University of Chicago Press.

Campbell, B. G., and R. L. Bernor. 1976. The Origin of the Hominidae: Africa or Asia? *Journal of Human Evolution* 5:441–454.

Cerling, T. E.; F. H. Brown; B. W. Cerling; G. H. Curtis; and R. E. Drake. 1979. Preliminary Correlations between the Koobi Fora and Shungura Formations, East Africa. *Nature* 279:118–121.

Curtis, G. H., and R. L. Hay. 1972. Further Geological Studies and Potassium-Argon Dating at Olduvai Gorge and Ngorongoro Crater. In *Calibration of Hominoid Evolution*, W. W. Bishop and J. A. Miller (eds.), pp. 289–301. Edinburgh: Scottish Academic Press.

Delson, Eric, and Peter Andrews. 1975. Evolution and Interrelationships of the Catarrhine Primates. In *Phylogeny of the Primates*, W. Patrick Luckett and Frederick S. Szalay (eds.), pp. 405–446. New York: Plenum.

Espenshade, Edward B., Jr., ed. 1970. *Goode's World Atlas*. 13th ed. Chicago: Rand McNally. 1971 printing.

Fleming, Stuart. 1976. Man Emerging. 1. The First 33 Million Years. *New Scientist* 71:6–8.

Haq, Bilal V.; W. W. Berggren; and John A. Van Couvering. 1977. Corrected Age of the Pliocene/Pleistocene Boundary. *Nature* 269:483–488.

Howell, F. Clark. 1978a. Hominidae. In *Evolution of African Mammals*, V. J. Maglio and H. B. S. Cooke (eds.), pp. 154–248. Cambridge: Harvard University Press.

1978b. Overview of the Pliocene and Earlier Pleistocene of the Lower Omo Basin, Southern Ethiopia. In *Early Hominids of Africa*, Clifford J. Jolly (ed.), pp. 85–130. London: Duckworth.

Howell, F. Clark, and Y. Coppens. 1976. An Overview of Hominidae from the Omo Succession, Ethiopia. In *Earliest Man and Environments in the Lake Rudolf Basin*, Yves Coppens, F. Clark Howell, Glynn Ll. Isaac, and Richard E. F. Leakey (eds.), pp. 522–532. Chicago: University of Chicago Press.

Jacob, Teuku. 1976. Man in Indonesia: Past, Present and Future. In *Modern Quaternary Research in Southeast Asia*, Vol. 2. Gert-Jan Bartstra and William Arnold Casparie (eds.), pp. 39–48. Rotterdam: Balkema.

Johanson, Donald C., and Maurice Taieb. 1978. Plio-Pleistocene Hominid Discoveries in Hadar, Central Afar, Ethiopia. In *Early Hominids of Africa*, Clifford J. Jolly (ed.), pp. 29–44. London: Duckworth.

Johanson, Donald C., and Tim White. 1979. A Systematic Assessment of Early African Hominids. *Science* 202:321–330.

Johanson, Donald C.; Tim D. White; and Yves Coppens. 1978. A New Species of the Genus *Australopithecus* (Primates: Hominidae) from the Pliocene of Eastern Africa. *Kirtlandia* 28:1–14.

Leakey, M. D. 1971. *Olduvai Gorge*. Vol. 3. Cambridge: Cambridge University Press.

1978. Olduvai Fossil Hominids: Their Stratigraphic Positions and Associations. In *Early Hominids of Africa*, Clifford J. Jolly (ed.), pp. 3–16. London: Duckworth.

1979. Footprints in the Ashes of Time. *National Geographic* 155:446–457.

Leakey, M. D., and R. L. Hay. 1979. Pliocene Footprints in the Laetolil Beds at Laetoli, Northern Tanzania. *Nature 278*:317–323.

Leakey, M. D.; R. L. Hay; G. H. Curtis; R. E. Drake; M. K. Jackes; and T. D. White. 1976. Fossil Hominids from the Laetolil Beds. *Nature 262*:460–466.

Leakey, Meave G., and Richard E. Leakey, eds. 1978. *Koobi Fora Research Project,* vol. 1. Oxford: Clarendon Press.

Morbeck, Mary Ellen. 1972. A Re-examination of the Forelimb of the Miocene *Hominoidea*. Dissertation, University of California, Berkeley.

Oakley, Kenneth P., Bernard G. Campbell, and Theya I. Molleson, eds. 1977. *Catalogue of Fossil Hominids,* part 1, *Africa*. 2d ed. London: Trustees of the British Museum.

Patterson, Bryan; Anna K. Behrensmeyer; and William D. Sills. 1970. Geology and Fauna of the New Pliocene Locality in Northwestern Kenya. *Nature 226*:918–921.

Patterson, Bryan, and W. W. Howells. 1967. Hominid Humeral Fragment from Early Pleistocene of Northwestern Kenya. *Science 156*:64–66.

Pickford, Martin. 1977. Pre-Human Fossils from Pakistan! *New Scientist 75*:578–580.

Pilbeam, David. 1976. Neogene Hominoids of South Asia and the Origins of Hominidae. *Les Plus Anciens Hominidés*, UISPP 9th Congress.

Pilbeam, David; Grant E. Meyer; Catherine Badgley; M. D. Rose; M. H. K. Pickford; A. K. Behrensmeyer; and S. M. Ibrahim Shah. 1977. New Hominoid Primates from the Siwaliks of Pakistan and Their Bearing on Hominoid Evolution. *Nature 270*:689–695.

Poirier, Frank E. 1977. *Fossil Evidence: The Human Evolutionary Journey*. 2d ed. Saint Louis: Mosby.

Sigmon, B. A. 1977. Contributions from Southern and Eastern Africa to the Study of Early Hominid Evolution. *Journal of Human Evolution* 6:245–257.

Tobias, Phillip V. 1975. New African Evidence on the Dating and the Phylogeny of the Plio-Pleistocene Hominidae. Royal Society of New Zealand, Bulletin no. 13: 289–296.

    1978. The South African Australopithecines in Time and Hominid Phylogeny, with Special Reference to the Dating and Affinities of the Taung Skull. In *Early Hominids of Africa*, Clifford J. Jolly (ed.), pp. 45–84. London: Duckworth.

Van Couvering, Judith A. H., and John A. Van Couvering. 1976. Early Miocene Mammal Fossils from East Africa: Aspects of Geology, Faunistics, and Paleoecology. In *Human Origins: Louis Leakey and the East African Evidence*, Glynn Ll. Isaac and Elizabeth R. McCown (eds.), pp. 155–207. Menlo Park: Benjamin.

Walker, Alan, and Richard E. F. Leakey. 1978. The Hominids of East Turkana. *Scientific American 239*:54–66.

Figure 3:11

Lyght, Charles E.; Chester S. Keefer; Francis D. W. Lukens; Dickinson W. Richards; W. Henry Sebrell; and John M. Trapnell, eds. 1966. *The Merck Manual of Diagnosis and Therapy*. 11th ed. Rahway, N.J., and West Point, Pa.: Merck Sharp and Dohme Research Laboratories.

Napier, J. R., and P. H. Napier. 1967. *A Handbook of Living Primates.* New York: Academic Press.

Schultz, Adolph H. 1931. Man as a Primate. *Scientific Monthly* 33:385–412.

—— 1960. Einige Beobachtungen und Malze am Skelett von *Oreopithecus;* im Vergleich mit Anderen Catarrhinen Primaten. *Z. Morph. Anthrop.* 50:136–149.

Figure 3:12

Albrecht, Helmut, and Sinclair C. Dunnett. 1971. *Chimpanzees in Western Africa.* Studies in Ethology. Munich: Piper.

Azuma, Shigeru, and Akisato Toyoshima. 1961–1962. Progress Report of the Survey of Chimpanzees in Their Natural Habitat, Kabogo Point Area, Tanganyika. *Primates* 3:61–70.

Baldwin, Lori A., and Geza Teleki. 1973. Field Research on Chimpanzees and Gorillas: An Historical, Geographical, and Bibliographical Listing. *Primates* 14:315–330.

Born, Carolynne. 1978. Dr. Jane Goodall's Latest Find: Violence in the Chimpanzee World. *Collage,* July, p. 2.

Bramblett, Claud A. 1976. *Patterns of Primate Behavior.* Palo Alto: Mayfield Press.

Busse, Curt D. 1977. Chimpanzee Predation as a Possible Factor in the Evolution of Red Colobus Monkey Social Organization. *Evolution* 31:907–911.

de Bournonville, D. 1967. Contribution à l'Étude du Chimpanzé en République du Guinée. *Bulletin de l'Institut Française d'Afrique Noire* 29:1189–1269.

Goodall, Jane van Lawick. 1971. *In the Shadow of Man.* Boston: Houghton Mifflin.

Hunt, Edward E., Jr. 1975. Population Dynamics of Wild Chimpanzees: A Lesson for Medical Anthropology. Paper presented at the 44th Annual Meeting, American Association of Physical Anthropologists. *American Journal of Physical Anthropology* 42:308ff.

Itani, Junichiro, and Akira Suzuki. 1967. The Social Unit of Chimpanzees. *Primates* 8:355–381.

Izawa, Kohsei, and Junichiro Itani. 1966–1968. Chimpanzees in Kasakati Basin, Tanganyika. 1. Ecological Study in the Rainy Season, 1963–64. *Kyoto University African Studies,* pp. 73–156.

Jones, Clyde, and Jorge Sabater Pí. 1971. *Comparative Ecology of Gorilla gorilla (Savage and Wyman) and Pan troglodytes (Blumenbach) in Rio Muni, West Africa.* Bibliotheca Primatologica, no. 13. Basel: Karger.

Kano, Takayoshi. 1971. The Chimpanzee of Filabanga, Western Tanzania. *Primates* 12:229–246.

—— 1972. Distribution and Adaptation of the Chimpanzee on the Eastern Shore of Lake Tanganyika. *Kyoto University African Studies* 7:37–129.

Kortlandt, Adriaan L. 1972. *New Perspectives on Ape and Human Evolution.* Amsterdam: Stichting voor Psychobiologie.

Marler, P., and L. Hobbett. 1975. Individuality in a Long-Range Vocalization of Wild Chimpanzees. *Zeitschrift für Tierpsychologie* 38:97–109.

McGrew, William C. 1974. Tool Use by Wild Chimpanzees in Feeding upon Driver Ants. *Journal of Human Evolution* 3:501–508.

—— 1975. Patterns of Plant Food Sharing by Wild Chimpanzees. In *Contemporary Primatology: Proceedings of the Fifth International Congress of Primatology,*

S. Kondo, M. Kawai, and A. Ehara (eds.), pp. 304–309. Basel: Karger.

McGrew, W. C.; C. E. G. Tutin; and P. J. Baldwin. 1979. Chimpanzees, Tools, and Termites: Cross-Cultural Comparisons of Senegal, Tanzania, and Rio Muni. *Man 14*:185–214.

Morris, Kathryn, and Jane Goodall. 1977. Competition for Meat between Chimpanzees and Baboons of the Gombe National Park. *Folia Primatologica 28*:109–121.

Nishida, Toshisada. 1979. The Social Structure of Chimpanzees of the Mahale Mountains. In *The Great Apes*, Perspectives on Human Evolution, vol. 5, D. A. Hamburg and E. R. McCown (eds.), pp. 73–121. Menlo Park: Benjamin/Cummings.

Nishida, Toshisada, and Kenji Kawanaka. 1972. Inter-Unit-Group Relationships among Wild Chimpanzees of the Mahali Mountains. *Kyoto University African Studies 7*:131–169.

Nissen, Henry W. 1931. *A Field Study of the Chimpanzee: Observations of Chimpanzee Behavior and Environment in Western French Guinea.* Comparative Psychology Monographs, no. 8. Baltimore: Johns Hopkins University Press.

Pierce, A. 1976. Inter- and Intra-Group Activities on Non-Provisioned Chimpanzees in Gombe National Park. Paper presented at the 6th Congress of the International Primatological Society, Cambridge.

Pierce, Ann Harden. 1978. Ranging Patterns and Associations of a Small Community of Chimpanzees in Gombe National Park, Tanzania. In *Recent Advances in Primatology*, vol. 1, D. J. Chivers and J. Herbert (eds.), pp. 59–61. New York: Academic Press.

Primate Society of Great Britain. 1974, 1975, 1977, 1978, 1979. *Primate Eye: Current Primate Field Studies.* Supplement to Newsletter.

Rahm, U. 1971. L'Emploi d'Outils par les Chimpanzés de l'Ouest de la Côte-d'Ivoire. *Terre et la Vie 25*:506–509.

Rand McNally. 1979. *Commercial Atlas and Marketing Guide.* Chicago: Rand McNally.

Reynolds, Vernon. 1972. Review of *Chimpanzees in Western Africa*, by H. Albrecht and S. C. Dunnett. *Folia Primatologica 17*:160.

  1975. How Wild Are the Gombe Chimpanzees? *Man 10*:123–125.

Reynolds, Vernon, and Frances Reynolds. 1965. Chimpanzees of the Budongo Forest. In *Primate Behavior: Field Studies of Monkeys and Apes*, Irven DeVore (ed.), pp. 425–473. New York: Holt, Rinehart and Winston.

Riss, David C., and Curt D. Busse. 1977. Fifty-Day Observation of a Free-ranging Adult Male Chimpanzee. *Folia Primatologica 28*:283–297.

Sabater Pí, Jorge. 1974. An Elementary Industry of the Chimpanzees in the Okorobikó Mountains, Rio Muni (Republic of Equatorial Guinea), West Africa. *Primates 15*:351–364.

Silk, Joan B. 1978. Patterns of Food Sharing among Mother and Infant Chimpanzees at Gombe National Park, Tanzania. *Folia Primatologica 29*:129–141.

Silk, J. B., and H. C. Kraemer. 1976. Comparison of Mother-Infant Proximity among Wild and Captive Chimpanzees. Paper presented at the 6th Congress of the International Primatological Society, Cambridge.

Struhsaker, T. T., and P. Hunkeler. 1971. Evidence of Tool-Using by Chimpanzees in the Ivory Coast. *Folia Primatologica 15*:212–219.

Sugiyama, Yukimaru. 1973a. The Social Structure of Wild Chimpanzees. In *Comparative Ecology and Behavior of Primates*, R. P. Michael and J. H. Crook (eds.), pp. 376–410. New York: Academic Press.

Suzuki, Akira. 1969. An Ecological Study of Chimpanzees in a Savanna Woodland. *Primates 10*:103–148.

Teleki, Geza; E. E. Hunt, Jr.; and J. H. Pfifferling. 1976. Demographic Observations (1963–1973) on the Chimpanzees of Gombe National Park, Tanzania. *Journal of Human Evolution 5*:559–598.

Tutin, Caroline E. G. 1975. Exceptions to Promiscuity in a Feral Chimpanzee Community. In *Contemporary Primatology*, Proceedings of the Fifth International Congress of Primatology, S. Kondo, M. Kawai, and A. Ehara (eds.), pp. 445–449. Basel: Karger.

Van Chi-Bonnardel, Régine. 1973. *The Atlas of Africa*. New York: Free Press.

Figure 8:1

Behrensmeyer, A. K. 1976. Lothagam Hill, Kanapoi, and Ekora: A General Summary of Stratigraphy and Faunas. In *Earliest Man and Environments in the Lake Rudolf Basin*, Yves Coppens, F. Clark Howell, Glynn Ll. Isaac, and Richard E. F. Leakey (eds.), pp. 163–170. Chicago: University of Chicago Press.

Boaz, Noel T. 1977. Paleoecology of Early Hominidae in Africa. Kroeber Anthropological Society Papers, no. 50:37–62.

Brain, C. K. 1978. Some Aspects of the South African Australopithecine Sites and Their Bone Accumulations. In *Early Hominids of Africa*, Clifford J. Jolly (ed.), pp. 131–161. London: Duckworth.

Brock, A.; P. L. McFadden; and T. C. Partridge. 1977. Preliminary Palaeomagnetic Results from Makapansgat and Swartkrans. *Nature 266*:249–250.

Brown, F. H., and R. T. Shuey. 1976. Magnetostratigraphy of the Shungura and Usno Formations, Lower Omo Valley, Ethiopia. In *Earliest Man and Environments in the Lake Rudolf Basin*, Yves Coppens, F. Clark Howell, Glynn Ll. Isaac, and Richard E. F. Leakey (eds.), pp. 64–78. Chicago: University of Chicago Press.

Cerling, T. E.; F. H. Brown; B. W. Cerling; G. H. Curtis; and R. E. Drake. 1979. Preliminary Correlations between the Koobi Fora and Shungura Formations, East Africa. *Nature 279*:118–121.

Howell, F. Clark. 1978a. Hominidae. In *Evolution of African Mammals*, H. B. S. Cooke and V. J. Maglio (eds.), pp. 154–248. Cambridge: Harvard University Press.

    1978b. Overview of the Pliocene and Earlier Pleistocene of the Lower Omo Basin, Southern Ethiopia. In *Early Hominids of Africa*, Clifford J. Jolly (ed.), pp. 85–130. London: Duckworth.

Howell, F. Clark, and Yves Coppens. 1976. An Overview of Hominidae from the Omo Succession, Ethiopia. In *Earliest Man and Environments in the Lake Rudolf Basin*, Yves Coppens, F. Clark Howell, Glynn Ll. Isaac, and Richard E. F. Leakey (eds.), pp. 522–532. Chicago: University of Chicago Press.

Oakley, Kenneth P.; Bernard G. Campbell; and Theya I. Molleson, eds. 1977. *Catalogue of Fossil Hominids*, part 1, *Africa*. 2d ed. London: Trustees of the British Museum.

Patterson, Bryan; Anna K. Behrensmeyer; and William D. Sills. 1970. Geology and Fauna of a New Pliocene Locality in Northwestern Kenya. *Nature* 226:918–921.

Tobias, Phillip V. 1975. New African Evidence on the Dating and the Phylogeny of the Plio-Pleistocene Hominidae. Royal Society of New Zealand, Bulletin no. 13:289–296.

——— 1978. The South African Australopithecines in Time and Hominid Phylogeny, with Special Reference to the Dating and Affinities of the Taung Skull. In *Early Hominids of Africa,* Clifford J. Jolly (ed.), pp. 45–84. London: Duckworth.

White, T. D., and J. M. Harris. 1977. Suid Evolution and Correlation of African Hominid Localities. *Science 198*:13–21.

Figure 8:2

Behrensmeyer, A. K. 1976. Lothagam Hill, Kanapoi, and Ekora: A General Summary of Stratigraphy and Faunas. In *Earliest Man and Environments in the Lake Rudolf Basin,* Yves Coppens, F. Clark Howell, Glynn Ll. Isaac, and Richard E. F. Leakey (eds.), pp. 163–170. Chicago: University of Chicago Press.

Eckhardt, Robert B. 1977. Hominid Origins: The Lothagam Problem. *Current Anthropology 18*:356.

Goodall, Jane van Lawick. 1971. *In the Shadow of Man.* Boston: Houghton Mifflin.

Howell, F. Clark. 1978a. Hominidae. In *Evolution of African Mammals,* Vincent J. Maglio and H. B. S. Cooke (eds.), pp. 154–248. Cambridge: Harvard University Press.

McHenry, Henry M., and Robert S. Corruccini. 1980. Late Tertiary Hominids and Human Origins. *Nature* 285:397–398.

Oakley, Kenneth P.; Bernard G. Campbell; and Theya I. Molleson, eds. 1977. *Catalogue of Fossil Hominids,* part I, *Africa.* 2d ed. London: Trustees of the British Museum.

Patterson, Bryan; Anna K. Behrensmeyer; and William D. Sills. 1970. Geology and Fauna of a New Pliocene Locality in Northwestern Kenya. *Nature* 226:918–921.

Patterson, Bryan, and W. W. Howells. 1967. Hominid Humeral Fragment from Early Pleistocene of Northwestern Kenya. *Science 156*:64–66.

Sigmon, B. A. 1977. Contributions from Southern and Eastern Africa to the Study of Early Hominid Evolution. *Journal of Human Evolution* 6:245–257.

Tobias, Phillip V. 1967. Pleistocene Deposits and New Fossil Localities in Kenya. *Nature 215*:479–480.

——— 1975. New African Evidence on the Dating and the Phylogeny of the Plio-Pleistocene Hominidae. Royal Society of New Zealand, Bulletin no. 13:289–296.

——— 1978. The South African Australopithecines in Time and Hominid Phylogeny, with Special Reference to the Dating and Affinities of the Taung Skull. In *Early Hominids of Africa,* Clifford J. Jolly (ed.), pp. 45–84. London: Duckworth.

Figure 8:5

Johanson, Donald C., and Tim D. White. 1979. A Systematic Assessment of Early African Hominids. *Science 203*:321–330.

Johanson, Donald C., Tim D. White; and Yves Coppens. 1978. A New Species of the Genus *Australopithecus* (Primates: Hominidae) from the Pliocene of Eastern Africa. *Kirtlandia 28*:1–14.

Leakey, Mary D. 1979. Footprints in the Ashes of Time. *National Geographic* 155:446–457.

Leakey, Mary D., and R. L. Hay. 1979. Pliocene Footprints in the Laetolil Beds at Laetoli, Northern Tanzania. *Nature* 278:317–323.

Leakey, M. D.; R. L. Hay; G. H. Curtis; R. E. Drake; M. K. Jackes; and T. D. White. 1976. Fossil Hominids from the Laetolil Beds. *Nature* 262:460–466.

Pfeiffer, John. 1980. Current Research Casts New Light on Human Origins. *Smithsonian* 11(3):91–103.

Protsch, R. 1976. The Position of the Eyasi and Garusi Hominids in East Africa. Ms. from Les plus anciens hominidés, UISPP, 9th Congress.

Figure 8:8

Aronson, J. L.; T. J. Schmitt; R. C. Walter; M. Taieb; J. J. Tiercelin; D. C. Johanson; C. W. Naeser; and A. E. M. Nairn. 1977. New Geochronologic and Paleomagnetic Data for the Hominid-Bearing Hadar Formation of Ethiopia. *Nature* 267:323–327.

Howell, F. Clark. 1978a. Hominidae. In *Evolution of African Mammals,* Vincent J. Maglio and H. B. S. Cooke (eds.), pp. 154–248. Cambridge: Harvard University Press.

1978b. Overview of the Pliocene and Earlier Pleistocene of the Lower Omo Basin, Southern Ethiopia. In *Early Hominids of Africa,* Clifford J. Jolly (ed.), pp. 85–130. London: Duckworth.

Johanson, Donald C. 1976. Ethiopia Yields First "Family" of Early Man. *National Geographic* 150:791–811.

Johanson, Donald C.; Yves Coppens; and Maurice Taieb. 1976. Pliocene Hominid Remains from Hadar, Central Afar, Ethiopia. Ms. from Les plus anciens hominidés, UISPP, 9th Congress.

Johanson, Donald C., and Maurice Taieb. 1976. Plio-Pleistocene Hominid Discoveries in Hadar, Ethiopia. *Nature* 260:293–297.

Johanson, Donald C.; Tim D. White; and Yves Coppens. 1978. A New Species of the Genus *Australopithecus* (Primates: Hominidae) from the Pliocene of Eastern Africa. *Kirtlandia* 28:1–14.

Johanson, Donald C.; Maurice Taieb; Yves Coppens; Hélène Roche. 1980. New Discoveries of Pliocene Hominids and Artifacts in Hadar: International Afar Research Expedition to Ethiopia (Fourth and Fifth Field Seasons 1975–1977). *Journal of Human Evolution* 9(8):583–585.

Johanson, Donald, and Maitland Edey. 1981. *Lucy: The Beginning of Humankind.* New York: Simon and Schuster.

Figure 10:1

Boaz, Noel T. 1977a. Paleoecology of Plio-Pleistocene Hominidae in the Lower Omo Basin, Ethiopia. Dissertation, University of California, Berkeley.

Brown, F. H., and R. T. Shuey. 1976. Magnetostratigraphy of the Shungura and Usno Formations, Lower Omo Valley, Ethiopia. In *Earliest Man and Environments in the Lake Rudolf Basin,* Yves Coppens, F. Clark Howell, Glynn Ll. Isaac, and Richard E. F. Leakey (eds.), pp. 64–78. Chicago: University of Chicago Press.

Chavaillon, J. 1976. Evidence for the Technical Practices of Early Pleistocene Hominids. In *Earliest Man and Environments in the Lake Rudolf Basin,* Yves

Coppens, F. Clark Howell, Glynn Ll. Isaac, and Richard E. F. Leakey (eds.), pp. 565–573. Chicago: University of Chicago Press.

Guilmet, George M. 1977. The Evolution of Tool-Using and Tool-Making Behaviour. *Man 12*:33–47.

Howell, F. Clark. 1976. An Overview of the Pliocene and Earliest Pleistocene of the Lower Omo Basin, Southern Ethiopia. In *Human Origins: Louis Leakey and the East African Evidence*, Glynn Ll. Isaac and Elizabeth R. McCown (eds.), pp. 227–268. Menlo Park: Benjamin.

1978a. Hominidae. In *Evolution of African Mammals*, Vincent J. Maglio and H. B. S. Cooke (eds.), pp. 154–248. Cambridge: Harvard University Press.

1978b. Overview of the Pliocene and Earlier Pleistocene of the Lower Omo Basin, Southern Ethiopia. In *Early Hominids of Africa*, Clifford J. Jolly (ed.), pp. 85–130. London: Duckworth.

Howell, F. Clark, and Yves Coppens. 1976. An Overview of Hominidae from the Omo Succession, Ethiopia. In *Earliest Man and Environments in the Lake Rudolf Basin*, Yves Coppens, F. Clark Howell, Glynn Ll. Isaac, and Richard E. F. Leakey (eds.), pp. 522–532. Chicago: University of Chicago Press.

Merrick, H. V. 1976. Recent Archaeological Research in the Plio-Pleistocene Deposits of the Lower Omo Valley, Southwestern Ethiopia. In *Human Origins: Louis Leakey and the East African Evidence*, Glynn Ll. Isaac and Elizabeth R. McCown (eds.), pp. 461–482. Menlo Park: Benjamin.

Merrick, H. V., and J. P. S. Merrick. 1976. Archeological Occurrences of Earlier Pleistocene Age, from the Shungura Formation. In *Earliest Man and Environments in the Lake Rudolf Basin*, Yves Coppens, F. Clark Howell, Glynn Ll. Isaac, and Richard E. F. Leakey (eds.), pp. 574–585. Chicago: University of Chicago Press.

Rak, Yoel, and F. Clark Howell. 1978. Cranium of a Juvenile *Australopithecus boisei* from the Lower Omo Basin, Ethiopia. *American Journal of Physical Anthropology 48*:345–365.

Figure 10:2

Boaz, Noel T. 1977b. Paleoecology of Early Hominidae in Africa. Kroeber Anthropological Society Papers, no. 50:37–62.

Brown, F. H., and R. T. Shuey. 1976. Magnetostratigraphy of the Shungura and Usno Formations, Lower Omo Valley, Ethiopia. In *Earliest Man and Environments in the Lake Rudolf Basin*, Yves Coppens, F. Clark Howell, Glynn Ll. Isaac, and Richard E. F. Leakey (eds.), pp. 64–78. Chicago: University of Chicago Press.

Day, Michael H. 1978. Functional Interpretation of the Morphology of Postcranial Remains of Early African Hominids. In *Early Hominids of Africa*, Clifford J. Jolly (ed.), pp. 311–345. London: Duckworth.

Goodall, Jane van Lawick. 1967. *My Friends the Wild Chimpanzees*. Washington, D.C.: National Geographic Society.

Guilmet, George M. 1977. The Evolution of Tool-Using and Tool-Making Behaviour. *Man 12*:33–47.

Howell, F. Clark. 1978a. Hominidae. In *Evolution of African Mammals*, Vincent J. Maglio and H. B. S. Cooke (eds.), pp. 154–248. Cambridge: Harvard University Press.

1978b. Overview of the Pliocene and Earlier Pleistocene of the Lower Omo

Basin, Southern Ethiopia. In *Early Hominids of Africa,* Clifford J. Jolly (ed.), pp. 85–130. London: Duckworth.

Howell, F. Clark, and Yves Coppens. 1976. An Overview of Hominidae from the Omo Succession, Ethiopia. In *Earliest Man and Environments in the Lake Rudolf Basin,* Yves Coppens, F. Clark Howell, Glynn Ll. Isaac, and Richard E. F. Leakey (eds.), pp. 522–532. Chicago: University of Chicago Press.

Leakey, Mary D. 1978. Olduvai Fossil Hominids: Their Stratigraphic Positions and Associations. In *Early Hominids of Africa,* Clifford J. Jolly (ed.), pp. 3–16. London: Duckworth.

Merrick, H. V. 1976. Recent Archaeological Research in the Plio-Pleistocene Deposits of the Lower Omo Valley, Southwestern Ethiopia. In *Human Origins: Louis Leakey and the East African Evidence,* Glynn Ll. Isaac and Elizabeth R. McCown (eds.), pp. 461–481. Menlo Park: Benjamin.

Merrick, H. V., and J. P. S. Merrick. 1976. Archeological Occurrences of Earlier Pleistocene Age, from the Shungura Formation. In *Earliest Man and Environments in the Lake Rudolf Basin,* Yves Coppens, F. Clark Howell, Glynn Ll. Isaac, and Richard E. F. Leakey (eds.), pp. 574–585. Chicago: University of Chicago Press.

White, T. D., and J. M. Harris. 1978. Stratigraphic Interpretation of the Omo, Shungura, and Lake Turkana Fossil Suid Record. *Science* 202: 1309.

Figure 10:3

Boaz, Noel T. 1977b. Paleoecology of Early Hominidae in Africa. Kroeber Anthropological Society Papers, no. 50:37–62.

Brain, C. K. 1974b. Some Aspects of the South African Australopithecine Sites and Their Bone Accumulations. Conference on the African Hominidae of the Plio-Pleistocene: Evidence, Problems, and Strategies. Sponsored by Wenner-Gren Foundation for Anthropological Research, New York.

1976. A Re-Interpretation of the Swartkrans Site and Its Remains. *South African Journal of Science* 72:141–146.

1978. Some Aspects of the South African Australopithecine Sites and Their Bone Accumulations. In *Early Hominids of Africa,* Clifford J. Jolly (ed.), pp. 131–161. London: Duckworth.

Brock, A.; P. L. McFadden; and T. C. Partridge. 1977. Preliminary Palaeomagnetic Results from Makapansgat and Swartkrans. *Nature* 266: 249–250.

Day, Michael H. 1965. *Guide to Fossil Man: A Handbook of Human Palaeontology.* London: Cassell.

1970. *Fossil Man.* New York: Bantam Books.

Howell, F. Clark. 1978a. Hominidae. In *Evolution of African Mammals,* Vincent J. Maglio and H. B. S. Cooke (eds.), pp. 154–248. Cambridge: Harvard University Press.

Klein, Richard G. 1977. The Ecology of Early Man in Southern Africa. *Science* 197:115–126.

Koenigswald, G. H. R. von. 1962. *The Evolution of Man.* Ann Arbor: University of Michigan Press. Reprint, 1976.

Le Gros Clark, W. E. 1964. *The Fossil Evidence for Human Evolution.* Rev. ed. Chicago: University of Chicago Press.

Oakley, Kenneth P.; Bernard G. Campbell; and Theya I. Molleson, eds. 1977.

Catalogue of Fossil Hominids, part 1, *Africa.* 2d ed. London: Trustees of the British Museum.

Partridge, T. C. 1978. Re-appraisal of Lithostratigraphy of Sterkfontein Hominid Site. *Nature 275*:285–287.

Pilbeam, David. 1972a. *The Ascent of Man: An Introduction to Human Evolution.* New York: Macmillan.

Poirier, Frank E. 1977. *Fossil Evidence: The Human Evolutionary Journey.* 2d ed. Saint Louis: Mosby.

Read, Dwight W. l975. Hominid Teeth and Their Relationship to Hominid Phylogeny. *American Journal of Physical Anthropology 42*:105–125.

Sigmon, B. A. 1977. Contributions from Southern and Eastern Africa to the Study of Early Hominid Evolution. *Journal of Human Evolution 6*:245–257.

Stiles, Daniel. 1979a. Early Acheulian and Developed Oldowan. *Current Anthropology 20*:126–129.

  1979b. Recent Archaeological Findings at the Sterkfontein Site. *Nature 277*:381–382.

Tobias, Phillip V. 1975. New African Evidence of the Dating and the Phylogeny of the Plio-Pleistocene Hominidae. Royal Society of New Zealand, Bulletin no. 13:289–296.

  1976. African Hominids: Dating and Phylogeny. In *Human Origins: Louis Leakey and the East African Evidence,* Glynn Ll. Isaac and Elizabeth R. McCown (eds.), pp. 377–422. Menlo Park: Benjamin.

  1978. The South African Australopithecines in Time and Hominid Phylogeny, with Special Reference to the Dating and Affinities of the Taung Skull. In *Early Hominids of Africa,* Clifford J. Jolly (ed.), pp. 45–84. London: Duckworth.

Vrba, E. S. 1975. Some Evidence of Chronology and Palaeoecology of Sterkfontein, Swartkrans, and Kromdraai from the Fossil Bovidae. *Nature 254*:301–304.

  1979. A New Study of the Scapula of *Australopithecus africanus* from Sterkfontein. *American Journal of Physical Anthropology 51*:117–130.

Figure 10:4

Brace, C. L.; P. E. Mahler; and R. B. Rosen. 1972. Tooth Measurements and the Rejection of the Taxon *Homo habilis. Yearbook of Physical Anthropology 16*:50–68.

Curtis, G. H., and R. L. Hay. 1972. Further Geological Studies and Potassium-Argon Dating at Olduvai Gorge and Ngorongoro Crater. In *Calibration of Hominoid Evolution,* W. W. Bishop and J. A. Miller (eds.), pp. 289–301. Edinburgh: Scottish Academic Press.

Day, Michael H. 1965. *Guide to Fossil Man.* 1968 printing. London: Cassell.

  1976. Hominid Postcranial Material from Bed I, Olduvai Gorge. In *Human Origins: Louis Leakey and the East African Evidence,* Glynn Ll. Isaac and Elizabeth R. McCown (eds.), pp. 363–374. Menlo Park: Benjamin.

Goodall, Jane van Lawick. 1975a. The Behavior of the Chimpanzee. In *Hominisation and Behavior,* G. Kurth and I. Eibl-Eibesfeldt (eds.), pp. 74–136. Stuttgart: Gustav Fischer.

Leakey, Mary D. 1971. *Olduvai Gorge,* vol. 3, *Excavations in Beds I and II, 1960–1963.* Cambridge: Cambridge University Press.

1978. Olduvai Fossil Hominids: Their Stratigraphic Positions and Associations. In *Early Hominids of Africa,* Clifford J. Jolly (ed.), pp. 3–16. London: Duckworth.

Leakey, Meave G., and Richard E. F. Leakey, eds. 1978. *Koobi Fora Research Project,* vol. 1, *The Fossil Hominids and an Introduction to Their Context, 1968–1974.* Oxford: Clarendon Press.

Oakley, Kenneth P.; Bernard G. Campbell; and Theya I. Molleson, eds. 1977. *Catalogue of Fossil Hominids,* part 1, *Africa.* 2d ed. London: Trustees of the British Museum.

Poirier, Frank E. 1977. *Fossil Evidence: The Human Evolutionary Journey.* 2d ed. Saint Louis: Mosby.

Rightmire, G. P. 1979. Cranial Remains of *Homo erectus* from Beds II and IV, Olduvai Gorge, Tanzania. *American Journal of Physical Anthropology* 51:99–116.

Stiles, Daniel. 1979a. Recent Archaeological Findings at the Sterkfontein Site. *Nature* 277:381–382.

1979b. Early Acheulian and Developed Oldowan. *Current Anthropology* 20:126–129.

Susman, Randall L., and Norman Creel. 1979. Functional and Morphological Affinities of the Subadult Hand (O.H.7) from Olduvai Gorge. *American Journal of Physical Anthropology* 51:311–332.

Figure 10:5

Cox, Allan. 1969. Geomagnetic Reversals. *Science* 163:237–245.

Day, Michael H. 1965. *Guide to Fossil Man: A Handbook of Human Palaeontology.* London: Cassell.

Day, Michael H., and J. R. Napier. 1964. Fossil Foot Bones. *Nature* 201:969–970.

Hay, Richard L. 1976a. *Geology of the Olduvai Gorge: A Study of Sedimentation in a Semiarid Basin.* Berkeley: University of California Press.

Leakey, L. S. B. 1961. New Finds at Olduvai Gorge. *Nature* 189:649–650.

Leakey, L. S. B., and M. D. Leakey. 1964. Recent Discoveries of Fossil Hominids in Tanganyika: At Olduvai and Near Lake Natron. *Nature* 202:5–7.

Leakey, Mary D. 1971. *Olduvai Gorge,* vol. 3, *Excavations in Beds I and II, 1960–1963.* Cambridge: Cambridge University Press.

1978. Olduvai Fossil Hominids: Their Stratigraphic Positions and Associations. In *Early Hominids of Africa,* Clifford J. Jolly (ed.), pp. 3–16. London: Duckworth.

Oakley, Kenneth P.; Bernard G. Campbell; and Theya I. Molleson, eds. 1977. *Catalogue of Fossil Hominids,* part 1, *Africa.* 2d ed. London: Trustees of the British Museum.

Rightmire, G. P. 1979. Cranial Remains of *Homo erectus* from Beds II and IV, Olduvai Gorge, Tanzania. *American Journal of Physical Anthropology* 51:99–116.

Tobias, Phillip V. 1967. *Olduvai Gorge, vol. 2, The Cranium and Maxillary Dentition of* Australopithecus (Zinjanthropus) boisei. Cambridge: Cambridge University Press.

Figure 10:6

Cerling, T. E.; F. H. Brown; B. W. Cerling; G. H. Curtis; R. E. Drake. 1979. Preliminary Correlations between the Koobi Fora and Shungura Formations, East Africa. *Nature* 279:118–121.

Goodall, Jane van Lawick. 1971. *In the Shadow of Man.* Boston: Houghton Mifflin.

Harris, John W. K., and Glynn Ll. Isaac. 1976. The Karari Industry: Early Pleistocene Archaeological Evidence from the Terrain East of Lake Turkana, Kenya. *Nature 262*:102–107.

Howell, F. Clark. 1978a. Hominidae. In *Evolution of African Mammals,* Vincent J. Maglio and H. B. S. Cooke (eds.) pp. 154–248. Cambridge: Harvard University Press.

Isaac, Glynn Ll., and John W. K. Harris. 1978. Archaeology. In *Koobi Fora Research Project,* vol. 1, *The Fossil Hominids and an Introduction to Their Context, 1968–1974,* Meave G. Leakey and Richard E. F. Leakey (eds.), pp. 64–85. Oxford: Clarendon Press.

Leakey, Richard E.; Meave G. Leakey; and Anna K. Behrensmeyer. 1978. The Hominid Catalogue. In *Koobi Fora Research Project,* vol. 1, *The Fossil Hominids and an Introduction to Their Context, 1968–1974,* Meave G. Leakey and Richard E. Leakey (eds.), pp. 86–182. Oxford: Clarendon Press.

Leakey, R. E. F., and B. A. Wood. 1974. A Hominid Mandible from East Rudolf, Kenya. *American Journal of Physical Anthropology 41*:245–249.

Oakley, Kenneth P.; Bernard G. Campbell; and Theya I. Molleson, eds. 1977. *Catalogue of Fossil Hominids,* part 1, *Africa.* 2d ed. Trustees of the British Museum.

Rightmire, G. P. 1979. Cranial Remains of *Homo erectus* from Beds II and IV, Olduvai Gorge, Tanzania. *American Journal of Physical Anthropology 51*:99–116.

Walker, Alan, and Richard E. F. Leakey. 1978. The Hominids of East Turkana. *Scientific American 239*:54–66.

Figure 10:7

See Figure 8:1.

Figure 10:11

Aronson, J. L.; T. J. Schmitt; R. C. Walter; M. Taieb; J. J. Tiercelin; D. C. Johanson; C. W. Naeser; and A. E. M. Nairn. 1977. New Geochronologic and Paleomagnetic Data for the Hominid-Bearing Hadar Formation of Ethiopia. *Nature 267*:323–327.

Boaz, Noel T. 1977b. Paleoecology of Early Hominidae in Africa. Kroeber Anthropological Society Papers, no. 50:37–62.

Brace, C. L. 1972. Sexual Dimorphism in Human Evolution. *Yearbook of Physical Anthropology 16*:31–49.

Brace, C. L.; P. E. Mahler; and R. B. Rosen. 1972. Tooth Measurements and the Rejection of the Taxon *Homo habilis. Yearbook of Physical Anthropology 16*:50–68.

Brain, C. K. 1974b. Some Aspects of the South African Australopithecine Sites and Their Bone Accumulations. Conference on the African Hominidae of the Plio-Pleistocene: Evidence, Problems, and Strategies. Sponsored by Wenner-Gren Foundation for Anthropological Research, New York.

1978. Some Aspects of the South African Australopithecine Sites and Their Bone Accumulations. In *Early Hominids of Africa,* Clifford J. Jolly (ed.), pp. 131–161. London: Duckworth.

Brock, A.; P. L. McFadden; and T. C. Partridge. 1977. Preliminary Palaeomagnetic Results from Makapansgat and Swartkrans. *Nature* 266:249–250.

Brown, F. H., and R. T. Shuey. 1976. Magnetostratigraphy of the Shungura and Usno Formations, Lower Omo Valley, Ethiopia. In *Earliest Man and Environments in the Lake Rudolf Basin,* Yves Coppens, F. Clark Howell, Glynn Ll. Isaac, and Richard E. F. Leakey (eds.), pp. 64–78. Chicago: University of Chicago Press.

Carney, J.; A. Hill; J. A. Miller; and A. Walker. 1971. Late Australopithecine from Baringo District, Kenya. *Nature* 230:509–514.

Day, Michael H. 1965. *Guide to Fossil Man: A Handbook of Human Palaeontology.* London: Cassell.

Day, M. H.; R. E. F. Leakey; A. C. Walker; and B. A. Wood. 1975. New Hominids from East Rudolf, Kenya. *American Journal of Physical Anthropology* 42:461–475.

Howell, F. Clark. 1978a. Hominidae. In *Evolution of African Mammals,* Vincent J. Maglio and H. B. S. Cooke (eds.), pp. 154–248. Cambridge: Harvard University Press.

Howell, F. Clark, and Yves Coppens. 1976. An Overview of Hominidae from the Omo Succession, Ethiopia. In *Earliest Man and Environments in the Lake Rudolf Basin,* Yves Coppens, F. Clark Howell, Glynn Ll. Isaac, and Richard E. F. Leakey (eds.), pp. 522–532. Chicago: University of Chicago Press.

James, W. Warwick. 1960. *The Jaws and Teeth of Primates.* London: Pitman.

Johanson, Donald C. 1978. Our Roots Go Deeper. *Science Year 1979:*43–55.

Johanson, Donald C., and Tim D. White. 1979. A Systematic Assessment of Early African Hominids. *Science* 202:321–330.

Johanson, Donald C.; Tim D. White; and Yves Coppens. 1978. A New Species of the Genus *Australopithecus* (Primates: Hominidae) from the Pliocene of Eastern Africa. *Kirtlandia* 28:1–14.

Klein, Richard G. 1977. The Ecology of Early Man in Southern Africa. *Science* 197:115–126.

Krantz, Grover S. 1975. An Explanation for the Diastema of Javan *erectus* Skull IV. In *Paleoanthropology: Morphology and Paleoecology.* Russell H. Tuttle (ed.), pp. 361–372. The Hague: Mouton.

Krogman, W. M. 1969. Growth Changes in Skull, Face, Jaws, and Teeth of the Chimpanzee. In *The Chimpanzee,* vol. 1, *Anatomy, Behavior and Diseases of Chimpanzees,* G. H. Bourne (ed.), pp. 104–164. Basel: Karger.

Leakey, Mary D. 1971. *Olduvai Gorge,* vol 3. *Excavations in Beds I and II, 1960–1963.* Cambridge: Cambridge University Press.

  1978. Olduvai Fossil Hominids: Their Stratigraphic Positions and Associations. In *Early Hominids of Africa,* Clifford J. Jolly (ed.), pp. 3–16. London: Duckworth.

  1979. Footprints in the Ashes of Time. *National Geographic* 155:446–457.

Leakey, M. D.; R. L. Hay; G. H. Curtis; R. E. Drake; M. K. Jackes; and T. D. White. 1976. Fossil Hominids from the Laetolil Beds. *Nature* 262:460–466.

Leakey, Meave G., and Richard E. F. Leakey, eds. 1978. *Koobi Fora Research Project,* vol. 1, *The Fossil Hominids and an Introduction to Their Context, 1968–1974.* Oxford: Clarendon Press.

Leakey, Richard E. F., and Roger Lewin. 1977. *Origins.* New York: Dutton.

Oakley, Kenneth P.; Bernard G. Campbell; and Theya I. Molleson, eds. 1977.

Catalogue of Fossil Hominids, part 1, *Africa.* 2d ed. London: Trustees of the British Museum.

Passingham, R. E., and G. Ettlinger. 1974. A Comparison of Cortical Functions in Man and the Other Primates. In *International Review of Neurobiology,* vol. 16, Carl C. Pfeiffer and John R. Smythies (eds.), pp. 233–299. New York: Academic Press.

Pilbeam, David. 1972a. *The Ascent of Man: An Introduction to Human Evolution.* New York: Macmillan.

Poirier, Frank E. 1977. *Fossil Evidence: The Human Evolutionary Journey.* 2d ed. Saint Louis: Mosby.

Read, Dwight W. 1975. Hominid Teeth and Their Relationship to Hominid Phylogeny. *American Journal of Physical Anthropology* 42:105–125.

Shantha, Totada R., and Sohan L. Manocha. 1969. The Brain of Chimpanzee *(Pan troglodytes).* In *The Chimpanzee,* vol. 1, *Anatomy, Behavior, and Diseases of Chimpanzees,* G. H. Bourne (ed.), pp. 188–237. Basel: Karger.

Sigmon, B. A. 1977. Contributions from Southern and Eastern Africa to the Study of Early Hominid Evolution. *Journal of Human Evolution* 6:245–257.

Swindler, Daris S. 1976. *Dentition of Living Primates.* New York: Academic Press.

Tobias, Phillip V. 1967. *Olduvai Gorge,* vol. 2, *The Cranium and Maxillary Dentition of* Australopithecus (Zinjanthropus) boisei. Cambridge: Cambridge University Press.

1971. *The Brain in Hominid Evolution.* New York: Columbia University Press.

1975. New African Evidence on the Dating and the Phylogeny of the Plio-Pleistocene Hominidae. Royal Society of New Zealand, Bulletin no. 13:289–296.

1978. The South African Australopithecines in Time and Hominid Phylogeny, with Special Reference to the Dating and Affinities of the Taung Skull. In *Early Hominids of Africa,* Clifford J. Jolly (ed.), pp. 45–84. London: Duckworth.

Vrba, E. S. 1975. Some Evidence of Chronology and Palaeoecology of Sterkfontein, Swartkrans, and Kromdraai from the Fossil Bovidae. *Nature* 254:301–304.

Name Index

Subject Index

Acheulian industry, see *Homo erectus*
advanced gracile australopithecine, see
    *Australopithecus habilis; Australopithecus
    africanus*
Afar, see Hadar Formation
African apes, see chimpanzee (common);
    chimpanzee (pygmy); gorilla
African rift system, East, 49, 51, 159, 169,
    173, 178, 253
albumin, 35, 39, 39n6, 42
altruism, evolution of, 162
American Sign Language (ASL), 117–119
amino acids, 34, 37
amino acid sequencing, 37, 42
ancestral population, adaptation to
    environment, 134, 137–139; behavior,
    137–139, 140, 264; bipedalism, 138,
    264; canines, bimodal distribution, 201;
    communication, 128; dating, 333; diet,
    137, 139–140, 264; food sharing, 264;
    foraging, 140; Lothagam, 171; mental
    capacities, 126, 142; model of,
    chimpanzee (common), 65–131, 264;
    model of, chimpanzee (pygmy), 58n10;
    mother-off spring, 264; radiation, 55; tool
    use, 138; see also chimpanzees (com-
    mon); chimpanzees (pygmy)
anthropoids, 43
ape-like ancestors, dating and location, 174,
    255, 276
apes, brain, 30, 31; evolution, 29–30;
    intelligence, 31; locomotion, 29, 30, 31,
    45; nonverbal communication, 33;
    similarities to humans (Darwin and
    Huxley), 29–31; teeth and jaws, 30,
    178–179, 180, 186–187, 200, 201; see
    also Miocene "apes"; chimpanzees
    (common); chimpanzees (pygmy); gorilla;
    orang utan; gibbon

Asian apes, *see* orang utan, gibbon
Australopithecus, Africa, 174; animal
    associations, 214; bipedalism, 55, 197–
    199; brain, 69; 206–208, 273;
    butchering, 220, 222–223; childhood
    duration, 208–209; classification, 185–
    187, 191n1, 192–193, 252–254;
    communication, 203, 207, 221; canine
    reduction, 202–204; cheek teeth, 204–
    205; China, 52, 276; cranial capacity,
    205, 208, 242–243; dating, 44, 170, 246,
    252–253, 255, 276; death process, 210;
    defense, 195, 196–197, 217–218; diet,
    193; food sharing, 221; gathering, 189,
    193, 220–221; generic adaptation, 11,
    193, 222–223; group size, 197, 209,
    219; hand and arm, 198–199; hunting
    hypothesis, 25, 193–195; invention of
    containers, 205; Java, 276; location, 255;
    locomotion, 197–198; maps, 174, 194,
    276; mating behavior, 202; meat eating,
    215; mother-offspring relationship, 198,
    208–209, 219; population density,
    139n3; predation and defense, 217–218;
    range size, 221–222; sexual behavior,
    207, 209–210, 257–258; sexual
    dimorphism, 220; social organization,
    195–197, 207, 209, 218, 219, 220;
    summary: species and sites, 225–227;
    teeth and jaws, 193; tools, 69, 205–
    206n14, 210–214, 215, 216, 217, 228,
    230–231, 236–237, 238–239, 241, 244–
    245, 259, 261, 262; variability and
    speciation, 193, 254–260; see also A.
    *afarensis; A. africanus; A. robustus; A.
    habilis*
Australopithecus afarensis (basal australo-
    pithecine), Hadar Formation, Afar Trian-
    gle or Depression, bipedalism, 173–178,

366